CAVEAT

Caveat is Alexander M. Haig, Jr.'s startling account of the machinations of the President's men in foreign affairs. It is also the most candid book ever written by a high-ranking former Cabinet member about an Administration still in office.

In *Caveat*, Alexander Haig writes about his eighteen controversial months as Secretary of State. It is the detailed account of Haig's battle with the President's men and the Byzantine and, at times, dangerous influence they have on foreign affairs.

Forthrightly and dramatically, Haig reveals his struggles with Richard Allen and his successor, William Clark, National Security Advisers; Edwin Meese, counselor to the President; James Baker, chief of staff; and Michael Deaver, deputy chief of staff. He shows how we conduct our foreign relations with the Soviet Union, China, Israel, Poland, Central and South America, and our European and Asian allies. You are there with the President and the Cabinet in the White House, with Margaret Thatcher at 10 Downing Street, with Deng Xiaoping in Beijing, with Andrei Gromyko in Geneva and New York, with Soviet Ambassador Dobrynin in Washington. *Caveat* is an intimate look at power relationships at the highest levels of government.

In his compelling memoir, General Haig also explains what he really meant by his "I am in control" statement following the attempt on the President's life. He discusses

(Continued on back flap)

CAVEAT

CAVEAT

Realism, Reagan, and Foreign Policy

ALEXANDER M. HAIG, JR.

MACMILLAN PUBLISHING COMPANY

New York

Macmillan Publishing Company
866 Third Avenue, New York, N.Y. 10022
Collier Macmillan Canada, Inc.

Library of Congress Cataloging in Publication Data
Haig, Alexander Meigs, 1924–
Caveat: realism, Reagan, and foreign policy.
Includes index.
1. United States—Foreign relations—1981–
2. Reagan, Ronald.   3. Haig, Alexander Meigs, 1924–
I. Title.
E876.H34   1984   327.73   84-936
ISBN 0-02-547370-0

10 9 8 7 6 5 4 3 2 1

Designed by Jack Meserole

Printed in the United States of America

The photographs are credited in the order in which they appear: *Time* magazine, Senator Howard Baker, White House photo, no credit, White House Photo, White House photo, White House photo, White House photo, no credit, no credit, White House photo, Kirstin Hodson, White House photo, no credit, no credit, no credit, no credit, United Press International photo, White House photo, no credit, no credit.

Macmillan books are available at special discounts for bulk purchases for sales promotions, premiums, fund-raising, or educational use. Special editions or book excerpts can also be created to specification. For details, contact:

Special Sales Director
Macmillan Publishing Company
866 Third Avenue
New York, New York 10022

To my wife, Pat,
and my children,
Alex, Brian, and Barbara

caveat . . . n. [L, let him beware] . . . 1: CAUTION. a: a warning enjoining one from certain acts and practices . . . b: a cautionary explanation to prevent misinterpretation.

—*Webster's Third New International Dictionary*

CONTENTS

ACKNOWLEDGMENTS

In the preparation of this volume, as in all my enterprises, I have had the unfailing and indispensable encouragement and astute advice of my wife, Patricia Fox Haig, and my children. Throughout the process of researching and writing *Caveat*, I have enjoyed the literary and editorial advice of Charles McCarry, without whose patience, professionalism, acumen, and wit this volume could not have been undertaken. Herein, as when he was with me at the State Department, first and foremost my friend and associate Sherwood D. Goldberg, together with Dr. Harvey Sicherman, has refreshed my memory, checked my recollections, and warned me about my enthusiasms. The staff of the Manuscripts Division of the Library of Congress, which has custody of my personal papers, has been unfailingly helpful.

To all of these I am grateful, but I have discovered that in writing a book, one has daily cause to be grateful to a great many people who reappear from the past to teach once again lessons that have been the unconscious guideposts of a lifetime. Among these I should like to mention my courageous mother, Regina Murphy Haig, my sister, Regina Haig Meredith, her husband, Edward, my brother, the Reverend Francis R. Haig, S.J., and my father-in-law, Lieutenant General Alonzo P. Fox (U.S.A. Ret.); General of the Army Douglas MacArthur, Presidents Lyndon B. Johnson, Richard M. Nixon, and Gerald R. Ford; Generals Creighton W. Abrams, Jr., Edward ("Ned") Almond, and Lyman L. Lemnitzer; David Bruce, Ellsworth Bunker, Arthur Burns, Joseph A. Califano, Jr., John Connally, Henry Kissinger, Joseph M.A.H. Luns, Nelson A. Rockefeller, and Cyrus R. Vance.

As this is a personal memoir, and because the Foreign Service of the United States is a quiet service that believes that brilliance effaced is brilliance preserved for another day, I have not described the work of the men and women who served with me during my time as Secretary of State in the detail or in the terms of praise it would otherwise demand. Suffice it to say that it would have been quite impossible to do so in any adequate fashion. Nevertheless, I should like to list here the names of many, though not all, of my colleagues who were part of the events I have described and whose names have not appeared in the text: Elliot Abrams, L. Paul Bremer III, Robert L. Brown, Joan Clark, Dean Fischer, Robert D. Hormats, Jonathan Howe, Hugh Montgomery, Powell Moore, Davis Robinson, and Ronald I. Spiers; and those whose personal contribution to me cannot be overlooked: Alvin P. Adams, Kathrine Backus, Dan Haendel, Michael Klosson, Michael Ledeen, Patricia McKee, Clayton E. McManaway, Jr., Joyce Nesmith, Keith E. Schuette, Raymond Seitz, Lora Simkus, and Anthony Wayne.

For any excellence in this book or in the work it describes, these men and women share the credit. The errors are my own.

AUTHOR'S NOTE

This book is neither autobiography nor formal history, but rather a personal memoir of the period in which I served as U.S. Secretary of State. In limiting myself to a description, from the point of view of a close participant, of the events of this remarkable period, I am aware that I have omitted subject matter that would form an important part of a more general work. The description of such questions belongs to future books. Herein, I have consciously limited myself to a description of the most vivid events of my incumbency at the State Department, because these are the episodes from which lessons of great importance to the United States and the American people must be drawn.

A.M.H.
Washington, D.C.
January 1984

CAVEAT

ONE

"Be My Secretary of State"

WHEN, on December 11, 1980, President-elect Ronald Reagan asked me to be his Secretary of State, I had spent no more than three hours alone with him. About an hour of that time had been passed in a Marine helicopter as I escorted Reagan, who was then governor of California, from the White House to Camp David and back again. The year was 1973, and he had come to confer with President Richard M. Nixon, who was at the time under severe attack because of Watergate and was seeking the support of prominent Republicans. There was little conversation in the helicopter; it was neither the time nor the place for it.

Reagan and I met again in the spring of 1979, at his house in California. On that occasion, we spoke mostly about Edgar Bergen. The famous ventriloquist had died, and Reagan had just returned from the funeral. Reagan's convivial spirit had been quietened by the sorrow of the occasion. He and Bergen had been friends for many years; saying good-bye at the funeral obviously had not been easy. Reagan was tired. His face was drawn; his thoughts were with his friend; there was a sad little smudge of theatrical makeup on the cuff of his shirt, the stigmata of the politician in this age of television. Reagan greeted me courteously, told an affectionate story or two about Bergen, and after a foreshortened cocktail hour, ushered me into the dining room.

This evening had been arranged by one of the other guests, Richard V. Allen, whom I had known as an uneasy member of Henry A. Kissinger's staff on the National Security Council. At the time, I was still Supreme Allied Commander in Europe, though I had announced my intention to resign from that post and to retire from the Army in a few weeks' time. In Europe, I had made some statements about U.S. policy toward the Soviets that the press had interpreted as being critical of the policies of my commander in chief, President Jimmy Carter. Thereupon, Allen had called me to say that Reagan would like to hear my assessment of the European scene the next time I was home. On this night, I had taken a commercial flight from St. Louis, where I had been on NATO business, in order to dine with the Reagans in their unpretentious home on the heights above Los Angeles.

Mrs. Reagan is, of course, one of the most charming hostesses in America. On first meeting, and sometimes subsequently, she gives an impression of guarded shyness, but she is possessed of a sprightly intelligence, a ready gift for conversation, and an unerring sense of her husband's mood. It was a small dinner party. The other guests besides Richard Allen were my aide, Major Seth Hudgins, and Peter Hannaford, a partner of Michael K. Deaver's in a Washington public relations firm and a leading lobbyist for Taiwan. As I have said, Ronald Reagan was distracted by the loss of his old friend. Clearly he was fatigued. Mrs. Reagan was attentive, even anxious, and sought to make her husband more comfortable by lifting the burden of the evening as much as possible from his shoulders. In this she was assisted, in a diffident but effective way, by Hannaford. It is common for assistants to shield the great men for whom they work from the importunities of outsiders. The tendency to protect Reagan, even to answer questions that were clearly addressed to him, went beyond the usual. As a result, Reagan was a rather quiet dinner companion. Though I understood why this should be so, I confess I was disappointed that he was not in better form. Reagan was just beginning to emerge as a serious candidate for the Republican Presidential nomination, and privately I believed that, barring the emergence of some right-wing McGovern, whoever the Republicans nominated would be the one elected. Though I was still on active duty and any discussion of politics, as such, would have been improper, I was intensely interested in Reagan's views on any number of questions of foreign and domestic policy. I had come prepared to ask questions.

Instead, I found myself answering them. Mrs. Reagan skillfully led the conversation. I discovered that she had a well-defined and sensible view of current events. We spoke of NATO, of the internal situation in allied countries, of the Soviet military buildup. From time to time, Dick Allen joined in with an observation. Allen is a comic manqué whose speech is marked by a habitual mirthful undertone, and his remarks brightened the somber atmosphere. Reagan himself was a hospitable presence, smiling at the jokes, contributing an occasional phrase, gazing with deep fondness and admiration on his wife.

The evening was so pleasant, and Nancy Reagan's table talk so captivating, that I was somewhat surprised when I realized, while driving back to the airport at the end of the evening, that I had hardly exchanged a word with the man who—as I already suspected—would be the fortieth President of the United States. I hoped that there would be another opportunity, but knowing the ways of the Presidential personality—and the ways of staff assistants who guard the doors of the powerful and the possibly-to-be-powerful—I wondered if Reagan and I would ever meet again.

The months passed. At the end of June I left NATO and ended my thirty-one years of Army service. My wife, Pat, and I had settled into an apartment in a suburb of Philadelphia, and it was rewarding after more than three decades of living as a stranger to be back again in my home city. It was a pleasant life. I conducted a seminar on the Presidency at the University of Pennsylvania and served as a director of the Foreign Policy Research Institute and of several corporations. As a means of expressing certain very strong views on defense and foreign policy that I had been obliged to suppress as an officer on active duty, I continued a series of speaking engagements before business and professional audiences. This activity took me to some forty states. My prime purpose in undertaking all this travel, apart from the satisfaction of speaking my mind, was the support of my family. To others, it continued to have the appearance of a run at the nomination; a Haig-for-President Committee was formed in Washington. Although I was not consulted by the people involved, I did nothing to interfere with their right under the First and other amendments to the Constitution to support anyone they chose for the Presidency. But I never imagined that I had a chance to be nominated.

In July, I fulfilled an engagement as lakeside speaker at Bohemian Grove, a summer encampment of prominent men that takes place in a magnificent redwood forest near San Francisco. Next morning, I was invited to breakfast in the Owl's Nest, Reagan's camp at the Grove, and was seated next to Reagan. Again, he was rather quiet, but the guests at the table formed a historical tableau in terms of the 1980 Republican campaign: besides Reagan, John B. Connally was there, along with Henry Kissinger. Afterward, John Connally, a man with many admirable qualities who was then regarded as a strong contender for the nomination, inquired about my availability as a Vice Presidential candidate. No doubt he spoke to others about their availability also; these conversations are the straws that go into political bricks.

In August, I received another call from Richard Allen. Reagan wanted to talk to me again. Could I come to the ranch? I agreed. But wishing this time to have the opportunity of asking my questions and of answering whatever questions Reagan might have, and thinking that this would save Reagan's time, I asked if he and I could meet alone. This request was granted, and I went to California.

At their ranch north of Santa Barbara, the Reagans have achieved a homely simplicity that is very restful. The arid scenery, as one looks out toward the Pacific and back toward the mountains, is mild and peaceful. On my arrival, after a twisting ride up the steep mountainside, the Reagans greeted me on the doorstep. They then gave me a tour of the property. I was struck by an atmosphere of frontier frugality. Ronald and Nancy Reagan built this place, or large parts of it, with their own hands. They put up the sturdy log fence that surrounds the corral. Together they rebuilt the small, one-story ranch house that they bought as a near-ruin. They take an enormous, and quite infectious, pride in their work. You have the feeling that the ranch is more than a retreat, that it is the place where the Reagans truly feel most at home.

The tour over, Mrs. Reagan said good-bye with her firm handshake. She explained, with pointed good humor, that she was about to go riding—"so that you two can talk alone," she said. I guessed that my request for a private meeting with her husband had caused a misunderstanding, but there was no chance to repair the affront. Mrs. Reagan mounted her horse and cantered away.

Reagan, in close-fitting twill riding breeches, worn with old-fashioned, buckled cavalry boots, exuded good health and good fellowship. He has the physique of a man many years younger than his age, and in his open-necked shirt gave the appearance of peak physical fitness. We settled down for our talk in the living room of the ranch house, surrounded by Indian artifacts and Western objects of art. Reagan seemed genuinely glad to see me. Certainly I was happy to see him. I had always had warm feelings for him, reaching back to the Nixon Administration when he and I had had a kind of telephone acquaintanceship. As part of my duties, I sometimes had to call key governors and others to ask for their support for certain Presidential policies or actions. These were nearly always controversial. It is not usually a rewarding task to ask a man to stick his neck out on an issue that can do him no political good and may even do him harm. But Ronald Reagan was, in the best sense of the word, a loyalist, a man who seemed instinctively to put country above party and party above self. When President Nixon asked for his support, he gave it. Sometimes he gave his support at considerable political cost to himself as governor of California, but he always gave it ungrudgingly, and he always had a personal word of encouragement for me, a bringer of unwelcome tidings whom he did not even know.

I had been invited to come here, I supposed, because Ronald Reagan and I had something in common. We were both perceived to be candidates for the Republican nomination for the office of President of the United States. Reagan, of course, was beginning to emerge as the front-runner. He was possessed of a large, loyal constituency built up over fifteen years of intense and highly effective campaigning. My "candidacy" consisted of a dash of media speculation, a gratifying enthusiasm among a small group of supporters, who were for the most part unknown to me, and a cameo appearance or two in the popularity polls. My chances for the nomination had not improved since I returned to civilian life. I had no expectation that I would be President and had said so repeatedly in public and private. Of all the truths that a public man can speak in American life, that is the one least likely to be believed, so I was not especially surprised that Reagan, or at least the men around him, should withhold judgment on my real intentions.

Conversation flowed easily. Reagan's affability, his habit of speaking plainly without metaphor or jargon, and, above all, the impression he gives of *liking* the person he is talking to, create a good atmosphere. Simply put, Ronald Reagan is a nice guy and one is aware of this every moment. This is no small gift for a man to be blessed with. Like old friends passing a Sunday afternoon, we spoke about the hostages, then held captive in the American embassy in Teheran by "revolutionary youths" associated with the Ayatollah Ruhollah Khomeini, and about the difficult future of Iranian-American relations. The Shah of Iran, seduced and abandoned by the American government, had been driven into exile, and we discussed this and what it meant to such men as Anwar Sadat, who had risked everything on a dream of peace and the friendship of the United States. We spoke about Watergate and Vietnam and how these two tragic chapters in American history had leached the nation's belief in itself. We spoke about the need to strengthen our defenses; we spoke about the economy and the frightening growth of inflation. We agreed on most things.

On one subject, the draft, we did not agree. Reagan, as a conservative, believes that compulsory military service is an invasion of the right of the individual to free choice. Urging him to moderate this doctrinaire view, I argued that our youth should grow up with a sense of obligation to the nation. Those who are selected need not undertake military service in every case; some form of socially useful work should suffice if conscience does not permit the bearing of arms. National service, administered with absolute fairness for all classes and conditions of citizens, would do much, in my view, to restore a sense of national community and purpose and break down the artificial ideas of social class that have sprung up among our young people since World War II and that are repugnant to the American idea. As a young officer in Korea, I was repelled by the policy of granting draft deferments on educational grounds and for other reasons that primarily benefit the white middle class. In Vietnam, the system produced even greater abuses. A draft that was openly designed to favor the rich and the educated filled the ranks with soldiers who were neither. As I know from having served with them in battle, these young men were brave, intelligent, indomitable soldiers. But very, very rarely were they the sons of doctors and lawyers, corporate executives and politicians. Had there been more of the latter in our infantry divisions, fewer would have died; the influence of their families would have caused the United States government to fight those two inconclusive wars in quite a different way—or perhaps to have pursued policies that would have preserved the American position without resort to arms in the first place.

Reagan could not accept my advice to moderate his opposition to a draft. But we found, at the end of our ninety minutes together, that we could accept most of what the other thought and said. At this time I had not committed myself to any candidate for the Presidency. Now Reagan asked me if I would support him—"join my team," as he put it. Of course, he was asking me to abandon my own candidacy, such as it was. In itself, that was not a problem. It was inconceivable to me that I could present any threat to Reagan's nomination. But I was not ready to swear fealty to a liege. I thought it better, for the time being, to go on as I was, stating the issues that interested me in my own terms, to my own audiences, free of the anxiety that I might utter some phrase that could be interpreted as being in conflict with some position of Reagan's.

I told Ronald Reagan that I could not, at this time, become a part of his political household. But I assured him that, as I went around the country speaking, he could rely on me to do nothing that would set the two of us in opposition. With the exception of the draft issue, I would be supportive of his basic policy.

Speculation about my own Presidential ambitions continued. There is no cure for this in a country that promotes absolute freedom of expression, but I tried to do nothing to make it worse. I was looking for a job; rumors that I had a yen for the Oval Office were not reassuring to potential employers. On December 22, 1979, after discussing the decision with those in Philadelphia and Washington, D.C., who had worked on my behalf, I formally announced to the press that I was not a candidate; I hoped that that would end the matter. On December 26, I was named president and chief operating officer of United Technologies Corporation in Hartford, Connecticut. Moving into this beautiful New England community, settling into a comfortable house where we hoped to dwell until the end of our lives, facing the challenge of leading a great public corporation, Pat and I felt a sense of hopeful new beginning. The long years of temporary duty and sudden transfer, stimulating and rewarding as they had been, were truly over.

There was one passing cloud. While playing tennis, I had noticed a pain in my leg. A preemployment medical examination in connection with the issuance of life insurance revealed blockages in my coronary arteries. This came as a surprise. Except for a case of infectious hepatitis during the Korean War, I had never had a sick day in my life. My retirement physical from the Army had revealed no sign of trouble. In late March 1980, at the Texas Heart Institute at St. Luke's Episcopal Hospital in Houston, a surgical team led by Dr. Denton Cooley performed a double bypass operation. Within a month I was fully active and feeling as well, at fifty-five, as at any time in my life.

My new work was absorbing. In Harry J. Gray, chairman of the board at UTC, I had a gifted teacher and a friend who made my adjustment to a new career seem like a homecoming. I had never been happier. Despite continuing invitations, I avoided making speeches whenever I could; I had said what I wanted to say. From time to time I talked on the telephone with such men as Richard M. Nixon and former Secretary of the Treasury William E. Simon, who had news and gossip from the political world, and Richard Allen, who had his finger on the pulse of the Reagan organization. But I had become a private man, and I thought that I had dropped off the political radar screen forever.

Then, in July 1980, I received a call from Mike Curb, the lieutenant governor of California and a member of the Reagan team. The Governor, Curb said, hoped that I would attend the Republican convention in Detroit, and deliver a speech on foreign policy. I had some misgivings. Former Connecticut governor John Lodge and other state Republican leaders urged me to go. Harry Gray consented. Therefore, wearing the badge of a delegate from Connecticut, I found myself on the floor of the convention. Like most delegates, I glimpsed Reagan only on television. At his staff's request, I spoke in my candidate's behalf before a number of the larger Reagan delegations, including the one from California, which I confess I regarded as an unexpected honor. Bill Simon, who was being mentioned as a possible Secretary of the Treasury, and George P. Shultz, who was regarded as a likely Secretary of State, were touring the delegations, too, and sometimes we appeared together. My old friends, former President Gerald R. Ford and Henry Kissinger, were in evidence, but they were not working the Reagan beat.

A curious feature of the 1980 convention was the suggestion that former President Ford should be nominated for the Vice Presidency under the nebulous understanding that in the new Republican Administration he would be a sort of co-President of the United States, with powers and duties defined in a written agreement between himself and the Presidential candidate. I could not believe that the men who were proposing this, or those who were attempting to cobble an agreement to bring it about, were serious. Constitutionally, it was chaos. In terms of human behavior, it was worse. The person has not been born who would share the power of the Presidency, and to introduce as second in command a man who had himself been President was a prescription for trouble for the nation and for great personal unhappiness for Gerald Ford. I felt strongly enough about this to call Kissinger and express an opinion. In the end, nothing came of this bizarre idea.

The Vice Presidency, someone has said, is like the last cookie on the plate: nobody wants it but someone always takes it. So unsettled was the question of the Vice Presidency at the 1980 Republican convention that highly placed gossips even whispered to me that my name was being considered. If true, this was a great honor, but I received the news with dismay and hoped that the plate would not be passed to me. In the end, Reagan made a sensible choice of running mate in George M. Bush, whose candidacy gave ideological and regional balance to the ticket. Before this happened, a man who claimed to represent Reagan asked me to give him, on a confidential basis, an assessment of George Bush. I inferred from his tone of voice and body language that he hoped for something less than a ringing endorsement. I doubted that the man in fact came from Reagan, though he may have been a messenger for those in the Reagan camp who opposed Bush's presence on the ticket. I told him I would respond, in person, to a direct request from Reagan himself, but that I would not manufacture hearsay by whispering value judgments about George Bush behind his back. The man went away.

My speech on foreign policy, though it was scheduled during prime time, was preempted by punditry about the Ford Vice Presidential candidacy. Yet the delegates seemed to receive what I said with interest. My remarks were based on the foreign policy plank in the Republican platform and on some of the things I had been saying around the country. It called for a policy very like the one I was later to advocate within the counsels of the Reagan Administration. Afterward, Justin Dart, a member of the kitchen cabinet and an old friend, shook my hand and said, "You're our next Secretary of State." After all that had happened, I was not at all surprised to hear this—the air in a convention quivers with hyperbole—but I did not take it as gospel. Before I went back to Hartford and my work, I saw Reagan once again when we were seated at the same table at a luncheon given by a Polish-American group in Detroit. Though I understood that I was there at Reagan's request, it was not an occasion for anything more than an exchange of pleasantries.

Back at UTC, there was no time in which to campaign for Ronald Reagan, but I wanted him to be elected, and so on Election Day I voted for him in the expectation that he would be.

At Christmastide 1980, those were my connections with Ronald Reagan and his campaign for the Presidency. In another society, they would probably not be deemed sufficient to warrant the offer of the highest Cabinet post in a newly elected government. Winston Churchill, during his long exile from power, surrounded himself with like-minded men who thought of themselves as the next rulers of Britain and to some degree functioned as a supernumerary government, sharing information, discussing policy, negotiating on one another's interests exactly as if they were real ministers of the crown. When at last they came to power at a time of great peril to the British people, they were able to save their country because they understood the issues and because they knew and trusted each other; like athletes or soldiers, they had practiced and practiced until the thing came naturally. We Americans do not function in that way. In almost everything we do, we come together as strangers. Usually, matters turn out pretty well. That is the origin of our reputation as innovators and improvisers and also the basis of the suspicion among foreigners that we do not always know exactly what we are doing.

After the election, Richard Allen, who expected to be Reagan's adviser for national security affairs—a job he had also expected to have under President Nixon in 1969, only to be beaten out by a more solemn man, Henry Kissinger—called me on the telephone. Allen, speaking for Reagan, said that I was a candidate for a Cabinet post. The first position mentioned was that of Secretary of Defense. I pointed out that military men are prohibited for a ten-year period after leaving active duty from becoming Secretary of Defense. General of the Army George C. Marshall was the only military man to be nominated as the Secretary of Defense, but to accomplish this, a special act of Congress had been required. In my view, General Marshall, as one of the greatest men in American history, was a fitting exception to the rule, and should be the only one.

Between the election and the inauguration, Allen invited me, on behalf of the President-elect, to attend a dinner at the Madison Hotel in Washington in honor of Prime Minister Edward Seaga of Jamaica. Before dinner, I was ushered into to a private room in the hotel to meet Reagan's aides, Edwin M. Meese III and James A. Baker III, and the President-elect's friend and adviser, Senator Paul D. Laxalt of Nevada. They were there, it seemed, to look me over. There was very little small talk. They asked, first, if I had anything to hide in connection with Watergate. I assured them that I had nothing whatever to hide. Then Meese asked me a second question: did I want to be President? I answered in the negative. It seemed a curious question. Meese's own man, a Republican, had just been elected by a landslide. Surely he was in no political danger from any other Republican. Later, at dinner, Meese leaned over to my wife and said, "Don't worry, he's going to make it." Passing along this mysterious tidbit, Pat commented, "My worry is that you *will* make it."

William Simon, who had good sources within the Reagan camp and who was himself a candidate for a Cabinet post, told me that I was going to be named Secretary of State. George P. Shultz, who was eminently qualified for the job, was still regarded as the leading contender. His colleague at the Bechtel Corporation in California, Caspar W. ("Cap") Weinberger, who, like Shultz, had a personal relationship with Reagan, had also been mentioned. In the end, Shultz remained in private life and Weinberger, a highly experienced administrator who was a former Director of the Office of Management and Budget as well as a former Secretary of Health, Education, and Welfare, was made Secretary of Defense. Later I learned that Shultz had never been asked to accept the post for which he had been mentioned in the press. With respect to my own possibilities, the phone calls and the rumors continued. I began to take them seriously when the familiar baritone of Richard Nixon came down the telephone line one day to say that Reagan had decided to ask me to be his Secretary of State. In matters Republican, Nixon usually knows what he is talking about. By this time, nearly all the Cabinet positions had been filled; I believe that only State and Labor remained when, finally, Reagan called me on the telephone.

It was a wintry Thursday afternoon, December 11. I was in my office with a cold that was turning into flu. The President-elect identified himself as "Ron Reagan" and in his pleasant way said, "Al, I'm calling to say that I'd like you to join my team and be my Secretary of State."

Without pausing, he went on to say that Richard Allen, as National Security Adviser, would act exclusively as a staff coordinator. "You know my feeling about the Secretary of State," Reagan said. "He would be *the* spokesman. I won't have a repeat of the Kissinger-Rogers situation. I'll look to you, Al."

Of course, I am quoting here from memory, but the words were so important, and I was so gratified to hear them, that they made a strong impression on me. In our talk at the ranch, Reagan and I had discussed the unhappy situation that had developed when Nixon's Secretary of State, William P. Rogers, one of his oldest supporters, was outmaneuvered in the bureaucracy, in the press, and, therefore, abroad, by Kissinger. Finally, Rogers, excluded almost entirely from the making of foreign policy, had to go. Nixon, who disliked unpleasant confrontations in any case and who certainly did not wish to fire a man he had liked and respected for half a lifetime, had asked me to break the news to Rogers.

This experience, along with others that were hardly less traumatic, had convinced me, as had my reading of history, that there could be only one official in the government responsible, under the President, for the formulation of foreign policy and for its public enunciation. That official could be the Secretary of State or he could be the National Security Adviser; for that matter, he could be anyone the President chose—John F. Kennedy conducted much of his foreign policy through his brother Robert, who happened to be the Attorney General, and Lyndon B. Johnson initially relied heavily on his Secretary of Defense, Robert S. McNamara. But whoever the man was, he had to be the President's man, chosen by the President, trusted by the President, and in daily contact and communication with the President. He, and he alone, had to speak for the President on matters of foreign policy on those occasions when the President chose not to speak for himself.

As Dean Acheson wrote, "[a President's] relationship with the Secretary of State will not prosper if the latter is not accepted as his principal adviser and executive agent in foreign affairs, and the trusted confidant of all his thoughts and plans relating to them." Two of the most successful recent Secretaries of State, Acheson under Harry S Truman and John Foster Dulles under Dwight D. Eisenhower, enjoyed this ideal relationship. The most celebrated National Security Adviser in history, Henry Kissinger, had a similar arrangement with Nixon, and when Kissinger became Secretary of State, he took with him to Foggy Bottom all the privileges that had eluded William Rogers. It should not be supposed that every hour these men spent together was free of tension and anxiety. Much of what a Secretary of State has to tell a President is unpleasant. "The problems are frustrating," Acheson wrote. "They are sure to provoke controversy in many quarters. Most of the desirable measures are distasteful to accept. All of the decisions are hard. So the Secretary of State has the makings of an unwelcome visitor."

This does not mean that a President should not have other advisers. Of course, he must have them. But a superpower must speak about its intentions in one clear voice lest it baffle its allies, mislead its adversaries, and, ultimately, lose its own way in a maze of conflicting policies. Press briefings and thoughtless answers to tricky questions are not—cannot be—policy.

Reagan seemed to grasp these truths. Once again, I admired his instincts. "I will look to you," he told me. Into this simple phrase I read the President-elect's understanding that to make foreign policy for a powerful state is, to a degree, to make the future. I was certain that Ronald Reagan understood what a solemn undertaking this was, and how important it was to go about the job with the right apparatus.

I asked Reagan if I could have a day to consider the matter and discuss it with my employer. In the hours that followed, I sought advice from my wife and from Harry Gray and his wife, Helen. It was not easy to ask Pat to give up a life she had learned to love. Nor was it easy for Harry Gray, who had taken a great chance only a year before in entrusting the corporation he had built to a man who had had no experience in the business world, to release me from my contract. Both told me what I had learned again and again in long years in uniform: when the commander in chief asks an American for help, he must give it. Besides, in one part of my nature I now wanted the job. I had been training for it, in a sense, for thirty-one years. I thought that I could perform it well, and that it was important that it be well performed.

I accepted. I accepted with a certain sense of loss, to go back to an old life that I knew was filled with difficulty and misunderstanding and implacable (and often unjust) judgment of character and perfor-

mance. I had served near to six Presidents. I had seen one of them fall
in dreadful disgrace, but I had seen Presidents, including Richard
Nixon, rise in triumph also. I had seen war as it was made in high
places and as it was fought on the battlefield. I did not want to see
any more of it. It seemed a good thing to do what one could to
prevent more wars from being made. Therefore, I accepted the post
Reagan had offered me with a glad and hopeful spirit.

I was certain that, in a broad way, the President-elect and I shared
a certain view of the world. Reagan had not revealed to me, in the
course of our brief conversations, a profound knowledge of international issues or an intimate acquaintance with foreign statesmen
among whom, a few weeks hence on his inauguration as the fortieth
President of the United States, he would assume his place as leader of
the Western world. I had not searched for these qualities in Reagan.
There was no reason to suppose that they would be present, nor was
it essential that they should be; of all our twentieth-century Presidents, only two, Eisenhower and Nixon, can be said without quibble
to have come to office with deep firsthand knowledge of the world
outside America.

Like the voters who elected him by one of the greatest majorities
in American history, I perceived in Ronald Reagan more significant
qualities than mere expertise: decency, optimism, a gift for self-edu-
cation, a sturdy commonsense affection for the United States and for
mankind, and a talent for communication that approached the artistic. Abraham Lincoln and Harry S Truman, possessed of similar
attributes, required in addition only a singular historical opportunity
in order to achieve greatness. Whether Ronald Reagan could be a
great President was unknowable. Like most Americans, I profoundly
hoped that he would be. I did know, everyone knew, that history
would test him most rigorously, and that civilization itself, under
powerful assault by forces of terrorism and doubt, would in some
measure survive or decline according to the quality of his answers.

I hoped that I could help him. "The relationship," Acheson
wrote, "is essentially one of partnership." The Secretary of State is
emphatically the junior partner. I realized that the new President and
I were not yet partners or even friends, except in the sense that men
of similar ideas are natural friends, and that he is a man who feels
most comfortable when surrounded by old friends.

Yet I was confident that the two essential elements of Acheson's "partnership" were present: Reagan had given me his trust and I had given him my loyalty. All else ought to have followed naturally.

BACKGROUND

There was another reason for my accepting the appointment offered by President-elect Reagan. The reason had nothing to do, and yet in a sense it had everything to do, with my duties as Secretary of State. A few days after my Hardingesque conversation in that room at the Madison Hotel with Baker and Meese and Laxalt, the *Washington Post* commenced a series of articles about me. These raised scurrilous questions about my service in the White House, my association with President Nixon, and the circumstances of his resignation. By both innuendo and more direct means, it was suggested that I had unjustly escaped public humiliation and hanging as a Watergate criminal, and that my appointment to the Cabinet might provide a good opportunity to correct this oversight.

My wife and children were distressed. My friends were appalled. I was infuriated, and in an earlier day, when the reputations of public persons were still protected by the law, might have sued for libel. When the alleged Watergate cover-up occurred, I had already left the White House and was vice chief of staff of the Army. After the event, Nixon called me back to be chief of staff in the White House. I had no connection with this tragic episode except to try to keep the White House machinery running and the indispensable authority of the President intact after the damage—irreparable damage, as it turned out—had been done.

But I could hardly run away from these false charges. Failing to confront them would be tantamount to saying that I was afraid of scrutiny because I did not think I could stand up to it. I knew perfectly well that I could stand up to it. I had stood up to exhaustive investigation before for the simple reason that I had done nothing illegal and had nothing to hide. The *Post* (and whoever its sources were) had now made it necessary for me to go through the whole dispiriting process again as a matter of honor to my family and pride in my career as an officer of the United States Army. Over the years, I have thought much about the press and its place in American life, but never more deeply and never more poignantly than in my time as Secretary of State, for these early articles in the *Post* were a harbinger of things to come.

"Remarks are not literature," Gertrude Stein is supposed to have said to the young Ernest Hemingway. Leaks to the press ought not to be read as policy, but they often are. Lately, there has been some justification for the practice.

All Presidents, all politicians (and not only politicians), hope to make use of the press. All arrive in Washington determined not to be unduly influenced by the press, and all fail to some degree. It is easy enough to remember, when one is greeting the voters in Indiana, that most Americans do not read the *New York Times* and the *Washington Post* or watch the evening news on ABC, CBS, and NBC—or, for that matter, necessarily believe everything they read or watch or hear. This memory tends to become submerged once the campaign is won and the candidate, as officeholder, takes up residence in Washington. Then the capital, with its curious mixture of high ideals and hard work and base ambition and blind vanity, becomes the universe: if I am so famous that the *Post* is writing about me, then, of course, the whole world is reading it.

Politicians live (and, as we know, sometimes die) by the press. The press lives by politicians. This symbiotic relationship is at the center of our national life. The relationship has always existed. Probably it came into being at about the same time as human speech, which permitted the first gossip to repeat the (suitably edited) sayings of the chief of the clan to the people in the next cave. It existed in America, an especially nourishing environment for all types of communication, before the Declaration of Independence. Thomas Jefferson wrote some of the same things that I shall write about the press— for example, the prime truth about it, which is that for all its follies it is indispensable to the preservation of liberty in this country.

The press is still, as it was in Jefferson's time, a powerful check upon the government, but the government has no tangible power over it. (The government has, of course, certain intangible powers, but we will come to that subject later.) The press is a peculiar, disembodied, melancholy creature driven by strange hungers, never happy with its triumphs, wanting always to be loved, and incessantly suspecting that it is not. In this, of course, it closely resembles the politician.

There the resemblance ends. The politician and his appointed assistants have an obligation to be responsible. The press has none. It prints what it is given. If some important national secret is betrayed in the pages of a great newspaper, as has often happened, it is nonsense to protest that the editors and reporters have no patriotism, no decency, that this is treason. The charges may be correct, but you have arraigned the wrong defendants. The failure of patriotism, the betrayal of decency, the treachery are real enough. But these are the trespasses of the public official who, having been trusted with the secret, could not keep it.

Why not? This is a question I have wrestled with over three decades of life in Washington. When, as a young major, I was by a lucky chance brought into contact with some of President Kennedy's closest advisers, I learned how quickly secrets that clearly were vital to the security of the United States found their way into the newspapers—and how angry this made the President and his aides. The phenomenon astounded me. At West Point, we had been taught that military secrets were as sacred as the lives of our men because soldiers died when secrets came into the possession of the enemy. Evidently civilians are not bound by such simplistic formulas, because in the Johnson, Nixon, Ford, and Carter administrations, the leaks were at least as great a problem.

In the Reagan Administration, they were not merely a problem, they were a way of life, and in the end I concluded that they were a way of governing. Leaks constituted policy; they were the authentic voice of the government. It is not surprising that this should have been so. The President's closest aides were essentially public relations men. They were consummate professionals—*wizards* is not too strong a word. In my view they were the most skillful handlers of the press since the New Deal. They had just completed a campaign—not simply a drive for the nomination and the election, but a campaign that went back beyond the governor's mansion in Sacramento, California. Now their long dream of power had become reality.

This is the classic dilemma of the campaign staff. How to translate rhetoric into policy? How to transform a political image into a historical personality? How to metamorphose the staff's suspicion of outsiders into an atmosphere of consultation and collaboration with a lot of strangers on whom the President must depend if he is to succeed? How to share credit, and even the affection of the President, with newcomers? These are not easy questions.

Reagan's staff decided to find their answers in the place they knew best—the press. For years, they had been communicating with their chief's friends and enemies through the press, rewarding the one and punishing the other. They had often communicated with each other in the same way. It seemed natural to them, now that they were in the White House, to communicate thus with other officials and agencies of the U.S. government, and even with foreign governments. From Inauguration Day, and perhaps even before, they communicated with me in this fashion.

At first, I did not realize that the *Times* and the *Post* and the networks and the news magazines had let themselves be converted into White House bulletin boards. When, for example, I would deliver a sensitive memorandum for the President's eyes only in the early afternoon, and then hear line-by-line quotations from it on the evening news, I would react with surprise and call up the White House to express my shock. How naive I must have seemed.

The men in the White House were not naive. They were grappling with a difficult problem, the most difficult faced by men trying to establish the authority of a new President since the election of Franklin Delano Roosevelt. Neither FDR in 1932, when Republicans controlled the press, nor Ronald Reagan in 1980, when liberal Democrats were the rule among journalists, had very many friends and sympathizers in the established press. How, in the face of a reflexive ideological hostility—not to say bigotry—toward Reagan and all that he stood for, were his men to get fair, even favorable coverage of his Administration? They were determined to get it, and to a truly admirable degree, they succeeded. How did they do it?

First, they had a bit of luck. As Reagan came to office, the press was nervous about itself. It had played a major role in bringing down three Presidents in a row—two of them Democrats even if they were Southerners, let it be remembered. Even within the press, some thought (though few violated tribal taboos far enough to say so outright) that there had been excesses. I may argue that the press has no obligation to be responsible, but the press doesn't necessarily agree. It has its standards and its degrees of respectability. Its practitioners are human; naturally, they want to belong to the company of honorable men. Besides, there is an ultimate control on the press and a very effective one: if its readers do not believe it and do not trust it or if they think it lacks a standard of fair play, they will stop heeding it and it will die. Therefore, the press was inclined to cool its ardor for a time, even to go so far as to show that it could be fair to a President whose policies much of it despised.

Second, the White House wizards understood the great intangible power that the government holds over the press. I have said that the press is disembodied; I meant that it has no life of its own, it lives on the acts of others. Action, to the press, is information; it is not interested in the parentheses of policy, forethought, and consequence. Information is power; manifestly, the press cannot live without information. It has no information of its own; it follows, then, that it must rely on others to manufacture the stuff.

The government is the great smithy of information. Appreciating this, Reagan's men exercised their intangible power. They opened the doors to the workshop and escorted reporters inside in a way hitherto unknown in Washington. They literally told them everything. For the first time in living memory, you could actually believe almost everything you read. For the press, always the outsider, always operating on suspicion and guesswork and animosity, it was a dream come true. It had never had sources like this. And, of course, it could not risk losing these sources by offending them, so it wrote what it was given.

"A Worldwide Climate of Uncertainty"

THERE IS a tendency to argue that Ronald Reagan is an aberration who does not represent the true will of the voters or the political center of the nation. This is a fallacy. His election was the culmination of a trend in American politics that began with the death of Franklin D. Roosevelt, a trend that has ever since, in election after Presidential election, steadily moved the political center to the right in this country.

Harry S Truman, in his famous victory over Thomas E. Dewey in 1948, did not win a majority of the popular vote (49.6 percent). Neither did John F. Kennedy in 1960 (49.7 percent). Lyndon B. Johnson won by a landslide in 1964, but Jimmy Carter mustered only a bare majority (50.1 percent) in 1976.

No Democratic President since Roosevelt has been twice elected in his own right. Truman and Johnson, Vice Presidents who succeeded deceased Presidents, chose not to run for a second full term after once being elected at the head of the ticket. Kennedy was assassinated in his first term. Carter was defeated after a single term.

In the same period, conversely, the two Republicans elected to the

Presidency before Reagan were reelected with an increased majority. Eisenhower increased his share of the popular vote from 55.1 percent (33,936,234 votes) in 1952 to 57.4 percent in 1956 (35,590,472 votes). Richard M. Nixon improved from 43.4 percent in 1968 (31,785,480 votes) to 60.7 percent in 1972, when he polled 47,167,319 votes and carried forty-nine of the fifty states. Running under staggering handicaps, our only appointed President, Gerald R. Ford, polled 47.9 percent of the vote, 2.1 percent less than Jimmy Carter. In 1980, Ronald Reagan won 50.7 percent of the popular vote (43,893,770).

In the nine Presidential elections since the death of Roosevelt, the Republicans have won five, the Democrats four. Overall, Republican candidates polled a total of 315 million popular votes or 52 percent, the Democrats 292 million or 48 percent.

These facts suggest that a conservative trend had been developing for at least thirty years before it propelled Reagan into office in 1980. In the process, it swept away the old Republican party, dominated by the Eastern Establishment, beloved in the Farm Belt, and despised both in the South and in the northern industrial cities as the party of Hoover. In place of the GOP arose what its present proprietors, if they were given to snappy phrases, might call the Grand New Party. At its heart is a coalition of former Southern Democrats and Western populists. It has its considerable share of blue-collar adherents, and it has kept the allegiance of its Establishment Easterners (not all of whom live in the East), baffled though they may be by the Laffer curve and the curious manners of some of Reagan's appointees. It has even attracted a class of intellectuals, called neoconservatives, who used to be liberal Democratic intellectuals and still sound like liberal Democratic intellectuals, as a Frenchman who learns English late in life will typically still sound like a Frenchman when he speaks our language. There are also some real conservatives in the party.

This itemization of Republicans demonstrates how thoroughly fractured is the Democratic party. It might not be an exaggeration to say that if it does not change, it will die—and if it changes, it will die. The Democratic party has become the party of orthodoxy. Its leaders, its rhetoric, its ideas belong to a stirring past that is nevertheless a past that will not come again. Yet Democrats seem to feel that if they stop paying incessant homage to their party's past, it will lose its soul. A veil of religiosity has been drawn across the seductive statue of liberalism; no heresy goes unpunished, no apostate goes unstoned.

Few things are sadder than the fiery reformer who in his old age begins to toy with the idea of burning reformers at the stake. However, the party of FDR as we knew it between 1932 and 1948 is no more. The Democrats have lost the South, and in the North, they have lost great neighborhoods of voters who no longer automatically believe in them. On the evidence of recent elections, they have lost the capacity to find within their once-dynamic party men and women who are comfortable with the future and realistic about the present.

Against this background, the lesson of Ronald Reagan's election in 1980 seems clear enough. The people were asking for realism. They were asking for an atmosphere of honest pride in the United States, an acknowledgment by their leaders of the astonishing things that America had accomplished for its people and for the rest of the world. They were asking for an end to doubt, for an end to vituperation. A victory as vast as Reagan's cannot be explained by the weakness of his opponent or the contumely that was heaped upon Jimmy Carter. It can plausibly be explained as a great act of popular trust, a signal from Americans to their leaders and opinion makers that it was time to start trusting one another again—which, in the most fundamental way, means believing in the nation once more.

The country had been through Vietnam and Watergate. It had been told that it was a cruel and greedy imperialist power that cared nothing for human life. It had been told that it was corrupt, that it was an unjust society that oppressed its masses, that freedom was being systematically destroyed by the institutions of the government. These charges contradicted the evidence of American lives as they were being lived. Americans looked on Vietnam after Saigon (renamed Ho Chi Minh City) fell to the Communists and saw the brutal oppression of a people Americans had tried to preserve from exactly this fate. They saw thousands of innocent men and women and children, mostly ethnic Chinese, put to sea in leaky boats to drown or otherwise perish if they could not reach a friendly shore. Next door in Cambodia, at least 1 million of the Khmer people, and probably many more than that number, were murdered by a regime composed of Marxist zealots, a force created by the Vietnamese Communists. Sensible Americans began to wonder if, after all, the United States had been the most malevolent force at work in Indochina.

In the matter of social progress within the United States, the record was equally clear. In decision after decision and enactment after enactment, the rights of the individual had constantly been expanded. The loathsome practice of racial segregation had been ended and the country was visibly on its way to becoming a truly integrated society. Freedom of speech and of expression had been broadened in such a way that it was possible to speak or publish with a liberty that had heretofore been unknown; for public figures, the laws of libel effectively ceased to exist—an uncomfortable state of affairs for many public figures, but a potent force for an open society.

In accepting the Republican nomination in 1960, Richard Nixon said, "I believe in the American dream because I have seen it come true in my own life." Those who detested Nixon writhed. But he spoke the truth—he *was* born poor, and by a combination of luck and brains and, above all, hard work, he rose to the highest office in the land. So, in my own lifetime, have six other men of humble origins—Truman, Eisenhower, Johnson, Ford, Carter, and Reagan. It is the common experience of Americans to improve their own lives and to provide the means for their children to do even better. It is taken for granted that an American boy, and now, at long last, a girl, can achieve almost anything within the limits of individual ability and effort. This is an extraordinary state of affairs, unknown to history before the founding of the democratic state, and still un-dreamed of in places where democracy has not taken root.

Some time ago, I encountered a professor at a great university who specialized in forecasting the future of nations. What, I asked him, is the nation of the future? "Clearly it is the United States—if we get back to work," he replied. It is our collective good fortune that hundreds of thousands of new immigrants are streaming into the United States in a great replenishment of the nation's human re-sources. Many of these new Americans come from Europe, but nearly half the annual total arrive from Latin America and Asia. These refugees from war and political oppression and poverty and class tyranny are finding in America exactly what our own forebears found: opportunity and freedom. Like our ancestors, they are eager to hope and willing to work. They believe that America is the coun-try of the future. The first generation will endure hard labor and practice frugality for the sake of the second. A nation is the sum of its families, and our new neighbors from overseas are reminding us that families and nations are built by work, and above all by a well-founded optimism about the future. Such an optimism can only be premised on a realistic assessment that the American present, though imperfect, is the very best mankind has so far invented for itself, and that violent departures from the past can jeopardize the future. If that truth is so clear to a peasant from the Mekong Delta, why should it evade an American youth who was educated at Berkeley or Harvard—or, for that matter, his professor?

Certainly it does not evade the vast majority of Americans. They look at the explosion of freedom and social justice in this country, they look at the vitality of our artistic life and the inventiveness of our technology (and the marriage of the two, for what were our ventures into space if they were not great works of art joining men and machine and the face of creation?), and they realize that, far from plummeting into an abyss, we are living in a renaissance.

It was that realization that gave Ronald Reagan his historic opportunity. He had the possibility of helping his own nation, at least, to see itself for what it really is and to act at home and in the world with the confidence that was justified by the reality of its economic, military, and, above all, moral strength. Better than any President since Kennedy, he had the surface qualities and the skills to do the job. In the epoch of television, Reagan, like Kennedy, was made for the camera. His looks, his geniality, his goodwill, the tone of his voice were superbly suited to the task at hand. (In this he held a great advantage over Richard Nixon, the President I knew best. Nixon, as a writer and speaker of English, was a considerable stylist; I have heard that a group of university researchers who examined the writings of various American Presidents for clarity and the absence of rhetorical tricks gave Nixon the top mark. I suspect that this must have been a blind tasting because I have thought that Nixon's basic problem as a communicator was a matter of musculature: on signal from his autonomic nervous system, of which he was not aware, his face formed expressions and his voice mechanism produced tones that had the unhappy effect of driving his multitude of detractors into new fits of exasperated disbelief.) Reagan, however, was a trained professional, a man who knew, as a matter of inborn talent and rigorous training and long experience, how to appeal to an audience.

In a demagogue, this would have been a dangerous thing. But Reagan was no demagogue. He was, it is true, a man of strong beliefs, but they were traditionally American and, oddly enough, essentially liberal beliefs. He was a man with an overdue political message. Politics is, after all, a way of explaining the meaning of life. Americans, everyone in the Western world, were eager to have contemporary life explained. It is evident that some enormous process of change was taking place. The United States, and with it the rest of the world, is changing from twentieth-century to twenty-first-century technology. The West is modifying its life as an industrialized society and is becoming something new, a technological society—one not based on production of tangible goods alone—as well as a society increasingly organized around services. This is not happening in any important sense as a result of wrong decisions or right ones taken in the field of government policy; it is happening because it is a natural evolution of human activity.

Reagan, when he came to office, was preoccupied by domestic questions, and so he should have been. The nation had not yet emerged from its long night of self-doubt. The economy was a shambles. He had to attack these problems, had to show himself to be a leader and an innovator. But it was my hope that the new President understood the intimate relationship between domestic and foreign policy, and that the one could not be made to succeed without the other. The United States and the other nations of the world are interdependent; no American Administration can deal with domestic economy without assessing the impact of its policies on the world economy. It was essential that this be understood from the beginning, that the principle of teamwork be applied to the creation of the integrated policy framework that would be needed if America's urgent problems, at home and abroad, were to be effectively addressed.

There was a sunny moment in history, from the end of the Second World War to the 1960s, when the United States was paramount in the world. As the richest and most militarily powerful state on earth, and probably in history, it could often decide what it wanted to happen on a global scale and then make it happen. America willed the recovery of Europe and made it happen through the Marshall Plan. It anticipated the demise of the French and the Dutch empires in Indochina and Indonesia and helped to bring it about. The list is very long and very familiar. On the whole, given the supernatural temptations inherent in the situation, the United States comported itself well, and with a degree of altruism that surprised the world and in some cases confused it, but anyway created an atmosphere of trust and admiration among our allies and friends that is a far more important element in our relationships with them than the exasperation that sometimes breaks out on both sides.

However that may be, the era has ended. Our wartime allies and enemies, mightily assisted by the United States, finally recovered from the ravages of the world war just before America began to immerse itself in a new war in Vietnam. Western Europe and Japan now dispose between them even greater economic power than the United States. The situation with regard to petroleum resources has profoundly altered the economic relationship between the United States and its allies and the Third World. We have become at least as dependent upon the Europeans for our defense as they have been upon us, and their contributions to NATO in men and materiel and money now surpass our own. The Soviet Union, at the time of Reagan's inauguration, possessed greater military power than the United States, which had gone into a truly alarming military decline even before the withdrawal from Vietnam accelerated the weakening trend. Reagan was, and remains, President of a United States that no longer deploys irresistible economic influence and military power.

America, in the late twentieth century, requires a more skillful and realistic diplomacy. But if it is weaker than it was, it is still a superpower. That is a fact of history and nature from which there can be no escape. The United States, if it does not wish to sow fear and confusion in the world and create conditions of the greatest danger for itself and for all of humanity, must behave like the superpower it is. For all but the final year of Carter's Presidency, it had refused to do this, apparently as a matter of conscience. I will not examine the metaphysics of this attitude; what's past is past and it is fruitless to dispute the wisdom of acts that cannot be retrieved. Because of Vietnam and Watergate, the U.S. had, for some time before Carter took office, been too distracted to act like a superpower.

The consequences were devastating. The whole balance of the world was disturbed. Our enemy, the Soviet Union, had been seduced by the weakness of the American will and extended itself far beyond the natural limits of its own apparent interests and influence. In 1968, Leonid Brezhnev, as a means of justifying the Soviet invasion of Czechoslovakia, promulgated the Brezhnev Doctrine, which held that the U.S.S.R. would use military means to intervene in any Soviet bloc nation where Communist rule was threatened. The Brezhnev Doctrine would be extended throughout the world as part of the Soviet Union's policy of supporting "wars of national liberation," i.e., Marxist insurgencies inspired and equipped by Moscow. This meant that Soviet military power, transformed from a continental to a global phenomenon, would be used to *establish*, not merely preserve, Communist rule wherever the U.S.S.R. decided to do it. We were witnessing the conjunction of Soviet ambition and a maturing Soviet global reach. President Carter chose not to resist this audacious assault upon American interests and, incidentally, upon the safety of legitimate governments and innocent people around the world.

Statesmen and others often speak of preventing World War III. One might instead suggest that World War III may actually have begun on that winter day in 1948 when Jan Masaryk was defenestrated in Prague, and that it has been going on ever since in a ceaseless testing of wills and exchange of blood to decide whether the future of mankind will be Marxist-Leninist or otherwise. The Greek civil war, Korea, the Berlin blockade, the Hungarian uprising, East Berlin, the Cuban revolution, Vietnam, Prague, Afghanistan, and, most recently, the rise of international terrorism and the bloody insurgency in El Salvador, are among the hundreds of skirmishes and battles in this unnamed and unrecognized war. Meanwhile, American military power declined, and our influence in the world continued to languish as the fear of "another Vietnam" paralyzed the will of the U.S. government.

In light of the foregoing, it might seem that the new President's Secretary of State would have had to paint for him a picture of the Soviet Union as a buoyant imperial power, having its way whenever and wherever it chose with an America that had come to the end of its moral capital. This was not the case. In fact, the Soviet Union was, and is, a deeply troubled and most vulnerable power. The problems on the surface are plain to see: across the board, Moscow is overextended militarily and economically. Its military procurement program is a prescription for permanent social deprivation; some analysts project that if the spending curve continues at its present rate, the military budget will consume almost the entire Soviet gross national product before the end of the century. The weapons this mindless buildup produces are not always of the first order of excellence, as was demonstrated, *inter alia*, by the feat of the Israeli air force in shooting down more than twenty Syrian MIG's in one engagement over Lebanon in 1982, without themselves suffering any loss. Afghanistan is a ghastly drain on Soviet treasure, manpower, and ideological credibility. It has cost them much in the sense that it has educated the Third World about the nature of Soviet policy. Terrorism has killed and maimed a great many innocent people, but it has not yet shaken the West in any important way; assuming a higher state of alert, the free nations can handle this new class of criminals without invading the rights of the rest of the population.

The Russians' underlying problems are even more serious. First of all, the Great Russians who have dominated what is now the U.S.S.R., first as tsars and now as commissars, are becoming a minority of the population. They are being outnumbered by the other peoples of the Soviet Union. No one can tell what this fact of demography may mean for the future in a state in which there are no established means for the orderly transfer of power, let alone for the peaceful evolution of a balance of ethnic identity and influence. It is a serious question, as all questions containing the threat of change are grave for the Soviet leadership, because Moscow has become the preeminent defender of the status quo in the world.

The Russian revolution has become a frozen orthodoxy. Moscow dares not change, it cannot change, and in this lies its mortal illness. In Poland, as earlier in Hungary, East Germany, and Czechoslovakia, we saw how little the Soviet Union has the capacity to transform itself. It may be seen by leftist visionaries as the agent of change, through the power of its scripture and of its guns, in Vietnam or Cambodia or Cuba or even Afghanistan. Nevertheless, its objective is not change but conformity: the war of liberation, the terrorists' bomb, are instruments for making other countries just like the Soviet Union.

But it does not profit a nation to be like the Soviet Union. The nations of Eastern Europe, who have had the longest experience of this unnatural condition, are in a state of rage over the economic deprivation and cultural starvation brought about by the replacement of their ancient nationhood by a "socialism" imposed and perpetuated by the Red Army. The satellites demand change. The Soviets will never give it to them. What can the outcome be? In the Third World, many states, on attaining independence from colonialism, adopted the Marxist model. This was understandable enough. The conditions in which human beings live under a colonialist regime (or under an oligarchy, which can be described as a form of domestic colonialism) arouse such rage as to make the most radical solution seem the most attractive. The rhetoric of the left is purgative and very satisfying emotionally. Marxist revolutionary technique provides a disciplined instrument with which to seize power and establish political control. However, it lacks long-term practical value as a means of reforming society because it is a system of lies about the nature of man and society that was invented to strike back at the hypocrisies of nineteenth-century capitalism. On its record, Marxism cannot stimulate economic development; it just does not work, and especially it does not work in developing countries that need education, technology, intensive capital investment, and, not incidentally, that fertilization of the political system which can only take place when leaders and people are not separated from one another by the apparatus of a police state.

There is another matter to be mentioned here. It concerns what happens after the war of liberation. The world knows what that is and saw it in the Soviet Union itself, where, according to Aleksandr Solzhenitsyn, 35 million persons died in the Gulag, snuffed out by their own government. More recently it was seen in Cuba, where hundreds were executed, thousands were imprisoned, and tens of thousands fled the country. We have spoken about the carnage in Vietnam and Cambodia. There are many other equally striking cases. The historical record shows that Marxists simply are unable to carry out political operations without committing murder. Sometimes this ideological homicide occurs on a mass scale, as in Cambodia; sometimes it is random, as in acts of terrorism; and sometimes it is selective, as when a political rival is executed by gunshot in the cellars of the Lubiyanka. But the fact is, the triumph of a Marxist revolution almost always brings hideous suffering down upon the people it has "rescued" from the previous oppressor. The world has noticed this; the refugees from communism, though not nearly as numerous as the dead, are everywhere in their millions.

Clearly, the Soviet Union, because it is the only other superpower and because it insists upon the struggle of opposites as a matter of dogma, is and must remain the first concern of any U.S. Administration. After the Carter experiment in obsequiousness, and the criticism and uncertainty it stimulated among our allies and friends, there was an imperative need to deal with the Soviet question. No frivolous playground test of manhood was involved here. Across the whole spectrum of our relations with the other nations of the world, a shadow had fallen. Certain foreign leaders who were our traditional friends, and some who were not, believed that the United States had accepted the Soviet assertion that communism was an inevitable historical condition, and that America was looking for a means of accommodating itself to that reality. In this, they were to some degree correct: there were people, honest and patriotic, in the permanent bureaucracy of the U.S. foreign policy establishment, who accepted the inevitability of a Marxist phase of ascendancy in the Third World, at least.

Even if this had not been so, there was plenty of evidence of our vacillation. We had coldly abandoned our faithful ally, the Shah of Iran, an act that sent a tremor of apprehension through every moderate Arab leader in the Middle East. The Persian Gulf was now threatened by a theocratic regime in Teheran that seemed to have abandoned reason, and the moderate Arabs wondered who would protect them if the Soviets gained control of the fundamentalist movement. That the Soviets had ambitions in the Gulf and beyond no one doubted. The Red Army occupied Afghanistan. Ethiopia and the Yemens were in the hands of Soviet clients. There were Cuban troops in three African countries, and it was an open secret that Soviet troops were present also. Muammar al-Qaddafi was arming an international conspiracy of leftist cutthroats with Soviet weapons and explosives, and he was threatening Chad and Sudan with conventional military power. Anwar Sadat, that great champion of peace in the Middle East, had sacrificed the goodwill of the Arab world at Camp David and was isolated. He, of all men, was not sure of America's friendship. Neither was Israel, and as her fear of betrayal and aggression grew, our influence upon her diminished and with it our ability to help advance the peace process and preserve her security. The fires of insurrection, fed by the Soviets and fanned by their surrogates, the Cubans, spread unchecked in Central America. In Europe, where a massive propaganda campaign designed to split us away from our NATO allies on the question of nuclear weapons had been launched, our allies urged us to take up our fallen leadership. In Southeast Asia, we had abandoned our influence almost totally, and if it had not been for the Chinese, who were doing America's work for it in that region, the rest of the dominoes might have fallen after South Vietnam and Cambodia and Laos. As for the Chinese, strategically the most important nation on earth, they had been promised much by both Democratic and Republican administrations and been given little. The Chinese leaders were wondering exactly what point or advantage there could be in a relationship with a United States too enfeebled by its malaise to resist the spread of Soviet hegemony throughout the Far East and to render even minimal assistance to a China that was attempting, at enormous risk, to find her way out of the economic and political impasse of Maoism.

There was, in short, a worldwide climate of uncertainty. This was dangerous in the extreme. Even the Soviets thought so. They and their surrogates chose the ground for revolution with bravado, but if no line were drawn, how could they know whether they had gone too far? Our friends felt fearful and alone; they did not know whether we would ever face up to the Soviets again. If we did not, if we had, in fact, accommodated ourselves to the inevitable loss of the world to Moscow, then what choice was left to them except to do what we had done and make the best deal they could while there was time?

The new President, in his first days, had to move against the uncertainty. He had to act decisively and directly on the Soviet Union. In his campaign, he had spoken about "linkage," the concept that any improvement in relations between Moscow and Washington had to be linked to an improvement of Moscow's behavior in the world. Unswerving advocacy of a code of international behavior that insisted on peaceful change was a sound starting point. As the first order of business in foreign affairs, the President had to tell the Soviets that they must choose between better relations with the U.S. and the destructive adventures they had undertaken, especially since Vietnam, across the face of the globe.

Our ability to direct events had been limited. With our military strength at the ebb and our economy in trouble, we had to proceed with care. Nevertheless, strong signals were needed. A new President has perhaps eighteen months to put the framework and substance of his foreign policy into place. After that, he will be shackled by his critics and distracted by the exigencies of the next election. At all times, a national leader must be resolute; he must make hard decisions and live with them within himself and within history. This is no easy thing; men want to be loved even when it is meet that they should be feared—and Presidents are only men. Perhaps they are most human just after a great victory at the polls, for it is then that they most want to avoid any act that might diminish the people's love for them.

"When armies are mobilized and issues joined," wrote the sixth-century Chinese sage, Lao Tzu, "the man who is sorry over the fact will win." The greatest victories are achieved not by war but by persuasion. But an adversary will not be persuaded to compromise, an enemy will not be persuaded to surrender, by a timid statesman who wants the love of his people more than he wants to preserve their interests. To make war is to admit failure. However, once you decide to make it, you had better win it. Otherwise you will earn a reputation for vacillation and surrender that will haunt the future of your diplomacy and of your nation.

Our primary adversary in Vietnam was the Soviet Union. North Vietnam and the Vietcong were Soviet surrogates. Without Soviet aid, they could not have mounted an effective offensive against South Vietnam, much less against American forces. If in the beginning we had been willing to go to the Soviet Union and demand an end to the aggression of Hanoi, and if Moscow had believed in our determination, there might very well have been no war. If ever there was a case in which the threat of our power might have achieved more in the beginning than the application of our power did in the end, this was it. Baffled by the ambiguities of the situation—would the Soviets escalate to nuclear war? would China intervene? was the Diem regime democratic enough to merit our unqualified friendship?—we chose not to do the obvious, and we are living with the consequences.

With the election of Ronald Reagan, the United States confronted another great opportunity. If it could shake off its lethargy and abandon its self-doubt, it could lead the free world into a new era of stability, peace, and social progress. My years in Europe had convinced me that our allies thirsted for American leadership. Other nations wanted the reassurance, the freedom to develop, that only a strong American advocacy of the rule of law and peaceful change can provide. The Third World was beginning to shake off the theories and the rhetoric that could neither solve its enormous social and economic problems nor discover and develop the potential of its people, and was ready to seek new areas of cooperation with the West. The Soviet Union was beset by problems that could not be solved by its atrophying system and its doctrinaire leadership.

Here was a historic chance to build a policy that acknowledged change and turned it into strength, that acknowledged the reality of interdependence and transformed it into unity. It seemed possible to join our strength with the strength of other nations that shared our values and to make mutual interest, based on the principle of peaceful change, the basis of the future. Opportunities do not last forever. We have little time to turn adverse trends, a decade in the making, toward a more favorable future. We can do so only with a disciplined, unified effort that was promised by the President's overwhelming victory. It may be, as I have been told, that when I arrived in Washington at the end of 1980 to face confirmation by the Senate and then to take up my duties, I seemed somewhat impatient, somewhat driven. If that was so, these were the reasons.

BACKGROUND

When a Roman emperor or general returned to the city after a great victory and was awarded a triumph, he passed among the populace wearing a hero's chaplet, followed by his soldiers, his booty, and his captives. Lest he be made drunk by glory and the cheers of the citizens, he was provided with a dwarf who rode beside him in his chariot and whispered into his ear, "Remember, you are mortal."

In present-day America, the press performs the dwarf's function. President-elect Reagan announced my nomination while on his way to get a haircut, thus performing two needful acts at once. To the press, even to me, this seemed faintly risible, and editors turned it into a reminder to the people that their new President and the person he wanted as his Secretary of State were only men: if one had just shown that his hair would soon grow down over his ears if he did not have it trimmed, could the other escape revealing similar telling details now that he was under the full light of public scrutiny?

Ordinarily, a confirmation hearing before a committee of the United States Senate is a serious search for the truth conducted by men of intelligence and experience who take their duty to the nation, and their responsibility to the reputation of the man or woman whom they are examining, with the utmost seriousness. A hearing can be an occasion for orotund mutual congratulation. Usually that happens when a senator or former senator is nominated for high office, but a President cannot always buy sweetness and light at this price or he will find himself with a Cabinet that behaves like a Senate. Accordingly, he must accept some acrimony.

Sometimes a hearing will be seen by both senators and press as a media event. The senators still want to discover the truth, but as a breed, they do not object to a bit of national exposure as they go about their solemn undertakings. Television lights are the modern equivalent of the toga; they are an emblem of the highest modern office, that of celebrity. The press, too, is interested in the truth, but it has learned from the long practice of its craft that forbidden knowledge sells better.

Forbidden knowledge played a central role in turning my confirmation hearings before the Senate Committee on Foreign Relations into a media event. Even after an orgy of revelation that had lasted for half a decade and more, appetites were still sharp for revelations about Richard Nixon. Henry Kissinger was likewise an object of curiosity. I had worked closely with both men. Perhaps, in the course of examining the question of my fitness for office, some horrendous new fact could be enticed out of hiding in order to justify, one more time, the wisdom and patriotism of those who had overturned the results of a national election and brought down an erring President.

The speculation began, as I have described, in the *Washington Post*. It was taken up, in somewhat more restrained fashion, by other newspapers and by the broadcasters. Then the ranking minority member of the committee, Senator Claiborne Pell, Democrat of Rhode Island, dropped an object into the soup as it boiled and bubbled. He wrote to Zbigniew Brzezinski, President Carter's special assistant for national security affairs, requesting that the White House supply, from National Security Council files, "all documents, correspondence, or memoranda authored by or directed to General Haig between 1969 and the present." Brzezinski refused, citing executive privilege on behalf of one incumbent President and two former ones, Nixon and Ford. This exchange of correspondence was released to the press. In an interview, Brzezinski said, "We are not going to be parties to some indiscriminate witch hunt." Presently, however, Carter's press secretary, Jody Powell, stated during an appearance on "Meet the Press" that the Carter White House would, after all, permit a search for the materials.

The materials sought by Senator Pell included the infamous Watergate tapes. This was forbidden knowledge with a vengeance. Would Richard Nixon, who had jealously asserted his Presidential prerogatives in regard to the tapes, go to court to prevent their release? Would the keeper of the National Archives yield them up? If he did, what would they contain? I told the committee that I had no objection whatever to their obtaining and listening to the tapes of conversations I had had with the President between May 4, 1973, the date I returned to duty at the White House, and July 18, 1973, the date on which I ordered the removal of the taping system.

The symbiosis between politician and press came into play. In this situation, anything the one did handsomely served the other. In both cases, the objective was to have a public hearing that would attract unusual attention. The senators, I repeat, wanted a vibrant encounter because they wished, for any number of reasons, to settle the matter of my suitability once and for all. It is also true that the Democrats, who had been in the majority in the Senate for twenty-eight years, were now in the minority as a result of Ronald Reagan's sweeping victory. They chafed at their new status. Some may have entertained the thought that it might be possible to paint Reagan with the Nixon brush through me. One or two disliked not only the associations that duty had thrust upon me, but also what they conceived to be my system of beliefs. Yet I question that even the most skeptical or hostile senator wanted me to turn out to be a scoundrel; the country had had a surfeit. For the press, however, there is no such thing as too many scoundrels. It must pay attention to dramatic values. It knows that villains are interesting. I had been cast as Iago.

Naturally, I would have preferred that the hearing be held under quieter circumstances. I don't mind being questioned, hectored even, but it is discomfiting to have to answer sharply in full view of the world. It is easier to administer humiliation in public than to accept it. Besides, a circus atmosphere elicits the clown in all of us. It is difficult, when on camera, not to play to the gallery. This cheapens the process, distorts the results, and causes otherwise good and thoughtful persons to make damn fools of themselves. To a significant degree, the television camera has driven the natural, the heartfelt, out of our national life. The rule used to be "What am I saying?" Now it is "How do I appear?" The hackneyed question of the television reporter—"How do you feel?"—has never been answered because the camera in some mysterious fashion takes away feelings and substitutes pretenses.

The controversy over the tapes and papers (though the papers were distinctly less thrilling than the tapes) went on for several days and accomplished its purpose. For the committee, it captured the attention of the people and showed the new Administration, even before it took office, that the Senate would insist on its privileges. For the press, it created an audience—and, incidentally, assured that the drama would be of high quality because no senator could now fail to be very rigorous in his questioning.

What it did for me, or to me, was irrelevant. There was never the slightest chance that Nixon would agree to release the tapes without the intervention of the courts, and everyone knew that from the beginning. In the end, Nixon did take measures to prevent the release of the tapes and the archivist kept the files requested by Senator Pell safely in the Archives, where no doubt they will defeat the attempts of future historians to understand why, in the 1970s, they had the power to hypnotize millions.

THREE

"No One Has a Monopoly on Virtue"

THE QUESTION that ought to be asked of nominees for high office is this: who are you and how did you become the person you are today? I am not suggesting that the Senate go in for amateur psychoanalysis. But in the life of every human being there are events that have had an important effect on the way in which he looks upon the world and lives in it. As a boy, I may have imagined that policy is made in a high-ceilinged room by gentlemen with snowy white hair sitting around a polished table in neat dark suits, in full possession of the facts. But, as I have learned in serving six Presidents, that is not the way it happens in the real world. Learning that has left its mark on me, and I should have been happy to explore this ground with the committee in full view of the American people.

However, it was unlikely, as the date of my confirmation hearing before the Senate approached, that anyone was going to join me in a philosophical exercise on the relationship between personal experience and policy making, though that was the quiddity of the matter. The primary subject would be Nixon. I was determined not to be Richard Nixon's judge. I had not been a witness to his misdeeds, only to their consequences and to his suffering. I am not insensible to the central lesson of Watergate, that a seemingly trivial act can take on such Aeschylean significance as to threaten the balance of the world. But it would be wrong to assign all the blame for that state of affairs to Nixon. There were abuses, and actions that were worse than abuses, on all sides. One need not describe the damage, not the least of which is that the United States now has a precedent for the removal of an elected President from office through a process of denunciation rather than due process of law. It is true that Nixon chose not to avail himself of the impeachment process, but there were reasons for that beyond the shrill quality of public discourse that made a fair trial moot. Not all of those reasons, which included an unselfish belief that the country would be sundered politically, economically, and emotionally by a protracted impeachment process, redound to Nixon's discredit.

Apart from Watergate, other questions were likely to arise. During my time as deputy to Henry Kissinger, many issues had stirred emotions. In 1969–70, on Presidential orders and in strict compliance with existing laws, the telephones of seventeen members of the White House staff and newsmen were tapped for reasons of national security. A leftist regime had been overthrown in Chile, and this had raised questions about the involvement of the American intelligence service. The bombing of the Cambodian sanctuaries and other events in the Vietnam War were likely to be discussed.

On none of these questions was there any need for a mea culpa, and I never considered making one. But in the sort of atmosphere that was building for the hearings, it is not always enough to be innocent. The Republican majority had recalled to duty Fred D. Thompson, who had been the minority counsel at the Watergate hearings seven years before. The Democrats voiced their intention to rehire a member of their own Watergate committee legal staff. Senator Howard H. Baker, Jr., of Tennessee, the leader of the Republican majority in the Senate, advised me to engage legal counsel.

I asked my old friend Joseph A. Califano, Jr., if he would represent me. In the days following the Cuban missile crisis, Califano had been legal counsel to Secretary of the Army Cyrus R. Vance, and I had been Vance's military assistant. Later, when Califano became special assistant to Secretary of Defense McNamara, I became Califano's deputy. Subsequently, Califano had been President Johnson's principal aide on domestic matters and, afterward, President Carter's

Secretary of Health, Education, and Welfare. Now he was engaged in the private practice of law in Washington. In addition to his legal skills and his friendship, he had a third, very important qualification: he had been on the other side in Watergate and understood the mind-set of the opposition.

Califano set to work immediately to chart the shoals that lay before me. In exhaustive conversations, sometimes in his office, sometimes in my temporary office on the first floor of the State Department, I told him everything I remembered about the days I had spent in the Nixon White House. In due course, though not in this book, I shall attempt to recount these facts for a considered review by the American people. Joe and a good part of his law firm gathered every available scrap of information—all the press coverage, all my testimony, all my depositions to investigators and Watergate prosecutors. The record was collected into a huge stack. Califano and his associates examined every scrap of it. Then Joe told me what I knew already: I was invulnerable to any charge of improper conduct.

Meanwhile, Howard Baker was giving me sage advice on the ways of the Senate. Baker embodies much of what is admirable in a great politician—knowledge, skill, a reasonable and honest mind, and an accommodating spirit. He was dedicated to doing everything he could to make the hearings go well for the President-elect and the party. Few public men acquit themselves with the ever-maturing statesmanship displayed by Howard Baker during a long career in the American political system. Baker led me to Tom C. Korologos, who had handled White House liaison with the House of Representatives in the Nixon Administration. Korologos helped me to find my way through the frustrating apparatus of senatorial courtesy and procedure. I attempted to call on every member of the committee, but some of the Democrats were not able to see me. Senator Baker had told me that there was great concern in the party about these hearings because of my connection to Nixon, and, of course, he was correct. If Democrats were obsessed with keeping the issue of Watergate alive as a matter of political survival, Republicans were equally obsessed with separating themselves from it for the same reason. One Republican senator told me that we had to be careful, as he put it, that my confirmation was not made to look like the reelection of Richard Nixon.

The man meant well, but this nettled. I had served on the staff of the National Security Council under military orders, and under military orders I had been summoned back to the White House by the commander in chief. The tragedy I had witnessed, and tried within the limits of legality and honor to help manage, was in the past. It had nothing whatever to do with my qualifications to be Secretary of State. In strategy sessions, it was suggested that I ought to volunteer in my opening statement that I, too, deplored Nixon's behavior, on the theory that this would somehow lay the issue to rest. A dignified tone and demeanor were recommended. Friends in the Senate advised the same course. I could not follow it. I was willing to answer the inevitable questions that would be put to me. But my purpose before the committee was to describe, as best I could, how the foreign policy of the United States would be administered by the new President and his Secretary of State, not to gossip about a former President or to be brought so low that I would seek to demonstrate my fitness for my post, or certify my own decency, by joining in the hurling of anathema upon him.

More than personal pride was involved in this. If I permitted myself to be hammered down, the cost would be severe. If I crawfished before my own countrymen, what could I be expected to do when dealing with America's adversaries? I had a chilling vision of the videotapes of such a performance being played in the Kremlin. The price was unpayable. I said so, more than once, with some heat, as we prepared for the hearings. I agreed with Edmund Burke that a public man in a democracy owes to the people who put him in office his wisdom and judgment, not mere obedience to the shifting whims of popular opinion. No one except my wife seemed to grasp my point. My lawyers and my staff looked worried and advised me to be a little less frank, a little more docile. I did not know how to acquiesce and still be myself.

The hearing before the Senate Committee on Foreign Relations began in room 1202 of the Dirksen Senate Office Building at ten o'clock in the morning on Friday, January 9, 1981. It is always a good thing, on these occasions, to have one's family nearby. My wife and our daughter Barbara sat in the first row behind the witness table, and so did my younger brother, the Reverend Francis R. Haig, S.J. Joe Califano was not at all unhappy to have Frank in his clerical collar watching over me; nor was I. Before entering the hearing room, we had met for a few moments with Senator Baker and with

Senator Charles H. Percy of Illinois, chairman of the committee, and with other Republican senators—Barry M. Goldwater of Arizona was there, offering encouragement. He told me that John Sherman Cooper, a former senator from Kentucky, was coming up to make a statement on my behalf. And most heartening of all to me, my old friend, Jacob Javits of New York, for so many years the lion of the Senate, came to the hearings.

In hearing room 1202, all the trappings of drama were in evidence—the crowd stirred by pleasant anticipation of a day of sport, reporters in their elaborate indifference, the cameras and lights and banks of microphones, the noble room itself with its mellow paneling suffused by the morning sun through the tall windows. In the first moments, the bustle of the cameramen and their blinding lights were distracting. Then the senators took their places at the committee table. The dignity of the chamber, the solemn sense that this hearing was joined in history to all the others that had taken place down through the long years of the republic's life, overcame the artificial and the ephemeral.

Senator Pell, the first member of the committee to speak after the opening remarks of the chairman, described the terms of the engagement from the Democratic point of view. Pell began by saying that he believed me to be intelligent, loyal, and competent. "Yet," he said, "General Haig's nomination to this senior, most conspicuous post is of concern to me because he carries with him, whether justified or not, the political baggage, scar tissue, if you will, from his service during a very distasteful period in our history, marked by gross abuses of Presidential power. . . . I do not recall a nomination that has come before us that has caused the concern and worry in the Senate that this one has."

Chairman Percy, discussing the committee's efforts to obtain the tapes and other materials, pointed out that there existed an "exhaustive record" already available to the committee, on the matters that were causing worry and concern. "A large proportion of the committee staff," he said, reading from a letter he had sent to Pell, "has now spent weeks reviewing these sources and to my knowledge has identified nothing that would disqualify this nominee to be Secretary of State. On the contrary, he emerges as a man of consistently distinguished service." Later, Percy introduced into the record the following letter, written by Leon Jaworski, the Watergate special prosecutor, to Major General Julius Klein, a constituent of Percy's:

. . . I made it clear on a number of occasions to members of the news media and to congressmen as well as to others that there was nothing in General Haig's conduct at the White House during the Nixon Administration subject to adverse criticism, in my opinion. I dealt with General Haig for almost a year. There was hardly a week that we were not in contact with each other and sometimes several times a week. I found him to be honorable in his own conduct and certainly fair in all his dealings with me.

Naturally, General Haig owed his allegiance to President Nixon and he demonstrated this allegiance until the very end. . . . Following Nixon's resignation, I talked to Senator John [C.] Stennis [of Mississippi], Chairman of the Armed Services Committee, and I made it ever so clear . . . to him that I not only found nothing improper in General Haig's conduct but that I personally admired and respected him greatly.

Of course, the cause for some of the criticism rests in the fact that some people are naturally vindictive and have little regard for ascertaining the facts. Others labor under mistaken beliefs. What is overlooked is that so long as General Haig served as chief of staff he had no alternative than to be loyal to his commander in chief. (In my own view, General Haig is a great soldier, who performed in the highest and noblest tradition.)

Thinking that it might provide some reassurance to the senators, I had requested that I testify under oath. This is not usual in confirmation hearings. In my opening statement, I pointed out that I had already testified under oath on eight separate occasions before committees of the Senate, the Watergate grand jury, and Judge John Sirica, on matters relating to Watergate, the national security wiretaps, covert operations in Chile, and the question of the $100,000 Hughes campaign contribution to Nixon's friend Charles "Bebe" Rebozo. "None of these investigations," I reminded them, "has found any culpability on my part." I told them that, although Watergate was obviously important during my tenure as White House chief of staff, I spent 90 percent of my time trying to assure that the other business of the Presidency was properly conducted. On the subject of Nixon, I said:

I believe that President Nixon, as the duly elected and duly constituted head of the executive branch, was entitled to the presumption of innocence, until proven otherwise, accorded as a constitutional right to every American citizen. In that context, I worked hard within the boundaries of the law and the advice of lawyers to support him.

Rather to my surprise, Nixon did not figure in the early questioning. The senators went, instead, directly to sensitive matters of policy. Reagan and I had conferred again a couple of days before, in a meeting at Blair House, and I felt that he and I were beginning to work toward an outline of his foreign policy. But no incoming Administration, until it opens the files and talks to the bureaucracy, can know all the subtleties and nuances in the situation it has inherited. In other words, it would be impossible to be specific about future actions when testifying before an open hearing even if were not unwise. Yet there is an obligation, and on my part there was a keen desire, to speak as frankly as possible. You have to tell the Senate what you see when you look at the world situation. You must describe your guiding principles. From that, they ought to be able to deduce what you are likely to do in a given situation.

Early in the afternoon session, Percy asked about a newspaper story. A warning bell rang in my mind. I was hearing it for the first time, but I would hear it again and again in the months ahead. Percy, a tone of concern in his rich voice, said, "I read . . . some words on the front page of the *Wall Street Journal* that disturbed me very, very much indeed and simply said, 'New Arms Talks Should Wait Six Months, Caspar Weinberger Says.' Now this is a designee for Secretary of Defense. . . . What bothers me about this statement is that . . . it looks like policy on arms control, which is the responsibility of the Secretary of State, is being established by the Secretary of Defense." In my opening statement I had said, expressing convictions that the reader will recognize:

The United States must speak to other nations in a single voice. . . . The authoritative voice must be the President's. A President needs a single individual to serve as general manager of American diplomacy. President-elect Reagan believes that the Secretary of State should play this role. As Secretary of State, I would function as a member of the President's team, but one with clear responsibility for formulating and conducting foreign policy, and for explaining it to the Congress, the public, and the world at large.

Earlier, Senator John Glenn, Democrat of Ohio, had jested about Richard Allen's heavy schedule of appearances on network talk shows. Obviously we were not off to a very good start on our policy of speaking with one voice on foreign policy. To Percy, I replied, mildly I hoped, that Weinberger's experience underlined the dangers I faced if I plowed new ground in these hearings before the Administration had had a chance to coordinate its policy and its views. The moment passed; but the bell I had heard was only that of the opening round, and the problem would remain.

To my knowledge, there had never before been a confirmation hearing that was so openly conducted on ideological grounds rather than merely political ones. For some men, there is a high emotive content in terms that apply to me: soldier, Republican, conservative, patriot. Add to that tinder the burning issues of Watergate, Vietnam, Cambodia, wiretaps, the CIA, Chile, and you have the makings of a pretty hot time. It seemed possible that two of the younger Democrats on the committee, Senators Paul S. Sarbanes of Maryland and Paul E. Tsongas of Massachusetts, were not so much interested in discovering my beliefs as in discrediting them. They had formed their conclusion before they talked to me; now they were looking for data that would prove their theses. Both are intelligent, articulate young men who had done their homework. In one sense, it was a pleasure to be questioned by them for the opportunities it gave to tell the truth while giving vent to a little honest emotion. In another, it was the symbolic equivalent of being thrown out the window, like some erring dean during a campus demonstration in the 1960s, by radicals who wish to rifle your files.

Sarbanes's first question was, in his own characterization of it, tangential. He asked if I had foresworn my political ambitions and would therefore not be tempted to use the office of Secretary of State as a springboard to the Presidency. I assured him that I had no such ambitions. In a truism that seems even apter now than it did then, I said that, judging by the fate of its recent occupants, the office of Secretary of State could hardly be described as a path leading to the Presidency. He then quoted from my opening testimony, in which I spoke of my belief in the Presidency and my view, during Watergate, that my overriding duty was to preserve that office in the national interest. Sarbanes asked me to define the obligation of a member of the executive branch to obey an order from the President. I stated my belief that an illegal order must be disobeyed and tried to reassure him that it had never been necessary for me to refuse to obey such an order because none had ever been given to me.

Sarbanes did not seem to be reassured: he concluded by noting that there was concern, based on this very point, about a military man becoming Secretary of State. How it might be possible for a civilian to disobey an illegal order in a way that was different from that of a military man doing the same thing was not entirely clear to me.

Nor would Senator Tsongas be lulled into any automatic trust in my word. Before Tsongas's turn came around, I had had the following exchange with Senator Jesse A. Helms of North Carolina:

HELMS: From your experience during those days—I am still referring to Chile—isn't it a fact that Communists from all over the world came into Chile to influence what was going on there?

HAIG: I can't speak categorically to that, Senator. I do know that there were many additional Communist elements that were either visitors, participants, or advisers with the Allende government.

To Tsongas's ear, I must have sounded categorical despite my disclaimer.

TSONGAS: Senator Helms referred to Communists that were associated with Allende, and you said that was true, and can you tell us who they were?

I did not hold in my hand a list of names, but I answered, on the basis of my recollection of the intelligence reports of the time, that Cuban and Soviet presence in Chile had increased substantially during the Allende regime. Tsongas had elicited from me the story of a Chilean woman, with whom I had had a conversation in Brussels, who had taken part in a demonstration against the Allende regime protesting the introduction of Marxist textbooks and teachers into the schools. The demonstration had been dispersed by police. My informant, and many other women, had been arrested, and some of them had been very roughly handled. This incident has been cited as the immediate cause of the military coup in Chile. Many of the women were married to members of the military, and they appealed to their spouses to save the country from dictatorship. Shortly thereafter, the Chilean armed forces, despite a very strong tradition against intervention in political matters, overthrew the Allende government.

TSONGAS: Let me say that your capacity to recall that conversation with the woman I think is remarkable, and I would hope that when we get into other issues regarding Chile, that we will have the same sort of recall.

Certainly my powers of recall were exhaustively tested. I doubt that any nominee has ever been asked to respond to so many matters of fact and opinion in a confirmation hearing. The committee had seventeen members, nine Republicans and eight Democrats. Each senator, in order of seniority, was allotted ten minutes in which to ask questions. Later, as the hearings expanded into five days, this portion rose to thirty minutes. Percy is an exceptionally patient, even indulgent, chairman, who was more than responsive to the wishes of the minority. Each senator had his own special interest. Percy is committed to arms control, and, quoting Reagan's campaign statements in support of strategic arms negotiations, including a promise, as reported in the *Washington Post*, to "immediately open negotiations on a SALT III treaty," he asked about our timetable for talks with the Russians on this subject.

This was not a question that could be discussed publicly beyond the giving of a general assurance that it would have the Administration's close and early attention. The time was not right to give the Soviets something they wanted as passionately as they wanted a treaty on strategic arms. Their international behavior did not warrant it. The condition of the American nuclear arsenal did not permit it. As I coincidentally told Senator Gary Hart, Democrat of Colorado, "The key issue facing the American people right now is that [the United States is] less capable than we should be in this area, and very early on in this decade we are going to be seriously less capable than we should be." With Pell, I was able to discuss the issue of the MX missile and its importance to the defense of the country and the future of negotiations.

In my opening statement, I had said that the foreign policy of the United States under Reagan would be built on the three pillars of consistency, reliability, and balance. I was examined at length on the practical meaning of this formula. Senators S. I. Hayakawa, Republican of California, and Joseph R. Biden, Jr., Democrat of Maryland, examined my views on China. I told Hayakawa that China was emerging as a stabilizing force in East Asia. Biden, with some irony, asked if the Administration intended to continue to support the Marxist regime in China, and I replied that it was in our strategic interest to do so. Senator Alan Cranston, Democrat of California, who is possessed of a tenacious mind, led me into a discussion of the conditions under which force might be used by the United States. We agreed that it should be used, as had been the consistent American policy, only as a last resort and only in defense of our security and that of our allies.

Senator Pell engaged me in a long colloquy on nuclear war. I assured him that I was against it, and as he voted for my confirmation, I must have convinced him. There was some doubt in my mind that I would be able to do so. Before the hearings, when I called on him at his office, he took the position that the prime if not the sole duty of a Secretary of State is to avoid nuclear war. After I had agreed that the avoidance of a nuclear holocaust was the first aim of any sensible foreign policy, I added that "some things are worse than war." I was not referring to nuclear war, or even advocating conventional conflict as anything but a last resort. But some things are worth fighting for; Americans have fought for them repeatedly, and generally believe that they have remained a free people as a result. Senator Pell raised this point in his questions. The clarification was probably worth making. The members of the committee asked for, and were given, assurances that I did not intend to breach the War Powers Act or the arrangements that had been made to consult committees of Congress in advance in cases where covert action was being contemplated. The discussion on the Soviet Union was exhaustive, for this is a subject in which every member is interested. Senator Christopher J. Dodd, Democrat of Connecticut, asked if I foresaw any improvement in our relations with Cuba. Not, I said, while the Cubans were carrying out terrorist activities in the Western Hemisphere designed to overthrow lawful governments by force. Sarbanes raised the question of aid to Nicaragua; already I had doubts about the wisdom of supporting a government that was working so assiduously against American interests.

On the whole, it was a thoughtful session in which questions were briskly asked and sometimes briskly answered. It seemed to me that the participants had, all unawares, turned what had been billed as a soap opera into an educational program. Certainly I was learning a great deal from the senators, and I had the feeling that they were learning much about me. As we talked, the early stiffness and wariness faded. We were getting to know each other, to understand each other's concerns. I was glad, for we would have to work closely together in the future.

Looking back on the hearings, it seems remarkable that so many of what were to become the key issues of American foreign policy in the Reagan years should have been raised. They were all there: Soviet adventurism, Soviet troubles; Poland; Cuba and its role in the de-stabilization of Central America; nuclear arms in Europe; the desir-ability of a strategic relationship with China and the Taiwan question; defense requirements; the tortured questions concerning the management of covert action and the interpretation of the War Powers Act; terrorism.

There was even discussion, lighthearted enough at the time, of the difficulties inherent in speaking with a single voice in foreign affairs in an Administration whose members were bursting with ideas and just coming out of the long enforced silence of opposition and private life. Of all the sound advice the Senate gave me in my five days and one evening of hearings before the Foreign Relations Committee, that was the most valuable. At the time, though, I did not know that. I was aware of the tendency among the President-elect's men to sing from different sheets of music, but I put it down to the exhilaration produced by the freshness of the candidate's triumph at the polls. I assumed that Reagan would control the garrulity.

If, in the hearings, much time was devoted to a sober discussion of how the future needed to be managed, the leitmotiv of Watergate also continued to be heard. Time after time, the events of the past were exhumed and reautopsied. I repeat: this was perfectly proper; the senators involved had to satisfy themselves, if they could, that the facts really had been established. However clear the existing case, they were obligated to conduct a diligent search for new evidence that would either corroborate or refute earlier findings by commit-tees of Congress, grand juries, the special prosecutor, and sundry investigators. But it is not especially enjoyable to be the cause for the rebirth of the doctrine of guilt by association. Besides, the hearings were not the only things in my life; between sessions, I was trying to deal with the transition of power at State, to find the right men and women to fill its senior posts, to come to terms with Reagan's men and with the Foreign Service on matters of administration, personnel, and budget. Negotiations for the return of the American hostages in Iran were in a final, delicate stage, and though this matter was in the hands of the outgoing Administration, I was monitoring it closely. Only a few days before, I had heard for the first time about a plan to sell AWACS aircraft to Saudi Arabia, and already the situation had grown tense with the Israelis and the Saudis alike. These talks had left me virtually no time to prepare for the hearings. Mine was a totally unrehearsed performance.

At length, I was overtaken by exasperation. This happened on the fourth day, after a long session in which the plowed and salted earth of the Nixon era—Chile, wiretaps, Watergate—was spaded again and again. In the third day's session, until two o'clock in the morning, these same issues had been gnawed and worried. Now Senator Sarbanes, after dwelling for a time on the resignation of Elliot Richardson in the matter of firing Archibald Cox as special prosecutor, turned once again to Nixon and his deeds. Why had I not resigned, like Richardson, as a matter of conscience? It hardly seemed necessary to say again that I had not been there when the misdeeds took place. So I suggested that one did not have the option of quitting when the republic was in danger: "I felt an obligation to do the best I could. I did that."

Sarbanes asked for my "value judgment" about the things that were happening. I repeated my assertions that there had been abuses on both sides, that Nixon had a right to the presumption of innocence like any other citizen. I mentioned the spectre of extra-constitutional solutions, which were more real than is generally recognized. "I wanted to be sure," I said, "that our system had an opportunity to work, and that populist or extraordinary measures driven by emotion or hate or bias, for whatever reason, did not become the standard of the land." Why, Sarbanes asked, wouldn't the overriding objectives have been to ensure that the Constitution and the laws of the country were maintained? I thought I had just said exactly that.

The exchange ran on. Sarbanes continued to press me for a "value judgment." It was a spirited episode. There is no need to reproduce it in its entirety. Those who watched it on television will remember. Others will deduce the tone and content from what has gone before in this chapter. The following excerpt is greatly shortened; in the unabridged version, Sarbanes asks me for a "value judgment" no fewer than four times:

SARBANES: . . . The difficulty is that every time a question is asked, you interpret it to mean that you had some involvement in what occurred. I want to know what you thought about what occurred. . . .

HAIG: . . . It is one of the greatest tragedies that has ever befallen our country . . . it would be an equal tragedy to try to resurrect it, to have it reborn. . . . What are you after, something you want me to say that you have been unable to get from somebody else with respect to that tragic period in our history?

SARBANES: What I am asking you for is some indication of your value judgment of what took place.

HAIG: I have answered the question completely. . . . Do you think I am going to endorse what was done? In no way, on either side. . . . No one has a monopoly on virtue, not even you, Senator.

Earlier in the hearings, when the back of my neck had turned red at some insult, Joe Califano had passed me a note that read, "Keep cool in Kabul." This bit of meaningless humor had the desired effect. Now, during the lunch break following my exchange with Sarbanes, there were no jokes. We were in a deserted committee room adjoining the hearing room. It was cool and quiet, a relief from the hectic atmosphere next door. Sandwiches and fruit, coffee and soft drinks had been laid out for our lunch. Barry Goldwater and Howard Baker stopped by to advise and commiserate. My lawyers, my staff, Baker—all thought I had made a disastrous error, perhaps even affronted the whole Senate, in my reply to Sarbanes. Joe is a brilliant lawyer, and Howard Baker is a profound student of the Senate, but I could not agree.

Someone said, "Tell them what they want to hear."

"What is our purpose here?" I said. "I can't tell them what they want to hear!"

"Get out what you feel," Califano advised. "It's not coming through. Say many acts were illegal and unconstitutional, but I would not render a personal judgment on Nixon after seeing what he went through."

That was what I thought I had been saying, repeatedly.

Tom Korologos told me, "We lost Sarbanes today. Try to smooth it over like Joe says. Don't raise your voice, don't preach to them. You must swallow your pride."

"But the attack was on my integrity," I said.

Korologos didn't have to tell me that I had lost Sarbanes. I knew it; but I doubted if I had ever "had" him. I told Joe I would go back to Hartford if necessary, without regrets. There are worse things than not being confirmed.

The night that Richard Nixon resigned the Presidency and his long ordeal was over, I did not want to leave him alone. His speech on national television had drained him. All Presidents must be aware of history because they are the limbs on its body. No President was more keenly aware of it than Nixon; better than anyone, he knew what had happened to him and how this event was likely to be viewed. We went together to the Lincoln Sitting Room, his favorite place. He did not turn on the lamps; the only light came from the flickering flames of a log fire on the hearth. One of the stately servants who look after the first family asked if the President wanted anything. He did not. Mrs. Nixon entered and embraced her husband. The President's daughters kissed him. They had wanted him to fight; he himself had wanted mightily to fight. But in the end, he had chosen the welfare of the nation above his own interests. Nixon began to talk. He spoke about his predecessors and the times of doubt and anguish through which nearly all of them had passed. Not a single word did he speak about his own tragedy. He uttered no recriminations. He had lost the thing he wanted all his life, but he seemed to be at peace. He said that he wanted to speak in the morning to his staff, to thank them and say good-bye. I would have advised him to spare himself this test of emotional stamina, but he was determined not to neglect what he saw as a final duty. I left him there, sitting alone in the dark. When I returned in the morning, shortly after dawn, Nixon was still in the same chair. He had a way of sitting on the small of his back, and that was how he was sitting now. The gray light of morning filled the room. There was the smell of a fire that had died. On a table before Nixon, lay a stack of books—the memoirs of Presidents. In each, he had inserted a slip of paper, marking a place where he had found something of interest. That is how Nixon had spent his last night as President of the United States. He had been seeking solace from the only men who could truly know what he was feeling—his kinsmen in history, the other Presidents.

Joe Califano had said it well: I simply could not render personal judgment on Nixon after seeing what he had gone through.

Nevertheless, it seemed right to explain to the committee how I felt. Califano and I decided that I must read a prepared statement when the hearings reconvened. Seated at the committee's horseshoe dais, in the chairs of the absent senators, we worked out a statement. Pat, who knew me best, contributed mightily. Califano and the staff made their suggestions, and by the end of the ninety-minute break, the statement was completed. It was very brief. It affirmed my belief that the actions leading to Watergate were improper, illegal, and immoral. It reiterated my conviction that the bombing of the Cambodian sanctuaries and the 1972 bombing of North Vietnam were not abuses of power. I said:

I cannot bring myself to render judgment on Richard Nixon or, for that matter, Henry Kissinger. I worked intimately for both men. It is not for me, it is not in me, to render moral judgments on them. I must leave that to others, to history, and to God.

The statement, when I read it before the committee, seemed to provide some sort of psychic punctuation mark. The hearings continued into the next day, but the acrimony had been drained away.

In retrospect, I do not think anything was lost by the incident with Sarbanes. In some circumstances, it is wrong to turn the other cheek. The Foreign Relations Committee voted, fifteen to two, for confirmation, with Sarbanes and Tsongas casting the negative votes. It is always, in the end, less complicated to speak your mind. I had done that, and so, according to their lights, had Sarbanes and Tsongas. There was nothing to regret.

According to a study by the committee staff, the hearings had lasted thirty-two hours over five days with one evening session. Among my recent predecessors, beginning with John Foster Dulles, only one, Henry Kissinger, had been subjected to more than one day of hearings. On January 21, the day after the inauguration of Ronald Reagan, the Senate voted, ninety-three to six, to confirm my nomination as the fifty-ninth Secretary of State.

BACKGROUND

It is diverting to attempt to identify the precise moment when the grain of sand enters the oyster, beginning the long process of irritation that ends with the pearl. In my case, the sea change that eighteen months later produced my resignation, though I should hesitate to characterize that act as a pearl, began almost at the start of my days as Secretary of State. It began in a jest. At my first news conference at the State Department, on January 28, 1981, I was asked to describe my concept of my role in the foreign policy establishment.

". . . . When I accepted this position," I replied, "I was assured by President Reagan personally that I will be his chief administrator, if you will, and I use the term 'vicar.' . . ." Seldom has a man made an unwiser public display of pedantry. In *Webster's Third New International Dictionary*, the word *vicar* (from the Latin *vicarus*, "substitute," "deputy") is defined as meaning "administrative deputy." Possibly the only other American to use the word in this sense and have it get into print was Paul H. Nitze, who employed it to describe the relationship of the Secretary of State to the President in testimony before the late Senator Henry M. Jackson's subcommittee on government reorganization more than thirty years ago. I stole it from Nitze.

I thought *vicar* a pleasing word, one that described with considerable accuracy the job President-elect Reagan had said he was giving to me. But the word caused the press to chortle and the White House staff to choke. In some minds it seemed to evoke the picture of a harmless ecclesiastical gentleman on a bicycle, in others that of an antipope. Very soon I lost my affection for it. With the dazzling speed that only words possess, it entered the vocabulary of the press and the consciousness of the Administration, and it played its part in creating first the impression, and finally the uncomfortable reality, of a struggle for primacy between the President's close aides and myself.

There had already been some straws in the wind. In facing the ordeal of the confirmation hearings, I had been left entirely to my own devices. No advice, no offer of help, no word of encouragement came to me from Reagan or his staff. When the hearings were over and it seemed that I had come through them all right, the President-elect did not congratulate me, nor did any of his people phone or write. Because Reagan is so instinctively kind and courteous, this surprised me. But each President has his own style, and in fairness there is no reason why I should have been praised for getting myself confirmed. That was the least I owed to my chief, who had risked much in nominating me. The hearings had generated a tremendous amount of print and television coverage, and for nearly a week had dominated coverage of the incoming Administration.

This exposure transformed me into a media figure, a role I had dreaded and shunned all my life. Suddenly, the papers and magazines were full of "think pieces," and my face kept popping up on television; getting in and out of a car became a theatrical event. The side effect of this treatment is loss of personal complexity. For ease of identification, you are simplified by the typewriter and the camera into a "personality." This personality has a single, simple characteristic that becomes the code by which the individual is recognized. The code for me was arrogant. Pictures in the press invariably showed me glaring, wagging a finger, clenching a fist.

Senator Tsongas, while explaining to me why he could not vote for my confirmation, had said, "You are going to dominate this Administration, if I may say so. You are by far the strongest personality that's going to be in there." This was nonsense, and if Tsongas had had my interests at heart, he would not have uttered it. But he had done so, on national television, and his words had been reprinted in the *New York Times*. That bestowed upon his statement an afterlife it might not otherwise have enjoyed. If the exact words were not remembered, if Tsongas was not remembered as their author, the sentiment, at least, was always vividly recalled.

Perhaps it lingered in the atmosphere on Inauguration Day when, dressed in formal attire, I dropped in at the White House to deliver the draft of a document for the President, as I had promised. It was received by Edwin Meese in the presence of James Baker and Michael Deaver. Also present were Caspar Weinberger, Richard Allen, and William J. Casey, the Director of Central Intelligence. The next day, the press contained gossip items suggesting that I had tried to thrust the paper into the President's hands and secure his signature only moments after he had taken the oath of office. Highly placed White House sources were quoted on the shock this "grab for power" on the first day of the Administration had produced in the President.

All this struck me as being distinctly odd. I could not conceive that any of the seven of us who had firsthand knowledge of the circumstances—the President's three senior aides, two members of his Cabinet, his adviser for national security, and myself—would be so mischievous, so numb to the requirements of the Presidency, as to plant such a story. I concluded that some journalist, or some junior member of the staff not yet accustomed to White House rules of discretion, had overheard something. This distortion was the result.

It was damaging to the President and to me. And it wasn't true. I called Ed Meese to make these points. He told me the matter wasn't worth worrying about. At my first news conference, the one in which

I burdened myself with the term "vicar," I was asked about "steps, or alleged steps, that you've taken to assert your predominance over the foreign policy bureaucracy." In reply, I made a joke, "I was discussing that just the other day as the President was taking his first shower in the White House."

After all, Meese and I had agreed that the matter was laughable.

FOUR

"A Strong Ring of Professionals"

AFTER the election, Reagan remained mostly in California in a long farewell to his adopted state and his earlier life. When his staff spoke of him, they called him the Governor, not the President-elect or President Reagan, as if they were as reluctant to take leave of the golden era of his stardom and governorship and triumphant candidacy as Reagan himself was to quit the shores of the Pacific. Early in January, however, Reagan returned to Washington and took up a brief residence at Blair House in order to meet his future Cabinet as a group and inspect the transition. At Blair House, on the morning of January 6, 1981, I called on him to discuss the current play of events in the world and, most particularly, the structure of his foreign policy.

Richard Allen met me as I came in, and together we went upstairs to a second-floor sitting room where Reagan awaited us. The meeting was scheduled for thirty minutes, and there was a great deal of ground to cover. In dealing with a President, one must (1) tell the absolute truth, no matter how unpleasant, and (2) conserve the President's time. Later, I was told that the President had found me brusque. Perhaps, in my ignorance about his way of doing things, I came a little too quickly to the point; maybe my speech was unadorned. This is a habit of speech instilled in West Point cadets and nothing in a life spent in the service of busy and impatient men had cured me of it. If Reagan was uncomfortable on this day, he gave no sign of it. Because of his habitual cheery courtesy, it is at times difficult to know when he is agreeing or disagreeing, approving or disapproving. On this day, on important matters, I had no doubts.

In its last days, the Carter Administration was negotiating frantically for the return of the American hostages from Iran, and I brought Reagan up to date on this. We discussed trade as a source of diplomatic leverage, and I expressed my view that the grain embargo, imposed on the Soviets by President Carter almost exactly a year before as a result of the invasion of Afghanistan, should not be lifted in the absence of some important concession from Moscow. We touched on energy policy, including sensitive questions of nuclear proliferation, and technology transfer, a vital element in the expansion of our relationship with China and an important question for our European allies, who had been engaged for some time in providing technology for a pipeline that would supply them with natural gas from the Soviet Union. We talked briefly about staffing the Department of State. President Chun Doo Hwan of Korea and Prime Minister Edward Seaga of Jamaica would be the first foreign leaders to visit Washington in Reagan's Presidency. During Chun's visit, the new Administration would want to mend the rupture in our relations with Korea caused, under Carter, by the threat of withdrawal of U.S. troops from Korea and by the human rights policies of Carter's Administration. Seaga, a moderate, had just defeated an extreme left-wing government in an election; it was in our interest to demonstrate support for the new regime and to do what we could to see that it succeeded in Jamaica.

But the essential point, the very first order of business, was the structure of the foreign policy establishment. The President had to decide who was going to do what, and put his decision into writing. Every President since Eisenhower, at the outset of his Administration, has approved and signed such a document. Without such a Presidential charter, the foreign policy machinery of the government cannot function in an orderly way. The alternative is dispute over territory, rivalry over precedence, loss of decorum, and a policy that lacks coherence and consistency.

Foreign policy is not the exclusive preserve of the State Department. Many issues—defense, trade, energy, food, technology transfer—cross departmental lines. Defense, Treasury, Commerce, CIA, and other agencies have vital foreign policy responsibilities. These must be coordinated.

To Reagan I said, "You must have a single manager who can integrate the views of all your Cabinet officers and prepare for you a range of policy choices. I believe it requires that the Secretary of State be your vicar for the community of departments having an interest in the several dimensions of foreign policy."

The President nodded after each point and agreed.

We discussed, at length, the importance of speaking with a single voice on foreign policy and agreed that Allen and his colleagues at NSC would have no independent contact with the press and that contacts with visiting foreign dignitaries should be the sole province of the Department of State.

Once again Reagan nodded, and with a glance at Dick Allen, repeated his desire that his National Security Adviser should be a staff man, not a maker of policy or a spokesman. If Allen had any quibble with this concept, he said nothing about it to the President on this occasion—or to me at any time before or after.

The issue of policy coordination is complex and the result of thirty-five years of historical development. The National Security Council was created by Congress in 1947. It is headed by the President. The statutory members are the Vice President; the Secretaries of State, Defense, and Treasury; the Director of Central Intelligence; the National Security Adviser; and whoever else the President wishes to appoint. In the Reagan Administration, the Permanent Representative to the United Nations was also a member. The NSC is supported by a staff, headed by the National Security Adviser, that varies in size according to the wishes of the President. Truman made little use of the NSC until the outbreak of the Korean War, and then it became the coordinating body for all important defense and foreign policy decisions.

Eisenhower, who had, of course, been one of the most brilliant staff officers in the annals of the Army, reorganized it as a military staff system, with two parallel bodies—a planning board to develop policy and an operations coordinating board to watch over the execution of policy. Crisis planning, in a rudimentary form, was introduced in the Eisenhower period. Army fashion, Eisenhower demanded a single recommendation for action from his staff after it had examined all the possibilities. Critics of the Eisenhower system said that in the turmoil of achieving consensus, it tended to limit philosophic clarity and dull the cutting edge of policy.

Kennedy, who seemed to have a natural antiorganizational bias, went in another direction, severely reducing the role of formal mechanisms. He assigned individuals, such as his brother Robert or Secretary of Defense McNamara, to find solutions to problems. He appointed politically sympathetic persons at the junction boxes of the government and sometimes set up ad hoc task forces to cut through the bureaucracy on specific foreign policy issues, and also did much foreign policy business during a regular Tuesday lunch with the Secretaries of State and Defense, the Director of Central Intelligence, and his special assistant for national security. Kennedy's methods introduced a breezy informality into the process, but the end result was to provide him with the advice he wanted to hear. At NSC meetings there frequently was no agenda. There were no formal decision memoranda recording the President's decision on a given question, with the result that every participant went back to his agency and issued instructions to the field that, in many cases, clashed with instructions coming from the other agencies involved. In any given case, this had the effect in our embassies overseas of sending the representatives of State, CIA, Commerce, AID, etc., scurrying off in different directions while the ambassador tried, and often failed, to find some way to coordinate all that zealous effort through the action of another Kennedy-era innovation, the "country team."

In 1966, after living with the Kennedy system during the early years of the Vietnam War, President Johnson commissioned a study by General Maxwell D. Taylor that led, among other efforts to formalize procedures, to the creation of Senior Interagency Groups (SIG's) and what were later called Interagency Groups (IG's) to study and formulate policy. Taylor's study designated the Secretary of State as the President's principal deputy in foreign policy—partly because LBJ found the incumbent Secretary of State, Dean Rusk, a congenial personality, more evidence of the importance of a personal bond between President and Secretary.

Nixon, as we have seen, gave Henry Kissinger the charter that had always belonged, at least nominally, to the Secretary of State. On January 20, 1969, Nixon's first inaugural, in a National Security Decision Memorandum, Nixon gave just one group chairmanship to the State Department, and the rest to Kissinger. That was the fundamental organizational reason why Kissinger, and not Bill Rogers, was the dominant figure in foreign policy during the Nixon and Ford administrations. Under Nixon, the option system was developed as a way of giving the President a range of choices of action, as opposed to the homogenized single recommendation of the Eisenhower method or the extreme informality that obtained under Kennedy. Kissinger brought in a very wide range of expertise and viewpoints to service the needs of a President who was in his own right a formidable expert in foreign affairs and a skilled strategic thinker and theoretician. This approach, with its mixture of the formal and informal, served Nixon well. President Ford left it intact and retained Kissinger to run it. President Carter made no far-reaching changes.

In organizational terms, the key to the system is the substructure of SIG's and IG's in which the fundamentals of policy (domestic as well as foreign) are decided. On instructions from the President, the IG's (as I will call the whole lot, for the sake of convenience), can summon up all the human and informational resources of the federal government, study specific issues, and develop policy options and recommendations. In foreign policy, this process may involve the development of a policy toward an entire country or the examination of a single issue: arms negotiations, say, or food policy. When the study is completed, options go forward to the President and he decides which option to approve. Thereupon, in theory at least, the whole weight of the U.S. government swings into place behind the President's chosen option, which then becomes policy. I also made the point that Presidential decisions must expeditiously be put into writing, so as to minimize misinterpretation.

There is a certain efficiency in this process. Built into it also is a high degree of bureaucratic competition and tension. IG chairmanships in the field of foreign policy are parceled out to State and other departments and agencies according to their interests and their influence. As Kissinger, that canny veteran of marches and countermarches in the faculty of Harvard University, recognized, he who controls the key IG's controls the flow of options to the President and, therefore, to a degree, controls policy.

That morning in Blair House there was no reason to discuss palace coups. Everyone involved—Reagan himself, Richard Allen, and I—had agreed on the identity of the vicar. It was now simply a matter of drafting a suitable document. Naturally, this document had to take into account Allen's advice and the wishes of the other Cabinet officers and agency heads involved. This was a matter for negotiation among colleagues. Reagan gave me leave to negotiate and draft the necessary paper, National Security Decision Document 1 (NSDD1). Heartened by the President's consistent support and understanding, I went away to do as he had ordered. There was never a question in my mind, after this discussion, that Reagan's view of how to organize and operate the foreign policy establishment was identical to my own.

There was a great deal to do besides NSDD1. I wanted to get a grip on the Department of State as soon as possible, to choose senior staff, to infuse it insofar as possible with the spirit of the new Administration. At this point, I had virtually no personal staff; the men I had worked with most recently were career officers in the Army or executives of UTC. Even if I had wished to do so, and I did not, surrounding myself with a military staff at the State Department would risk creating a troublesome symbolism and a climate of mistrust between two professional elites.

Less than a week after being nominated, I had asked an indefatigable young Philadelphia lawyer named Sherwood D. ("Woody") Goldberg to join me as my executive assistant. Woody and I had first met in Vietnam in April 1967. The outfit I had been commanding, the First Battalion of the 26th Infantry, First Infantry Division, had just fought a major engagement on the Cambodian border. Then the colonel commanding the Second Brigade of the First Division was wounded by a mortar round during an enemy attack on brigade headquarters, and I was ordered to replace him. The headquarters, when I arrived to take command, was a shambles, splintered and scorched by mortar and small arms fire. Through this sea of confusion, wearing a steel helmet and puffing on a pipe, moved a calm young captain who seemed to be putting things to rights. It was Woody Goldberg, the headquarters commandant. In no time, and with no fuss, he had supervised cleaning up the mess, reorganized the headquarters, and restored efficiency. It was an impressive performance. Twelve years later, following my retirement and his own departure from the Army after thirteen years of active duty, Woody volunteered to join me at the Foreign Policy Research Institute in Philadelphia. As I observed Woody working far into the night and inspiring others to work almost as hard, I understood that he had not lost his touch for bringing order out of chaos. I wanted him by my side at State. Also from Philadelphia came Harvey Sicherman, Ph.D., of the Foreign Policy Research Institute. My speechwriter and policy analyst, he also took it upon himself to make sure that the more amusing aspects of any situation did not escape my notice.

Mrs. Muriel Hartley, who had worked with me during the difficult years at the White House and, among many other assignments, had accompanied me to China in January 1972 to make the first preparations for President Nixon's historic visit in that year, became my personal assistant. It has been said that Mrs. Hartley was the only person at the White House who made Henry Kissinger timid; I have not checked this statement with Kissinger.

Until the Second World War, the three departments charged with preserving the interests and the safety of the nation abroad were housed in a single building, the old State, War, and Navy Building, which adjoins the White House on Pennsylvania Avenue. Evidently the space was adequate: the United States won the wars of the period and, in general, carried out an effective diplomacy. Total administrative personnel of all three departments in 1940 was probably no more than a few hundred. Now the Department of State alone has about 24,000 employees, 8,000 of them working in the department's headquarters—a rather dowdy, utilitarian structure lying near the Potomac within eyeshot of the Lincoln Memorial. The rest are posted abroad in 280 embassies, missions, consulates, and other diplomatic stations.

The Foreign Service, the professional diplomatic corps of the United States, numbers 3,800. They are a remarkable group of men and women, scholarly and sober and versed in foreign languages and the nuances of foreign culture and politics. They work hard. The indolent government servant, caring for nothing except his vacation and his pension, is a myth. Workaholism is endemic in the higher bureaucracy. In recent history, the Foreign Service has undergone a certain amount of battering. Its esprit was damaged by the recriminations of the McCarthy era, which inflicted on it an intellectual timidity and a professional diffidence that persists to the present day: if you are going to be pilloried twenty years from now for expressing an honest opinion or advocating a policy that fails, it is prudent to equivocate. Morale had been damaged most recently by a long period in which the making of foreign policy had been preempted by the White House. Every Secretary of State since the redoubtable Dulles, with the exception of Kissinger, had to some degree been a bystander. State had increasingly become a housekeeping agency, charged with the errands of foreign policy. The creation of policy was in the hands of the National Security Council staff, or sometimes the Secretary of Defense or some other agent chosen by the President of the day. (Furthermore, the turnover in Secretaries of State had earned them, in Bill Rogers's phrase, the status of "endangered species." In 1969, only Dean Rusk carried the venerable title "former Secretary of State"; today there are six of the defrocked extant.) To a degree, even Kissinger had made bystanders of the Foreign Service. As Secretary of State, he had run things with a personal staff, largely excluding the wider bureaucracy from the romance of important issues.

Under Reagan, I believed, all this was going to change. The problem was, how to make the Foreign Service and the rest of the department's staff believe this, too? The first step was to convince them that State would in fact once again be first in the President's heart. The second was to bring the Foreign Service into the thick of the action, and to do this quickly. I wanted a strong ring of professionals around me in key jobs. I needed their experience and their competence. The Foreign Service is the historic memory of American foreign policy, and this memory helps to preserve political appointees who temporarily reign over the department from error. It is also true that appointing professionals to significant jobs helps to ensure the loyalty of the Foreign Service to an Administration. There is nothing cynical in this. It is just a fact of organizational life that people whose views are not sought, whose competence is not respected, have little alternative beside disaffection.

The most difficult management problem faced by any incoming Administration is the inertia of the bureaucracy. It is like an asteroid, spinning in an eccentric orbit, captured by the gravity of its procedures and its self-interest, deeply suspicious of politicians who threaten its stability by changing its work habits. This is a greater problem for Republicans than for Democrats. The Foreign Service, the civil service as a whole, is not infected by Republican sentiment. Perhaps because they believe more fervently than Republicans in the power of bureaucracy to perfect the human condition, more young Democrats tend to make careers of federal service. Republicans are more likely to regard a few years in Washington as a civic duty to be performed while on leave of absence from the more lucrative private sector.

I found no great enthusiasm in the Department of State for the Reagan Administration. Reagan's transition team, headed by Robert G. Neumann, a native of Vienna who had been U.S. ambassador to Afghanistan and Morocco, had necessarily raised hackles simply by doing its job, which was to study the department and identify its strengths and weaknesses. I thought Neumann and his people had done an excellent job, and many of their findings were complimentary to the department and its personnel. No draconian changes had been proposed. Nevertheless, the fear was abroad that a legion of right-wing activists were going to march in and start conducting American diplomacy according to the rules of a political rally. Some early nominations, made before my own nomination as Secretary— that of the neoconservative Mrs. Jeane J. Kirkpatrick as ambassador to the United Nations, for example—had been read as signs of a trend in this direction. This was unjust, but the perception existed.

It is true that the Administration wanted to appoint people who were loyal to Reagan and sympathetic to his ideas. There was nothing strange in that. To the fullest extent possible, I, too, wanted the President to have his own people at State. There were about eighty high-level posts to be filled; twenty-four of these were at the sub-Cabinet level—a deputy secretary (formerly called the under secretary); four under secretaries, fourteen assistant secretaries, a counselor, a legal adviser, an executive secretary, a director of policy planning, and a director of political-military affairs. The top salary was approximately $60,000 a year. As it is virtually impossible to find in the outside world eighty fervent partisans of any persuasion who possess the expertise to fill these posts and are at the same time willing to give up what they are doing in order to join the government at a loss in earnings, it was inevitable that some, if not most, appointments must go to professionals.

Neumann's transition team had drawn up a list of candidates for all important appointive posts at State. (An interesting feature of the Neumann list was the choice of Ernest Lefever, who later had such troubles as the nominee for assistant secretary for human rights, as under secretary for political affairs, the third-ranking position.) Neumann's list had been combined with others to produce a final list that was in the possession of Dick Allen and John F. Lehman, who was himself to become Secretary of the Navy. The names on this list, it was understood, were the ones with which Reagan was comfortable.

I worked from the Allen-Lehman list. This meant, of course, that

Dick Allen was furnishing me with the men who would be my most trusted associates. Given the recent history of relationships between National Security Advisers and Secretaries of State, this might have touched a nerve. But I saw no reason for paranoia. From the beginning, Allen had said all the right things to me: he was going to be a staff man; he was here to help me and help me communicate regularly with the President. I believed him. Apparently he had been my greatest advocate in the Reagan camp for a long time. Moreover, I knew many of the men he was recommending from earlier days; others, such as Walter J. Stoessel, Jr., a candidate for under secretary for political affairs and a former ambassador to Moscow and Bonn, had had distinguished careers in the Foreign Service. It was a good list. I spent many hours interviewing the men and women named on it, and in the end, after asking the President for his approval, chose the ones I wanted. Reagan never demurred over one of my choices or in any way tried to influence my decisions in this matter.

The key appointment is that of deputy secretary of state. This is the number-two position in every sense of the word. The post has no defined duties; the Secretary and his deputy can make of it whatever they want. I wanted an alter ego in the job, a man who would share every detail of my work and to whom I could give my deepest confidence. He must also be a Reagan loyalist. One name, that of Justice William P. Clark of the California Supreme Court, was mentioned frequently by persons close to Reagan. It came up in an official way one day, early in January, when Dick Allen and I were going over his much-amended list of candidates. In one of the most significant decisions of my life, I seized upon it.

Clark had a single overwhelming qualification: he was an old and trusted friend of the President. I was not, and in an Administration of chums, bonded together by years of faith and hope and hard work on the campaign trail, this was a handicap. I assumed that in time, or so I hoped, Reagan and I would develop a closer relationship. Meanwhile, we would both benefit from the services of an interpreter. I reasoned that Clark could explain the President and his methods to me. I was already somewhat puzzled by the methods of the President's aides; perhaps Clark, who had known these men for years, could explain them, too. No less important, he could explain me to them.

In our meeting on January 6, I had discussed personnel matters with Reagan and given him a preliminary list of my choices for important posts. At that time I had made no overtures to anyone to be deputy secretary. I asked Reagan if he had any preference. With an air of mild surprise, he said he had not—the appointment was mine to make. Next day, when I saw Reagan during a luncheon for his Cabinet-designates, I found an opportunity to ask if he would approve of the appointment of Bill Clark as my deputy. He seemed delighted that I had thought of this, but at the same time he did not appear to be enthusiastic and I wasn't left with the impression that he was fully behind what I proposed to do. But he did not discourage me in any way, so I went ahead.

On January 8, I asked Woody Goldberg to get in touch with Clark and arrange a meeting. This was accomplished in secrecy. Because of the speculation surrounding Clark's name, it seemed wise to keep him away from the press so as not to embarrass the President with an outburst of new speculation. Clark came to Washington and slipped in a side door of the State Department. He is a very tall man with a boyish face and the simple manners of a rancher, which indeed he is; he wears a Stetson and Western boots. As Clark described his background, I took a great liking to him. He has a very manly and open and easygoing manner. "I don't know a thing about foreign policy," he told me with amiable candor. I knew that already. It didn't matter: the Department of State abounds with experts in foreign policy. I needed a man who understood how the President did things. Clark knew; he had been Reagan's chief of staff in Sacramento. "I know the Governor's ways," he said. In Clark's way of talking and thinking, I saw similarities to Reagan—the casual manner, the ready smile, the friendly tone, the easy equality—and understood why the two men were friends. It seemed to me that Clark and I could work together.

The response to our inquiries in California about Clark had not been altogether positive. Questions had been raised about his ability to grasp complex issues, and there was talk of an unfavorable book in the making. Also, he had not completed law school. I discounted these reports. Most public men are thought to be less intelligent than in fact they are. Bad publicity tends to arouse my sympathy for its object. Some of the most successful personages in history—Churchill, Patton, Eisenhower—had been indifferent students. Obviously the President-elect had great confidence in Clark. Reagan had appointed Clark to the highest court in California, and there had been reports—and not only in the press—that he was under consideration for the Supreme Court of the United States. I offered him the job.

Though acceptance meant giving up a lifetime appointment on the California bench, he said yes without hesitation. (Later, Clark may have had second thoughts. While an emissary was on his way by car to the California state capitol in Sacramento, carrying Clark's resignation from the supreme court, Clark tried to reach him by telephone, apparently to stop him from delivering the resignation. After failing to get through to the car telephone, Clark appeared at the door of his office and sadly said, "I couldn't reach him, so I guess it's all over.")

In the department, there was some anxiety about Clark's confirmation by the Senate Foreign Relations Committee, as he lacked even the rudiments of an education in foreign affairs. I asked two of the ablest foreign policy experts in Washington, David M. Abshire and Amos A. ("Joe") Jordan, to tutor Clark. They set to work at once, but did not have sufficient time to fill the empty vessel. Clark flunked the senatorial quiz. Clark himself did not seem to be consternated by this public display of ignorance. In his disarming way, he avoided deeper trouble by frankly admitting that he did not know the answers.

Meanwhile, we were encountering delays at the White House in the approval of my nominations for other positions. John H. Holdridge, my choice for the post of assistant secretary of state for East Asian and Pacific affairs, was resisted on grounds that he was not sufficiently pro-Taiwan. Lawrence S. Eagleburger, an old colleague from the NSC staff, whom I wanted as assistant secretary for European affairs, found disfavor because he was regarded as a Kissingerite. Among many other assignments in a distinguished career, Larry had been Kissinger's executive assistant both at the White House and at State. There was a certain determination to exclude men and women who had been closely associated with Kissinger from the foreign policy apparatus under Reagan. As these and other appointments were stalled, I asked Ed Meese and Jim Baker who, exactly, was opposing them. Senator Jesse A. Helms of North Carolina, they replied.

Politically, Helms, a Republican member of the Foreign Relations Committee, was decidedly to the right, and the right had its problems with Kissinger. There should have been no problem in these cases. Eagleburger was a thoroughgoing professional and a strong-minded individual unlikely to have been brainwashed even by so powerful an intellect as Kissinger. Nor could any question be raised about the objectivity of Holdridge, a speaker of Chinese who had been stationed in Beijing. Helms's obstructionism, if that was what it was, puzzled me. He was a friend of the Administration and of the State Department. He had been friendly to my nomination, and I was as closely identified with Kissinger as any man alive. If he had an animus, I, not Eagleburger, ought to have felt it. Still, Helms was cited by Meese and Baker as the source of the delay. Oddly, I never heard directly from Helms. On four occasions, I scheduled meetings with the senator, but each time Helms's office canceled at the last minute. Thoroughly puzzled and somewhat frustrated, I finally got through to Helms on the telephone. We talked about the men in question. To my surprise, Helms said he had no problem in accepting them. Other phone conversations followed, always with the same result: Helms had no objection to the appointments I was proposing. Yet later, when there were further delays, Helms was again cited as the cause. I was never able to unravel this mystery.

The delays caused by these tests for political purity, added to the stringent legal requirements that had grown out of the experience of Watergate and the normal delays of security clearance, were maddening. It was spring before some of our candidates were confirmed. But in the end, Holdridge and Eagleburger and all our other choices were cleared by the White House and confirmed by the Senate. We assembled a good team. Later on, the White House informed me that I had appointed a higher percentage of its preferred candidates than any other member of the Cabinet. Of a total of twenty-nine high-level appointments, twenty had come from the lists compiled by the transition team and the White House; eight had been my choices, and one had been a career officer who remained in his job.

The appointment of ambassadors was a longer, and in some ways a more delicate, process. I recommended to Reagan that he keep Mike Mansfield, the former Democratic majority leader of the Senate, as ambassador to Japan. Mansfield's patriarchal mien, his honesty, and his distinguished past had captured the respect of the Japanese, and he was as fine an ambassador as he had been a senator. Reagan himself appointed John J. Louis, who had no diplomatic experience, as ambassador at the Court of St. James's while at breakfast in Palm Springs, California, after being introduced to him at dinner the night before. Arthur A. Hartman, a veteran of the Foreign Service who had been ambassador to France under Carter, went to Moscow. A suitable number of career diplomats is needed in these posts, but an appointment on grounds of political allegiance or personal friendship often works out better than critics of this practice sometimes concede. Langhorne A. Motley, Reagan's ambassador to Brazil and later assistant secretary of state for inter-American affairs, was a great success in Brasilia though he had no previous diplomatic experience, and an old friend of the President's, the former actor John Gavin, has done well in Mexico despite sharp questions about his qualifications.

Incoming Secretaries of State work in an office on the first floor of the State Department. Upstairs, Edmund S. Muskie, the incumbent, continued to deal with the day-to-day business of the department. The most pressing issue, of course, involved the negotiations for the release of the hostages. These were in their last, delicate stages, and Muskie, with the courtesy that characterized all his dealings with me, kept me closely informed. There was a useful doubt in the minds of all those involved as to how the new Administration might handle this situation once it came to office. The Iranians (and some others involved in the negotiations) feared that Reagan might avail himself of options that the forbearing Carter had eschewed. We did nothing to disabuse the parties of their anxiety; it could only speed the return of the captive Americans. Muskie and the other Carter people were determined to complete the negotiations before Inauguration Day. Naturally, the new Administration would honor any agreement the old one made with Iran. That, at least, was my view of the matter. As I would discover on Inauguration Day, that was not necessarily the view of all my colleagues.

Meanwhile, I dealt with the details of setting up house. The Reverend Billy Graham called to wish me well, and so did my many other old friends. Richard Nixon phoned and advised me to insist on frequent personal contact with the new President. Former Secretary of State Dean Rusk, a man whose tenacity and intelligence I had admired, telephoned; I told him that if I could accomplish as much as he had done in the office, I'd feel good. Mrs. Kirkpatrick called on me to complain about the inadequacy of her office, her limousine, her personal staff, and her security detail. She made a very strong first impression with her determined stride, her obvious intelligence, and her crackling personality and manner of speech. I gave orders that she was to go first class at the State Department, and she received quarters and a car that were better suited to her needs. I had breakfast with Henry Kissinger. I asked Philip C. Habib, a man I thought would be useful to the President in the Middle East, to come by for a chat.

Robert C. ("Bud") McFarlane, a member of the transition team and an old and trusted acquaintance who was to be counselor of the department, started staff negotiations on a draft of NSDD1. The issues of the first days of Reagan's Presidency identified themselves. In Poland, the Soviets edged closer to repression of the exuberant nationalism represented by the Solidarity movement. In El Salvador, the insurgency quickened and I felt concern about the suitability of our ambassador. Pressure built within the Administration to lift the grain embargo against the U.S.S.R. The sale of arms to Taiwan troubled our relationship with China. The possibility grew that Pakistan, isolated from the U.S. and under threat from the Soviet occupation of neighboring Afghanistan, might develop a nuclear weapon.

I drove the staff toward solutions to these problems, and in the process sometimes proposed courses of action that I knew to be outrageous. I perceived that this style of leadership caused some consternation among those who had not worked with me before. This was my intention. It is very difficult to compel subordinates to exercise freedom of speech. A leader must insist that they do so, or he will find himself alone with his own opinions, surrounded by a crowd of sycophants. The habit of the bureaucracy is caution, and in the end caution must apply. But if in the formulation of policy you do not suggest bold and even outrageous courses of action, imaginative solutions may not suggest themselves to you. It is easier to climb down from an extreme suggestion than to clamber upward from a supine acceptance of the status quo. Group decisions come out of reaction. But there must be something to react to. In early days, and in some cases to the end of my time at State, eyebrows would fly upward at some of my statements. These were designed to produce resistance, to compel argument, to stimulate creativity. That was not always the result, but it was always the intent.

I spoke to the assembled personnel and told them of the President's plans for the department. The news that State would once again be at the center of events seemed to energize its people. The first tremor of enthusiasm could be detected. More privately, I spoke to the senior staff, outlining what I expected of them and what they could expect from the President and me. Within the inner circle, they had total liberty to propose, to amend, to object, to oppose as fiercely as they liked. But they must support decisions once they were made—or leave if they could not. I warned against any temptation to police the press and urged a disciplined reticence in dealings with reporters. I asked for precise memos no more than two pages in length, free of advertising gimmicks. I wanted a sense of urgency. The staff were to get to a decision fast, without needless equivocation— better a mistake than a frozen mentality. Their competence, their absolute loyalty, were assumed.

State was the President's best resource, I told them. The President, I said, wanted the State Department to be at the center of his foreign policy. This desire and intention would last as long as we performed.

As I spoke, I believed what I said. But already I saw signs that the President's intentions might be resisted.

BACKGROUND

When, on my second day as Secretary of State–designate, I dismissed Neumann's transition team, I had no ulterior motive whatsoever. The team's final report was due on Monday. It was delivered to me on that day. I read it, noted its many excellences, including a provocative essay by Myer Rashish on economic policy, and called the team together on Tuesday to thank them and bid them Godspeed. A transition team is designed to get you from one point to the next; it is not by definition an enduring institution. I asked six of the members to stay on. Rick Burt was to be director for political-military affairs; Chet Crocker, assistant secretary for African affairs; Neumann, ambassador to Saudi Arabia; McFarlane, counselor of the department; Paul Wolfowitz, chief of the policy planning staff; and Rashish, under secretary for economic affairs. The rest of the team left because its work was done.

Lots of people in the State Department, and in the press, were glad of that. Neumann's team was regarded by the outgoing Carter appointees and their allies in the bureaucracy as being excessively ideological, a view that was enthusiastically endorsed by some of the press. I reaped an ironic reward, and one that I would have been glad to do without, out of this situation.

Merely by informing Neumann's team that its mission had been accomplished, I became a sort of culture hero. Headlines proclaimed that I had "dismissed" Neumann and his people and, by implication, had saved the State Department from ideological thuggery. The *Washington Post* reported that "the former general had acted boldly to take charge within days of his nomination. . . . 'It was a very skillful performance by a man who knows how to use power,' according to one transition official. . . ." State Department professionals, who, according to the *Post*, feared that the transition team had turned the department into a place "full of innuendo, of vindictiveness, with ominous implications of purges," were said to be reassured by my action.

I was glad of that even if I thought the sentiment hyperbolic. It was nice to be loved, however briefly, by the *Washington Post*. But the right wing of the Reagan constituency, and the hardliners on his staff, could not have been pleased to think that my first act as Secretary-designate was to punish Reaganites and rescue liberals. It did not make me look like a team player.

FIVE

"Al, It's Just Newspaper Talk"

THERE WAS not a single memorable phrase in Ronald Reagan's inaugural address, and that was its strength. There had been enough of the ambrosia of high rhetoric in American politics. It was time for plain American speech. From the rather distant bleacher seats to which the Cabinet had been assigned, I watched Reagan take the oath, and then, in the mild midwinter sunshine, describe the country as he saw it and as he hoped it would be. As he does in private, he used few figures of speech; he did not strive for effect but made whatever emphases he thought necessary through the superb instruments of his flawless delivery and, above all, his friendly regard.

The release of the hostages was near. As Reagan spoke, a kind of diplomatic Russian roulette was being played out in Teheran, with the government of Algeria working feverishly to complete the final details of extremely difficult and complex negotiations. The deadline set for the release of the fifty-two captive Americans was noon, the hour when the Carter Administration ended and the Reagan Administration began. The moment passed with no word from Teheran. But six minutes after the inaugural and thirty-five minutes after the deadline, as President Reagan lunched in the Capitol according to tradition, news came that the plane carrying the fifty-two Americans had taken off. It seemed a good omen.

Since my meeting with Reagan at Blair House on January 6, we at State had been working with the Department of Defense, the NSC, and, in the latter stages, the CIA to produce a mutually agreeable version of NSDD1, the Presidential decision memorandum establishing the structure of foreign policy. My counselor, Bud McFarlane, and Richard T. Kennedy, the under secretary for management, had handled much of the staff work for State; Kennedy had been involved in drafting similar documents in the Nixon and Ford administrations. As is the usual method, each of the interested parties—State, Defense, NSC—produced a draft. These were compared and modified by the staff to take into account everyone's revisions. This compromise draft was then handed on to Cap Weinberger, Dick Allen, and me. William J. Casey, the Director of Central Intelligence, joined in at this point to shepherd through a section that defined the role of the CIA. Sections were drafted that defined the roles of the Secretary of State and the Secretary of Defense. In identical language, each was described, according to the President's wishes, as his "principal foreign [or defense] policy adviser; as such, he is responsible for the formulation of foreign [defense] policy and for the execution of approved policy." The NSC was described as "the principal forum for the coordination of national security policy issues requiring Presidential decision." State was awarded the chairmanship and Defense the vice chairmanship of all SIG's and IG's dealing with foreign policy. Defense, naturally, was given all chairmanships of defense-oriented committees. This arrangement was accepted without demur by Weinberger and Casey, and, especially, by Allen, who, when in my hearing, was not simply cooperative but enthusiastic about this definition of roles.

So it was with confidence, even camaraderie, that we four met at the White House after the inaugural ceremonies to deliver the agreed draft of NSDD1 to the President. Reagan did not need to be prodded to sign this document; he understood its importance. It was obvious that, unless the President wanted to amend it in some way, it had to be among the very first documents that he executed. Otherwise there would be no formal, legal authority for the conduct of foreign and defense and intelligence policies during the fishbowl period of the first days of Reagan's Presidency.

We did not seek to see the President, who was fully occupied with the personal joy and the public ceremony of his inauguration. Instead, we gave the document to Edwin Meese, counselor to the President. But Meese did not merely accept custody. Instead, he invited us into his office. At first, I thought he just wanted to inject a little warmth into our first official encounter as members of the Reagan Administration. James Baker, the White House chief of staff, and his deputy, Michael K. Deaver, were already present. There was a slight stiffness in our behavior. We were barely acquainted, and if I was a newcomer to a circle of familiars, Meese, Baker, and Deaver were strangers in the Executive Mansion, a place I knew well. We were all wearing formal clothes; it seemed faintly comical to be doing business while dressed in this way.

A certain festivity was in the air and a certain solemnity, too. We were living through the first hours of a new era, and if the heart of the government is anywhere, it is in the White House. I was familiar with these corridors, these rooms, with the views from the windows. There is a republican modesty about the interior of the White House, with its low ceilings and smallish rooms and homely furniture and kindly portraits of the Presidents. At the end of an Administration, it has an air of shabbiness, poignant to those who remember the paint when it was new and the furniture before it was battered. A new President's first day in this house compels memories of men who have been here before and of the optimism of their arrivals and the stoicism of their departures. No one, I imagine, has left the place more threadbare than Jimmy Carter.

Meese seemed very much at ease, very sure of his authority. Baker and Deaver, favorites of Mrs. Reagan's, seemed to be lesser players, hanging back a bit. Normally, the chief of staff is the principal figure on the White House staff, but in this case, Meese seemed to hold that position. Baker was cautious, reticent. He had reason to go slow; he, too, was an outsider. A Princetonian and a lawyer from a prosperous family of Houston lawyers, he had worked for John Connally's campaign before assisting Bush in his campaign to deny the nomination to Reagan. By the standards of Reagan's more excitable supporters on the right, Bush and everyone connected to him were liberals who deserved to be treated like vanquished enemies. Baker's appointment to such a high post on the White House staff had shocked the right wing, in the first of a series of such affronts to conservatives.

Meese gestured us to seats around the conference table. This was

Henry Kissinger's old office, and this was the identical table over which I had labored far into countless nights a decade before. Meese's desk already groaned under teetering stacks of documents. We all sat down and, under Meese's chairmanship, began a point-by-point discussion of the document. He appeared to think that the Secretaries of State and Defense, the Director of Central Intelligence, and the National Security Adviser had to clear this paper with him. This came as a great surprise to me. NSDD1 represented a great deal of work and delicate compromise by officers of the executive branch whose responsibilities are constitutionally defined. The counselor to the President has no constitutional authority, no responsibility for foreign affairs. These facts did not seem to be uppermost in Meese's mind. With lawyerly meticulousness, he conducted a dogged critique of the paper. In the process, my earlier understanding with the President—and Weinberger's, too—were disappearing in a haze of nit-picking. The compact Reagan and I had had on lines of authority was in danger of being obscured. Worse, and this seemed no remote possibility, the understanding was in danger of being reversed. Surely the President did not know about this, surely he did not want his counselor editing communications from the Cabinet, or muddying Presidential instructions.

Once before, when the Cabinet-designates met in Washington on January 7, I had sensed in Meese a tendency to assume an unusual measure of authority. The meeting, as I remember it, was largely taken up with an interesting if somewhat discursive lecture on the nature of conservatism by Mrs. Kirkpatrick. But the President's aides spoke, too. Meese, as the first among them, naturally had the most to say. In a sort of primer on Cabinet relations with the White House, he explained the President's ideas, the President's procedures, the President's priorities. Reagan himself spoke very little, content apparently to let his staff define these matters. When Reagan did intervene, it was usually to recall an incident from his days as governor of California that was in some way relevant to the subject at hand.

At length, Meese finished his examination of NSDD1 and tucked it into his briefcase. I would like to be able to say that something in his manner warned me that the document would stay there, unsigned, for well over a year. But the truth is, I never dreamed that he would not hand it to the President at the start of the next day. However, insights were not denied to me altogether: I left the White House that day with the distinct feeling that Ed Meese and his colleagues perceived their rank in the Administration as being superior to that of any member of the Cabinet.

On January 21, the day after the inauguration, Reagan called a meeting of the National Security Council. Iran and El Salvador and Libya were discussed, among other urgent questions. We heard the first accounts by the hostages of their treatment at the hands of their captors, and these stories opened the wound of national humiliation that had been inflicted by the long imprisonment of our citizens. El Salvador did not arouse high passions, but there was a sober understanding that this situation represented a serious escalation of Soviet and Cuban adventurism in the hemisphere. The President was a listener, absorbing the views of his advisers. On this first day, these were not invariably well organized or expressed. Weinberger spoke with great force on questions that interested him, but not always with precision. Dick Allen operated in his own bailiwick with the same puckish style that he exhibited everywhere. Unlike some of his predecessors, Reagan made no decisions on the spot, and gave little indication of his own position on the issues; instead, he rose at the end of the meeting and left.

Afterward, Weinberger, Allen, Casey, and I were asked to join the President and Attorney General William French Smith in the Oval Office for further discussion of the hostage situation. Former President Carter had gone to Frankfurt, where the liberated hostages were being temporarily housed on a military base, to welcome them back into the nation. This arrangement had the virtue of giving Carter public credit for the deliverance of the hostages while separating him from the nearest media center by the width of the Atlantic and the Rhine. Already, some member of the White House staff, still attuned to the public relations requirements of the campaign, had suggested that the President meet the hostages when they landed in the United States. Reagan rejected this unworthy gesture. At State, where planning for the return of our citizens was centered, we were determined that these men and women should come home in the greatest possible degree of privacy and dignity. The President could not put his own sense of the appropriate at risk by seeming to bask in the outpouring of patriotic joy that was inspired by the return of the hostages. These Americans and their families had suffered. One of my first acts on coming to Washington was to put myself at the disposal of the families and to make certain that all arrangements for the return met with their approval and protected their welfare. The choice of West

Point, quiet and remote and historic, as a first point of return was an inspired idea. The request by the media for television coverage of the reunion of the hostages with their families at Stewart Air Force Base, New York, was not allowed. An offer from Mayor Ed Koch of New York City for a ticker-tape parade was declined. There would be no circus atmosphere.

But these were not the questions raised at the meeting in the Oval Office. In addition to the President and the members of the Cabinet and Allen, the triumvirate was there—Meese, Baker, and Deaver. Without preamble, it was suggested that the agreement with the Iranians for the return of the hostages, negotiated by the Carter Administration, be abrogated.

This amazing proposition won the support of many in the room. Insofar as Baker's reaction could be interpreted, he appeared to be in sympathy. So did Deaver. The President did not seem to be surprised by the suggestion; evidently he was prepared, in his remarkable equanimity, to listen to the most audacious ideas. It was clear that everyone in the room was angry with the Iranian terrorists and the regime of the Ayatollah Ruhollah Khomeini; these were understandable sentiments in which most Americans shared. Questions were raised about the legality of an agreement obtained under duress; some suggested that there was a legal basis for abandoning the agreement. The fact that a gesture of this kind would have a huge propaganda impact abroad and a salutary effect on public opinion at home hovered in the background, a consideration that was brought to the President's attention by Baker and Deaver.

When it was my turn to speak, I had to say that I was appalled that such a cynical action could even be considered. The agreement, however bitter, however deeply flawed, was a binding contract. In accepting it, the Carter Administration had pledged not merely its own solemn word, but the honor of the United States government. Half a dozen friendly nations, out of their goodwill for the United States and their trust in its word, had committed their own honor to the process. Administrations changed, but the government of the United States must continue uninterrupted. No incoming Administration had the right to renounce lightly a solemn international contract entered into by its predecessor. We just couldn't do it.

Again, the President, in his quietude, was nodding agreement. He seemed to agree with me. Those who supported the contrary view obviously did not agree. Reagan had listened to their views with impartial receptivity. Once more, he made no decision. How could he have made one? He had heard no facts, only recommendations for a course of action that seemed proper to its advocates and unthinkable to me—and, incidentally, to Reagan's other foreign policy advisers, Dick Allen and Bill Casey. Much theory had been talked, but few facts had been adduced. We did not even have before us a clear explanation of the details of the agreement. Obviously, Reagan needed accurate information on which to base his eventual decision. Once he saw the facts, I had no doubt which way he would decide. I volunteered to compile the facts; Reagan agreed that State should do so, in coordination with the Department of Justice. I rushed back to the department and commissioned Paul Wolfowitz, director of policy planning, and Richard R. Burt, director of politico-military affairs, to write a "bible" for the President on the Iranian hostage agreement. They and their staffs set to work at once, and in collaboration with Bill Smith's experts at Justice, produced a masterly paper. In the end, the agreement with Iran was honored.

One does not regard such outcomes as personal victories or defeats. It is the duty of the President's advisers to give him wholehearted advice so that he will have a range of choices. It is in the nature of the process that one view will prevail over others. I admired the frank, unapologetic way in which the proponents of scuttling the agreement presented their arguments to Reagan. If, as in the matter of Iran, they had not had a good idea, they nevertheless offered good assessments. However, the encounter in the Oval Office was disturbing for another reason altogether. Of the many destructive effects of Vietnam and Watergate, none is worse than the tendency for a new Administration to believe that history began on its Inauguration Day, and its predecessor was totally wrong about everything, and that all its acts must therefore be canceled. This produces a policy of recrimination rather than a policy of renewal; it causes men and women to look back in anger rather than to look forward, as they should, in hope and confidence.

It seemed important to establish, early in Reagan's Presidency, that smallness of spirit would not be his way. Until Vietnam, the existence of a bipartisan consensus in foreign affairs was largely taken for granted. Usually, if not always, politics did stop at the water's edge. A Vandenburg could support a Roosevelt or a Johnson could rally to an Eisenhower, however much the one man deplored the other and his program, when the vital interests of the nation were at stake. Further, congressional discipline usually permitted the leaders of the House and Senate to commit their committee members, regardless of party, to a course of action hammered out with the President in the confidence that all would close ranks. As late as 1969, a President could summon the leadership of Congress and explain his policy to them, and if they could not wholly believe in it, they would nevertheless refrain from reviling it because, as the President, he was entitled to this indispensable courtesy. Popular opinion disciplined itself in a similar way. But since the failure in Vietnam, foreign policy has been politicized. There has been a steady legislative takeover of foreign policy at the very time when the congressional committee system has lost its power to discipline unruly or irresponsible members. Like Presidents, committee chairmen in the House and Senate have lost the right to the respect and deference that once passed with the office as a matter of inheritance. Congress and public opinion have fallen away from the old assumption of decency in an opponent, so that one side thirsts for a public accounting of failures while the other lives in fear of it.

President Mohammad Zia ul-Haq of Pakistan once remarked that being the friend of the United States is like living on the banks of a great river: the soil is wonderfully fertile and there are many other benefits, but every four years or eight years, the river, flooded by storms that are too far away to be seen, changes its course, and you are left in a desert, all alone. These irrational changes of course, produced by a political vengefulness that is alien to American life, are a great danger. They confuse our friends, mislead our adversaries, and confound our own plans for a more manageable world.

Believing this, I may have snatched the issue of the Iranian agreements out of the White House staff hands a bit too brusquely. But their style was new to me; I had never encountered anything quite like it; possibly, my subconscious mind was struggling to understand it while my conscious mind was busy with the day's agenda. Earlier, the first Cabinet meeting had been held. On entering the Cabinet room, I saw that Meese and Baker were seated at the Cabinet table. This, too, was a startling departure from tradition. Robert Haldeman and John Ehrlichman, at the height of their pride, would never have dared such an act of lese majesty. They were aides, not members of the Cabinet, and they sat against the wall, in the chairs provided for aides, as all other aides have always done. Mike Deaver was seated there now—but this, too, would change. A meeting or so later, he was ensconced at the table with the others.

In the Cabinet meeting itself, Meese took the part usually played by the President. He formulated issues, led discussions, summarized remarks. Baker, once again, was quiet and circumspect. Notes passed between the two; from time to time, Deaver would leave his perch along the wall and place a leaf of paper in front of Meese or Baker.

The question of the Soviet grain embargo arose. John R. Block, the energetic young West Pointer who was Secretary of Agriculture, pressed for its immediate end. In this, Block was, with absolute propriety, advocating the interests of his constituency. I had favored handling this issue in the National Security Council, in line with my view that for all its political and economic importance within the United States, it was an even more significant foreign policy issue. During the campaign, Reagan had promised to lift the embargo on the grounds that it was an unfair burden on the farmer. Naturally, he felt compelled to keep his promise. Eventually he would have to do so, but the time was not now. Seventeen million tons of grain, the amount withheld by the U.S. from sale to the U.S.S.R. (together with all soybeans and soybean products), was a significant bargaining chip. To give it away to Moscow, especially at a time when the Poles were living in the shadow of a Soviet invasion, would be perceived as a sign of weakness and unwisdom. Such a course would give the Soviets something for nothing and throw away whatever advantage had been gained by the American farmer's year of sacrifice.

However, the preoccupation of the Administration, like its expertise, lay in domestic policy. Reviving the economy, restoring confidence, reforming the relationship between the government and the private sector—these were the issues of the moment, along with building up military strength. And so they should have been, because without these things, little was possible in other policy areas. But if there was a case for enthusiasm for the President's priorities, there was a case also for judicious exceptions when these were clearly vital to the national interest. Weinberger, Allen, Mrs. Kirkpatrick, and William E. Brock, the trade representative, joined me in my opposition to an immediate lifting of the grain embargo. The President took the question under advisement, but it was obvious that the grain embargo was going to loom large in the first days of the Administration.

Certainly Ed Meese, and to a much lesser degree than was later true, Jim Baker and Mike Deaver, loomed large in the dawn of the Reagan era. During the first Cabinet meeting, I wrote on my notepad: "Government by Cabinet or troika?"

The President had laid much emphasis on the concept of Cabinet government, and on February 13, Meese announced the formation of five Cabinet councils: economic affairs, commerce and trade, human resources, natural resources and the environment, food and agriculture. The Secretary of State was given membership only on the first two. With the fate of the grain embargo, as well as the whole question of food policy as an aspect of foreign policy, in mind, I wrote to Meese suggesting that State be made a member of the council on food and agriculture and noting my assumption that "the functional Cabinet councils will deal only with domestic aspects of these questions . . . [while] foreign policy implications will be dealt with in the NSC mechanism." But there was no entry for State to the council on food and agriculture, and the question of the grain embargo, including its foreign policy aspects, remained in the Cabinet.

The Cabinet council system was vigorously advocated by the President's men, and it was Meese who controlled it. On its face, it was an innovative approach to policy making. The idea was that committees of Cabinet officers would convene to study questions of basic policy in areas where their responsibilities overlapped in order to develop information and a range of possible solutions for the President. This would have been an excellent system if it had stimulated more direct communication between the President and his Cabinet members. In that case, the President's desires would have been understood, the ideas and the experience of the Cabinet would have been brought to the surface of policy, and a powerful new element of creativity would have been harnessed. In practice, the chairmanship went to the Cabinet officer with the strongest vested interest in the subject at hand, an efficient method for setting the fox among the chickens and producing solutions that were politically loaded in favor of the major domestic vested interest concerned.

For that and other reasons, it did not lead to government by Cabinet, but to government by staff. It was not Ronald Reagan but a White House staffer who was the point of contact. Did a demand for action by a Cabinet council come from the President himself? Did the results of the action go to the President himself? It was impossible to know. Normally, it was the staff, not the President, who handed out assignments and received the finished homework. That in itself vitiated the enthusiasm of the Cabinet. It is one thing (and a most gratifying thing) to give the President what he needs. It is another to fill up an assistant's briefcase with papers that may never be read.

There are three main levers of power in the White House: the flow of paper, the President's schedule, and the press. Meese did not get a firm grip on any of these. In the early days of the Administration, he was preoccupied with the Cabinet, the NSC, and the other collegial devices that support the President. Accompanied by Baker and Deaver, he attended every conceivable meeting where policy was likely to be discussed, even the most sensitive meetings of restricted groups from within the NSC. These were usually held in the White House situation room, which lends a certain extra zest to secret discussions. The triumvirate's schoolboyish habit of scribbling and passing notes, which I had noted in the first Cabinet meeting, never abated. Baker and Deaver were always jotting things down and passing them on.

Meese expressed his own position on any given issue with great frankness. In this he was different from the elusive Baker, who was reluctant to reveal his opinions and hardly ever expressed a strong preference in clear terms. Ed Meese was by no means a bungler when it came to questions of foreign policy. He possesses a logical mind and is capable of keen insights. But his experience in these matters was thin, and this was a handicap to him until he learned the ground a little better.

Meese, in the early days, maintained a high profile in the press. He was often on television, frequently interviewed, ceaselessly sought after. At length, overwhelmed by his Cabinet work and perhaps distracted by the demands of being a public personality, he let the situation get away from him. Baker and Deaver, at first tentative allies, became ever closer. One by one, Baker gathered the levers of power to himself, and as Meese receded from the news and from his early predominance, Baker, in closer and closer collaboration with Deaver, became more and more the puissant figure next to the President. But all that was months in the future.

Meanwhile, we were attempting to get policy in motion. NSDD1 had not been signed. Where was it? I asked Dick Allen. His reply: "Meese has it." Had the President seen it? Allen did not know, and when I told him over the telephone on January 23 that I would call Reagan direct if the memorandum was not signed on that day, he seemed unable to share my sense of urgency. I explained that, absent the signed document, we had no structure and no mandate on how to do business. "The situation contains the seeds of disaster," I said. Allen did not protest or demur, but he just couldn't get the memorandum signed or even find out what had happened to it.

This was an early sign that the factor that would bring Allen down, and in the end bring me down, too, was already at work: neither Allen nor I had direct, regular access to the President. Allen had to go through Meese. No route at all had been pointed out to me, no arrangement made for regular contact. It is a wry experience, recalling the many attempts I made to communicate with the President through Allen. I was petitioning for access to the Oval Office to a man who himself had no access. If this bothered the happy-go-lucky Allen, he gave no sign of it. "It doesn't matter," he said to me, of being marooned, "because I will win in the end." Events did not vindicate his optimism.

The Presidency is the ultimate university. The chief executive must be a diligent student, and to a degree his subordinates must be his tutors. They search out the subject matter, digest it, lay it before the President, answer his questions. If a President does not have a grasp of the issue, it puts a great burden on his aides and on himself. Some Presidents have a greater vocation for learning than others, but in the end, all become scholars. Preparation is all: not even the most brilliant President can master the detail of a complicated matter of policy during the course of a meeting. He must come into the room with the essential facts already absorbed, then rule with a composed mind and a firm hand over contending recommendations for decision.

Allen wanted the job of providing the facts of foreign affairs to President Reagan on a day-to-day basis. That was all right with me. There would be plenty of opportunity, or so I assumed, for me to present my views on major issues. As a means of keeping the President abreast of the work of the State Department, I continued a long-standing policy of sending him Night Notes; these were a terse summary, usually only one or two pages long, of the significant events and actions of the day. Perhaps because of my military background, I am intensely sensitive to the need to tell the boss everything, to keep him fully in the picture. The last thing I wanted or intended was to get out ahead of the President on policy or anything else. It was essential that he control the process and be fully informed.

If from the earliest moments there were problems of communication with the rest of the White House, there were none with Dick
Allen. We spoke on the telephone as many as five times a day. We saw
each other frequently when Allen came to my office at State or when I
went to the White House for NSC meetings. He was unfailingly
cheerful, always cooperative, never abrasive, invariably sympathetic.
Institutionally, Allen was in an impossible position from the start
because he reported to the President through Meese. If Allen believed
that something was urgent, he had first to convince Meese, and Baker
and Deaver as well, of its urgency before he could lay it before
Reagan. To live on this sort of sufferance defeats efficiency. By definition, Allen was not a member of the inner circle. According to the
remorseless standards of judgment that apply in such cases, Allen
was therefore regarded by his colleagues as being irrelevant. In time, I
am sorry to say, I came to regard him in that light, too.

It was clear after several days of fruitless search that the copy of
NSDD1 we had given to Meese was lost forever. Therefore, on February 5, Weinberger and I submitted it again to the President with our
recommendation that he sign it. This version disappeared also. We
then decided that we would proceed as if the document *had* been
signed, and set up the SIG's and IG's. But some of the members,
especially those from Defense, were reluctant to do business on such
an informal basis. Thereupon, Weinberger and I instituted a weekly
breakfast at which, over eggs and coffee, we discussed policy objectives and formulated recommendations for the President. In fact, we
were getting things done. In those early days, all of the issues that
have preoccupied the Administration in foreign affairs ever since
were identified. Policies emerged, actions were recommended and
taken. The course of the nation was set for the voyage through the
Reagan years. But to me, the White House was as mysterious as a
ghost ship; you heard the creak of the rigging and the groan of the
timbers and sometimes even glimpsed the crew on deck. But which of
the crew had the helm? Was it Meese, was it Baker, was it someone
else? It was impossible to know for sure.

Admittedly, I complained about that. Plaintively, Dick Allen said
to me one day, apropos of what I do not recall, "Al, why don't you
just worry about the State Department?" That was precisely what I
was worrying about, and it was all that I was worrying about. Things
were not as they should have been. Not only had our charter as the
President's principal instrument of foreign policy not been signed,

but far from speaking with a single voice on foreign policy, the Administration was becoming a sort of Babel. I was reminded of Mark Twain's note to the reader at the front of *Huckleberry Finn*, in which he lists the various exotic dialects spoken by the characters and explains that he has done this lest anyone think that the people in the book are all trying to talk alike and not succeeding. In all charity, I think that my colleagues in the Reagan Administration were trying to talk alike. But they seldom succeeded, and the results were vexing.

Meese and Baker were frequent talk-show guests. Allen is a bona fide expert on foreign affairs, so his infrequent appearances were never a problem in the sense that he seldom put his foot in his mouth, but they certainly were a departure from the original concept that he would be a silent and invisible adviser and staff expediter in the White House. In their television appearances, Meese and Baker were often asked questions that touched on foreign policy, and in their urgent desire to oblige the press, they answered. Generally, their statements were responsible and accurate. But sometimes the things they said contradicted existing policy or complicated the process of putting a new policy into effect. Because they were known to be very close to the President, every word they said was examined in foreign capitals for policy implications. No one knew if what they were saying was the President's policy; I myself was never altogether certain on this point. The world diplomatic community is, figuratively speaking, a gigantic monastery teeming with dedicated friars whose labor is devoted to wringing every nuance and hidden meaning out of such screeds as the transcripts of television shows. Often the statements of Meese and Baker lacked precision; frequently they were badly timed. Policy is a delicate plant that requires a quiet environment until it is mature; if you bring it into the public arena too young, it often withers. It was difficult to get these points across to Meese and Baker. Sometimes, after hanging up the phone, I would have the impression that they regarded me as some sort of naif who did not understand that publicity is the engine of politics. In fact, it was Allen's job to police the public statements of the White House staff in the field of foreign affairs. Mostly, I relied on Allen to do this. As always, he was sympathetic to my needs, but either he could not do what was necessary, or would not.

On February 3, the fourteenth day of the Administration, the Secretary of Defense told the press that the United States was going to proceed with deployment of the neutron warhead. This was a very foolish statement. It was not foolish to suggest that deployment of this weapon was in the interests of Western security. Clearly, it was. In the spirit of detente, President Carter had abstained from production of the neutron bomb on the assumption that the Soviets would exercise a corresponding restraint. They had not done so. But our European allies were already nervous over questions of nuclear policy and uncertain as to how the new government in Washington was going to deal with this issue. Weinberger's statement sent them the worst possible message at the very outset of the Administration. The message was that the United States believed itself at liberty to take decisions that affected the security of the entire Western alliance without bothering to consult with its allies.

I talked the matter over with Weinberger and told him that I thought it best to correct the record and reassure our allies. With large-minded generosity, he agreed that this must be done. Immediately, I sent off cables of reassurance to our allies, then issued a public statement that corrected the record as gently as possible. The neutron bomb, a weapon designed to kill enemy soldiers while leaving property relatively unharmed, has developed into an issue fraught with emotion and distorted by propaganda. I feared greatly that Weinberger's words might bring dangerous political pressures on certain European governments and endanger the consensus in the alliance that supported the deployment of a new generation of American missiles on European soil. As Weinberger spoke, the Soviets had well over 1,000 warheads, most of them on advanced medium-range SS-20 missiles, targeted on West European cities and installations. The alliance had 108 obsolete short-range Pershing missiles. This was precisely the sort of imbalance the President and Weinberger, and I, too, wanted to redress. That was our first priority. The so-called neutron warhead represented a lower priority.

It is not easy to convince other governments or the public that the minister of defense of a superpower is talking off the top of his head on issues of war and peace. Caspar Weinberger is a capable man, immensely likable and honest, a talented administrator, and a stubborn fighter for what he believes is right. The defense policy that he and President Reagan have devised for the United States is a long-needed corrective and will heighten the chances of keeping the peace in small ways and large. But his tendency to blurt out locker-room opinions in the guise of policy was one that I prayed he might overcome. If God heard, He did not answer in any way understandable to me. The arduous duty of construing the meaning of Cap Weinberger's public sayings was a steady drain on time and patience.

These contretemps in the first days held a certain dramatic interest, and I understood from the beginning that they must have a serious effect on my ability to function. Yet they consumed only a small part of the day and, at the time, constituted petty annoyances rather than major problems. The primary goal was to establish the substance and the atmosphere of the Reagan foreign policy. In the first days of the Administration, opportunities to establish the atmosphere of the new policy abounded. Even after a very few days, a feeling of momentum was beginning to build.

Our old friends the Moroccans, threatened by Soviet tanks and antiaircraft missiles in the hands of the Polisario insurrectionists in Western Sahara, asked for the immediate delivery of U.S. tanks and aircraft, the shipping of which had been suspended in 1980. The Moroccans got their arms—and other support, which will be described in the next chapter. I called in the Algerian ambassador (Algeria and Morocco had severed diplomatic relations in 1976 over the question of support to the Polisario rebels) and explained that what we had done for the Moroccans was in no way directed against Algeria. On the other hand, Colonel Qaddafi received the first of what were intended as a series of increasingly intense warnings that the United States intended to oppose him in his campaign to destabilize the region.

We decided on new approaches to important negotiations on the Law of the Sea and the question of Japanese auto imports, approaches that later resulted in important gains for the United States. The Fisheries Treaty, which contained provisions that were harmful to the interests of U.S. fishermen, was withdrawn from the Senate, where it had little chance of ratification.

We reassured our friends in northern Africa and reasserted our friendship and support for Pakistan, which had been so far isolated from the United States as it attempted to cope with the aftermath of its conflicts with India and the Soviet invasion of Afghanistan—which had driven hundreds of thousands of refugees across its northern frontier—that it had contemplated building its own nuclear weapon.

From intelligence reports and other data, we pieced together evidence that showed an unmistakable pattern of Soviet, Cuban, and Nicaraguan involvement in organizing, training, and arming the guerrillas who were seeking to overthrow the legal government of El Salvador. In meetings of the NSC and in conversations with the President, we started the process that would result in a suspension of aid to Nicaragua and a new policy of increased support of the government headed by José Napoleon Duarte Fuentes, a moderate Christian Democrat. (Twenty U.S. military advisers had been sent to El Salvador by Carter in 1980.) Our ambassador in San Salvador, who did not sympathize with the new policy, was replaced. Larry Eagleburger went to Europe to discuss our plans and our concerns with our NATO allies; Vernon ("Dick") Walters, a man of many languages and matchless contacts, traveled to Mexico to brief President José Lopez Portillo and the leaders of Brazil, Argentina, and Chile. We consulted fully with the Congress, and I discussed policy with the members of the House Foreign Affairs Committee at breakfast. A series of briefings was held for the ambassadors of allied and friendly nations.

I made plans for an early journey to the Middle East to reassure our friends there that the United States would once again be a reliable partner in that troubled region and to set the stage for overdue progress in the Arab-Israeli peace process, which had largely lain dormant since Camp David. I learned that a Defense Department team in the previous Administration apparently had committed the United States to providing some form of airborne warning and control system aircraft and enhancements in the form of fuel tanks and bomb racks for F-15 fighters to Saudi Arabia. Ambassador Ephraim Evron had already expressed Israel's anxiety about this decision, which promised to generate difficult problems involving our friends in the Middle East. New approaches to the peace process, and especially to the solution of the question of autonomy for Palestinian inhabitants of the West Bank and Gaza, were explored. We spoke for the first time of including U.S. troops in a peacekeeping force when the Sinai was returned to Egypt in a few months' time.

The Seventh Annual Economic Summit meeting of the leading economic nations, in Ottawa in March, offered an opportunity to explore ways to use economic relationships to bolster the alliance. We worked, successfully, to restructure the agenda in order to emphasize terrorism, energy security, and East-West relations instead of North-South issues, which would be covered at another summit. As Reagan's first trip abroad, and his first chance to negotiate with a large group of foreign leaders, the Ottawa summit was important.

Delivery to Congress of the report on human rights prepared by the previous Administration was delayed until President Chun of Korea, who had encouraged our hopes for a liberalization of his country's practices, had completed his visit to Washington. We told Argentina that it had heard its last public lecture from the United States on human rights. The practice of publicly denouncing friends on questions of human rights while minimizing the abuse of those rights in the Soviet Union and other totalitarian countries was at an end. The U.S. decided to vote for Argentina in the U.N. Human Rights Commission. We knew that the Europeans would likely not vote with us and that there would be unfavorable press reaction, but Argentina had dramatically improved its record, and, in our judgment, further improvement was more likely to be achieved by recognition of that fact than by reducing one of the most important nations in the hemisphere to the status of pariah. In the face of controversy that continues to this day, I identified international terrorism as the ultimate violation of human rights, but this was an effort that never won the full support of the White House.

Prime Minister Wojciech Jaruzelski of Poland called in our ambassador and other Western ambassadors and told them that Western financial assistance was vital to his government's stability. The enormous Polish debt would come due in a matter of weeks, and default was probable if the debt was not rescheduled. The impact of default would be serious on financial institutions in the West and devastating to Poland. The Europeans wanted to reschedule the debt; we studied that option, and at the same time began considering contingency plans, including a trade embargo, should the Soviets move into Poland directly or by proxy. Immediately on assuming office, I had sent a letter to the Soviet foreign minister, Andrei Gromyko, expressing American concern over the threat to the Polish movement for social justice.

A meeting between the Chinese ambassador and myself, originally scheduled for thirty minutes, expanded to an hour and a half of frank discussion concerning the strategic relationship between China and the United States. President Reagan and I had spoken at length about China and its profound strategic importance, and about Taiwan, with its equally profound emotional and political significance in both Washington and Beijing. Out of these talks, and a later trip to China, the elements of a policy emerged. In Thailand, our ambassador met with Son Sann, a leader of the anti-Vietnam resistance in

Kampuchea (formerly Cambodia), as a means of demonstrating U.S. sympathy with those who were resisting the Vietnamese occupation of that country. In the United Nations, we took the difficult decision to continue to support the Khmer resistance movement as a means of opposing the Vietnamese military presence in Kampuchea. Son Sann and Prince Sihanouk were two of the leaders of this movement; the third was Pol Pot, and it was with considerable anguish that we agreed to support, even for overriding political and strategic reasons, this charnel figure.

We successfully defended the State Department budget from an attempt by the Office of Management and Budget to cut $2.6 billion from a foreign aid budget of $8 billion. In Prime Minister Edward Seaga, one of the earliest official visitors to Reagan's White House, we perceived a prime candidate for a creative aid program. It was vital that he should succeed, and be seen to succeed, as a friend of the United States. During his one-day visit on April 7, 1982, few fresh ideas were advanced by the White House. Seaga's aides expressed disappointment and frustration, and in order to allay this reaction and salvage our original purpose, I went back to my desk and, with the help of the staff, put together overnight a package that provided for trade opportunities, tax incentives to U.S. firms to locate in Jamaica, and aid. The private sector was brought into play in an especially effective way when David Rockefeller accepted an invitation to form a committee of businessmen. Serendipitously, this late-night effort provided the model for the regionwide program, prepared by State's Bureau of Inter-American Affairs, that was afterward called the Caribbean Basin Initiative.

My days began soon after dawn and ended near midnight. They were continuously interesting, continuously challenging. Not a single under secretary or assistant secretary had been confirmed (and it would be early summer before some of them were finally legitimized), but the staff was functioning well. Each day, my report of the day's activities went to the President. I could not discover if it reached him or if he read it. The second submission of NSDD1 by Weinberger and me produced no result. The paper remained unsigned. I continued to inquire after its fate, and in so doing perhaps intensified the suspicion on the part of the President's aides that it represented an attempt to grab power. In fact, it was an attempt to contain power within a structure ordained by the President.

This and other points did not seem to register on the triumvirate.

Allen understood my arguments but did not sympathize with my insistence on form. In retrospect, I realize that the fundamental difficulty was a conflict in manners. Persistence was not part of the California style. Nevertheless, I persisted. On February 6, I sent a memo to the President suggesting that he set aside one hour a week in which to discuss foreign policy issues with me. "My daily report to you is a useful way to brief you on the directions I am pursuing . . . ," I wrote. "But that format necessarily precludes an in-depth discussion of major policy questions. And, of course, it does not permit the kind of give and take between us that would allow me to have a more intimate sense of the overall policy framework within which you wish me to operate."

There was no reply.

BACKGROUND

If I had some difficulty in wrenching opinions from the White House staff when I spoke to them in person, its members conversed with remarkable fluency through the press. In the *Washington Post* I learned, early in February, that Bill Clark had not, after all, been my choice as deputy secretary of state, but rather that he was "expected to function as the White House eyes and ears in the State Department, especially on behalf of those in the Reagan inner circle who are suspicious of Haig's ambitions for the Presidency." From the *New York Times* I discovered that my "take-charge" style had earned me the nickname CINCWORLD, or commander in chief of the world. The *Times* ran a sort of checklist of secret Cabinet discussions and confidential conversations, summarizing the events of the opening days of the Administration.

From these and other printed reports, it appeared that I had raised hackles by defending the State Department budget, by pointing out the foreign policy implications of the grain embargo and auto imports, by reassuring our allies on our plans with respect to the neutron bomb, and by the nature of my personality. Neither the

President nor anyone else had brought this to my attention in real life. The fanciful story of my thrusting a "twenty-page memorandum" (NSDD1) into Reagan's hands as he returned from his swearing-in took root in the press and demonstrated once again that gossip is a hardier plant than truth. In *Time* magazine, I learned that Meese had "set to work on an amended version [of NSDD1] that gives some protection to the other agencies." If true (as it turned out to be, in a development that brought me to the brink of resignation), this was an insight into Meese's methods and intentions that I had not been able to ascertain by asking him direct questions.

Plainly, someone in the White House was attempting to communicate with me through the press. This seemed very strange. The Administration was less than three weeks old. The appearance of unity and mutual respect ought to have held up longer than that. One would have thought that it would have been more efficient, and less embarrassing to the President, to have discussed these things man-to-man. I called up Meese and asked him the meaning of these stories. "Al, it's just newspaper talk," he said. "Don't pay any attention." Baker gave me the same advice.

But the phenomenon had seized my attention. Few things are more stimulating than to be able to hear what is being said about you behind your back. Was my own deputy a plant, and if he was, why was his cover being blown in the newspapers? An amused Bill Clark, veteran of the Sacramento, California, newsprint wars, dismissed the story as nonsense. But there were new stories, or recycled old stories, on this subject almost daily. Rumor, to paraphrase Marx's remark about money, has a life of its own; it feeds on its own body. I feared that great damage was being done—to the President's leadership, to my credibility, to the integrity of the White House's deliberative mechanisms, and to poor Bill Clark, who was being dangled before the world as some sort of Scarlet Pimpernel.

Even at this very early stage, it was clear that the press had exceptional sources in the new Administration. Line-by-line quotations from my report to the President on a conversation with the Soviet ambassador were put into the hands of a television commentator in time for the evening news on the very day they were delivered to the White House. A story in *Newsweek* contained direct quotes from deliberations in the National Security Council. An NSC decision on Libya appeared in the papers on the day it was made. Plans for covert action in Central America were leaked to the *Washington*

Post, then backgrounded to the major media. A secret submission to the NSC by James L. Buckley, the under secretary of state for security assistance, was leaked. I learned that my memoranda to the President were being transmitted by a hidden hand to Senator Helms and, thereafter, were being made available to reporters in a method of leaking-by-proxy that suggests the Byzantine complexity of the methods involved in the craft of leaking.

What it all meant, what it all served, who was turning the faucets, were questions that could not be answered with certainty. My protests—to Meese and Baker and Allen, to Vice President Bush, and, finally, to the President himself—that this use of the press was hurting the President and undermining his policy brought about no changes. Confidentiality is the basis of diplomacy. If this torrent of secrets continued to pour into the press, we were going to have trouble getting the rest of the world to believe in our discretion.

The situation, with its overtones of soap opera, diverted attention from real problems. People in the State Department, in their attempts to understand the motives and the wishes of the White House staff and to predict the next twist in the plot, began to resemble kremlinologists: texts were construed, photographs were analyzed, the connections between certain reporters and certain officials were speculated on, a belief grew that auguries could be read from this steaming mess of startling indiscretion, sly innuendo, and half-truth.

If that was the reaction it produced in those who could distinguish between a betrayed national secret and a piece of malarkey, what effect was it having on the rest of the world, which could not know the difference?

"Signals to Moscow"

SOVIET DIPLOMACY is based on tests of will. Since Vietnam, the United States had largely failed these tests. Like the assiduous students of tactics and Western vulnerabilities that they are, the Russians would send out a probe—now in Angola, again in Ethiopia, finally in El Salvador—to test the strength of Western determination. Finding the line unmanned, or only thinly held, they would exploit the gap. From unstable situations of this kind, routs develop. It was time to close the breach and hold the line. From the experience of the 1970s, I was convinced that the Soviet Union did not want war. But where the United States was soft or inconsistent or ambiguous in its policies, the Russians were increasingly willing to take risks. We had to change that pattern of cause and effect.

Mere confrontation should never be the aim of our policy. If the Reagan Administration came into office with the determination to resist Soviet adventurism, it arrived also with the idea of reopening a realistic dialogue with Moscow. We wanted to identify questions on which the U.S. and the Soviets could accommodate their interests in ways that advanced peace and social justice. But before that could happen, the Soviets must believe that it was better to accommodate to the United States and the West then to go on marauding against their interests and security. Rhetoric would not lead them to this conclusion. Only a credible show of will and strength could do so. Even with the American military in a temporary state of post-Vietnam dysfunction, the United States and its friends had enough assets to be able to deal with the Soviets and their proxies with confidence. No one knew this better than the Soviets.

Elsewhere, there was less confidence in our fundamental strength. Especially in the Third World, deep doubts existed about the United States and its capacity to project its power in defense of its own interests—or, at times, to see clearly what these interests were. Vietnam and its aftermath had made a deep impression. More recently, the United States had not merely countenanced the fall of its steadfast ally, the Shah, it had accepted that his overthrow was not just inevitable but, in some inexplicable sense, moral and desirable. The humiliating consequences to the United States of this miscalculation had not gone unobserved by the rest of the world. While giving the Soviets and their clients leave to violate all norms of international behavior, we had placed bewildering restrictions on our own freedom of action. Insecure, nervous states look for steadiness, strength, and purpose in a greater power. For more than a decade, the Soviets had been outmatching America in this regard. This was especially true with respect to arms supply. Moscow provided arms quickly and in large amounts to its friends; Nicaragua was only the most recent example of this policy. Washington, by contrast, was usually late and often hesitant. The idea that arms are intrinsically evil is an article of faith to many in the West, in and out of government. However, conflict is never the consequence of arms per se, but more often of an imbalance of arms. In the absence of a universally accepted code of international conduct, the provision of arms to a threatened smaller power can be a bona fide of intentions, a signal that you are ready to defend a principle.

In the morning of an Administration, the air is fresh and still relatively quiet, and friends and adversaries are alert and watchful. It is the best time to send signals. Our signal to the Soviets had to be a plain warning that their time of unresisted adventuring in the Third World was over, and that America's capacity to tolerate the mischief of Moscow's proxies, Cuba and Libya, had been exceeded. Our signal to other nations must be equally simple and believable: once again, a relationship with the United States brings dividends, not just risks.

Even before Inauguration Day, we had sent an old-fashioned sort of signal to the Russians and to an old friend in Africa that served both these purposes. During the transition period, King Hassan II of Morocco sent a delegation to me in my temporary office at the State Department asking for just such a display of American will as we wished to make—and wished to make early. The Moroccans had seized, and subsequently released, some Soviet fishing trawlers. Moscow had responded by stationing several Soviet warships in the Atlantic, off the southern Saharan coast. In light of heavy Soviet support to the Polisario insurgents in the Western Sahara, the Moroccans regarded this as a serious threat both to themselves and to neighboring states.

Here was an opportunity to show support for Morocco, to demonstrate opposition to a leftist insurgency, and to warn the Soviets early on. I talked the situation over with Secretary Muskie and with the Department of Defense. There happened to be a U.S. Navy guided missile cruiser in the vicinity. The outgoing Administration diverted the cruiser and its escort vessels on a training exercise toward the coast of Morocco, and the Soviet ships withdrew from the area.

King Hassan's concern over the presence of Soviet warships off the coast of his country was understandable. Polisario guerrillas in the Western Sahara were equipped with Soviet arms. Recently, guerrilla attacks had intensified and there were reports of the arrival of Soviet tanks and SAM missiles. Now the Moroccans were pressing for delivery of American M-60 tanks and OV-10 aircraft. Sale of these weapons had been approved by Congress and committed by the Carter Administration, but delivery had been suspended by the executive branch pending a solution of the situation in the Western Sahara and of certain financial details.

In the first of many such episodes, the Near East affairs bureau of the State Department argued against delivery of the weapons to Morocco on grounds that this action would offend Algeria. With fluctuating enthusiasm, Algiers had supported the Polisario insurgency, and relations between Algeria and Morocco had been troubled as a result of their differences over this situation. The Algerians had, of course, been most helpful to the United States in the negotiations for the release of the hostages. Certain State Department bureaucrats,

whose sympathies clearly lay with Algeria, the revolutionary republic, rather than with Morocco, the kingdom, maintained that
concessions to Algiers would encourage the friendlier trend in our
recent relations following many years of gingerly contacts. I raised
this matter with Bud McFarlane, who had done outstanding staff
work on this question. I decided that the issue of Morocco's defense
against a Marxist insurgency and Soviet intimidation was so important in itself, and as a means of alerting Moscow and the world at
large to the revival of American will, that some other means of
acknowledging our genuine gratitude to Algeria would have to be
found. I explained our policy to the Algerian ambassador and released the aircraft and tanks already approved for delivery to Rabat.
Although I had apprised President Reagan of my action in the regular
night note, Richard Allen protested that this should have been a
matter for a priori Presidential decision.

Other signals went to Moscow. The level of propaganda on the
Polish question was building, a sign that the Soviets were preparing
world opinion for yet another suppression of human rights in Eastern
Europe, and events were moving inexorably in that direction. The
President agreed that the Russians must understand that the United
States was not in a state of paralysis on this issue. With Reagan's
approval, I sent a letter to Andrei Gromyko, the Soviet foreign minister, in which American concerns were plainly stated, as was our
displeasure over cynical and unhelpful Soviet propaganda in connection with the hostage situation in Iran. Gromyko himself was on
vacation, but the acting foreign minister, Korniyenko, replied for him
in the interim, expressing personal disappointment that the first communication between the new American Administration and the government of the U.S.S.R. should have dealt with such discomfiting
issues. When Gromyko returned, he wrote a letter expressing similar
thoughts, and released it to the press.

There was more discomfiture to come. I sent an options paper to
the President, recommending that he lay down a marker on the question of Cuba. Reagan, despite some sentiment among his advisers to
do otherwise, decided to abide strictly by the understandings on the
status of Cuba reached by the U.S. and the U.S.S.R. in the aftermath
of the Cuban missile crisis. These understandings did not include the
right of Moscow and Havana to inspire, train, equip, and arm insurgencies in Central America or anywhere else in the world. With
Cuban troops in three African countries and Cuban advisers swarm-

ing into Nicaragua in support of the El Salvador Marxists, we wished to remind the Soviets and the Cubans of that fact.

In Washington, with its fluid social atmosphere in which the most bitter adversaries are likely to meet in the perfumed no-man's-land of the cocktail party, occasions for diplomacy often arise at unforeseen times. A few days after the inauguration, I attended the annual Alfalfa Club dinner. These entertainments provide the members of the Alfalfa Club, who include some of the most prominent men in the country, with a chance to engage in an evening of broad political humor and boyish pranks, satirizing the political "in's" of the moment. It is always a thoroughly enjoyable show.

I found myself seated next to the Mexican ambassador. Mexico, whose governments had combined a glacial rate of domestic social improvement with an exuberantly revolutionary rhetoric in international affairs, was eager to act as an intermediary between the Salvadoran insurgents and the Reagan Administration. Now, in the midst of the Alfalfa Club's antic evening, the Mexican ambassador leaned over and made me an offer. Would the new Administration like to open a discreet line of communication with the rebels in El Salvador? I exploded: no longer, I said, would Washington deal secretly with insurgents who were attempting to overthrow legal governments in the Western Hemisphere. The Mexican ambassador was startled by my vehemence. Moreover, I continued, in the next four years, the Americas would see a determined U.S. effort to stamp out Cuban-supported subversion. The days of Cuban terrorism in the Americas are over, I said.

Months earlier, when I was a private citizen, President Lopez Portillo had told me that the difficulty he had had, in a domestic Mexican sense, in dealing with the Carter Administration was that, in his words, "a president of Mexico cannot survive by taking positions to the right of the President of the United States." Evidently I had relieved the Mexican ambassador of this worry. He gripped my hand warmly. "For years," he said fervently, "I have been waiting for an American to speak words such as these. Tonight I will go home and sleep well!"

Later, I encountered Rita Delia Casco, the fiery young ambassador of the Sandinista regime, at a Washington soiree. In that fiscal year, Nicaragua was scheduled to receive $75 million in American economic aid. The ambassador expressed confidence that there would be no change in U.S.-Nicaraguan relations as a result of the election. I stated bluntly that this confidence was misplaced. While the Sandinistas betrayed their neighbors, there would be no business as usual. America was prepared not only to cut off all aid, but to do other things as well. Ambassador Delia was shocked by my blunt words, but these were carefully chosen. I knew that they would be repeated in Havana and Moscow as soon as she could get back to her embassy's code room.

Anatoliy F. Dobrynin, the Soviet ambassador to the United States, and I had encountered each other before. In 1970, while President Nixon and Henry Kissinger were at the Puerto Rican Conference on Economics with President Georges Pompidou of France, I was ordered by the President to deliver a strong demarche to the Soviets concerning their violation of the American-Soviet Understandings on Cuba. We had discovered that the Soviets were building a base for nuclear submarines at Cienfuegos, on the southern coast of Cuba. Certain Soviet submarines were routinely carrying nuclear weapons capable of destroying targets inside the United States. The American ultimatum told the Soviets to cease and desist and to dismantle as much of the base as had so far been built.

Dobrynin is a cordial man, admired by Washington hostesses for his charming mimicry of bourgeois social graces, but on that occasion I saw the steel in his character. We were in a dimly lit room behind the perpetually drawn shutters of the Soviet embassy on Sixteenth Street. In arctic silence, Dobrynin listened to the message I had delivered to him, then lifted a face that was tense with anger and resentment. He said that this demarche was totally unacceptable. His demeanor was cold and threatening. On instructions from the President, I told him that the Soviets would either remove the base at Cienfuegos or the United States would do it for them. Perhaps, in carrying out my instructions, I used a less modulated tone than another American might have. Dobrynin's response was equally tough. In the end, because they did not want another Cuban missile crisis any more than we did, the Soviets complied. But I was left with no doubts that Dobrynin was a formidable personality and a man totally dedicated to his country and its purposes.

Dobrynin is the dean of the Washington diplomatic corps. In nearly a quarter of a century in Washington, he has developed an encyclopedic knowledge of American affairs. He is a brilliant man, possessing that rare intellectual combination: a retentive mind and a gift for the quick, apt reply. He schools himself on every aspect of every issue and more often than not knows more about almost any subject than the ever-changing combinations of American officials with whom he deals. It is impossible not to admire his diplomatic skills. Beyond that, the witty, well-tailored "Doby" and his wife, Irina, a formidable person in her own right, are welcome everywhere. No Soviet ambassador (and few others) has developed such a wide social and professional acquaintance in official Washington.

So special was Dobrynin's position that he had been accustomed to entering the State Department by driving into the basement garage and then riding a private elevator to the seventh floor, where the Secretary's office is located. This trivial but highly symbolic perquisite acknowledged the special nature of the relationship between the United States and the only other superpower. Dobrynin was the only diplomat in Washington routinely accorded this privilege; the other 150 ambassadors accredited to the U.S. government drove up to the main entrance on C Street, walked across the lobby, and rode in a public elevator. All this changed at five o'clock in the afternoon on January 29, when Dobrynin called on me for the first time. In a maneuver that was savored for its subtle nuances and vivid symbolism, Dobrynin's car was made to back out of the garage and proceed to the C Street entrance, where the flustered ambassador of the Soviet Union dismounted into a thicket of microphones and cameras.

I wish that I could claim credit for this inspired gesture, which conveyed so aptly the change in American attitudes toward Moscow. But the situation rose not from geopolitical considerations but from bureaucratic pique. While Dobrynin was being showered with privileges in Washington (including a direct telephone line from his desk in the Soviet embassy into the Secretary of State's switchboard), American ambassadors in Moscow were being kept in sterile isolation. The Soviet desk of the Bureau of European Affairs had been smarting under this unequal state of affairs. The chief of the desk, Robert German, applied to Assistant Secretary George Vest for permission to take away Dobrynin's parking privileges as a means of getting the Russians' attention. Vest quite properly approved without consulting me. German thereupon called up the Soviet embassy and informed them of the decision. On January 29, Dobrynin's secretary called my office, which knew nothing of this quiet little protocol skirmish, and asked where her boss could park. "Oh, in his usual place, I suppose," said the person who answered in all innocence. Dobrynin naturally drove into the garage. But German had stationed one of his officers there in case there should be just such a test of wills, and the Soviet limousine was halted and made to back ignominiously into the street.

Dobrynin must have thought that he had been deliberately humiliated, but as he entered my office, I was not aware of his parking problem. He managed to conceal any chagrin he may have felt as a result of being treated as an ordinary mortal. He looked well-fed, bearish, and smiling. Among the furnishings in the Secretary of State's office are two red brocade chairs, episcopal in their size and dignity, in which I suppose the decorator intended that the Secretary of State and visiting foreign ministers should sit. I offered one of these chairs to Dobrynin: "Here, Anatoliy, sit in my big red chair!" With a fleeting smile over my imagery, Dobrynin shook my hand. "It's good to see you back in Washington, Al," he said. "You belong here." This was a nice compliment; Dobrynin is never at a loss for the right phrase. He and I had hardly been on a first-name basis in the past, since I had been so often cast in the villain's role during the Nixon Administration. But the use of given names among members of the higher diplomatic corps is universal, whether the people involved know each other well or not; the atmosphere of fellowship it implies makes it easier to say the hard things to one another that diplomats sometimes must.

Dobrynin settled down into the red chair and placed the black leather envelope he had brought with him on his lap. He then began to make the points he had come to make; this was no idle social call. The first weeks of the new Administration, he observed, had been interesting. He wondered where it would all lead. Carter had stressed human rights, and in the end not much had come of it. In his first news conference, on January 29, President Reagan had had firm words for the Soviet Union:

. . . so far, detente's been a one-way street the Soviet Union has used to pursue its own aims. . . . I know of no leader of the Soviet Union since the revolution and including the present leadership that has not more than once repeated . . . that their goal must be world revolution and a one-world Socialist or Communist state . . . the only morality they recognize is what will further their cause, meaning they reserve unto themselves the right to commit any crime: to lie, to cheat . . . when you do business with them, even at a detente, you keep that in mind.

My own public remarks about the Soviets, while somewhat less theological, had been scarcely more flattering. "This will cause great puzzlement in Moscow," Dobrynin said. "I hope it will not continue."

"The United States and the Soviet Union had begun to understand each other in the 1970s," I replied. "But because of various Soviet actions—in Africa, in Afghanistan, in support of Cuban interventionism—differences have developed. These activities on the part of the Soviet Union have destabilized the international situation and caused a loss of freedom for many people."

Dobrynin made no direct reply to this. He said that the policy of the new Administration looked like the old pre-Carter policy. I said it was different because it was backed by a great popular consensus.

Reports from Poland, I said, were causing great distress in the Administration. Recent statements by the Polish government were very threatening; a heavy hand seemed to be developing. But the situation must be worked out by the Polish people alone. Dobrynin's steel showed through: Nothing happened in Poland today. We have put off consideration of the Polish problem until tomorrow.

I raised the question of the transshipment of Soviet arms through Nicaragua to the insurgents in El Salvador. "All lies," said Dobrynin.

"Photographs don't lie," I replied. "The United States is profoundly disturbed by Cuban activities in the Caribbean and elsewhere in the world."

Dobrynin said he was not familiar with the Nicaraguan scene, but this was certainly no way to start an Administration. Quiet dialogue was better than an exchange of news conference statements. How, he asked, should the United States and the Soviet Union begin to develop a dialogue?

"I'll ask the President," I said. "But it is not acceptable to talk peace while acting differently. One statement we can never accept is Brezhnev's insistence on your right to support so-called wars of liberation whenever and wherever targets of opportunity develop."

This was a flash point. Dobrynin said he could recall no such policy. It would be very unfortunate, he added, if the Soviet leadership formed the impression that the Reagan Administration was hostile to the U.S.S.R., because first impressions often persisted.

"Not hostile," I said. "Offended by Soviet excesses. Confident, determined, prepared to do what is necessary. The Soviet leadership must know that there must be change, for the future good of both sides."

Dobrynin opened his black leather envelope and removed a document. This was Gromyko's reply to our demarche on Poland and Soviet exploitation of the hostage situation at a time when the lives of the Americans were at risk. It was an unyielding document. While Dobrynin waited, I read the translation, with its minor misspellings and small grammatical errors, prepared by the Soviet embassy. Gromyko denied any fault in the hostage situation: One could not help asking for what reason all this was being done and whether any thought was being given as to how we should regard such distorted interpretations. The question in Afghanistan, from Moscow's point of view, was not the Soviet takeover of the country, but armed incursions into the territory of the Democratic Republic of Afghanistan by Afghan resistance fighters. On Poland, the language was unequivocal: First of all, the internal affairs of a sovereign socialist state could not be a subject of discussion between third countries, including the U.S.S.R. and the U.S.A. If one were to speak, however, of outside attempts to exert influence on the internal situation in Poland, then it would be necessary to state that such attempts do take place and that they were being undertaken precisely on the part of the U.S.A. and other Western powers. In this regard it was sufficient to mention at least the provocative and instigatory broadcasts of the "Voice of America" . . . those broadcasts were, inter alia, aimed at generating among the Polish population unfriendly sentiments with regard to the Soviet Union. Here again a question arose: what purpose then was being served by the attempts of the American side to introduce the Polish topic into the Soviet-American dialogue and to make at the same time inappropriate warnings addressed to the Soviet Union? How often in our dealings with the Soviets had we encountered this mixture of truculence, accusation, and suspicion that jammed the normal frequencies of civilized discourse? Gromyko is a master of the form. At the end of this letter, he came at last to its real business: he would like once more to confirm Soviet readiness for an exchange of views on a wide range of issues.

In the silence, the grandfather clock against the wall ticked strongly away. When I had finished reading, Dobrynin and I said good-bye to one another.

This first conversation with Dobrynin had constituted what is termed "a useful exchange." Each side had made the points it considered essential. The United States had served notice that Soviet behavior must improve before relations between Moscow and Washington could improve, especially on matters pertaining to Poland and the developing world. The Soviet Union had told us that it was disturbed by American rhetoric and uncertain about the new course of American policy; that the crushing of Polish aspirations would not take place immediately, but probably would take place eventually; and that it intended to continue to deny any involvement in the bloody events in Central America. On the whole, Dobrynin had been surprisingly docile. He might well have protested more vigorously against the Administration's rhetoric about the Soviet Union or injected a shriller note of threat or contempt into his denials. Clearly the Soviets had been impressed by the public statements of the Administration. I hoped that they would be even more impressed by its actions.

Gromyko's interest in talks was no surprise. It was to be expected that the Soviets would suggest substantive, high-level discussions with the new Administration, including a summit. There were many matters they wanted settled and chief among these, because in important areas they now enjoyed a strategic advantage, was nuclear arms control. The Soviet concern over the vocabulary being used by the new men in Washington to describe the activities of the U.S.S.R. reflected this. The Russians did not want to go so far in condemning us that they would have to swallow their pride in order to talk to us. If my advice to the President prevailed, there would be no summit at an early stage. But we must communicate with the Soviets constantly. From the first day of the Administration, that had been done. Despite reports to the contrary, we were talking to the Russians at many levels. The Russians simply did not like what they were hearing. But at this early stage there was nothing substantive to talk about, nothing to negotiate, until the U.S.S.R. began to demonstrate its willingness to behave like a responsible power. That was the basis of our early policy toward Moscow.

Certainly there could be no summit while the shadows of Budapest and Prague fell across Poland. Every bit of leverage and influence we possessed must be mustered in an effort to influence

Soviet calculations and modify Soviet actions. To sit down with the Soviets at the moment when they were laying plans to crush the spirit of the Polish people would be to ratify—to become, in the moral sense, a party to—this brutal act. No American President could do that and keep the support of his own people or the respect of the world. Gromyko's charges of American and Western interference in Poland's internal affairs, especially through the scrupulously re-strained news broadcasts of the Voice of America, were disin-genuous. Though we had the capacity to do so, official U.S. policy was to desist from fishing in the Soviet Union's troubled waters in Eastern Europe. Perhaps Moscow feared that this might not always be so. The existence of a Polish state, policed by the Red Army, in which the mere expression of patriotism was a crime, was propa-ganda point enough.

In Eastern Europe, the Soviets asserted a sphere of influence that the Western powers had acknowledged at Yalta, near the end of World War II. Was the bargain struck at Yalta ineluctable? This was a question worth raising. Did the universal application of the Brezh-nev Doctrine mean that past understandings, however abused, no longer applied? Or was the Soviet strategy of wars of liberation a prelude to the suggestion of condominium between the superpowers? Certain Chinese leaders, among others, believed that U.S. diplomacy in the later Vietnam period had moved America toward strategic partnership with the Soviet Union through such measures as the Helsinki accords, SALT, detente, and increased credits and trade. They were not alone in fearing, however wrongly, a deal between the United States and the Soviet Union to divide the world. China never lost sight of the possibility of such a superpower stratagem, and Europe is ever restive over such a prospect—as are we with regard to their respective Soviet policies.

It was essential that this never happen, either in perception or in reality. The prevailing climate of terror and insurgency and promis-cuous intervention at the expense of the miserable must not be per-mitted to reawaken the idea of spheres of influence. It was my night-mare that some credulous American leader would be seduced into splitting up the world with the Soviet Union. To strike such a deal would be to shatter the Western alliance and the strategic connection to China, Japan, and the rest of the Far East: to abandon the idea of shared goals and ideals based on human liberty; and to condemn hundreds of millions of human beings to the perpetual winter of totalitarianism. Clearly, such a solution would not guarantee security, but would simply, and at last, give Moscow the economic and geopolitical base it needed to complete the revolution when, in due course, its half of the world became strong enough to devour the other half.

If, when the United States draws nearer to the Soviet Union, its friends fear that superpower freemasonry will come into play, the act of drawing away from the U.S.S.R. instills fear that war or economic dislocation will be the result. A steady course, based on firm principles and on the economic and military strength that alone make possible a realistic diplomacy, will steer us around either disaster. The Soviet Union, as Reagan came to office, was in an expansionist period, but already, as the Russians themselves would suggest, the point of excess had been reached. America and the West might wait for this historical phenomenon to subside; but we and our friends could not wait in idleness. We must do what we could, and that was a very great deal, to arrest Soviet imperialism by confronting it, by containing it, by describing it for what it is—and, when it was in harmony with international stability and the cause of freedom, by joining with the Soviets to make one small peace after another in the countless places where they have made their small and deadly and unnecessary wars.

"All I ever hear from you," Anatoliy Dobrynin said to me, "is Cuba, Cuba, Cuba!"

It is true that I raised the subject often. Cuban troops in Ethiopia were the praetorian guard of a regime whose policy had caused inestimable suffering, including mass starvation, among populations displaced by their military adventures. Cuban troops in Angola were the chief impediment to a settlement that might bring peace to that country and independence to neighboring Namibia. These were vitally important matters. But it was the role of Cuba in the insurgency in El Salvador that engaged our attention in the most urgent manner.

All these points I made to Dobrynin the next time we met. Less than a week had passed since our encounter at the State Department. Our meeting this time was in less official circumstances. Senator Percy, chairman of the Senate Foreign Relations Committee, had invited us to dinner at his house in Georgetown. For a pleasant hour or two at the table, Doby—the soul of affability, reason, and wit as he sipped his wine—made small talk about his country place in Maryland and his prowess as a weekend bicyclist. Now, while

Loraine Percy and Irina and Pat chatted in the living room, Dobrynin and Percy and I retired to the upstairs sitting room. Here the mood changed. Dobrynin repeated his earlier complaints about Reagan's rhetoric and about the lack of communication with the new Administration (now just two weeks old). We had scrapped SALT II. What did it all mean?

The Russian was taken aback when I recited the litany of Soviet excesses—Poland, Afghanistan, Kampuchea, the Yemens, Africa, and, once again, Cuban activities in the Western Hemisphere. On the subject of Central America, Dobrynin remained unresponsive, again pleading ignorance of events in that part of the world. He was silent and forbidding on the subject of Poland; softer on Afghanistan, hinting that Moscow may have made a mistake, but what is will be— there was no turning the clock back. He expressed a certain impatience. Dobrynin had not come here to discuss these issues, but to talk about arms negotiations. Senator Percy was an enthusiastic advocate of such talks. He sought to elicit from me some commitment that the Administration would consent to a resumption of strategic arms negotiations. Dobrynin clearly read Percy's advocacy as an encouraging sign that he had a valuable ally, and pressed for a commitment to begin talks on almost any subject.

Once again, I said that there could be no business as usual. The United States and the U.S.S.R. must, first of all, reach an understanding on standards of international conduct. Especially, Moscow must control its client, Cuba, in this hemisphere. Dobrynin still was not prepared to talk about that, but he had something to offer—a new direction in Afghanistan, perhaps even a withdrawal of Soviet forces and the establishment of an autonomous state. But what did autonomy mean? Was it genuine independence? We both knew that the withdrawal of Soviet forces and the establishment of an Afghan state that had even a scintilla of genuine autonomy would mean the fall of Moscow's puppet and the slaughter of his followers by outraged Afghan patriots in a matter of days. The Administration, I repeated, had to see some evidence of Soviet restraint. Then we could begin to think about dialogues on arms control, trade credits, technology transfer.

In the days that followed, we began to receive signals in return. We heard rumors, which I did not altogether credit, that the Soviets were telling their friends to slow down support to insurgencies and urging restraint in their dealings with the United States. Brezhnev wrote to Reagan, employing softer language to reiterate Gromyko's inflexible position on Poland. The President, with his excellent instinct for the right gesture, replied with a handwritten note that established human contact, if not rapport, with the Soviet leader. The Soviets read this as a hopeful sign. Dobrynin told me that it might be possible for Gromyko and me to meet in September in New York, when we both attended the United Nations General Assembly.

"Can't we work out our differences?" Dobrynin asked. He suggested subjects for talks that were of interest to the U.S.S.R.

"The key is illegal intervention," I reiterated. "You must demonstrate goodwill if we are to discuss these matters." If Cuban interventionism continued, we would have to take action to protect our interests and our friends in the Western Hemisphere.

I mentioned Chad, where Colonel Qaddafi was conducting military operations, and this carried over into additional comments about the role of Qaddafi in destabilizing African regimes and in giving aid and comfort to terrorists.

In response, Dobrynin made it clear that Libya was an American problem.

We received further indications that Qaddafi might be expendable. An American delegation returned from Moscow to report hints from members of the Politburo that they were not sure they could control Qaddafi. An important Soviet diplomat told a high U.S. official that Qaddafi was "a madman." Before he was deposed, First Deputy Prime Minister Mieczyslaw Jagielski of Poland, in a meeting at the State Department in Washington, said that it was his government's policy to avoid the use of force and to proceed with social renewal and democratization; at the same time, he asked for American help in rescheduling the Polish debt, for an additional $200 million in Commodity Credit Corporation guarantees, and for assistance in purchasing agricultural produce. These were interesting signs.

By small gestures and large, we maintained our position. On my recommendation, President Reagan froze economic aid to Nicaragua two days after taking office, and indefinitely suspended all aid to the Nicaraguan government (while continuing $5.6 million in support for a wide variety of nongovernmental organizations that directly assisted the Nicaraguan people) on April 1. The visa of a Soviet Americanologist, Georgiy Arbatov, who had sought entry into the United States to appear on the "Bill Moyers Show," was canceled to protest lack of American access to Soviet television. Under constant pressure from Richard Allen and Richard Pipes of the NSC staff, President Reagan took a personal interest in the seven members of the Vashchenko and Chmykhalov families, Pentacostalists who had sought asylum in the American embassy in Moscow, but even in the face of a Presidential request, the Soviet authorities refused to allow their safe emigration. Every official of the State Department, in every exchange with a Soviet official, emphasized American determination that the U.S.S.R. and its clients—especially Fidel Castro and Qaddafi—must moderate their interventionist behavior, and that Poland must be spared. The Soviets showed an interesting tendency to register flexibility on every subject except one: Poland.

In southern Africa, an area where superpower vital interests were not directly engaged, there appeared for a time to be a real prospect for a realistic accommodation. The problem here was to provide for the independence of Namibia without, at the same time, permitting another Soviet-dominated government to be installed in this mineral-rich strategic region. My conversations with Dobrynin, and later with Gromyko, began a process that may well have led to the twin events of Namibian independence and withdrawal of Cuban troops from Angola. As with El Salvador, Namibia was a question with local, regional, and global connotations. I entertained the hope that this opening could form the basis of a new dialogue with Cuba, touching on problems in the Western Hemisphere, and gradually open the way to habits of consultation and accommodation that may have alleviated tensions in such places as Afghanistan. The Russians seemed to agree with me that the possibility of such a trend existed. However, these initiatives, which involved efforts by Britain, France, Canada, and West Germany as members, with the United States, of the Contact Group that had been seeking a diplomatic solution to the Namibian problem since 1977, fell victim to the increasing brittleness in Soviet-American relations, to our unwillingness to put effective pressure on Cuba in the Caribbean—and above all, to the suppression of Solidarity in Poland.

In regard to Poland, on April 24, the Administration misplayed the strongest card it held when President Reagan lifted the grain embargo against the Soviet Union. Some issues rise from the grass roots and drive government policy in unexpected directions. Others are imposed upon the grass roots from above. The grain embargo issue was an example of the second type. To an appreciable degree, it was an issue fed by Farm Belt legislators and commodity interests to relieve the plight of their constituents. That is a perfectly legitimate approach, but it leaves out the dimension of sophisticated patriotism at the grass roots. I believed and argued that the issue could be explained to American farmers in such a way that they would accept a delay in lifting the embargo in the national interest. There was little desire to make these explanations, but nothing before or since has altered my confidence in the patriotism of the American farmer.

On January 4, 1980, in reaction to the Soviet invasion of Afghanistan, President Carter had embargoed the sale of U.S. agricultural products to the U.S.S.R. In order to honor the Soviet-American Grains Agreement, negotiated in 1975 to forestall large unexpected Soviet purchases such as the "great grain robberies" of the 1970s, Carter allowed annual sales of 8 million metric tons of wheat and corn. This had the effect of denying Moscow 17 million metric tons of American grains for which the Soviets had already contracted in the United States. Canada and Australia and the European Economic Community agreed not to replace U.S. grains in their sales to the U.S.S.R.

During the campaign, Reagan had not criticized the grain embargo as such, but he had said that it imposed an inequitable burden on farmers, and he had promised to lift it. Secretary of Agriculture Block reminded him of that promise, as I have reported, at the very first Cabinet meeting. With the support of Ed Meese, Block continued to press his case vigorously. I admired him for that. A full-scale recession was in progress and promised to get worse before it could be cured. The farmers had had an especially hard time economically, and Block wanted to offer them some relief. Meese took the uncomplicated position that the President had made a campaign promise and must keep it. My attempts to persuade Block and Meese, and ultimately Reagan, that the embargo was a very important foreign policy issue did not succeed. It was viewed almost exclusively as a domestic issue. (As a matter of fact, I would have opposed imposing the embargo in the first place. To use food as a weapon is bad policy. Moreover, the grain embargo was selective; in order to be effective, economic sanctions must apply across the trade spectrum. But now that the embargo was in place, lifting it involved worldwide consequences.)

Obviously, a decision to continue the embargo would not, in and of itself, have influenced events in Poland in any decisive way. But it was one of the principal pieces on the board. We had been telling the Soviets that there would be no business as usual so long as it continued to trifle with the national life of other countries. Now, Warsaw Pact troops were maneuvering along the Polish frontiers. The military regime installed in Warsaw by the Soviet Politburo was assuming an increasingly threatening posture toward Solidarity. This moment, pregnant with the possibility of a Soviet invasion of Poland, was not one to choose to resume selling the Soviets grain and other foodstuffs that we had denied to them because they had invaded Afghanistan.

Yet it was inevitable that we should end the embargo. Canada had already announced that it would not limit 1981 sales to the Soviets; Australia was wavering; President Valery Giscard d'Estaing of France, facing a strong challenge for reelection, warned us, confidentially, that he would be obliged to sell 600,000 metric tons of grain to Moscow as a gesture to the powerful French agricultural sector. All of this, added to ongoing Argentine sales, created commercial anxieties. In Block's eyes, and Meese's, the embargo was irrelevant because the Soviets would soon be able to find all the grain they wanted on the world market. If the Russians were going to get the grain anyway, shouldn't distressed American farmers profit from the sale?

By February 3, I was telling the staff that the President would be forced by domestic political considerations to lift the embargo. Accepting this, we concentrated on the timing of the action. It should be preplanned in such a way as to give ample notice to our allies. State advised the White House that at least sixty to ninety days' advance notice would be required to consult with our friends. I asked Myer Rashish, the under secretary for economics, to develop a game plan, suggesting what we might be able to extract from the Soviets in exchange. They wanted talks on any subject. Why should we not talk to them about the grain embargo as if it were an issue for negotiation?

The Japanese, meanwhile, told us that their trade restrictions against the U.S.S.R. would be lifted as a matter of political necessity if the United States lifted the grain embargo. If we were not receiving specific warnings from other nations, it was because the cause and effect was so obvious as to require no explanation.

I continued to advise delay. Action should be taken with the state of the Polish crisis firmly in mind. On March 23, in the Oval Office, I

On the aggressive Haig "image" created by the news media: "The 'take-charge' image had taken hold. . . . My photograph (jaw jutting, arms akimbo) had been on the cover of *Time* magazine."

Haig *(center)* at the exhausting Secretary of State confirmation hearings: "The primary subject would be Nixon. I was determined not to be Richard Nixon's judge."

January 1981: Haig (with Mrs. Haig) at an austere White House swearing-in ceremony.

Haig with President Reagan,
Vice President George Bush,
and the original Cabinet.

Haig *(far right)* with the President and the President's men: Deputy Chief of Staff Michael Deaver *(far left)*; Chief of Staff James Baker *(second from left)*; Defense Secretary Caspar Weinberger; Reagan; Vice President George Bush; Presidential counselor Edwin Meese *(on Haig's left)*; National Security Adviser William Clark *(back to camera)*.

Above: At a frenzied press conference just after the attempt on President Reagan's life: "My remark that I was 'in control... pending the return of the Vice President' was a statement that I was the senior Cabinet officer present."

Relieved and relaxed Haig *(center)* in the White House situation room moments after the assassination crisis had passed: with National Security Adviser Richard Allen *(second from left)*; CIA Director William Casey *(seated, second from right)*; and Defense Secretary Weinberger.

counseled the President to go slow. "Hold off, there's no rush," I said. "Let me meet with Dobrynin and feel the vibes. If we can't get a concession, then we can go ahead." The talk around the White House on that day was that the embargo might be lifted before the end of the week. On the way out, I stopped in on Ed Meese and told him I had advised the President that it would be a mistake to lift the embargo before we had attempted to wring whatever foreign policy advantage possible out of the issue, or at least to limit the substantial damage that would surely ensue. Subsequent explorations with Dobrynin convinced me that the Soviets would not be manipulated by such obvious self-serving tactics. It is an enduring truth that you can never negotiate successfully by making concessions that your negotiating partner knows about in advance.

When, finally, the embargo was lifted, it came as a sudden action. At 6:50 P.M. on Tuesday, April 21, Meese summoned me to the White House. Secretary Block was on the point of leaving Meese's office. Speaking for the President, Meese informed me that the grain embargo would be lifted on Friday, April 24. This left virtually no time to consult with other governments, even to inform them of our intentions. There was no provision for a decent interval in which our friends and allies could do all the things that are necessary to minimize the political and economic shock of an action of this kind. I said that we needed more time; to act in such rude haste would undermine the Administration's reputation as a responsible partner. Meese replied that the decision had been made; the timetable could not be changed. Moreover, the President had decided to seek a new five-year agreement on grain sales with the Soviets and to ask them if they wished to make an immediate purchase of American grain. Only that morning, seeking to find the means of salvaging some shard of advantage, I had suggested calling in the Soviets and asking if they wanted to make purchases, rather than just precipitously lifting the embargo. It was too late now even for such patchwork measures as that.

Meese informed me that the President wanted me to call in Dobrynin that very evening and inform him of the decision. Exhilarated by his victory, Block said he wanted to be present at this meeting with the Soviet ambassador. I replied, as gently as I could, that I planned to discuss with Dobrynin a number of sensitive issues in addition to the grain embargo. Block said he would leave after we had talked about the grain embargo. I referred to the delicate questions of protocol involved, to the importance of keeping domestic and foreign policy unmingled, to the mischief an unguarded word from a Cabinet officer could cause. Still Block insisted. Ed Meese intervened, and after some more discussion, Block reluctantly gave up the idea of accompanying me.

Returning to the State Department, I asked the staff to prepare messages to other nations saying that we would end the grain embargo very soon. My assistants immediately pointed out that lifting the grain embargo opened the question of lifting existing embargoes on sales of phosphates and energy-related technology to the Soviet Union. It would be pointless to embargo phosphates if grain sales were freed of restraint; it would be difficult—a point Cap Weinberger had raised with some heat—to embargo technology, for the same reasons. One of the assistant secretaries, a man intimately acquainted with the ways of Europeans, drafted the necessary language on a pad held on his knee. Finishing his work, he looked up and said, "They'll laugh in Europe when we propose restraints on technology transfers to the Russians." The pipeline was not yet visible as the divisive question it later became, but these were prophetic words.

Dobrynin came to my office at 7:15 P.M., as twilight was deepening into darkness. I understood the political necessity behind my instructions from the President, but speaking to Dobrynin on this issue was the most distasteful thing I had had to do since coming to Washington. I told him that the embargo would be lifted as a gesture of goodwill because the Soviets had restrained themselves so far in Poland. The United States was prepared to negotiate a new agreement for Soviet purchase of U.S. agricultural products. American grain was available to Moscow for immediate purchase.

Dobrynin knew Washington and the United States; he understood the situation perfectly in all its nuances. He is a consummate professional; his face was a blank. The Soviets now had their prize. Their next move would be to demand assurances that any future grain deals with the United States must contain guarantees that the shipments would not be subjected to future embargoes motivated by foreign policy considerations. Even this blatantly unacceptable Soviet demand would later be accommodated.

"Are there any restrictions at all?" he asked.

"The decision could be affected by any surprise move on the part of your government," I replied.

I nearly choked on the words.

BACKGROUND

On the day after President Reagan lifted the grain embargo, I told the press that, if the Soviet Union invaded Poland, the Administration would impose a total ban on all U.S. trade with the U.S.S.R. and would reimpose the grain embargo.

Though I had made this statement with the President's blessing, and though it constituted nothing more than a restatement of established U.S. and NATO policy, it created a flurry in the White House. Clarifications were issued by James Baker's White House spokesmen, which raised doubts that I had been speaking for the President in this matter.

Reagan is a great watcher of the press, and what he reads in the morning or sees on television can affect his mood for the remainder of the day. On this day he appeared to be annoyed. In the Oval Office, he told me that he was upset by this latest flurry in the media. He had questioned the staff. They had told him that they had attempted to moderate my remarks because they weren't aware that these reflected the President's position.

The President, they explained to the President, had been having private telephone conversations with me and they didn't know the resulting decisions and had had no guidance. In other words, they had been prevented from policing the chief executive's relationship with me and, therefore, could not be held responsible for any unfortunate results.

Baker's messengers sent rumors of my imminent resignation or dismissal murmuring through the press. I read that John Block believed that I had given the French "permission" to sell those 600,000 metric tons of wheat to the Soviet Union, a misconception that showed that the Secretary of Agriculture did not yet fully understand French *amour propre*. A "senior Presidential aide" was quoted in a syndicated column as saying, "We *will* get this man [Haig] under control." A television report sought, in a flight of lighthearted slander, to read my character by suggesting that I was taking personality-altering prescription drugs. (I wasn't even taking aspirin.) An anonymous White House source was quoted as saying that the President didn't think my jokes were funny. It was reported in print that James Baker had sounded out Donald H. Rumsfeld, a former White House chief of staff and Secretary of Defense, on his availability to replace me as Secretary of State; Rumsfeld, in a letter to me, said that this was "just flat untrue."

Even the press was beginning to worry a bit. "Like a whispering campaign," wrote the columnists Evans and Novak, "the effort to tame Haig's ambition and limit his power cannot now be stopped by the high Presidential advisers who started it." What good effect could this have on the conduct of foreign policy?

Only a few days before, the President had told reporters on the South Lawn:

The Secretary of State is my primary adviser on foreign affairs and in that capacity he is the chief formulator and spokesman for foreign policy in this administration. There is not, nor has there ever been, any question about this.

But there was a question, and a deeply troubling one, implanted in the press. Did I, or did I not, speak for the President? If, every time I spoke, one or more of the President's anonymous assistants readjusted the statement so as to fine-tune its meaning or even to reverse its intention, then doubts would result. A negotiator must have the confidence of his principals, and be known to have it, or he cannot negotiate.

Even in normal Administrations, the press is a vitally important instrument of policy. In this Administration, it was already beginning to be perceived as the supreme instrument of policy. I told the President that this pattern of back-fence gossip was a self-inflicted wound on the Administration's capacity to win confidence abroad and, hence, to succeed in the policies he had defined. "This is hurting you, Mr. President," I said. "It's not a battle over turf. It's a question of having someone clearly in charge of foreign policy."

The President nodded. "I'm with you, Al," he told me.

SEVEN

Central America: "The Will to Disbelieve"

TO UNDERSTAND the circumstances of life in a nation like El Salvador is to wish to change those circumstances. No one could be unmoved by such a spectacle of poverty and social injustice and cultural deprivation. Annual per capita income is $650, the inflation rate is 30 percent, illiteracy is 60 percent, six babies out of every hundred die in infancy, life expectancy for men and women alike is less than sixty years. For most of its history, El Salvador has been an oligarchy. Until very recently, fourteen families owned most of the country, and all but a fraction of its 4.67 million population was excluded from education and any but menial employment.

Merely by taking up arms against these conditions of life, the Salvadoran insurgents, with a leadership drawn mostly from the affluent classes and entirely from the violent left, won a measure of idealistic international sympathy and trust. What the rebels had done in fact was to add murder, terrorism, and inestimable sorrow to the miseries of the people. In the first year of the rebellion, 10,000 soldiers and civilians were killed, with the guerrillas claiming to have slain 6,000 of that number. As the Reagan Administration came to office in January 1981, the Salvadoran insurgents were launching their "final offensive" against the central government. Many in the bureaucracy and in the press doubted that the junta could withstand the attacks being mounted against it by several thousand well-armed guerrillas. In the end, though difficult battles were fought, the army prevailed and the government remained in power. No one imagined that the war was over. The fundamental question remained. Could there be economic reform and democracy in El Salvador, or would one of the stark alternatives—leftist totalitarianism or a return to rightist oligarchy—be visited on the people of this unfortunate country?

The answer, which was bound up with some of the most complex strategic issues ever to face an incoming Administration, was largely in the hands of the new President. If he seized the situation, and dealt with it in a determined and clearheaded way, I was convinced that he would create a momentum that would help to bring about the strengthening of an international order based on peaceful change under the rule of law. But if, for lack of resolve or because he was given advice that did not serve his needs—or information that did not describe the case—he reproduced the miscalculations of the past, then it seemed to me that the brutality and rapacity that had marked international life in recent years must continue, with results that could not be calculated. For, grave though its plight might be, El Salvador was not merely a local problem. It was also a regional problem that threatened the stability of all of Central America, including the Panama Canal and Mexico and Guatemala with their vast oil reserves. And it was a global issue because it represented the interjection of the war of national liberation into the Western Hemisphere.

It was typical that Americans would be reluctant to treat El Salvador as a strategic problem with global implications. Historically, we have been slow to think and act in these terms. It has cost us dearly. Over the past forty years, circumstances have brought me close to many decisions that Presidents and others have made. And because I started young and lasted a relatively long time as an observer, and sometimes as a collaborator, of great personages, time has given me the opportunity to witness the consequences. After World War II, an American Secretary of State declared that Korea was not within the U.S. sphere of interest. A short time later, North Korean troops attacked across the 38th Parallel and drove American forces back on Pusan. As a young aide-de-camp in General Douglas Mac-Arthur's headquarters in Tokyo, I was present when he announced his daring plan to the Joint Chiefs of Staff to mount an amphibious assault at Inchon against their unanimous advice and that of President Truman. A few months later, entering Seoul with elements of X Corps, I saw evidence of Soviet military presence down to the battalion level in the North Korean army. Still later, near the Cho'san Reservoir, at a moment when it was an article of faith in Tokyo and Washington that no Chinese regulars were present in this area, I saw regular divisions of the Chinese army attack across our thinly held and foolishly divided front in overwhelming numbers and with stupefying bravery, and I looked on dead Americans, some of whom had frozen to death at their positions as they held out with scarcely believable heroism in the murderous cold of the Asiatic winter. Our armies retreated, and then retook the lost ground back to the 38th Parallel mile by bloody mile. We never returned to the Yalu or even seriously considered a policy that would clear Korea of Chinese forces or Soviet influence. We scaled down our objectives, put limits on the use of our power, and politicized the solution. In the context of our newly acquired global responsibilities, this was something entirely new in the American experience. Nearly three years passed before an armistice was signed—and then only after a new American President, Dwight D. Eisenhower, sent the enemy a message containing the veiled threat that nuclear weapons would be used on the battlefield unless an agreement was concluded.

A decade later, as a lieutenant colonel serving as a military assistant to the Secretary of Defense and his deputy, I was asked to collaborate with another officer in drafting a list of possible U.S. actions in Vietnam. This was in the period following the Gulf of Tonkin incident, just subsequent to the bloody Vietcong attacks on American billets in South Vietnam, but before the landing of U.S. Marines at Danang in the spring of 1965. My fellow officer and I presented our superiors with a list of some thirty different levels of American response to the intensifying Communist insurgency in Vietnam. These ranged from full American mobilization and the credible threat of an invasion of North Vietnam, accompanied by an ultimatum to the Soviet Union, as the power behind Hanoi's war effort, down to such token actions as the insertion of limited forces into South Vietnam and a campaign of psychological warfare to win (in a phrase newly minted) the hearts and minds of the people. Our chiefs and their civilian superiors presented only the weakest options to President Johnson, with the recommendation that he apply progressively harsher methods if the Vietcong and the North Vietnamese did not respond. Thus was incrementalism born—and with it, the pernicious idea that a President can have it both ways by masking an unpopular action with measures that tend to exacerbate rather than solve a problem.

Only a short time before, I happened to be in close proximity to the decision makers when the first bombing raid on North Vietnam was ordered by President Johnson following the Gulf of Tonkin incident. Having thus been present when the United States entered the war as a belligerent, I afterward commanded a battalion of the First Infantry Division at the battle of Ap Gu, on the Cambodian border. I watched at close hand as President Nixon took his decisions to bomb the Cambodian sanctuaries and authorize the Christmas bombing of North Vietnam and the mining of Haiphong Harbor. I carried the messages to President Nguyen Van Thieu that persuaded him to accept a peace that he accurately feared would be shattered by his enemies, and later I failed in my efforts in the spring of 1975 to persuade President Ford to resist, or at least make the attempt to resist, when North Vietnamese divisions poured into South Vietnam in violation of the Paris agreements and at last destroyed a South Vietnamese army that had been so far abandoned by its American allies that many of its units ran out of ammunition on the field of battle.

In 1950, it was the judgment at supreme headquarters in Tokyo, in which Washington nervously acquiesced, that the Chinese would not attack our forces in Korea. Supreme headquarters in Tokyo held the stubborn belief that no regular units of the Chinese army were present in northern Korea or in adjacent areas of China. Both judgments flew in the face of the evidence. U.S. Marines, moving into the gap near the Cho'san Reservoir between X Corps to the east and the Eighth Army to the west, had already engaged regular Chinese troops and taken prisoners. A young X Corps intelligence officer had spotted Chinese cavalrymen moving between the Eighth Army and X Corps and had identified them from their distinctive sashes, sabers, and other uniform markings as an elite reconnaissance unit that operated in conjunction only with Chinese regular army groups— formations of at least three armies, numbering as many as 150,000 men. President Truman, in a speech on Korea in June 1950, had referred to an American intention to draw a line around the Nationalist Chinese islands of Quemoy and Matsu, and MacArthur had sent a team to what was then called Formosa to consult with Chiang Kai-shek's military; I had been a junior member of the team. When X Corps landed at Inchon, shattered the North Korean armies, and advanced toward the Chinese frontier, Peking may have sensed the development of a pincer movement that could threaten its survival. It reacted with predictable violence—but the American leadership, intent on bringing the troops home for Christmas, was not in the mood for such black predictions and chose to ignore the evidence.

Times changed after the Korean War, but official American perceptions of Chinese interests and Chinese intentions did not. Thirteen years later, in Vietnam, and for years afterward, it was the judgment in Washington that Chinese military forces would enter North Vietnam and oppose any American Army fighting there. This, too, flew in the face of contemporary evidence. The Chinese, by now estranged from Moscow for reasons of ideology and pragmatism and preoccupied with the threat of Soviet forces along its northern borders, feared and opposed the extension of Soviet hegemony anywhere in East Asia; by the late 1960s, Peking viewed the North Vietnamese and their Vietcong proxies essentially as surrogates of the Soviet Union. A North Vietnamese victory over Saigon, which must inevitably lead to the domination of all of Indochina by a client of the Soviet Union, would run counter to the strategic interests of China. As the United States had no diplomatic relations and essentially no communication with China, the American Presidents involved could not know this. In this period, a growing dependence on the gathering of intelligence by technological means downgraded the role of the human analyst. We came more and more to define a fact as something that a camera or an electronic device had recorded. The role of human intelligence, informed by history and experience and sensibility, was relegated to a secondary role because it was "fallible." If President Johnson had gone to any American town and asked the first thirty people he met if he should get involved in a land war in Asia, most of them would undoubtedly have said "no." Unhappily, he did not get that sort of sage advice from data banks—any more than he received proper advice on what it would take to prevail in such a ground war.

The United States, unlike the Chinese, stubbornly refused to treat the Vietnam insurgency as anything other than a local problem. We knew, as well as the Chinese knew, that if the war was, in important measure, an expression of North Vietnamese imperialism, that it nevertheless could not take place without the approval, the encouragement, and the massive support of the U.S.S.R. Yet we chose not to take the issue to the Soviet Union or even, in a meaningful way, to Hanoi. We chose, instead, to tangle ineffectually with the puppets, rather than the puppet masters.

From these two miscalculations, the first in Korea and the second in Vietnam, one can draw two morals:

1. He who refuses to believe the evidence before his eyes in order to protect an illusion will suffer for his mistake.
2. A President who does not know the whole truth cannot enjoy a full range of policy choices.

These lessons were much on my mind as, in the very early days of the Reagan Administration, we began to consider the question of Central America. No game is so sterile as the game of "what if?" and I would not suggest that President Truman or President Johnson would have taken some other course of action in Korea or Vietnam (or President Kennedy at the Bay of Pigs or President Carter with regard to wars of liberation) if they had been briefed in a somewhat different way. It is impossible to know what they would have done or what the consequences might have been. But we do know that they acted, to a greater or lesser extent, in the absence of all the facts and in the absence of unflinching advice from experienced subordinates. I was determined that President Reagan *would* have all the facts, and that he would have, at least from me, the best advice of which I was capable.

There could not be the slightest doubt that Cuba was at once the source of supply and the catechist of the Salvadoran insurgency. Cuba, in turn, could not act on the scale of the rebellion in El Salvador without the approval and the material support of the U.S.S.R. I believed that our policy should carry the consequences of this relationship directly to Moscow and Havana, and through the application of a full range of economic, political, and security measures, convince them to put an end to Havana's bloody activities in the hemisphere and elsewhere in the world. Indeed, it is in just such sensitive areas where Soviet vital interests are not directly engaged—as they are, for example, in Poland—that opportunities for amelioration of conflicting superpower policies are most promising.

Only a determined show of American will and power—and an overdue rebirth of American clearheadedness—could accomplish these goals. The hard, indeed the agonizing decision before President Reagan was: shall we commit ourselves at a high level of intensity at the beginning, with all the risk that this entails, or shall we start small and accept comfortable rationalizations about the enemy, and once again commit the errors of judgment and the failures of will that cost us so much in blood and spirit first in Korea and later, with profounder consequences, in Vietnam?

The strategic considerations were clear. Wars of liberation had not been confined to mere targets of opportunity. They had taken place in the most strategic areas of the world—in Southeast Asia, with possible control of the Straits of Malacca added to the other consequences of a North Vietnamese victory; along both littorals of Africa, threatening the lifelines of Western commerce; in Ethiopia and the Yemens and (with the help of the Red Army) in Afghanistan to form a noose around the Persian Gulf. Central America was another strategic choke-point.

We knew that the Cuban government had been deeply involved with the Salvadoran guerrillas from the beginning. In 1979, Cuban intermediaries had integrated the four separate Salvadoran leftist movements into a coordinated front under the domination of the Communist element. The head of the Communist party of El Salvador had traveled to Moscow for consultations and had then gone to Hanoi, where North Vietnamese officials promised to provide 60 tons of captured American arms. When Salvadoran guerrillas told the world press that they had "purchased arms on the world market," that was what they meant; when they claimed on other occasions that they were using arms captured from the Salvadoran army, they did not explain how they obtained arms that had never been in the inventory of the Salvadoran military. The Soviets had shipped arms through Cuba to the guerrillas; many of these weapons had subsequently passed into El Salvador concealed in secret compartments in cargo trucks and by air and sea. In 1980 alone, the Cubans trained up to 1,200 guerrillas for the fighting in El Salvador. Through Cuban good offices, the Palestine Liberation Organization (PLO) had also provided training in its camps in the Middle East for a small number of guerrillas. Cuba and Nicaragua had set up Liberation Radio, the propaganda voice of the insurgency, in Nicaragua. There was other, even more conclusive, evidence that revealed the pattern of Cuban activities in Central America and the clear presence of Soviet support of these activities. The central question was: where was the money coming from? It is a very expensive proposition to fight even a guerrilla war on this scale. Cuba was semibankrupt, but was available to launder funds, and, in fact, did so in the case of very large sums, including one gift of half a billion dollars from a radical Arab state. The insurgents, evoking the legend of Robin Hood, said that they financed their war with the proceeds of bank robberies and ransoms obtained from the rich relatives of kidnapped members of the exploiting classes. Those who wished to accept these explanations were free to do so; many did. But, ultimately, Moscow was the banker.

I never envisaged the landing of Marines in Central America. This was not necessary; there was no popular consensus to support such an act, and in any case, it was not possible under the War Powers Act without the consent of Congress. Every realistic being knew that such consent would only be given in case of catastrophe. It risked inflaming the xenophobia of neighboring states and all the consequences this implied. The Salvadoran armed forces needed equipment and training so that they could guarantee the safety of their government while the process of land redistribution and social and economic reform was completed. So far, this process had been carried forward with little efficiency and evident reluctance. Patience was required. Honduras, which was moving steadily toward democratic elections and the restoration of full civilian government, and Guatemala, the strategic key to the region, needed reassurance and assistance. So did Costa Rica, an unarmed liberal democracy in a region bristling with weapons and revolutionary slogans, and Belize, which was just coming to independence after 140 years as a British colony. Stability must be restored, for instability could only produce oppression, no matter which side won, no matter what solution was imposed. I did envisage noticeably higher levels of U.S. aid, the introduction of reasonable numbers of military advisers, and, most important, an augmented U.S. military presence in the region. A carrier group, or two, maneuvering between Cuba and the Central American mainland would have been a useful reminder of the revival of keen U.S. interest in these waters and coasts and of our ability to blockade Cuba if that became necessary. Reinforcement of Army and Air Force units already in the region, and their advancement into a higher state of readiness, would have been desirable.

Plainly, the adoption of these measures, modest though they seemed given the stakes of the game, would present difficulties. Others within the Administration would foresee, as I did, opposition in Congress, outcry in the press, and pressure from other Presidential advisers to concentrate energies on different, more congenial issues. Very nearly the first words spoken on this subject in the councils of the Reagan Administration made reference to the danger of "another Vietnam." Indeed this danger existed, if Reagan repeated the errors of the past and resorted to incrementalism. To start small, to show hesitation, was to Vietnamize the situation. To localize our response was to Vietnamize the situation. Such a policy, in my view, could only lead us into the old trap of committing ever larger resources to a small objective. If it is easier to escalate step by small step, it is easier for an adversary to respond to each step with a response that is strong enough to compel yet another escalation on our part. That is the lesson of Vietnam. If an objective is worth pursuing, then it must be pursued with enough resources to force the issue early. El Salvador, vital though the preservation of its democratic future is, represents a symptom of dangerous conditions in the Americas—Cuban adventurism, Soviet strategic ambition.

Once before in recent times, resolute U.S. action in the Caribbean had driven Castro back to Havana. After the Sovietization of Cuba and the Cuban missile crisis of 1962, there had been a surge of terrorism and guerrilla activity in the region. President Kennedy had opposed this with a program of economic aid, education, and military assistance including extensive counterinsurgency activity (also an extremely active covert element), managing the effort himself and calling for weekly reports from the field that were delivered through his brother Robert. But this was clearly inadequate and American security in the region continued to deteriorate while U.S. influence declined. When the rash of subversion broke out again in the Dominican Republic in 1965, President Johnson introduced 22,000 U.S. troops into the country. Only then did the Cubans and the Soviets flinch. They remained relatively quiescent until 1978, when they began to exploit the hesitancy in American policy that resulted from the double traumas of Vietnam and Watergate, as well as a historic American insensitivity to the economic needs of the region.

The government of El Salvador was worthy of support. The junta, headed by President José Napoleon Duarte Fuentes, a civilian and a genuine Christian Democrat, was imperfect. In a situation convulsed by political terrorism, incidents of repression had unquestionably occurred. The United States could not condone such episodes, but neither did President Duarte, and as a matter of historical fact, civil wars are not usually fought under conditions conducive to the full respect of civil rights. Whatever else it may have been, the Duarte government, which included military officers as well as civilians who represented every political tendency in the country except those of the far right and the violent left, was the only hope for the transfer of power by democratic means. If it survived, elections could follow. No one—least of all the insurgents themselves—imagined that the leftist insurgents, if they won, would hold free elections to decide the future of the country.

Though this was not a point likely to be credited by many people outside of that country, the military was the guarantor of a democratic solution in El Salvador. In certain Latin countries with what may be called the romantic political tradition, the army is regarded as the protector of the liberty of the people. As a matter of historical experience, it is viewed as the remover of tyrants. El Salvador belongs to this tradition. Young military officers overthrew President Carlos Humberto Romero on October 15, 1979. The judiciary remained independent and fully functional. The first junta, also composed of two civilians and one military officer, was dissolved in January 1980 after the far left, moving into open confrontation, accused it of being a puppet of the United States, and the far right organized to block reforms. Violence escalated.

The young officers who had overthrown Romero persuaded the Christian Democrats to join them in an interim coalition until a new government could be freely elected. In March 1980, this junta, headed by Duarte, announced a land reform program that expropriated all estates larger than 1,250 acres and promised to grant 90 percent of all other arable land to peasant cooperatives or sharecroppers. The junta also nationalized the banks and exports. These measures broke the control of the old oligarchy over El Salvador's economy.

An outburst of violence from the left followed. The leftist opposition, after negotiations in Havana, coalesced into the Unified Revolutionary Directorate (DRU) and issued a manifesto calling for the establishment of a Marxist, totalitarian government in El Salvador. The left refused an invitation by the junta to enter into a peaceful dialogue and also refused an offer by the Catholic church to negotiate an end to the violence that, by late 1980, was consuming 800 lives a month. On October 15, 1980, the government proclaimed an amnesty for all its opponents willing to lay down their arms. But terrorist violence and guerrilla warfare continued.

As a first signal that U.S. policy was in new hands, President Reagan and I agreed that our ambassador in El Salvador, a career Foreign Service officer named Robert E. White, should be replaced. White disagreed with our policy and had spoken indiscreetly to the press. His removal and replacement by a more tough-minded ambassador was justified on the merits of the case, and this action would also have symbolic value. White was called home and subsequently retired to become a vociferous public opponent of our policy in El Salvador. Dean R. Hinton, a courageous and very able professional, was appointed in his place.

Beginning on January 23, El Salvador was discussed in an anguishing series of meetings in the National Security Council. In these discussions, the President was a robust partner. Most of the 120,000 Cubans who fled their homeland in 1979 to seek asylum in the United States were honest citizens. But Fidel Castro, in one of the most contemptuous insults ever offered by one country to another, had also emptied out his jails in order to send us what appeared to be the entire Cuban criminal and degenerate classes. The Department of Justice reported that our prison system had never before encountered such unmanageably violent criminals. Reagan was determined to find some way out of this dilemma, in which our law and practice obliged us to bear the enormous expense and the incalculable social consequences of being the unwilling hosts to the dregs of Cuban society.

Beyond that, the President understood the strategic problem and, I believed, sympathized with this solution. He knew that his opportunity to act would not last long, that if was to have an effective policy in Central America and throughout the world, he must put its elements in place in the first months of his Administration. But in the NSC and out of it, he was buffeted by the winds of opinion and tugged by the advice of those who doubted the wisdom of a decisive policy based on the strategic considerations I have outlined. Some advisers, especially his highest aides, counseled against diluting the impact of his domestic program with a foreign undertaking that would generate tremendous background noise in the press and in Congress. The Secretary of Defense genuinely feared the creation of another unmanageable tropical war into which American troops and

American money would be poured with no result different from Vietnam. Weinberger, who was already moving to restore American military strength, was acutely conscious of its present weaknesses. Our forces, he argued, were already spread too thin. He counseled caution in opening a new strategic theater that would draw down on military strength needed elsewhere in the world. The Joint Chiefs of Staff, chastened by the experience of Vietnam, in which our troops performed with admirable success but were declared to have been defeated, and by the steady decline of respect for the military and of military budgets in the post-Vietnam period, resisted a major commitment. I sensed, and understood, a doubt on the part of the military in the political will of the civilians at the top to follow through to the end on such a commitment.

If it is difficult for politicians to do bold things, it is almost impossible for them to do nothing. Instead, they will take small, cautious steps. When we spoke of putting twenty military advisers into El Salvador (as opposed to the 2,000 and more Cuban, Soviet, and East European personnel in Nicaragua who were advising some 4,000 Salvadoran guerrillas), we devoted a full hour to a discussion of guidelines and ground rules on the comportment of the U.S. military in El Salvador. Would they be allowed to carry rifles or should they be limited to sidearms? Should they appear in uniform or in civilian clothes? Large segments of time were devoted to methods for consulting Congress and handling the press.

The Reagan Administration, let it be remembered, had inherited the American commitment to El Salvador. In 1980, the Carter Administration had committed $25 million in aid for El Salvador. More than fifty U.S. military advisers were already in the country. Now we discussed, as a matter requiring Presidential decision, the provision of $5 million in spare parts to the Salvadoran military. In the NSC and in private meetings with me over breakfast, Cap Weinberger insistently raised the spectre of Vietnam and worried over the possibility that the President would be drawn into "involuntary escalation."

The President's advisers were divided into two camps. In one camp, which favored a low-key treatment of El Salvador as a local problem and sought to cure it through limited amounts of military and economic aid—which would be granted step by step—along with certain covert measures, were the Vice President, the Secretary of Defense, the Director of Central Intelligence (with reservations), the President's aides, Richard Allen, and most of the others.

In the other camp, which favored giving military and economic aid to El Salvador while bringing the overwhelming economic strength and political influence of the United States, together with the reality of its military power, to bear on Cuba in order to treat the problem at its source, I was virtually alone. In my view that the strategic gain that could be achieved by this combination of measures far outweighed the risks, and that the United States could contain any Soviet countermeasures, I was also isolated. In my view, direct military action was neither required nor justified, and, I repeat, I never contemplated it. But it was obvious that Cuba, an island nation of 11 million people lying 100 miles off the coast of a United States with a population of 230 million, simply could not stand up to the geostrategic assets available to the larger country. Clearly we could influence Cuban international behavior if we chose to do so, and also have an effect on the global aspects of the problem as long as right was on our side. Firm, prudent handling was needed. Military strength was one of our assets: a credible willingness to apply it to the degree necessary simply could not be disregarded.

I drove my arguments forward because the President was sympathetic. Reagan understood the problem. He knew that Moscow and Havana were behind the troubles in Central America. He understood that in a crisis of this kind you have to take bold and dramatic steps. He knew that if the United States conducts itself in its day-to-day affairs in a way that ignores violations of international law, terrorism, the routine use of force, and the contemptuous destruction of legal governments, it invites miscalculation by its enemies and defection on the part of its friends. He knew that a failure to carry through on this challenge at the heart of our sphere of interest would result in a loss of credibility in all our dealings with the Soviets. Reagan's problem, and it is the problem of all Presidents, was how to gather the facts and how to manage them once they were in his possession.

The discussions continued. On March 23, I told Ed Meese that whatever we were going to do in Central America, we must get it started in ten days. Together with Baker and Deaver, Meese continued to be the leading voice for caution and slow decision. His keen legal mind detected the risks; his deep loyalty and affection for the President made him protective. I understood that Meese's approach reflected a lawyerly passion to protect his client absolutely. Combined with this was the populist tendency that appeared to be the key to the style of Baker and Deaver and others among the President's closest advisers. These men were intensely sensitive to the public mood and reluctant to take any action that might alter it in the President's disfavor. When it was a question of alienating popular affections or of creating controversy, they would draw back. They doubted, as sometimes the President doubted, that the American people were ready to pursue the Cuban problem to its source. Weinberger seemed to agree. So did the Vice President.

In the State Department, after freewheeling discussions with Thomas O. Enders, the assistant secretary for inter-American affairs, and other senior staff, we were close to producing a plan of action that would, as a first step, seek to seal off the export of arms from Cuba to Central America. At the same time, the staff was engaged in writing a White Paper, bringing together such intelligence as could be made public on Soviet and Cuban involvement in the El Salvador insurgency.

To explain our policy, we sent emissaries abroad to consult with our allies and other friendly and interested countries. In February, Ambassador Walters visited Mexico, Argentina, and Chile. Larry Eagleburger toured European capitals. Both returned with reports that highlighted the political difficulties involved. President Lopez Portillo, reflecting the ambivalence that is a historic feature of Mexico's relations with the U.S., told Walters that he feared a U.S. military adventure in El Salvador, and that the United States could not, in the long run, prevail over the Soviet Union. Walters replied that, for the time being, we were not prepared to permit the U.S.S.R. to overthrow a government in the Americas by force. The Europeans, including Socialists and Social Democrats, by and large understood our objectives and sympathized with our concerns; but, they warned, what we were doing would arouse emotions on the left, and in their need to deal with that constituency, their open support for our efforts could only, at best, be muted.

The protracted nature of our discussions did not produce total paralysis. Such actions as were taken in the Caribbean by the Reagan Administration in these early days were mild enough—a measured amount of aid for El Salvador, the assignment of a few additional advisers. The nuclear carriers *Eisenhower* and *Kennedy* with their battle groups totaling some thirty ships were sent on routine Atlantic

Fleet maneuvers in the waters around Cuba. Half a dozen additional ships, carrying out separate maneuvers off Puerto Rico as part of a NATO exercise, staged an amphibious landing at Vieques. An existing task force on Key West, Florida, was upgraded to the status of Caribbean Command, "to reflect continuing U.S. interest in the vital Caribbean area." Even these limited actions, low on the scale of options, produced results. Castro ordered antiaircraft guns placed on the roofs of Havana during our naval exercises. From many sources we heard that the Cuban was nervous, that he desired contacts with the Americans. The flow of arms into Nicaragua and thence into El Salvador slackened, a signal from Havana and Moscow that they had received and understood the American message.

Castro had more reason to be nervous than he knew. In my conversations with Dobrynin, I continued to press the question of Cuban adventurism in the Americas and in Africa as well. Dobrynin's response convinced me that Cuban activities in the Western Hemisphere were a matter between the United States and Cuba, while reaffirming Soviet insistence on adherence to the 1962 Soviet-American Understandings on Cuba. Castro had fallen between two superpowers. The way was open to solve the problem in Central America, and solve it quickly, through the unequivocal application of pressure. The question was, had we the will to do it promptly, while the President still enjoyed the freedom of action he had won at the polls?

Despite this sign that the United States could defend its interests in the Caribbean with a relatively free hand, the President's advisers continued to seek some solution that might bring success in Central America without subjecting the President to the risk of what they judged might become a protracted minor war or even a superpower confrontation. When exercises ended around the first of December, the *Eisenhower* and the *Kennedy* and their escorts were withdrawn from the Caribbean. The Joint Chiefs of Staff were reluctant to station fleet units in the Straits of Florida or to move increased numbers of tactical aircraft to Florida on a permanent basis. The units were needed elsewhere, where, in the judgment of military planners, the threat potential was higher. Some of Reagan's advisers regarded Central America as a sideshow, an unimportant minor issue that diverted attention from more important matters, such as the restoration of the economy. But Central America was a far more significant issue, one that could overshadow domestic policy and, indeed, become a dominating issue of Reagan's Presidency. As always, he listened patiently, courteously to both sides. But as time passed, he reserved his decision.

Reagan believed that some sort of direct contact with Castro, or even with the Soviet leaders, might produce a desirable result. We were already talking to the Soviets on this issue and there was little doubt that they were repeating what we said to Havana. I advised leaving Castro in isolation a little longer as a means of reinforcing his anxiety—and Moscow's, too. But Reagan persisted, and it may have been his interest in this subject that led one of Richard Allen's staff assistants, in late February 1981, to take the unusual step of trying to arrange a meeting with Fidel Castro through the good offices of Jack Anderson, the syndicated columnist. Anderson, it seems, knew a Cuban exile in Miami who claimed to have arranged for the passing of messages between the Castro regime and previous U.S. Administrations. Roger Fontaine, one of Allen's staff assistants at the NSC, met the Cuban in Anderson's office. The question of opening a secret channel to Havana was discussed. The President's name was invoked. The possibility of a trip to Havana by Anderson and the Cuban was discussed. It was suggested that Castro had already given his blessing to such an enterprise.

When word of this encounter reached me, I telephoned Ed Meese, Allen's effective superior, to discuss its implications. We had spent three weeks putting fear into the hearts of the Cubans and getting results. This diversion undermined the whole effort. Meese seemed to understand my objections. The President could not have been aware of this, he said; he had told Allen not to meet with foreigners without prior clearance from the State Department.

As the weeks passed, Castro's approaches to the United States became more frequent. Messages came through two Latin American heads of state and from a contact Dick Allen maintained in Florida—perhaps Jack Anderson's friend. It appeared to some of us, in Dick Walters's phrase, that Castro was trying to signal that he was a victim of the Soviet Union. Some Latins suggested to us that it might even be possible to break Castro out of the Soviet orbit. President Lopez Portillo and his foreign minister, Jorge Castañeda, became leading advocates of reconciliation and what the latter termed "a cease-fire of silence." Mexico suggested that all Caribbean nations, including Cuba, should be included in the Caribbean Basin initiative, and that all, including Cuba, should be eligible for American aid. During his visit to Washington in July, Lopez Portillo volunteered officially to mediate between Cuba and the United States. When this proposal arose at a Cabinet meeting, Allen whispered in Reagan's ear and discussion ended. If he was advising the President that the time was not yet ripe for mediation, he was correct. Castro was just beginning to feel the pressure. There could be no talk about normalization, no relief of the pressure, no conversations on any subject except the return to Havana of the Cuban criminals and the termination of Cuba's interventionism.

To test Castro's sincerity, I sent him a message suggesting that Cuba accept the return of the criminals. It was carried to Havana by the Mexican foreign minister, Castañeda. A few days later, during a meeting on the island of Cozumel, Castro told Lopez Portillo that he was willing to discuss this issue—or even all issues outstanding—with the United States. I did not believe that the time had come for talks with the Cubans, but as summer wore away into autumn and each side in the NSC endlessly repeated its arguments, and as the early tentative pressures on Cuba began to subside in scope and impact, it began to seem that nothing could be lost by testing the waters. The Cuban vice president, Carlos Rafael Rodriguez, and I met in Mexico City.

This encounter was handled in strict secrecy. Only the President and a handful of others knew that it would take place. Before my departure, on November 22, Reagan and I discussed the vital importance of avoiding leaks, and the President himself decided on the short list of people who would be informed. Arrangements in Mexico City were handled with delicacy. Rodriguez is a famous man in Mexico, and my presence in the capital became known: soon after my arrival, some 5,000 demonstrators, members of the Mexican Movement for Peace, marched past the embassy, chanting "¡Cuba si! ¡Yanqui no!"

Jorge Castañeda, who had helped to arrange this meeting, loaned us his house in an elegant suburb for the purpose. Using an inconspicuous car, I left the embassy at the appointed hour in the early evening. Rodriguez was already there, waiting in a sitting room. Casteñeda introduced us, then departed. In the half light of early evening, Rodriguez seemed less a fearsome revolutionary than a cosmopolitan member of the privileged classes. Freshly barbered, he wore a well-cut suit, polished shoes, an expensive watch. He had the easy manner, the self-assured speech, the surface good humor of a man who is at ease with great affairs and famous people.

Though he is not well known in the United States, Rodriguez is a powerful figure in the Cuban hierarchy. Educated by the Jesuits, trained as a lawyer, a Castroite from the first days and a trusted collaborator of the Soviet Union, Rodriguez is an intelligent and dedicated man. His responsibilities include foreign affairs, and he had been at the center of events in Ethiopia, Angola, and, most recently, Nicaragua. A fervent Marxist with friends high in the Kremlin, he is likely the guarantee in human form that the Cuban revolution will outlive Castro.

Negotiations between nations, even between hostile nations, are carried on by human beings. The aim should be to reveal, not to hide, the human factor. It is essential to be truthful, even blunt. Usually, simple language is best. The possibilities for misunderstanding are great; nothing must be done to increase them. It was not my intention to threaten or intimidate Rodriguez. He knew well enough what the relative strengths of our two countries were. At this moment, two nuclear carrier groups were off the coast of Cuba, and the timing of their arrival greatly influenced my decision to attend this meeting. The uncompromising rhetoric of a new American President whose election filled Cubans with anxiety had already reached their ears. Rodriguez was used to living with these facts and with the fact of Cuba's economic debility, but I did not expect him to quail. Whatever else they may be, the Cuban Communists are not uncourageous. I simply wanted him to understand, without equivocation, how the Reagan Administration viewed the situation in El Salvador, and I wanted to suggest to him, as truthfully as possible, what measures the United States might take to defend its interests and preserve the government in El Salvador.

There were formidable difficulties in convincing him of our seriousness of purpose. Based on the experience of the last twenty years, the Cubans must have believed that the United States was weak and a candidate for defeat in Central America. Otherwise, Havana would never have undertaken her adventure in El Salvador in the very shadow of American power. Though he waited politely for the interpreter's Spanish, Rodriguez listened with great attentiveness as I spoke. I told him that in the view of the United States, the only acceptable solution in El Salvador was that the people should decide their own future through free elections. The road ahead for our two countries was one of choice. The American national mood was strong and optimistic. Defense spending was on the rise. U.S.-Cuban relations were devoid of natural hostility; our peoples had always been sympathetic to each other and the success of the Cubans who had come to the United States after the revolution demonstrated this in a dramatic way. There wasn't even an ideological problem—Cuba could have the same sort of relations with the United States as other small Communist countries. The difficulty was geopolitical—Cuba's willingness to carry out Soviet strategic designs in the Caribbean and elsewhere.

Rodriguez spoke of Cuba's inalienable sovereignty, its right to trade, its close friendship with the U.S.S.R., and its common ideology with Moscow. These factors were compatible with good relations with the U.S. Cuba had no troops in the field in the hemisphere. Its expeditionary forces were far away, in Angola and Ethiopia. He told me, at length and in confiding tones, about the history of Cuban involvement in Africa and about his own role in these events. He described Cuba's high sense of duty and sense of fair play in international affairs.

Rhetoric doesn't solve problems, I told him. We have proof of your involvement in Nicaragua. The United States does not accept your right to teach the Nicaraguans these bloody skills. Cuba cannot go on exporting revolution. The rule of law and peaceful change must prevail, not bloody terrorism. Sincerely, time is running out.

Rodriguez said he didn't want to argue facts and figures. But Cuba was not involved in the El Salvador insurgency. There were 2,759 [sic] Cubans in Nicaragua, of whom 2,045 were teachers, 240 were technicians, 150 were doctors, and 66 were nurses. There were no soldiers. Some Cuban military people were helping to organize and train the Nicaraguan army—nothing more. Cuba was sending no arms to El Salvador from the Soviet Union or anywhere else. If the CIA was saying that, it was wrong. The CIA had been wrong before; remember the Bay of Pigs. The Soviet Union didn't want a guerrilla war in El Salvador. Cuba did not have the authority to give away one piece of Soviet candy. Cuba never lies; Fidel never lies.

The exchange was not devoid of humor. I questioned Rodriguez's statement that there were more than 2,000 teachers in Nicaragua. It seemed more likely that they were soldiers. What do they teach, I asked, Marxist-Leninist theory? Please don't worry about that, Rodriguez said. These are *primary school* teachers. It's very hard to teach Marxism to kids! (Later, in talks with Andrei Gromyko, I raised the subject of these 2,000 Cuban soldiers. "They are teachers," said Gromyko stolidly.)

In the end, it came down to a question of American intentions. The last thing Cuba wanted, Rodriguez said, was a confrontation with the United States. The United States was mistaken, even irrational, to think that Cuba was involved in El Salvador. Cuba could not renounce its right to solidarity with revolutionary masses elsewhere in the world, but Cuba did not want a confrontation by mistake. Therefore, the United States must admit its mistake: "This statement about time running out is very worrisome."

Clearly the Cubans were very anxious. They had read the signs of a new American policy. Now they wondered if we would have the staying power to carry it out. Rodriguez and I spoke of another meeting, this time in Havana a few weeks hence with Castro himself. As we said good-bye and Rodriguez drove off into the evening to make his report to Castro (and no doubt to whatever Soviet official he consulted in Mexico City), I knew that by the time our emissary reached Cuba, our warships would have withdrawn from the Caribbean. I feared that our discussions in Washington would still be debating the fateful choices before the President—and that the energy that had shaken the Cubans and won a response from the Soviets would begin to drain out of the situation.

In March 1982, at the President's request, I sent Dick Walters to Havana. Without interpreters, he and Castro spent five hours together discussing the situation in Central America. Rodriguez also was present the whole time. Although American pressure on Cuba had by this time lessened appreciably, Castro was clearly apprehensive as to what steps the United States might take next. Walters told him that the United States wanted Cuba to cease its support for the El Salvador insurgents, end its military and security assistance to Nicaragua, and accept the return of the criminals. Castro made no attempt to deny Cuban involvement in Central America, stating that the question of the criminals was a solvable problem, but El Salvador and Nicaragua were "more difficult." There was, however, no movement toward a solution. Reagan, agitated by the reports of the Justice

Department on the criminals, continued to demand a solution. The legalities were complicated. At length, I recommended that the United States warn Castro that he must take the criminals back or face unspecified U.S. action. If he failed to respond, we would simply load them aboard an expendable ship, sail it into a Cuban anchorage under escort of the U.S. Navy, and inform Castro that we had returned his citizens to him. Neither this solution to the problem, nor any other, ever was approved.

Violence continued unabated in El Salvador. Many uniformed soldiers were killed by the guerrillas in the first six months of 1981. A campaign of destruction against the economic infrastructure of the country was launched by the insurgents, who began systematically destroying the 1,300 pylons of the power grid that carried electricity to the interior. By late August, one-third of the country was without electricity. Later, bridges and highways and trucks carrying food to market would be destroyed. The guerrillas perceived that it was impossible for the United States to match their destructive acts with economic assistance. Ambassador Hinton reported that $50 million in additional aid would be needed to meet the shortfall in the economy while he worked feverishly with limited local assets. In the meantime, Colonel Qaddafi had given $300 million to Nicaragua, a sum the United States could not match in this fiscal year, and Soviet shipments of arms into Cuba in the first seven months of 1981 amounted to 40,000 tons, more than double the total for all of 1981 and more than the amount shipped in any previous full year since 1962.

The war in El Salvador seemed to be a stalemate. No stalemate could have existed without the massive support of outside sources. In a localized conflict, the Salvadoran government could win in the end. Victory might take years, but if the insurgents were convinced that Cuba was out of the struggle, and that Nicaragua was wavering, their defeat was inevitable. The rebels could not sustain the struggle alone. But neither could the government of El Salvador survive alone, as we desired, if it must do battle at second hand with Havana and at third hand with Moscow.

BACKGROUND

During the autumn of 1981, several months after the events described in the foregoing chapter, I found myself riding through the streets of Berlin while, a few blocks away, thousands of demonstrators attacked the police and shrieked their hatred of the United States. The demonstrators, some with their faces painted white, had seized upon my visit to Berlin as a propaganda opportunity. (I rely on television coverage for this description of the crowd; the police of West Berlin kept the demonstrators far away from my car and I never saw them in the flesh.)

Judging by the slogans on their placards, the demonstrators believed that America, which had deployed no new land-based nuclear missiles in Europe, was a threat to Europe's survival, while the U.S.S.R, which had already deployed 1,100 new warheads aimed at European targets and was putting more warheads in place at the rate of six a week, was not. "Communists," said a companion. "No, they're not Communists," I replied. "It's worse than that; they've blinded themselves. As a matter of faith, they won't believe anything good about us or anything bad about the other side."

The will to disbelieve our own governments is a very strong force in America and in the West. No doubt scholars of the future will study it as an interesting event in the history of mass psychology and identify its origins. In the meantime, we can speculate that it had its beginnings in the radical and anarchist movements of the late nineteenth and early twentieth centuries. These political movements were, in a sense, new religions, promising enlightenment and salvation in the here and now. The smashing of idols and the burning of scripture are important components in any new religion.

In due course, the will to disbelieve—to reject, as a matter of automatic faith, anything that what is now called the establishment said and to suspect everything that it did as a trick to delude or defraud the common people—infected the entire left. Finally, it spread beyond the left into the ranks of essentially apolitical men and women who live by the entirely praiseworthy idea that injustice ought to be eradicated and the miserable ought to be uplifted. Millions of the world's most intelligent people came to think, as did those hysterical demonstrators in Berlin, that the best way to express their own decency, regardless of the evidence, was to believe nothing good about the West and nothing bad about the East.

Vietnam and Watergate, those ubiquitous agents of social corrosion, gave a powerful new impetus to the will to disbelieve. By the time Vietnam was lost, by the time Nixon had resigned, the ability of the intelligentsia—and especially of the press—to believe in the truthfulness of the government or in the integrity of public officials had virtually disappeared. In a speech before the Berlin Press Association, I spoke about this phenomenon:

I detect a growing double standard in the West toward appropriate norms of international behavior; one is a supercritical standard applied to those who cherish diversity, tolerate dissent, and seek peaceful change. . . . [But] the Soviet Union has occupied Afghanistan since 1979. The Afghans' religion, culture, and national life are in danger of destruction. One-fifth of the entire nation has been exiled. . . . Why are the voices of conscience . . . so muted? Vietnam, which inspired such widespread concern in the West not long ago, has enslaved its southern populations, has seized Kampuchea. . . . Where are the demonstrations against these outrages?

We ran into the will to disbelieve with a bang earlier when, on February 23, 1981, we published a State Department White Paper called "Communist Interference in El Salvador." The White Paper was a summary of some of the intelligence the U.S. government had gathered over a period of a year or more from human agents and by technological means, such as satellite photography. It was a sober, even a pedestrian treatment of the available information, which included details of arms smuggling and Cuban tutelage of the guerrilla movement, and concluded that:

Cuba, the Soviet Union, and other Communist states . . . are carrying out . . . a well-coordinated, covert effort to bring about the overthrow of El Salvador's established government and to impose in its place a Communist regime with no popular support.

This touched a nerve. A writer for *The Nation* summarized the approved response:

The White Paper fails to provide a convincing case . . . its evidence is flimsy, circumstantial, or nonexistent; the reasoning and logic is slipshod and internally inconsistent; it assumes what needs to be proven; and, finally, what facts are presented refute the very case the State Department is attempting to demonstrate.

This approach had the useful effect of diverting attention from the White Paper data: the guerrillas themselves had claimed the killing of no fewer than 6,000 of the 10,000 persons who had been slain in El Salvador in 1980, including noncombatant "informers" as well as government officials and military personnel, and that North Vietnam had given the insurgents more than 2,000 captured American weapons and over 2 million rounds of ammunition. The guerrilla leadership emphatically denied that it had received arms from any government. They explained that they purchased them on the international market, or captured them in combat; some were "manufactured by our own combatants." No proof of the truth of these statements was offered.

The White Paper was combed for errors and traces of conspiracy. Were the captured documents quoted in the White Paper forgeries? Were the photographs of captured weapons genuine? The White Paper was subjected to the sort of burning scrutiny that only a heretical document can provoke. Mistranslations and other small errors, which should not have occurred but in no way affected the authenticity of the other information cited, were discovered. These were used to discredit the entire document. Courtroom rules of evidence applied to the statements of the U.S. government. The White Paper's critics brought in the Scottish verdict: not proved. At the time this happened I was abroad, and no very vigorous defense was offered by those who had been left behind in the State Department. Perhaps no defense would have been equal to the task of quieting the outrage. We had told impermissible truths.

Elsewhere, Dan Rather, the CBS anchorman, testifying in his own defense against a charge of libel, described how he had weighed the evidence available to him and made the judgment of complicity that led to the lawsuit: "If it looks like a duck, walks like a duck, and quacks like a duck, you've got a duck." He was acquitted.

EIGHT

"As of Now, I Am in Control Here"

As the third month of the Administration approached its end, the habit of regular private conversations on foreign policy between the President and myself had not been established. In fact, as March 1981 came to a close, Reagan and I had rarely talked alone, though we had had many exchanges of views in the Cabinet and the NSC. Several times I had been called to his office to discuss one foreign policy matter or another, or had myself sought such a meeting, but on each occasion, Meese or Baker or Allen or all three drifted in and took part in the discussion. It grew increasingly difficult, in the face of resistance by his staff, to reach the President directly by telephone.

The National Security Decision Memorandum establishing the structure of the foreign policy mechanism had not yet been signed. Some progress had been made since the first draft was submitted on Inauguration Day. On February 25, during a meeting in Meese's office, a final draft had been approved. Meese, Baker, and Allen were present in addition to Weinberger, Casey, and myself. As a matter of symmetry, a new section had been added, designating the Director of

Central Intelligence as the President's principal adviser on intelligence matters in the same terms as the Secretaries of State and Defense were his principal advisers in their fields. Otherwise, this version of the decision memorandum was essentially the same as the original. It established Senior Interagency Groups (SIG's) for foreign policy, defense policy, and intelligence under the chairmanships of State, Defense, and the CIA. Foreign policy interagency groups (IG's) were set up for each geographical region and for political-military and international economic affairs; each was under the chairmanship of an assistant secretary of state. Similarly, the Defense and Intelligence IG's were to be chaired by officials from those agencies.

The details of this meeting were released to the *New York Times* on the day after it took place. I do not recall that the question of crisis management came up during the meeting, but in the newspaper's account, Meese was quoted as saying that "under a new setup, crisis management would remain under President Reagan or, in his absence, Vice President Bush." This suggested that things would remain as they were. For obvious reasons, the ultimate crisis manager must be the President. In a severe crisis, the fate of the nation is at stake, and only the President can deal with that question. In 1973, during the Yom Kippur War, the United States received an ultimatum from the Soviet Union: either the Israeli forces that were driving across the Sinai withdrew, or the U.S.S.R. would intervene, possibly with airborne troops. The Secretary of State, Henry Kissinger, suggested to me that this crisis could be managed in the State Department. As the White House chief of staff, I insisted, on instructions from the President, that it must be brought under control by the President, in the White House, with the support of State and other appropriate agencies. In the event, the Soviet challenge was handled in the West Wing situation room of the White House. U.S. strategic forces went to a higher state of readiness, a strong reply to the Soviet ultimatum was sent to Moscow, and the President won out. In the Reagan Administration, I envisaged the State Department providing whatever assistance the President required in the area of crisis management, in support of whatever system he decided he wanted to use. But no preeminent role was ever envisaged or sought for the State Department or the Secretary of State.

On Sunday morning, March 22, 1981, I read on the front page of the *Washington Post* that

. . . in an effort to bring harmony to the Reagan high command, it has been decided that Vice President Bush will be placed in charge of a new structure for national security crisis management, according to senior Presidential assistants. The assignment will amount to an unprecedented role for a Vice President in modern times. . . . "The reason for this [choice of Bush] is that the Secretary of State might wish that he were chairing the management crisis structure," said one Reagan official, "but it is pretty hard to argue with the Vice President being in charge."

This was the first indication I had had that any such move was contemplated. To place a Vice President in charge of crisis management would be a departure from precedent, but the Vice Presidency can be almost anything the President wants to make it. Nixon, who literally "learned" the Presidency in eight years under Eisenhower, isolated Spiro T. Agnew as if he were a bacillus. In at least one White House meeting that I attended, with members of the NSC and congressional leaders present, President Johnson allotted the loquacious Hubert H. Humphrey five minutes in which to speak (*"Five minutes, Hubert!"*); then Johnson stood by, eyes fixed on the sweep second hand of his watch, while Humphrey spoke, and when the Vice President went over the limit, pushed him, still talking, out of the room with his own hands.

Reagan, on the other hand, respected Bush's experience and listened to his views. Bush had been congressman, envoy to China, special representative to the United Nations, director of the CIA. Earlier in March, Reagan had surprised the State Department by putting Bush in charge of preparations for the Ottawa summit, and he had made it clear in other ways that Bush would be an exceptionally active Vice President. Nevertheless, Bush had a small staff. It lacked the skills and the resources to handle the complex tasks and the mass of work required of a proper crisis management team. Obviously, it would take some time to bring the Vice President up to speed in this new role. None of these considerations was mentioned in the *Post* article. Yet I was already so inured to reading the results of secret deliberations in the daily press that I thought it was distinctly possible that the *Post*'s information was accurate.

On Tuesday, I was scheduled to testify on the State Department budget before the international operations subcommittee of the House Appropriations Committee. The article was almost certain to come up in the course of the hearing. So that I would be prepared with the facts if I was called upon to reply to questions, I phoned Ed Meese on Monday morning and asked if there was any truth in the article in the *Post*. "None whatsoever," Meese replied.

I was glad to have this unequivocal reassurance. The article, by Martin Schram, had not confined itself to a discussion of the Vice President's appointment. It went on, quoting the usual anonymous Presidential aides, to say that "White House officials were unhappy with what they felt to be ill-timed and ill-considered actions by Secretary of State Alexander M. Haig, Jr., that placed the brightest spotlight on El Salvador at a time when the Administration was trying to focus maximum attention on Reagan's economic proposals." My performance in a number of other areas was also criticized, and I should have been sorry to think that these represented a truthful account of what was being said about the Department of State and about me in the White House.

Next day, during the subcommittee hearing, the chairman, Representative Dante B. Fascell, Democrat of Florida, mentioned the article in the *Post*, as I had anticipated. Fascell asked if I felt that I might be "bypassed" by the appointment of Vice President Bush as crisis manager. With Ed Meese's words of reassurance clear in my memory, I replied:

I read with interest and, I suppose, a lack of enthusiasm the same newspaper reporting that you refer to. [I do not] think a decision has been made . . . at least, it has not been discussed with me if it has been made, which would pose another set of problems.

Subsequently, I would read in the press that my words before the Fascell subcommittee had offended President Reagan, but when I spoke to him later in the day, he gave no such indication. I had gone to the White House directly from the subcommittee hearing to attend a meeting between the President and Foreign Minister Masayoshi Ito of Japan. Before he received Ito, Reagan called me into the Oval Office. He wore an expression of concern. "I want you to know," he told me, "that the story in the *Post* is a fabrication. It means that George would sit in for me in the NSC in my absence, and that's all it means. It doesn't affect your authority in any way."

When I returned to the State Department, at about five o'clock, the President called me on the telephone. Evidently he thought it necessary to reassure me a second time. "Al," he said, "I want you to know that you are my foreign policy guy." He went on to say that the ground rules had not changed. The Secretary of State was his deputy in all matters having to do with foreign policy.

At about five-thirty, the department's press spokesman, William Dyess, came into my office in a state of puzzlement. The State Department press corps had picked up a rumor that Vice President Bush was going to be named crisis manager before the end of the day. "There's no truth in it, Bill," I assured him. "I've just spoken to the President about it." Dyess went back to the press room and told the reporters that they were onto a false scent.

Half an hour later, James S. Brady, the President's press secretary, made the following statement to White House correspondents:

I am confirming today the President's decision to have the Vice President chair the Administration's "crisis management" team, as a part of the National Security Council system. . . . President Reagan's choice of the Vice President was guided in large measure by the fact that management of crises has traditionally—and appropriately—been done in the White House.

This was a stunning sequence of events. I called in my deputy, William Clark, who knew the mind of the President and knew his methods. I could not understand how Brady's statement could have been issued in the face of direct assurances from the President that appeared to contradict it. Unless there had been a misunderstanding, this revealed a fundamental problem and I should depart from the Administration.

Clark was as nonplussed as I. "Something is wrong here," he said. "The President wouldn't do a thing like this. Let me go over to the White House and find out what happened."

By now it was nearly seven o'clock. I had been away from my desk for hours, and it was overflowing. Aides were waiting for decisions. We were on the verge of cutting off aid to Nicaragua. We had told the Sandinista government that it was obligated to protect Americans in Nicaragua, but we could not be certain that our citizens would be safe in case of unrest. Some in the U.S. government thought the risk was so great that Americans should be evacuated before the announcement was made. Instead, we had taken certain precautions, including the formation of a military rescue force, to be sure that there would be no repetition of the disgrace of Teheran. This plan was before me. So were decisions having to do with the grain embargo and Central America. Dobrynin would be in the next day for what would prove to be a pivotal discussion on Cuba and arms control; I needed to prepare myself for that. The staff came and went. I called my wife and told her what had happened; she had already heard the news on television. "Don't unpack, honey," I told her, with forced cheeriness. At nine o'clock I went home and, after a late snack, slept fitfully. There were no more calls from the President, and no word from Bill Clark.

By six-thirty the following morning I was at my desk, and soon afterward I began dictating the draft of a letter of resignation:

Mr. President: Regretfully I have concluded that, following our discussion in your office yesterday morning, your subsequent telephone conversation with me in the afternoon, and Mr. Brady's later announcement on "crisis management," my ability to function as your Secretary of State has been irreparably damaged. . . . Members of your personal staff have consistently undermined your stated intention that the Secretary of State be your principal foreign policy adviser. Under these conditions it is impossible for me to discharge my responsibilities as I swore to do. . . . Consequently, I hereby tender my resignation. . . . I urge you to take prompt action to spare my successor the circumstances that have . . . proven to be so harmful to the successful conduct of our foreign policy and which have compelled me to take this step.

The typed letter was placed before me. I did not sign it immediately. The possibility that matters could be explained still existed. The night before, Bill Clark had attended a meeting in the White House. Meese, Baker, and Deaver had also been present, and Vice President Bush had stopped in. Clark reported that the President had been shocked by the misunderstanding. Reagan would clear it up and we would continue.

Word of my "threat to resign" had already leaked to the press. Early in the day, I called Vice President Bush. "The American people can't be served by this," I told him. "It's an impossible situation for you and me to be in. Of course, you chair the NSC in the President's absence. We didn't need to say it. This is staff mischief. Why the hell did they do this without discussing it with me?"

That, of course, was the heart of the matter. George Bush was eminently qualified to handle crisis management in the absence of the President. That was not the point.

"I have been dealt with duplicitously, George," I told the Vice President. "The President has been used. I need a public reaffirmation of my role or I can't stay here."

Bush said that he would talk to the President. Soon Reagan called me. In fact, he was able to explain the misunderstanding. He believed that I had known about the existence of the decision memorandum naming the Vice President as crisis manager. When he talked to me in his office, and afterward on the phone, he had supposed that his aides had told me of its existence and that it would be released for publication. Reagan regarded the appointment as a mere housekeeping detail, a formality: when the President was absent at a time of crisis, the Vice President sat in his place in the NSC until he returned.

Thus it appeared that Reagan's intention, in talking to me the day before, had been to make these points and to assure me that the decision did not threaten my authority in the field of foreign affairs. On the other hand, I had assumed, on the basis of my discussion with Meese before the House appearance, that he was talking about the appointment itself when he characterized the *Post* article as a fabrication. Reagan, however, had been talking instead about the rest of the story, in which it was suggested that he had lost confidence in me and intended to limit my role in the Administration and undercut my authority. It was a classic case of two men talking past one another. Notwithstanding this misunderstanding, I am still unable to comprehend why the crisis management announcement was issued before issuing NSDD1, which established basic procedural structure.

Lack of communication, aggravated by staff mischief, was the root problem. This was not the first time far-reaching decisions affecting foreign policy had been taken without the participation of the State Department. "I don't understand, Mr. President," I said. "These moves were never discussed with me. The situation got out of hand because we were not seeing each other. We need to sort it out, but I must have an expression of your confidence." The President replied that I could have that, but what was done, was done. Now that the matter had become public, there was no room for compromise, no possibility of negotiation. That, of course, is what is wrong with government by newspaper. To gain an edge in personal influence that could last only a short time before it was forgotten, an assistant had deprived the President of freedom of action. Reagan asked me to come to his office in the afternoon for a longer talk.

In the Oval Office, alone with Reagan, I thought it best to deal first with the underlying causes of the problem. Both the President and I had suffered grave embarrassment as a result of this planted story. He had subsequently told me that the statements about his judgment of me and my performance were untrue. This was a serious matter—even, potentially, a fatal matter. If recent history teaches us anything, it is that the Presidency can live only in an atmosphere of unpolluted truth.

I gave him a sheaf of clippings that showed the pattern of the most damaging leaks and advised him to read them. "Mr. President, the simple fact is, I can't do what you want me to do under these circumstances," I said. "If your perceptions on foreign policy are different from mine, then you'd be better served by another man. The matter must be clarified."

Reagan, the clippings in his hand, heard me out. "It will be clarified," he said.

"Please read the National Security Decision Memorandum that Cap and I sent over to you four weeks ago," I said. "It reflects the consensus reached by Weinberger and Casey and me. Baker and Meese agreed at the time. It must be promulgated now." I said that the decision memorandum on foreign policy structure must be issued as it stood: "Otherwise I cannot serve you."

"You know that I can't back away on this," Reagan said.

Of course I knew that. The situation was intolerable for both of us. What ought to have been an affair within the President's official family, settled in quiet amicability, had instead become a subject for gossip and speculation. What had begun in public must now be settled in public; otherwise its shadow would fall over both the President and myself for the remainder of our respective incumbencies. We were at a deadline; the cameras were outside. Both of us had been manipulated into intolerable positions. My conversations with Ed Meese, together with other information, had convinced me that he had been as misled as the President. Meese was a formidable defender of the policies he believed in, but he was a decent and honorable man. His loyalty to the President was too deep, and his instinct to protect the President's true interests was too strong, for him to have put Reagan in this distressing condition. The trouble lay elsewhere in the President's staff. I gave Reagan my opinion on this matter.

Reagan did not respond for a moment. Mildly, he said that it was true that he had received complaints from other Cabinet officers about "steamroller tactics" in connection with issues that interested me. I could well believe that this was true. Perhaps the President agreed with them. If this was the case, then now was the time for him to say so and for me to make it easy for him to speak out.

"*Do* we have different conceptions of what your foreign policy should be, Mr. President?" I asked.

Reagan, exasperated, raised his voice. "Damn it, Al," he said, "we have the same views, and I need you!"

Early that afternoon, as he boarded a helicopter on the South Lawn of the White House, the President was surrounded by reporters. They shouted questions about his meeting with me. Reagan, who carried a prepared statement in his pocket, handled the exchange with his usual skill and equanimity:

THE PRESIDENT: One of the principal responsibilities of a President, as we all know, is the conduct of foreign policy. In meeting this responsibility, let me say what I said a number of times before. The Secretary of State is my primary adviser on foreign affairs, and in that capacity, he is the chief formulator and spokesman for foreign policy in this Administration. There is not, nor has there ever been, any question about this.

Q: Mr. President, why, when you're in charge of foreign policy . . . do you need a crisis manager? Aren't you the ultimate crisis manager?

THE PRESIDENT: . . . it could do with an earthquake . . . a flood in any one of our states, a disaster of that kind . . . there is no conflict. . . . There has been some confusion. . . .

Q: Mr. President, can't you give us your own reaction to what you read about the Secretary's testimony on the Hill yesterday? . . .

THE PRESIDENT: I don't know whether you would like my reaction . . . my reaction was that maybe some of you were trying to make the news instead of reporting it.

That settled the matter, but it was not the end of it. Of course, the press was not attempting to make the news. It was the White House staff that was succeeding in making policy by manufacturing news. The press was simply reporting, with admirable accuracy, what it was being told. By resolving our misunderstanding, the President had eased the symptom, but the disease raged on. The problem was conceptual. When I was White House chief of staff, I regarded myself as a liaison between the President and his Cabinet. The chief of staff has an obligation to conserve the President's time and make certain that he is able to concentrate on the vital issues by protecting him from trivia and redundancy. But he has also a duty to understand the needs of the Cabinet and to be the Cabinet's advocate before the President.

The Cabinet should believe that the chief of staff is its friend in camp. President Reagan's senior aides seemed to take a different view of the matter. They appeared to regard themselves as managers of the Presidency, deciding through control of the schedule who the President would see, deciding through the control of the flow of paper what documents the President would read and sign, and deciding through manipulation of the press which policies and which servants of the President should be advanced and which defeated. This produced an atmosphere of uncertainty and mistrust. This pattern of staff behavior was, and remains, a grave and dangerous imperfection in the Reagan Presidency. To use a kindly phrase, it produced confusion in the relatively minor matter of the appointment of the Vice President as crisis manager. What might it produce another time, when peace and war were at stake?

To tolerate so glaring a flaw rather than rectify it early invited the most serious future difficulties, because the techniques used by the Reagan staff substituted form for substance and appearance for reality. The crisis management memorandum was promulgated not to establish an effective crisis management apparatus, but to chalk up on the public mind a petty gain and a petty loss in a game of palace influence. That in itself was meaningless. The consequences might not be. Because the Vice President had no adequate staff to support him for the time being, the practical effect was to establish the shell of a crisis management operation and delay the essential painstaking work of planning, staffing, and activating a mechanism that would automatically spring to life in time of crisis.

In the cloudless morning of a popular Administration, it may well have seemed that there was time to spare, license to improvise. But three days later, the nation would be facing the profoundest of all crises, an attempt on the life of the President.

At 2:35 P.M. on Monday, March 30, 1981, the State Department command center informed me that the television networks were reporting that a gunman had fired shots at President Reagan and his party a few minutes before as they left the Washington Hilton Hotel, where the President had addressed a luncheon meeting of the AFL-CIO. The President had escaped injury, but James Brady and two other men had been wounded.

I picked up a telephone connected to a direct White House line. James Baker told me that the first report was inaccurate. The President had been struck "in the back" by a bullet. The doctors were examining him. "It looks quite serious," Baker said. "I'm going right to the hospital."

Vice President Bush was in Texas. "I will move immediately to the White House," I said. "We should bring the Secretaries of Defense and Treasury, the Attorney General, and the Director of the CIA to the White House situation room at once and set up a command post."

Baker agreed. "You will be my point of contact," he said.

I then telephoned Richard Allen and told him that I was on my way to the White House. I did not repeat what Baker had just told me about the condition of the President, nor would I, in the hours ahead, confide this information to anyone except the Vice President. At 2:59 P.M., accompanied by Woody Goldberg, I left the State Department. I instructed the escort not to sound their sirens. In the car, my mind filled with memories of the day on which President Kennedy was assassinated and the sense of shock and sorrow that overcame the nation. Now the terrible blow had fallen again. We did not know whether the President's assailant had acted alone or whether he was part of a conspiracy. We lived in a day when acts of political terrorism were commonplace; I myself had narrowly escaped death less than two years before in Belgium, when a terrorist bomb, detonated by remote control, exploded a split second after my car had passed over it. It was essential that we get the facts and publish them quickly. Rumor must not be allowed to breed on this tragedy. Remembering the aftermath of the Kennedy assassination, I said to Woody Goldberg, "No matter what the truth is about this shooting, the American people must know it."

On arrival at the White House, three minutes after leaving the State Department, I learned that all of the President's senior aides, including his chief of staff, had rushed to the hospital. Richard Allen met me and together we went upstairs to James Baker's office, the logical place to find whomever Baker had left in his place. David R. Gergen, the White House staff director, was there. Seconds later, Secretary of the Treasury Donald R. Regan joined us. He was in direct moment-to-moment contact with the Secret Service. Richard Darman, a White House assistant, came in.

"Has the Vice President been informed?" I asked.

The answer was no. Gergen suggested that we telephone George Bush. All planes in the Presidential fleet are equipped with an open voice channel to the White House. Some are equipped with secure voice channels, which theoretically cannot be overheard; others are not and rely on scrambled written messages. There was no time to find out which kind of phone was installed on the Vice President's airplane. I could not discuss the President's condition with Bush on an open channel. Instead, I called for a stenographer and dictated the following message:

Mr. Vice President: In the incident you will have heard about by now, the President was struck in the back and is in serious condition. Medical authorities are deciding now whether or not to operate. Recommend you return to D.C. at earliest possible moment.

As soon as this message was dictated and on its way to the communications room for transmission, I turned to the telephone and placed a call to the Vice President's aircraft. Bush came on the line. Aircraft-to-ground telephones are seldom perfect. This time the connection was very poor. Bush's voice, thin and muffled by atmospheric noise, was barely audible. He could not hear me at all. "This is Secretary Haig," I said. Bush said, "What? I can't hear you." I tried again: "This is Haig, Mr. Vice President." Still he could not make out my words. I bellowed, "*George! This is Al Haig!*" At last, he seemed to hear me. "Mr. Vice President," I shouted, "we have had a serious incident and I am sending you the facts that we now have by classified message. I recommend that you return to Washington at once." Bush's voice, when it came back on the air, was faint, but I heard him say that he would return to Washington immediately.

To Allen, the senior White House staff member present, I suggested that the Secretary of Defense, the Attorney General, and the Director of Central Intelligence be asked to join Secretary Regan, Allen, and me in the situation room. Allen gave instructions that they be called. Other members of the Cabinet could participate if they wished, but these six men were the key figures in a crisis. Normally, the chairman of the Joint Chiefs of Staff would be included, but on this occasion his presence would have been ominous and inappropriate.

The situation room, located in the basement of the West Wing, is really two rooms—a conference room perhaps 25 feet long by 15 feet wide, and a larger L-shaped adjoining communications room. A table, equipped with telephones, runs down the center of the conference room; straight chairs are arranged along the walls. There are map cases on the walls and a single television screen. It is an austere place, especially compared to similar rooms elsewhere in the government that are much more evocative of the cinema, but it is equipped with an impressive array of state-of-the-art communications gear, and it is manned around the clock by a superlatively competent and efficient watch staff.

The situation room was designed for small meetings; seldom are more than a dozen persons present at one time. On this day, some twenty people had crowded into the room by the time we arrived. Most were junior White House staff members who had no function to perform but wanted to be near the heart of this tragic event. Their voices were raised in a steady, wordless murmur. In a palpable atmosphere of numbed shock, they exchanged the small talk of commiseration. There are no windows. The air conditioner could not overcome the heat of so many bodies in so small a space. The room became steadily hotter. I suggested to Allen that the room be cleared, and some of the onlookers departed. As the afternoon passed, many drifted back in and were cleared out again in a continuing cycle.

A working group—Woody Goldberg and White House aides Gergen, Darman, and Craig L. Fuller, the assistant for Cabinet affairs—formed around Regan, Allen, and me. Our primary task was to remain at the nerve center of the government and maintain its authority and its communications with the wounded President and with the rest of the world until the Vice President returned. It was essential that this be done in an atmosphere of calm control. When the other key members of the Cabinet arrived, we would constitute a full crisis team. But this would be an ad hoc group; no plan existed, we possessed no list of guidelines, no chart that established rank or function. Our work was a matter of calling on experience and exercising judgment. As the senior Cabinet officer present, I was, in Baker's phrase, "the point of contact" between the situation room and the hospital. Under this arrangement, as a matter of efficiency, Baker would speak only to me, and I would pass his information on to my colleagues.

It was essential that we communicate effectively with the American people and with the world beyond. It was literally true because these events were being telecast by satellite throughout the globe, that the whole world was watching. It was our duty to ascertain the true facts and get them out accurately and rapidly. The people must be told, as quickly as possible, everything that we knew, short of endangering the safety of our leaders or the security of our defenses. When an assassin strikes at the living symbol of the nation, the people have a right to know every detail about the criminal and his crime—whether he acted alone, whether he was part of a conspiracy. The damage that can be done by telling the truth in such circumstances is nothing compared to the havoc wreaked by an inadvertent distortion or concealment of the facts, which inevitably produces lingering speculation and unquenchable conspiracy-mongering. It was now nearly 3:30. A clear statement of the facts must be made to the press as soon as possible. I asked Gergen to draft a brief summary of what we knew, and Regan, Allen, and I reviewed and cleared it. Someone asked if we should say that the Vice President was en route to Washington. It was my opinion that if those were the facts, then that was what ought to be said; we need not say that he was coming from Texas.

If the attack on the President was part of a conspiracy, obviously the safety of the first family was at risk. All were under the protection of the Secret Service as a matter of routine. This protection was increased. We ordered that the whereabouts of all members of the President's immediate family be determined, and that the situation room be kept fully posted on this and all other details concerning their movements.

We had had no further word of the President's condition or that of the other wounded men. In the first of many such conversations we were to have that day, I called Baker at the hospital. He told me that the President had been struck in the left chest. He had walked into the hospital. The doctors were examining his wound. Reagan's condition was stable, but once again Baker gave the impression that the President's wound was serious. Omitting any reference to the gravity of the injury, I passed this information on to Regan and Allen and Gergen and Darman.

After I hung up, someone raised a doubt about the condition of the President. The television film, he said, seemed to show Reagan being carried into the hospital on a stretcher. Some onlookers remained in the room. Their presence increased the danger that our discussions might be leaked to the press. This was precisely the sort of false statement that could be transformed into an uncontrollable rumor. "That is absolutely wrong," I said in a loud voice. "Jim Baker personally told me that the President walked into the hospital, and Jim Baker would not tell me that unless he knew it for a fact."

The text of a cable to foreign ambassadors, drafted in the State Department, arrived for approval. The original text reflects the anxiety and shock felt in these moments:

Flash. Please deliver following message to government to which you are accredited: You will have heard that on March 30 there was an attempt on the life of President Reagan. His condition is stable and you should inform the government that in spite of this terrible event, the government in Washington continues to carry out its obligations to its people and its allies.

The last part of the final sentence would do little to allay the anxieties of foreign governments. I changed it to read:

His condition is stable and he is conscious. The Vice President is returning to Washington this afternoon.

I asked that the White House switchboard reach the Speaker of the House, the majority and minority leaders of the Senate, and the minority leader of the House. In the next few minutes, I spoke to Senators Baker and Robert C. Byrd, Speaker Thomas P. O'Neill, Jr., and Representative Robert H. Michel one after the other, telling them what we knew. Later, I placed similar calls to former Presidents Nixon, Ford, and Carter.

Secretary Regan had now received a preliminary report on the assailant from the Secret Service, and he gave us the essential facts: a white male identified as John W. Hinckley, Jr., had been disarmed and taken into custody at the scene of the shooting. He was 5 feet 10 inches tall and weighed 175 pounds. A Texas Tech student identification card that he carried identified him as a resident of Evergreen, Colorado, born May 29, 1958. The business cards of two psychiatrists had been found on his person. Across one of these cards was written: "Call me if you need me." Hinckley had so far refused to talk to officers or identify any groups he belonged to.

Caspar Weinberger arrived at 3:37, at about the same time as William Casey, who had made the 10-mile drive from CIA headquarters in Langley, Virginia. We went around the table and each member of the crisis team in his turn gave the newcomers a report on his activities. Weinberger and Casey read the cable to foreign posts and the press statement and approved. By this time Gergen was briefing reporters in the White House press room, and his image flickered on the television screen attached to the wall behind me. Weinberger seemed somewhat self-conscious. Perhaps he was embarrassed by his late arrival. The attack on the President had taken place slightly more than an hour before.

Abruptly, Weinberger said, "I have raised the alert status of our forces."

I was shocked by his words. Depending on the nature of the instructions issued by Weinberger, any such change would be detected promptly by the Soviet Union. In response, the Russians might raise their own alert status, and that could cause a further escalation on our side. The fact that this was happening would be reported on television and radio, and the news would let loose more emotion, exacerbating the existing climate of anxiety and anger and fear. Moreover, the Soviet leaders might very well conclude that the United States, in a flight of paranoia, believed that the U.S.S.R. was involved in the attempt to assassinate the President. Why would we alert our military forces if a lone psychotic had been responsible? The consequences were incalculable.

"Cap," I said, "what do you mean? Have you changed the Defcon [defense condition] of our forces?"

I cannot recall Weinberger's exact words, but his reply did not answer my question. He appeared, instead, to be quibbling over my choice of words.

"This is important, Cap," I said. "Will you please tell us exactly what you've done?"

Here I again used the term "Defcon" and other shorthand terminology to describe different states of strategic military readiness. This jargon is commonplace to all who have been involved in the Presidential management of strategic, that is to say nuclear, forces. Weinberger did not respond in a way that suggested he was fully familiar with these terms. This was natural enough: he had not dealt with such matters in the past, and he had been Secretary of Defense for barely ninety days, hardly long enough to absorb the complete vocabulary of the job. I kept pressing him for a clear description of his actions. At length, he said that he had ordered pilots of the Strategic Air Command to their bases. "Then you've raised the Defcon," I said.

He disagreed. This raised the temperature of the conversation. I began to suspect that Weinberger did not know whether he had raised the Defcon or, if he had raised it, to what level. Once again, in the plainest possible language, I asked Weinberger to describe the action he had taken.

"I'll go find out," he said. He left the room in order to telephone in private. He was absent for perhaps ten minutes. When he returned, he told us, unequivocally, that he had not formally raised the alert status of our forces. He had merely sent a message to field commanders informing them officially of the situation in Washington. Most important, U.S. strategic forces remained in their normal defense condition.

Fred F. Fielding, the White House counsel, had joined us, bringing with him an analysis of the Twenty-fifth Amendment to the Constitution, which provides for the transfer of Presidential authority to the Vice President in case the chief executive is incapacitated. While Weinberger was out of the room, Fielding and Attorney General Smith described the legalities and discussed the way in which the situation was handled in the most recent instance, when President Eisenhower suffered a coronary thrombosis in 1955. At no time did those present in the situation room consider invoking the Twenty-fifth Amendment, which had been ratified in the aftermath of Eisenhower's heart attack. Discussion of the transfer of authority was premature and inappropriate and I believed it should be avoided. Certainly the preparation of papers on the subject was ill-advised. The Dairy Bill was due for signing on the following day. If the President was able to sign it, and was seen doing so, then all doubt as to his capacity would effectively be dispelled. So far, there was little reason to believe that he would not be able to sign the bill and otherwise perform his duties. Weinberger, Regan, and Smith held the same views and expressed them forcefully.

The Attorney General received information that the assailant's weapon had been identified as a .38 caliber revolver. This is a powerful weapon (.38 is the standard police caliber) and this news, coupled to the anxiety generated by Jim Baker's continued description of the President's condition as "serious," was unsettling. It was not until 4:10 that we learned that the bullets that wounded the President and the other three men were actually much less powerful .22 caliber long rifle cartridges. The bullet that was removed from the President was badly distorted, which suggested that it might have been a ricochet.

At 3:55, we were informed by the Air Force that Vice President Bush's plane would land at Andrews Air Force Base in approximately 2½ hours.

I had taken a chair on one side of the conference table. The television screen was at my back. Moments after we had received news of Brady's condition, I noticed that Allen, who was sitting opposite, was watching the screen with a look of growing puzzlement. Other viewers shared his expression. Larry Speakes, the assistant White House press secretary, seemed to be briefing the press. "Where is Larry speaking from?" someone asked. "He must be at the hospital," another voice replied. "No," said Dick Allen, "he's upstairs in the White House press room. But what is he saying?"

At this point I turned my chair and craned my neck in order to see and hear Speakes. The room was hushed. It was oppressively hot. It appeared that Speakes had been waylaid by the press as he returned to the White House from the hospital. Reporters hurled hard questions at him.

SPEAKES: . . . I can only say what we said earlier, that the President has a gunshot wound in the left side of his chest, is in stable condition. . . .

Q: Is the President in surgery?

Q: Are they in surgery yet?

SPEAKES: I can't say. . . .

Q: We have gotten confirmed reports, so have other network news, so have the wires. Can't you help us with that, Larry?

SPEAKES: As soon as we can confirm it we will. . . .

Q: Larry, his brother's been called by the White House and has been told that the President is in surgery right now. Is your information going to be that far behind what we're getting from other sources?

SPEAKES: Leslie, we will do our very best to keep it up. As you know . . . our initial report was that the President was not hit. That's what we run into when we are not [one] hundred percent sure. . . .

Q: Is that the extent of what you know, what you've said now? . . .

SPEAKES: That's the extent of what I can say at this point.

Q: Has the U.S. military been placed on any higher alert readiness?

SPEAKES: Not that I'm aware of. . . .

Q: Would [the Vice President] assume emergency powers?

Q: Would there be a division of labor of any kind?

SPEAKES: Not that I'm aware of. We just haven't crossed those bridges yet. . . .

Q: Who's running the government right now?

Q: If the President goes into surgery and goes under anesthesia, would Vice President Bush become the acting President at that moment or under what circumstances does he?

SPEAKES: I cannot answer that question at this time. . . .

Q: Larry, who'll be determining the status of the President and whether the Vice President should, in fact, become the acting President? . . .

SPEAKES: I don't know the details on that.

The official White House spokesman was being asked who was running the government at a time of national crisis, and he was responding that he did not know. He was being asked if the country was being defended, and he was saying that he did not know. This was no fault of Speakes's. He had not been part of our group. He had no current information. "This is very bad," Allen said. "We have to do something."

"We've got to get him off," I said. Allen agreed. It was essential to reassure the country and the world that we had an effective government. I asked Allen to join me, and, together, Allen and I dashed out of the situation room and ran headlong up the narrow stairs. Then we hurried along the jigsaw passageways of the West Wing and into the press room.

When Allen and I arrived, Speakes was already off camera. After my strenuous approach to the cameras and the microphones, I was somewhat out of breath. With Allen at my side, I made the following statement:

HAIG: I just wanted to touch on a few matters associated with today's tragedy. First, as you know, we are in close touch with the Vice President, who is returning to Washington. We have in the situation room all of the officials of the Cabinet who should be here and ready at this time. We have informed our friends abroad of the situation. The President's condition as we know it, is stable, [he is] now undergoing surgery. And there are absolutely no alert measures that are necessary at this time that we're contemplating. Now, if you have some questions, I'd be happy to take them.

Q: The crisis management, is that going to be put into effect when Bush arrives?

HAIG: Crisis management is in effect.

Q: Who is making the decisions for the government right now? Who's making the decisions?

HAIG: Constitutionally, gentlemen, you have the President, the Vice President, and the Secretary of State, in that order, and should the President decide he wants to transfer the helm, he will do so. He has not done that. As of now, I am in control here, in the White House, pending return of the Vice President and in close touch with him. If something came up, I would check with him, of course.

Q: What is the extent of the President's injury?

HAIG: Well, as best we know, he's had one round enter his body, in the left side, into the left lung, and there is surgery underway to remove the round now. When the President entered surgery, he was conscious. His signs were stable. . . .

Q: What's the reaction of the Soviets on this? Any reaction?

HAIG: I don't anticipate any reaction. . . .

Q: Will you remain in charge here until the Vice President returns?

HAIG: We will stay right where we are until the situation clarifies.

Q: Any additional measures being taken—was this a conspiracy or was this a . . .

HAIG: We have no indications of anything like that now, and we are not going to say a word on that subject until the situation clarifies itself.

Q: Do you anticipate from what you know of the President's condition that the Vice President will have to for a period of time take the role of acting President?

HAIG: That is a fundamentally premature question.

On my return to the situation room, Weinberger expressed displeasure at my statement on the alert status of American forces. I was surprised and asked if I had not been correct in my understanding of what he had told the crisis team earlier on this subject. Weinberger gave no clear answer. I said, "Cap, are we or are we not on an increased alert status?" Instead of answering my question in direct fashion, he referred to the status of Soviet submarines off our coasts. Weinberger added that Ed Meese had told him on the telephone that the Secretary of Defense was third in line of command after the

President and the Vice President. On defense matters, this was quite true, but the question was moot. The Vice President would be landing in Washington in little more than two hours.

At 4:55, the Secret Service erroneously informed Secretary Regan, based on a report from the FBI, that Jim Brady had died of a head wound. This news produced shock and strong emotion in everyone present. Brady is an exceptionally likable man, witty and honest, with a wise appreciation of life and human foibles. Before he was engaged as the President's press secretary, I had asked him to become the assistant secretary of state for public affairs, and he had accepted. That he should have been wounded in the brain, the seat of so many of his most attractive qualities, seemed especially cruel. A deep hush fell over us. No doubt the strength of our response to this terrible news was related to our fears for the life of the President. Within minutes, the false report of Brady's death had been leaked to the press and was being reported on television. At 5:35, the erroneous report of Jim Brady's death was corrected.

Moments later, James Baker phoned from the hospital and told me that the President was still in surgery and was expected to remain there for some time. Surgeons were probing for the bullet.

We now expected that the Vice President would land at Andrews Air Force Base at about 6:30. Admiral Daniel J. Murphy, the Vice President's chief of staff, was prepared to brief him on the condition of the President, the status of defense forces, current intelligence, legal and constitutional questions, and press and foreign reaction.

At 6:15, James Baker entered the situation room and reported that the President was in good condition. A bullet had been removed from his lung, and the incision was now being closed. The President would spend the night in intensive care, but the doctors were confident that he would recover fully from his wound. The President, Baker reported, had not realized at first that he had been wounded; he thought that he had suffered a broken rib as a result of having been pushed with great force into the limousine. He walked into the hospital unaided. "Then," said Baker, holding up a yellow legal pad, "he turned yellow when apparently his lung collapsed." Even so, he had been able to wink at Baker when, wearing an oxygen mask, he was wheeled away on a rolling stretcher. Later, to Mrs. Reagan, he had said, "Honey, I forgot to duck." To the surgeons, as they prepared to operate, he said, "I hope you're all Republicans." Seeing Meese and Baker by his bedside, he asked, "Who's minding the store?" As Baker recounted each of the President's sallies, I looked around the table and saw in the faces of my colleagues a mixture of affection and admiration and profound relief.

At 6:30, Vice President Bush landed at Andrews Air Force Base. The Vice President decided that he would not helicopter directly to the White House and land on the South Lawn. Such a dramatic arrival would intensify speculation, and therefore mislead public opinion, on the question of a transfer of Presidential authority. The Vice President instead flew by helicopter to his residence and then proceeded to the White House by car. At 7:00, he arrived in the situation room. Allen, bypassing Admiral Murphy, briefed the Vice President, and in the course of his remarks raised the question of a "shift in authority." Bush replied that since reports on the President's condition were positive, there was no need to discuss the matter.

The Vice President asked about the alert status of U.S. forces and about the Polish situation. The next day, he would preside over a Cabinet meeting and an NSC meeting, brief the leaders of Congress, and meet Prime Minister Andries A.M. van Agt of the Netherlands, who was in Washington on an official visit. Bush asked if my trip to the Middle East, scheduled to begin on April 3, should be postponed, and we agreed that this would depend on the President's condition. We agreed that an official statement containing all of the confirmed information we possessed must be released to the press, and that no one must cloud the true facts by speaking individually to the press. "The more normally we behave, the better off we are," said the Vice President with stout good sense. He suggested moving out of the situation room and meeting instead in the Roosevelt Room upstairs.

As he spoke, Dr. Dennis S. O'Leary of Georgetown University Hospital appeared on television and described in detail the President's condition and the medical measures that had been taken to preserve his life. "The President," said Dr. O'Leary, "is in the recovery room. He is in stable condition and he is awake. He was at no time in any serious danger. . . . He has a clear head and should be able to make decisions by tomorrow, certainly."

The crisis was over. It seemed to me, as I rode home that night after briefing the staff at the State Department on the day's events, that the President had reason to be proud of his Vice President and of the men he had chosen to serve on his Cabinet and staff. Secretary of Agriculture Block and Secretary of Transportation Andrew L.

("Drew") Lewis, Jr., had joined the original group and everything they said and did strengthened us.

But the true credit belonged to the President himself. By virtue of his astonishing physical stamina and his courageous character, he had in the end vanquished the crisis by dispelling the nation's fears for his own life and unimpaired capacity. No grievously wounded man ever behaved more gallantly. By his quiet courage, sunny humor, and unfailing generosity to others, and by the force of his faith, Ronald Reagan steadied and rallied the nation.

BACKGROUND

Only minutes after Jim Baker had arrived from the hospital with the first news that the President would recover from his wounds, a correspondent appeared on the television screen in the White House situation room and announced that I had taken control of the White House. In the lighthearted relief of the moment I replied, "And the world was saved." Laughter filled the situation room. It was the first time for many tense hours when anyone present had felt like laughing.

If I watched my own image and listened to my own words on the screen that night, I do not remember it. No matter; there would be plenty of opportunities to see this segment rebroadcast in days to come. My appearance became a celebrated media happening. Edited versions were played and replayed many times. Even if I wished to do so, it is now far too late to correct the impressions made, but I may be forgiven for saying that I regard the way in which the tape was edited, especially by CBS, as the most effective bit of technical artistry to appear on television since that unfriendly makeup man touched up Richard Nixon's five o'clock shadow before his first debate with John F. Kennedy in 1960.

Perhaps the camera and microphone magnified the effects of my sprint up the stairs. Possibly I should have washed my face or taken half a dozen deep breaths before going on camera. The fact is, I was not thinking about my appearance. I was wholly intent on correcting any impression of confusion and indecision that Speakes's words may have inadvertently created. Certainly I was guilty of a poor choice of words, and optimistic if I imagined that I would be forgiven the imprecision out of respect for the tragedy of the occasion. My remark that I was "in control . . . pending the return of the Vice President" was a statement of the fact that I was the senior Cabinet officer present. I was talking about the arrangements we had made in the situation room for the three- or four-hour period in which we awaited the return of the Vice President from Texas. Less precise, though in the same context, was my statement that *"constitutionally . . .* you have the President, the Vice President, and the Secretary of State, in that order." I ought to have said "traditionally" or "administratively" instead of "constitutionally." If, at the time, anyone had suggested to me that I believed that the Secretary of State was third in order of succession to the President, the press would have had the pleasure of even more vivid quotes. For many months, in this same house, I had lived hourly with the question of succession in case of the removal first of a Vice President and then of a President; I knew the Constitution by heart on this subject.

The *New York Times* suggested that I had "appeared tense" and had used "tough-sounding language." The *Washington Post's* Martin Schram wrote of a "shaky, emotional claim over national television of a constitutional authority in the line of the Presidential succession."

On ABC's "Nightline," on April 1, Ted Koppel raised the question with his guests, Edwin Meese and James Baker.

KOPPEL: . . . it would be noted that Haig had misstated the constitutional line of authority. Constitutionally, the Secretary of State is not third in line but fifth. . . . Mr. Meese . . . if you were distressed, why so?

MEESE: I want to make it clear that there was not one second . . . when there was . . . a lack of anybody being in charge . . . and I must say at no time were any of us displeased with Mr. Haig or what he did or with any of the other people there. . . . Al felt it was important to reassure our allies and other people . . . that there was a continuity of government. . . .

BAKER: I personally had discussions with Haig in which we agreed that he would be our point of contact here in the situation room at the White House as he quite properly should have been as the senior Cabinet officer. . . .

The "take charge" image had taken hold even before the events of March 30. Only a few days before, my photograph (jaw jutting, arms akimbo) had been on the cover of *Time* magazine. With the insouciant hyperbole for which that publication is famous, the caption read "Taking Command." Inside, under a bold line reading "The 'Vicar' Takes Charge," the editors devoted several pages of snare-drum prose to an account of my life and a description of the Reagan foreign policy. Barrie Dunsmore of ABC reported:

The sight of Alexander Haig taking command on the cover of *Time* magazine was more than some of the President's aides could take and since its publication there have been several obvious White House putdowns. . . . the problem seems to be that some of Mr. Reagan's closest advisers see Haig as a political competitor who must be reminded that while he may be vicar, he is not the pope.

In days to follow, my vicarhood was recertified by "officials" and "Presidential assistants" with more zeal than was perhaps good for it. On April 1, the *Times* headlined its front-page story, "Haig Pictured in Key Role; Administration Hoping to Guard Effectiveness." The writer, Hedrick Smith, told his readers that

White House officials went to extraordinary lengths today to praise Mr. Haig for acting as the coordination point immediately after yesterday's shooting. . . . as one official put it, Mr. Haig [should] be presented to the world as "a vital player" enjoying White House confidence rather than an overeager Cabinet member sometimes at odds with the White House and the Pentagon.

In its editions of April 1, the *Post* picked up this same theme:

. . . top Presidential assistants lauded Haig's performance in the situation room. . . . "I worked at his side in the situation room from 2:30 to 8:30," said White House staff director David Gergen, "and he was steady, very steady. He did a hell of a job."

When I departed two days later for a diplomatic tour of the Middle East, the White House, in an official statement, assured reporters and the world that "the Secretary of State leaves today in the full colors of the Secretary of State and with the full confidence of the President."

Time described the issuance of the foregoing statement as an "extraordinary step." So it was. Never had I passed through a two-day period in which so many anonymous people were so eager to reassure the world in such an intensive way that I was not only competent, I was also quite "steady." But newsmen, canny skeptics that they are, were stimulated by all this reassurance to ask themselves, and their readers, a question: if this fellow is *really* all right, why do they insist on telling us that he's all right?

NINE

Israel and Saudi Arabia: "The AWACS Controversy"

ISRAEL has never had a greater friend in the White House than Ronald Reagan. Yet in the early months of Reagan's Presidency, the assumption that the United States would always unreservedly support Israel in a contest of interests with its Arab neighbors ceased to apply. In protecting what it saw as its interests and security, Israel administered a series of violent shocks to the Administration and to public opinion. Though Reagan's response was measured and understanding, the atmosphere of American-Israeli relations underwent a change. Israel came under unprecedented and sometimes exasperated public criticism from officials of the Administration. The power of Israel and its friends to influence American policy in the Middle East weakened. All this happened not because American policy, as a matter of conscious choice, suddenly changed to Israel's disadvantage. Rather, it happened because events that had been long in the making and policies that had been compelled by those events suddenly became visible.

Always dependent on American economic, military, and political assistance, Israel had become more so since the 1973 Yom Kippur

War. During the same period, the energy crisis had developed and the
United States had become steadily more interested in improving its
relations with the Arab countries. The fall of the Shah and the Soviet
invasion of Afghanistan reawakened in all parties a sense of the
strategic significance of the Middle East. In the Israelis, it awakened
the anxiety that the United States would deal with its strategic concerns in the region at the expense of its relations with Israel. Obviously, the best way to resolve the difficulties generated by this
anxiety was to achieve peace between Israel and her Arab neighbors.
No one expected that to happen soon. Our entire diplomatic experience since the 1973 war had taught us that we could sometimes
reduce tensions and even break through walls of animosity, as at
Camp David, but that we could not do away with the conflict with a
single comprehensive stroke. In pursuing the peace process, our goal
was to strengthen and complete the Camp David accords, which
provided the best hope of preventing the outbreak of another Arab-
Israeli war. At the same time, we had to pursue our strategic interests,
finding ways to work with each of our friends in the region so that
the forces that threatened us all could be contained.

To a considerable degree, the establishment of stronger ties to
Arab states depended on the sale of sophisticated arms. The lightly
populated but very rich states of the Persian Gulf believed that advanced technology was crucial to the solution of their difficult defense problems. This was especially true of the most important country on the gulf, Saudi Arabia. The question was, how could we
supply such equipment to our Arab friends without weakening Israel's security? The great AWACS controversy of 1981 sprang from
this question. It originated in a decision made by the Carter Administration, and inherited by Reagan, to sell airborne warning and
control (radar surveillance) aircraft to Saudi Arabia, along with
other military aviation items. These planes can detect and track other
aircraft at distances up to 350 miles. "I will open my heart to you,"
Prime Minister Menachem Begin said in Jerusalem. "Israel is surrounded by hostile Arabs, most of whom believe that a Jew is born to
be killed." Saudi Arabia, with comparable emotion, insisted that the
future of Saudi-American relations depended on delivery of the
equipment it had been promised. "Saudi Arabia," said the Saudi
minister of defense, Prince Sultan bin Abdul Aziz, "cannot accept
refusal of any of these items."

As a matter of historical practice, the United States has preserved

Israel's qualitative military superiority over all other nations in the Middle East. This bedrock American commitment to the security of Israel did not alter under the new Administration; more than once, even in the midst of the most bitter differences of opinion, Reagan promised the Israelis that this would never change while he was President.

However, the security of the Middle East, and especially that of the Persian Gulf, was a matter that required the urgent attention of the new American leadership. Nowhere in the world had the post-Vietnam hesitancy of the United States been more visible, or more sweeping in its consequences, than in this region. Especially since the events in Iran, the moderate Arab states had questioned the purposes and the resolve of the United States. We wanted to open a strategic dialogue with the moderate Arab states, among which Saudi Arabia was the most influential, and to establish a stronger relationship with them in the interests of the entire region. We wanted, at the outset of the Administration, to make some substantial gesture to the moderate Arabs as an earnest of American friendship and resolve. The sale of the aircraft to Saudi Arabia provided that opportunity. We believed that Israel's security would be enhanced, rather than threatened, by our policy, and that the peace process would be advanced by it.

My first objective in visiting the Middle East in April 1981 was to reassure our friends in the region that the United States was once again a reliable friend and ally. This was no simple task. The fall of the Shah, after thirty years of the closest friendship with America, had created profound uneasiness. So had the advance of Soviet influence and the climate of revolutionary ferment in the region. Few in the Middle East failed to make the connection between the decline in American will and strength and the rise in tension and disorder. Some tangible evidence was needed that attitudes had changed in Washington, and that the benefits of friendship with the United States could outweigh the risks.

I visited Egypt, Saudi Arabia, Jordan, and Israel. In every capital, I was given the same urgent message: dangerous forces had been let loose in the region, and only a credible new assertion of American influence, coupled with the influence of moderate Arab regimes, could oppose them. There was, in a real rather than a theoretical sense, a strategic consensus in the region. This had nothing to do with American phrase making or with an American tendency to turn the Middle East into a theater for East-West confrontation. Three great fears ran through the region: fear of terrorism, which was endemic; fear of Islamic fundamentalism, which had broken out in Iran in fanatical form; and fear of the Soviet Union. In reality, this was one consolidated fear: that terrorism and fundamentalism would so destabilize the region that the Soviets would either subvert the Islamic movement for their own purposes or seize control of Iran and possibly the whole gulf in a second revolution after the Iranian revolution collapsed under the political and economic weight of its own excesses.

The corresponding fear that ran through the West, and especially Europe, was that the oil of the Persian Gulf would be lost. From Israel's point of view, the product of this fear was a distortion of Western policy toward Israel. The sympathy of liberal opinion, which had always before largely belonged to Israel, was in considerable measure transferred to the other claimants to the soil of Palestine, the Palestinian Arabs. Acts of terrorism against Jews and even against synagogues aroused less indignation than Israeli acts of reprisal. The tendency to focus on the Palestinian issue distracted the West from consideration of the fact that many Middle East conflicts, and especially those around the gulf, had little to do with Israel and could not be solved by Israeli concessions. Israel was attacked in international forums and her very right to belong to the community of nations was questioned. Few beside the United States stood by her. Western businessmen, including many in the United States, were enamored of the commercial opportunities that the oil wealth of the Arab states provided. Western governments, fearing another worldwide oil shortage, consciously and unconsciously adjusted their policies and actions in such a way as to placate those who controlled the oil supply. In the circumstances, the Israelis were understandably worried about the future and disinclined to take risks with their security.

Certainly the oil supply was vulnerable. In Iran, the most strategically important country in Asia minor, a theocracy had succeeded the Shah, announcing that it intended to establish an Islamic state modeled on the seventh-century caliphate of the great Shiite martyr, Ali, son-in-law of Muhammad. While he reigned, the Shah's strategic forces had anchored the security of the Persian Gulf, site of one-third of the West's proven oil reserves. The Shah's successor had not taken up that burden. Saudi Arabia and the gulf sheikdoms were surrounded by unfriendly or unstable neighbors: revolutionary regimes in the Yemens to the south, heavy Soviet forces in Afghanistan to the east, Iran in its atavistic frenzy across the gulf, radical Ethiopia on the other side of the Red Sea. Iraq and Iran were engaged in a bloody war (in which each side had attacked the other's oil installations), ostensibly over the navigation rights in the Shatt al Arab, the estuary formed by the confluences of the Tigris and Euphrates rivers, which constitutes part of the boundary between the two countries.

To the north, in Syria, the Russians maintained a high political and military profile. The Palestine Liberation Organization was sufficiently a Soviet client that Moscow's ambassador to the United States and the Soviet foreign minister both thought it natural to attempt to deliver messages from the PLO to the U.S. government in talks with me. As Menachem Begin passionately charged, the PLO was bombarding Israeli settlements in northern Israel with shells and rockets provided by the Soviet Union. The Israelis retaliated with devastating air attacks—using the most modern American warplanes—on Palestinian camps within Lebanon. In 1975–76, 60,000 Lebanese had died in a complex civil war between Christians and Muslims. In 1976, the Syrian army invaded to prevent a victory by radical Arab forces that, it feared, might constitute themselves into a rival state similar to Iraq. The Syrians, along with token (and temporary) Saudi and Kuwaiti forces, remained as a peacekeeping force under the auspices of the Arab League. Now Lebanon was in danger of losing the last shreds of its sovereignty. The PLO, driven out of Jordan in the 1971 war between the guerrillas and King Hussein's forces, had become a militarized state within a state in Lebanon. The Syrians, who had initially entered Lebanon as allies of the Christians, increasingly became sponsors of the PLO. Israel regarded this as an intolerable threat to her security.

In this atmosphere of war and the threat of war, the region's greatest man of peace, Anwar Sadat, was isolated. His symbolic visit to Israel in 1977, followed by the signing of the Camp David accords in 1978 and the peace treaty with Israel in 1979, reestablished human contact between the two ancient peoples and brought an end to a generation of war. But Sadat's act of reconciliation, involving as it did explicit recognition of Israel's existence and sovereignty, alienated him—and Egypt, so long as he ruled—from most of the rest of the Arab world. He had staked everything on the moral and historical rightness of an act that preserved his people from further suffering and opened the way to a peaceful solution of the whole range of problems between Israel and the Arabs, and he had paid the price established over a third of a century by the march and countermarch of hatred and injustice and bloodshed.

But if, in the spring of 1981, Sadat was isolated politically from other Arabs, he was at one with them in their judgment of the dangers facing the Middle East. Sadat was a zealous student of history and geopolitics; the strategic realities affecting Egypt were in his blood in a way that few Americans, raised in a land protected by oceans and bordered by peaceable neighbors, can fully understand. The Soviets, he argued, were following a "two crescents policy" in the Middle East and Africa. The first crescent ran through Iraq, Syria, the Yemens, Somalia, and Ethiopia. The second was being put in place in southern Africa. This would enable them to cut Africa in half and isolate moderate Arab regimes, which would be caught in a vise between radical states under the influence of Moscow. In Qaddafi and the PLO, the Soviets had clients who possessed the means to destabilize through terror. Qaddafi had already sent more than one squad of assassins into Egypt with the mission of murdering Sadat. The Libyan leader, possessed of billions in oil revenues, had turned his country into a nest of terrorists. He supplied them with arms and refuge and cash. Together with the Palestinian terrorists, these guerrillas were present in every moderate Arab country—and in some that were not so moderate—like so many political time bombs.

In other Arab capitals, I heard similar arguments. Especially in the countries on the gulf, I detected a will to end the isolation of Egypt, to rejoin the oldest and most populous of the Arab countries and its leader in a coalition of moderate Arab powers. Every argument favored the encouragement of this trend. Absent such a reconciliation, it was possible to imagine Egypt, after Sadat, drifting back into the radical world with all the consequences that could follow: the dismantling of the peace process, a further loss of American prestige and influence, and a flight by the rest of the moderate Arabs into neutralism or accommodation with the forces they most feared—radicalism and the Soviet Union.

Certainly Prime Minister Begin and his government agreed that Soviet influence and the instability in which it breeds were mortal enemies of Israel's national safety, and national safety is ever the deep-lying question on which Israeli elections are fought. Begin had called parliamentary elections for June 30. There was some doubt that his Likud coalition, which had governed the country since 1977, could be returned to office. He faced intractable issues: economic problems, including severe inflation; the social and psychological toll exacted by more than thirty years of conflict, including heavy loss of life in the 1973 war, and Israel's isolation and dependence on the United States. However, Menachem Begin, learned, tenacious, canny, an orator in five languages, was never a man to be discouraged by adversity. His primary constituency, the non-European Jews who in recent years had become the majority of the Israeli population, admired his strength and understood his uncomplicated approach to their fundamental concerns. The tragic history of his people is the passion of Begin's life. "I myself," he has said, "who lost my mother and my father and my brother and my two nephews, whose children never knew their grandparents, suffer from Holocaust trauma. From the day I became prime minister, I swore that no one would shed Jewish blood with impunity."

Once again, this was the prime issue. Would Jewish blood be spilled again? There was reason for apprehension. Begin had given much in the cause of peace at Camp David and afterward. Israel had pledged herself to return the Sinai to Egypt by April 25, 1982, and the surrender of this buffer of occupied territory, held since the 1967 war, was profoundly troubling to a nation that believed itself surrounded by enemies. The prime minister was preoccupied also with the complicated issue of granting some form of local autonomy to Palestinian settlements on the West Bank of the Jordan River, as provided in the Camp David accords; in proposing the principle of autonomy, Begin had compromised deeply held convictions on the sanctity and sovereignty of what he called the historic Land of Israel. Fighting between Christians and Muslims in Lebanon was on the increase. The Israelis had noted a buildup of Syrian armor, heavy artillery, ground-to-ground Scud rockets. Begin feared that these would be used, in Begin's words, to slaughter innocents. The American decision to sell advanced military technology to Saudi Arabia added another element to the threat.

It has been said that Begin used the AWACS affair to win the Israeli election. No doubt he saw its value as a campaign issue, but this interpretation is far too cynical. One of the most skillful politicians in the world, famed for his sense of timing, Begin chose to engage an American President on his home ground on an issue the President could not afford to lose, and at a moment when he was at

the height of his popularity. A man of Begin's sagacity would hardly
have done that unless his convictions were engaged. After six months
of painful public controversy and intensive private negotiations, Begin nearly won. But in the process he lost the sympathy of powerful
figures in the Administration and sorely tried the tolerance and understanding of the President, with consequences for Israel and the
United States and the fate of the Middle East that have not yet
entirely revealed themselves.

The AWACS controversy, as it came to be called, originated in the
Carter Administration. Between Election Day and Inauguration Day,
Secretary of State Muskie and Secretary of Defense Harold Brown
told me that the Carter Administration had gone far toward committing the United States to providing Saudi Arabia with equipment that
would enhance the capabilities of sixty-two F-15 fighter-bombers that
had been approved for delivery to the Royal Saudi Air Force. That
additional equipment included fuel tanks that would increase the
range of the F-15's by about 200 miles, an improved Sidewinder air-
to-air heat-seeking missile that could be fired at an opposing aircraft
even head-on and still find its target, and a bomb rack that would
improve bombing accuracy. To support the enhanced F-15's, the outgoing Administration intended to sell the Saudis some form of radar
surveillance aircraft or "airborne warning and control system"
(AWACS).

Israel already possessed a number of F-15's, which were among
the most advanced combat aircraft in existence. They also had an
AWACS system, the E-2C Hawkeye. This is a two-engine, propeller-
driven aircraft that has good capabilities, but is considerably less
effective than the top-of-the-line E-3A Sentry AWACS used by the
U.S. Air Force and some NATO countries. The E-3A is one of several
military versions of the Boeing 707. It is equipped with a large disk-
like rotating radar dome and with electronic equipment that can
detect and track aircraft at high and low altitudes. The manufacturer
claims that the system can improve the defensive capability of combat aircraft by 200 percent and offensive capability by 400 percent.

Though he did not specify which system, Secretary Brown had
told the Saudis in December 1980 that the United States was "favorably disposed" to provide an aerial surveillance system. If this did not
amount to an absolute commitment, it created a state of affairs in
which an abrupt American withdrawal would compromise the trust

and friendship that both the Carter Administration and the Reagan Administration wanted to establish with Saudi Arabia and the rest of the moderate Arab world. Moreover, a study of Saudi air defense needs had been carried out by the U.S. Air Force. On the basis of this study, the Pentagon bureaucracy had decided that the more sophisticated E-3A, or simply AWACS as it came to be called, was what the Saudis needed. The Saudis knew this. I did not know it, and I do not believe that Muskie or Brown knew it, either. The judgment had been made by men deep in the American bureaucracy talking to counterparts in the Saudi defense establishment on the basis of technical needs rather than political considerations. The Saudis had already had opportunities to observe the capabilities of the AWACS during the Yemen conflict in 1978 and at the height of the Iran-Iraq war, when four U.S. Air Force AWACS had been sent to monitor these events. The American planes were still based at Riyadh.

Muskie and Brown had no wish to embarrass the new President. They offered to take the proposal to Congress and fight it out during the final days of the Carter Administration. In my opinion, they were almost certain to lose. The political capital of the Carter Administration was spent; its time was short. If the measure was killed, it might be impossible to bring it back to life. I took the problem to Reagan, telling him that it was a bad and dangerous situation, but that we must fight the issue ourselves if it was going to be fought. In my opinion, it must be fought. The Saudis would certainly regard it as a test of future relations. Reagan agreed.

In the discussions that followed within the Administration, much early support for the sale was evident. Many of the President's advisers perceived great value in a policy that was more favorable to Arab countries. Caspar Weinberger was especially enthusiastic. However, in light of the assurances that had been given to Congress by the previous Administration (Brown had told Congress in 1978 that the Carter Administration did not intend to sell the Saudis armaments or systems that would increase the ground-attack capability of their F-15's), we knew that it would be difficult to obtain the necessary congressional approval. At this time, discussion centered on the F-15's. The question of AWACS hardly arose. We proceeded still on the assumption that the choice between the Hawkeye and the far more sophisticated AWACS was still to be made. Airborne warning and control systems can be defensive in nature; so can Sidewinder missiles. But enhancements that are designed solely to improve the accuracy of air-to-ground missions are clearly not defensive in nature.

Before Inauguration Day, I informed the Israeli ambassador, Ephraim Evron, that the Reagan Administration planned to go ahead with the sale. Early in February 1981, with the President's approval, I told Sheikh Faisal Alhegelan, the Saudi ambassador, that the Administration would seek congressional approval for the sale of an airborne warning and control system to his country, together with fuel tanks and Sidewinder missiles for the F-15's, but that we could not provide bomb racks. These were only the opening conversations. I expected difficult negotiations, but because both the Saudis and the Israelis realized that the Reagan Administration was dealing with an inherited problem, I also expected, in the early blush of a new Administration, that we would quickly and quietly compose our differences. That would permit us to put this problem behind us, leaving us free to encourage the peace process and carry forward our plans for strategic cooperation.

We had hardly begun when, without notice, on February 3, Weinberger told the press that he supported the sale to Saudi Arabia. The next day, Ambassador Evron called on me to express Israel's distress over Weinberger's remarks. "We are very much aware of your wider interests in the region and the importance of Saudi Arabia in your overall strategy," Evron said. But Israel would need an additional fifteen F-15's of its own to offset the "threat" posed to Israeli security by an upgraded Saudi air force and maintain the military balance in the area. Evron did not mention AWACS, but the aroma of compromise was now in the air.

On February 24, the Israeli foreign minister, Yitzhak Shamir, visited Washington. When we met, I described American intentions, asked for his understanding, and pointed out the desirability of avoiding any action by Israel that would complicate congressional reaction to this issue. I told Shamir that radar surveillance aircraft would be included in the Saudi arms sale, but formal discussion centered on the F-15's. Israel knew the capabilities of these aircraft and regarded them as a serious threat. Later, in a meeting with President Reagan, Shamir was firm in delivering the message he had brought from Begin: Israel was adamantly opposed to any augmentation of the offensive capacity of any Arab state. The President told him unequivocally that he would never permit Israel to fall behind its neighbors in the quality of its weapons. In the end, however, a tentative understanding emerged with Shamir: the United States would supply to Israel an extra squadron of fifteen F-15's at a cost of $300 million; in return, the Israelis would mute their opposition to the sale of arms, including an aerial surveillance capability, to the Saudis. Although the sale was denounced by the Israeli cabinet as a danger to the security of Israel, this arrangement reflected a sound judgment on Shamir's part that there was little virtue in challenging the President so early in his term on a weapons sale that had been committed by Reagan's predecessor and would not decisively affect the balance of power with the Arabs—provided some compensation could be worked out for the Israelis.

The way now appeared clear to get the entire business behind us. I began briefing congressional figures on the F-15 "add-ons." The Saudis were informed by both Weinberger and me that the United States intended to sell them the F-15 equipment (except for the bomb racks) and also airborne surveillance aircraft of a type and number to be decided by the two governments. This was duly announced on March 6. We had not yet decided on the best time for notification of Congress.

There then occurred in Israel a leak to the press. The media carried a report, attributed to U.S. sources, that AWACS were to be sold to the Saudis. The information available to the press included details, some of them grossly exaggerated, of the radar and other electronic devices aboard these aircraft. Very soon, the government and the opposition parties were competing with each other to provide details of the capabilities of an aircraft that could circle over Saudi Arabia and yet look deep into Israel. The Labor party accused Begin of giving the appearance of acquiescence to an arms sale that was a danger to Israel. The discourse, taking place as it did during an election campaign, overheated.

In the American press, meanwhile, anonymous sources, clearly in the Pentagon, were quoted as saying that the Saudis would be provided with five E-3A Sentry AWACS, together with up to seven KC-135 tankers to refuel them in flight. This fleet of aircraft would be supported by a large number of ground radar stations. This was the first time I had heard that E-3A's would be provided to Saudi Arabia, much less that a fleet of tankers was included in the deal. At this stage, it appeared that the planes would be sold to Saudi Arabia without the restrictions on use and the requirement for sharing of information that governed deployment of AWACS to our closest NATO allies. All of this surprised me greatly.

So far as I knew, Weinberger was as surprised as I. Understandably, he defended his people at the Pentagon in their judgment that this equipment was what the Saudis needed—and that it was what the United States needed in the Persian Gulf region. As mentioned, four U.S. Air Force AWACS had been based in Riyadh since the war in Yemen in 1979. It was anticipated that American airmen would be aboard the Saudi AWACS during a period of training that would last for a number of years, and that the product of the Saudi radar surveillance of the gulf region would be shared with us. But there was no firm understanding with the Saudis on these points and others. It was known, too, that if the Saudis did not buy this equipment in the United States, they could easily buy it elsewhere. The British had developed a radar surveillance aircraft called Nimrod that was comparable to the E-3A AWACS. The value of the contracts for the entire arms package amounted to $8.5 billion. It must be said that the argument that American workers and manufacturers should benefit from the sale in terms of wages and profits played a persuasive role in our deliberations.

If we in the Administration were surprised by the revelation that AWACS would be sold to Saudi Arabia, the Israelis were astonished. They demanded to know why they were not given the courtesy of advance notice on such a sensitive issue. A storm of controversy arose in Israel. Its representatives in Washington told us that all deals were off. Selling AWACS to the Saudis would "alter the intelligence balance" in the Middle East and pose an unacceptable danger to Israel. The government of Israel would go all-out to prevent the sale.

I supported the sale of an airborne warning and surveillance system in principle, partly because I believed that it need not represent a real danger to Israel. We would also have to have important restrictions on its use. But the Pentagon had gone too far and too fast. The carefully wrought, though still tentative, understanding with Israel had been wrecked. The Israelis and their friends in the United States constituted a formidable lobby. It was not certain that the President could win a fight in Congress. Under the law, the Administration was required to notify Congress of its intention to make the sale. Congress then would have thirty days in which to defeat it by a majority vote in both houses. Therefore, if one house failed to defeat the measure, the sale would go forward. We believed that we had little or no chance to carry the House of Representatives. The Senate was controlled by the Republicans, but in July 1980, sixty-eight senators had sent Carter a letter opposing the sale of F-15's and AWACS to Saudi Arabia; fifty-five of these senators returned when the new Congress convened. It was decided, nevertheless, that we must concentrate our efforts on the Senate. I recommended that we separate AWACS and F-15 elements of the sale in the hope of achieving a quick resolution of the controversy. In this I was overruled when, on April 1, two days after the President was wounded, the National Security Council, with Vice President Bush in the chair, recommended the sale of enhanced F-15's (less the bomb racks) and also five AWACS aircraft together with seven KC-135 tankers to refuel them. The President approved this decision from his hospital bed.

With this clarification of approved policy in hand, I prepared for my visit to the Middle East, only to read in the newspapers the day before I left yet another leak—the NSC decision reported in detail.

When I arrived in Israel a few days later, Begin confronted me with his fears. He had invited me to his home, a simple, even Spartan house decorated with the drawings and cut-outs made by Israeli children. "If you sell these planes to the Saudis," he said, "Israel will be militarily transparent." Earlier, I had met with the Israeli cabinet. Its members attributed fantastic capabilities to AWACS, including the power to track tank columns on Israeli roads. In fact, the system cannot detect objects on the ground, or anything moving slower than 80 mph. I told the Israelis this. A full account of Israeli apprehensions and grievances was made by Foreign Minister Shamir when we met alone. He immediately asked why the United States was doing what it was doing. Once again I explained the strategic considerations involved. I spoke of the deep friendship between Israel and the United States and of the importance of American influence on the Arabs to the security of Israel. I insisted with conviction that the Saudi royal family recognized better than any Arab state the true nature of our common menace, and that they, too, needed reliable U.S. assurances. Shamir was not reassured. "Mere words for Israel," he said bitterly, "but arms for the Saudis! Saudi Arabia is no moderate nation where Israel is concerned." I described the sale as an element in the defense of the free world; Shamir spoke of holy war and Saudi anti-Semitism. Shamir contended that the Arabs would not fight the Soviets but that Israel alone would. Referring to the mutuality of interests between Israel and the United States, I described

Israel as a "strategic asset." Shamir interrupted, "Israel doesn't need to be called a strategic asset. We don't need it. We are in a life-and-death situation."

The issue was now irrevocably joined. It was clear that a very tough fight lay ahead of us. In Washington, the indomitable Senator Laxalt told the President and the press that there was deep division in the Senate over the issue, and that a majority of members would probably vote against the sale if the vote were taken immediately. The always judicious Senator Baker, just back from Israel and Saudi Arabia with the news that the Saudis had rejected any suggestion of a conciliatory gesture toward Israel, warned of the danger of "cataclysmic" differences of opinion in the Senate. He suggested that AWACS be manned by joint Saudi-American crews and advised that the sale be delayed. On April 21, the United States announced that the sale would in fact take place, subject to congressional approval. The next day, the Israeli cabinet denounced this decision and Prime Minister Begin informed the American ambassador, Samuel W. Lewis, of his government's "profound regret and unreserved opposition."

The situation in Lebanon continued to deteriorate. From early April, heavy fighting had been going on between Syrian forces and the Christian Phalange near the Christian town of Zahle, in the Beka'a Valley in central Lebanon. Over the weekend of April 25, the Syrians landed airborne troops on strategic ridges of the Sannin Mountains and dislodged the Phalange forces that had been holding this high ground. The Israelis, who followed a policy of supporting the Christians, shot down two Syrian helicopters. The Syrians responded by installing several batteries of highly effective Soviet-made SAM 6 antiaircraft missiles in the valley. The Israelis then threatened to destroy the missiles if they were not removed. At my urging, President Reagan sent Philip C. Habib, a retired under secretary of state and a gifted negotiator and stalwart patriot, to the Middle East as his personal emissary to confer with Israeli, Lebanese, and Syrian leaders in an attempt to prevent a further escalation of the violence in Lebanon.

There was reason for apprehension. In Israel a couple of weeks before, I had received reports of a cabinet meeting in which an incursion into Lebanon by Israeli troops had been approved. Military movements were under way. Later that evening, Begin described the turmoil and the communal violence in Lebanon and remarked that

Israel might intervene "as a matter of conscience." In very strong terms, I told him that neither the United States nor the world at large would understand such an action when Israeli security was not directly threatened. By coincidence or not, there was no Israeli invasion. But I warned the President that Israeli columns could cross the border at any time.

Meanwhile, Saudi Arabia designated Prince Bandar bin Sultan, a pilot in the Royal Saudi Air Force and the son of the minister of defense, as the coordinator of its efforts on behalf of the arms package. The press resounded with debate over the issue. It was suggested that American honor could be satisfied by giving the Saudis a "Stone Age" version of the aircraft, that the planes must be crewed by Americans, that the Saudis might use the equipment to attack Israel or to help other Arab states to do so. Saudi sensibilities were inflamed by such statements, and one representative of that government complained to the State Department that his country was being "treated like a second-class citizen" and being held up as unworthy of the trust the United States extended to other friendly nations. We were informed that King Khalid would not be able to visit the United States for the time being owing to the controversy surrounding the case. Meanwhile, Weinberger and I met for ninety minutes with the president of the Conference of Presidents of Major American Jewish Organizations. They urged the Administration to reconsider the sale and, in a deeply felt argument, stressed the danger of entrusting highly secret U.S. military hardware to what they regarded as an unstable regime. (Earlier, Prince Bandar had been asked by a U.S. senator how stable his country's regime was. In reply, he produced a photograph of his grandfather standing beside Franklin D. Roosevelt.)

As it prepared for the showdown in the Senate, the Administration betrayed little sense of urgency or organization. The Defense Department set up briefings for some forty key senators, but not all of the briefings took place. As always, there were problems of communication between Defense and State and the White House. Early in June, Weinberger and I took this problem to Edwin Meese. It was my opinion that Vice President Bush ought to be in charge of organizing strategy and action for the Administration. In the meantime, we should ask senators to keep an open mind on the issue until they had heard the President's final case, negotiate with the Saudis to allay concern on the "threat" to Israel and the security of AWACS technology, and develop a rationale on the costs and benefits of the sale with respect to American interests. It was imperative that the White House be fully engaged. On June 15, the President signed an order appointing not George Bush but Richard Allen as chairman of a new committee to coordinate the Administration's efforts on behalf of the arms package.

For a short while, it seemed that we might be able to proceed with a minimum of acrimony between ourselves and Israel and with a reduced potential for embarrassing the hypersensitive Saudis with the rough-and-tumble of an all-out American political battle. Then, on June 7, aircraft belonging to the Israeli air force bombed and destroyed Iraq's Osirak nuclear reactor, located about ten miles outside Baghdad. Later, the Israelis told me that they had agonized over the question of giving the United States advance warning of this raid and in the end decided not to do so on grounds that we would only have told them not to do it. In this judgment they were correct.

The raid took place on a Sunday. When the first word of it was brought to me at 4:50 P.M. by Woody Goldberg, I was at home. I immediately notified the President. The first question that came to my mind was the natural one. Had radiation been released? Would it affect the population of Baghdad and other nearby communities? Did we have aircraft available that could detect such radiation? Did we have decontamination teams and other resources available? If so, could we find a way to offer these as a humanitarian gesture to Iraq, with which we had no diplomatic relations? The State Department staff began working on the answers to these questions while I was en route to the operations center. When I arrived, I notified the leaders of Congress and our principal European allies, giving them the bare facts as we knew them. Obviously, the Israelis had used American-made aircraft and probably American-made "smart" bombs to carry out the raid. I called Ambassador Evron and asked for detailed information on the raid. Clearly, this was going to be a very thorny issue. Evron told me only that the reactor site had been destroyed. I believed him.

With superb efficiency, the intelligence staff at State immediately produced the basic facts. There had been two reactors, one Soviet-supplied, the other installed by the French. About fifty foreign workers were employed on the site, but normally only on weekdays; no doubt that was the reason why the Israelis had attacked on a Sunday. The reactor core contained about 12 kilograms (26.4 lbs.) of weapons-grade U-235. Experts forecast minimum contamination and no dangerous effects outside the immediate area. I called the President and gave him this information together with confirmation, from Ambassador Evron, that the Israelis admitted responsibility for the raid. Although this was a startling and dangerous action, it was not technically an attack on a peaceful nation: Iraq and Israel had been in a state of war with each other since 1948. There were obvious dangers for the United States in this situation. American equipment, delivered to the Israelis for defensive purposes only, had been used in the attack. The Arabs would suspect collusion. Our public position was simply to tell the truth: we had not been notified in advance and the United States was ready to help the victims. At 8:50 P.M., Evron called back from the Israeli embassy. No foreign experts had been injured in the raid. The Israelis believed that there was no danger of contamination; the reactor was not yet "hot." That was the reason for the timing of the raid—the reactors were near to activation and the Israelis wanted to strike first, to minimize the danger of the escape of radioactive debris. Israel believed that the reactor was a cover for nuclear weapons research, and if they had not destroyed it, Iraq could have produced effective nuclear weapons within five years. Later, Begin said that Israel had "lived with this nightmare for two years" and decided on the action several months before; he believed that three Hiroshima-size bombs would destroy Israeli cities with the loss of 600,000 lives.*

After passing this information on to the President, I drafted, on a yellow pad, an official statement on the episode in which the raid was condemned as an act that could not but worsen the tense and dangerous situation in the Middle East. The statement also acknowledged that equipment and armaments originating in the United States had been used in the raid. Israel's action had been shocking, and there would be consequences. Not only could the United States not condone the raid, it would have to take some action against Israel.

---

*In the postmortem, we discovered that the Israelis had notified both the Carter Administration and the government of France in 1980 of their fears that the reactor would be used to make bombs and asked both governments to take action to prevent this result. The Israelis then went quiet on the issue. It was never discussed with the Reagan Administration. In line with Israeli practice on such matters, Begin had consulted the opposition before taking the decision to attack the reactor. In May 1981, François Mitterrand was elected president of France. Evidently fearing that if he lost the election the new prime minister would not attack the reactor, Begin ordered its destruction.

Yet my feelings were mixed. The suspicion that Iraq intended to produce nuclear weapons was hardly unrealistic. In that context, Begin's action in destroying the plant where they might be made was understandable and might well be judged less severely by history than by the opinion of the day.

Protocol made it difficult for me to communicate directly with the Iraqis. They had no ambassador in Washington, and I could hardly place a call on the international telephone lines to the foreign minister of a country we did not recognize. Then Dick Allen remembered that the Iraqi foreign minister, Sa'dun Hammadi, had recently escaped death when an elevator in which he was riding fell a long way down its shaft in a New York City skyscraper. I phoned Hammadi, and after offering the truthful observation that I was glad that his life had been spared, expressed the concern of the United States for the well-being of the people who had been near the site of the bombing, and offered whatever assistance might be possible. The Iraqis, in their public statements about the raid, never suggested that the United States shared any blame in the incident.

Within the Administration, reaction to the Israeli raid combined astonishment with exasperation. Some of the President's advisers urged that he take strong, even punitive, measures against Israel. I argued that, while some action must be taken to show American disapproval, our strategic interests would not be served by policies that humiliated and weakened Israel. The President's deep natural sympathy for Israel and his understanding that she depended on American friendship, came into play also. In the end, the President decided to delay the shipment of four F-16 aircraft (the type used in the raid) to Israel. Weinberger revealed this action to the press before it had been officially communicated to the Israeli government. If any further exacerbation of the situation were possible, this accomplished it. "Cap, you have an obligation to tell us about your concerns," I told him on the telephone, "but not to go public. Please, let's have no more press briefings at the Pentagon on this subject."

The Osirak raid had a sharp impact on the AWACS controversy. The Israelis revealed that they had overflown Saudi territory on their way to bomb the reactor. This prompted Saudi officials to talk publicly of their need for AWACS for defense against Israel and of their pan-Arab responsibilities to warn others of impending Israeli attacks if detected. Our effort to downplay the significance of AWACS in the Arab-Israeli conflict became a casualty of the raid.

Meanwhile, opposition in the Senate took a dramatic turn. On June 24, a Republican senator, Bob Packwood of Oregon, sent the President a letter expressing "deep concern" over the sale. "It is our strong belief that this sale is not in the best interests of the United States and therefore recommend that you refrain from sending this proposal to Congress," Packwood wrote. The letter was signed by fifty-four members of the Senate, including twenty Republicans. This evidence of preemptive Israeli support on Capitol Hill presented the President with great difficulties: after three months of effort, the opposition seemed even stronger. A procedural problem also arose: how could he send notification of intent to sell the Saudis arms after a majority of the Senate had asked him *not* to send it? Senators Baker and Percy, joined by Senator John G. Tower of Texas, the chairman of the Armed Services Committee, sent another letter to Reagan, asking that he delay notification until July 20, and that he include assurances to the Senate on security of the equipment, information sharing, joint use by Saudi and U.S. crews, and operations. This solution to the procedural problem also indicated the only way to pass AWACS: the Saudis must agree to important restrictions on the use of the equipment.

Meanwhile, the Administration's forces remained in a state of disorganization. To members of the State Department who worked with him on the issue, it appeared, as one of them reported to me, that Richard Allen was "overwhelmed by the enormity of the problem and not yet seized of the urgency of taking control . . . and moving out." On June 25, a close associate who liked and respected Allen told me that he was convinced we would lose AWACS with Allen in charge. This impression was afterward fortified when, in full view of the television cameras, Allen accompanied Prince Bandar on a round robin of calls to senators. Coordination continued to falter. A memorandum of understanding on use of AWACS was drafted in the Defense Department and given to Prince Bandar, but not shown to the Department of State.

Toward the end of June, Bud McFarlane suggested that a mission be sent to Israel, ostensibly to discuss the suspended shipment of F-16 aircraft, but in fact to explore the possibility of another compromise on AWACS. McFarlane himself subsequently undertook this mission, but produced no vivid results, possibly because it followed closely on the delivery to Israel of an oral note expressing American displeasure over the Israeli attack on the Iraqi reactor. Begin had been offended by the note, a fact that he made plain to the American ambassador. On June 30, Menachem Begin's Likud had won a slim majority in the Israeli parliament, and Begin formed a new government. Over the following weekend, we learned of Begin's intention to destroy the Syrian missiles in the Beka'a Valley. We strongly discouraged this plan and, for the time being, Begin desisted. As we struggled to gain time in the resulting "missile crisis," events in the south of Lebanon added a new dimension to the situation. While Habib selflessly shuttled between capitals, attempting to find some basis for a cease-fire in Lebanon, Israel reported that its northern settlements were being bombarded by rockets launched from PLO bases within Lebanon. On July 17, again without prior notice, Israeli bombers struck PLO headquarters in downtown Beirut with heavy loss of life. A week later, owing partly to the very effective application of influence and persuasion behind the scenes by the government of Saudi Arabia, Habib achieved an agreement for a cease-fire in southern Lebanon.

As August approached, the Administration's tactics and strategy on the contest in the Senate still had not formed. I sent a memorandum to the President recommending a line of action. The foremost recommendation was that the President himself must become fully engaged. Allen sent me a note on August 4, quoting the comment Reagan had scribbled across the face of my paper: "I'll help. I agree with every word in the memo." When Congress returned from recess on September 9, it was given the first, informal twenty-day notification of the President's intent to sell the arms package. This meant that final and formal notification would take place on or about October 1, with the vote coming sometime in the following thirty days.

Earlier in September, Menachem Begin had paid an official visit to the United States. Some members of the White House staff believed that the President should seize the occasion to tell Begin outright to stop making difficulties for the United States. The President, however, understood that Begin believed that he was saving Israel, and that it was fruitless to question his basic assumptions. The two men spent thirty minutes alone at breakfast in the White House before meeting with aides. There were, of course, limits on the success Reagan could wring from this difficult situation. At the end of the meeting, which was sometimes passionate, he was still going to sell Saudi Arabia AWACS and Begin was still inalterably opposed to his doing so.

The Israelis had given us assurances that Begin and the other members of his government who accompanied him would not violate the President's hospitality and lobby against the Saudi arms package during their visit to Washington. On the day of his departure, accompanied by his minister of defense, General Ariel Sharon, and others, Begin paid a visit to Capitol Hill for a luncheon at the request of the Committee on Foreign Relations. The senators asked Begin for his views on AWACS. It was not his intention, Begin replied, to interfere in the debate, but he had a duty to present the fact: Israel was opposed to the sale. As part of its effort to allay the fears of the Israelis with regard to AWACS, the Pentagon had sent a team of Israeli military observers on a flight in the aircraft. The scheme went awry. On landing, the Israelis had been more convinced than ever that the aircraft were a mortal danger to their homeland. Now one of Begin's military aides unrolled a map and demonstrated Israel's vulnerability to surveillance by AWACS. "It is a real concern," Begin said. "I say to you, we face a serious danger." General Sharon, a man who does not mince words, was asked what he thought of the possibility of the Saudis buying Nimrod aircraft from the British in case the sale of AWACS should not occur. He replied that the Israelis would prefer the Saudis to have British planes. If Americans were flying in certain aircraft, the Israelis would have to be cautious about shooting them down.

That afternoon, as I returned to Andrews Air Force Base, Bill Clark met me and told me excitedly that James Baker had informed the President that Begin had been lobbying in the Senate against AWACS. Baker had offered a second report suggesting that Begin had given a "hit list" of senators opposed to AWACS to the Reverend Jerry Falwell, the evangelist. A third report from Deaver had Henry Kissinger informing the White House that he had found Begin "euphoric" and confident that AWACS could be defeated. All this, said Clark, in a tone of bitterness and reproach, constituted a serious breach of the assurances the Israelis had given us regarding Begin's political activity while he was a guest of the United States. It seemed to me possible that a mistake—even a series of mistakes—had been made. Sam Lewis, our ambassador to Israel, had made the rounds with Begin, and he had reported no such activity. I called Reverend Falwell, who denied that he and Begin had even discussed AWACS. The minutes of the meeting with the members of the Foreign Relations Committee confirmed that Begin had not initiated the discussion of AWACS and confined himself to answering questions put by the senators. I took this information to the White House, and in a meeting in the Oval Office attended by his principal aides, laid it before President Reagan. But by now Reagan was very disturbed. At this hour, Begin was in New York, preparing to depart for Tel Aviv. The President instructed me to fly to New York and ask Begin for an explanation. In a small government jet, I landed at John F. Kennedy International Airport. Begin received me in a private room in the El Al terminal. In obedience to the President's wishes, I spoke very frankly. Begin, somewhat taken aback, was uncharacteristically docile. He denied that he had acted improperly. I believed him. In official dealings, Begin can be combative, even harsh, but he is scrupulously truthful. Before we parted, I used the occasion to caution him once again that, in case Israel was contemplating an invasion of Lebanon, its government should realize that unless there was a clear, internationally recognized provocation—and even then, unless Israeli reaction was proportionate to the provocation—any such course would have very grave effects in the United States. This was a message I had occasion to repeat over and over again during the next nine months.

In late September, the Saudis informed us that they could not accept some of the proposed restrictions on use of the AWACS. They felt that they had been humiliated by detailed press coverage of what they had supposed were secret negotiations. Soon afterward, Richard Allen and Baker conceived the idea of sending a congressional delegation to Saudi Arabia to discuss the matter. I never fully understood the reasoning behind this suggestion. The Saudis were infuriated by it. On hearing about it after emerging from talks with Andrei Gromyko in New York, I flew back to Washington and, in the Oval Office, urged Reagan not to approve the idea. Congress has no power to negotiate with a foreign government. It is unwise to carry on diplomatic negotiations before the press. Crown Prince Fahd, afterward King Fahd, solved the dilemma by telling Reagan on the telephone that Saudi Arabia could not accept the delegation if it was bringing a message having to do with restrictions on the use of AWACS. Fahd indicated that if the President needed such a visit for political purposes, it would be acceptable. The congressmen did not go.

On September 24, Senator Baker informed the Administration that twelve senators would have to switch their votes in order for

AWACS to pass. This did not appear to be achievable. Senator John Glenn, Democrat of Ohio, had been attempting to work out a compromise in which the Saudis would be supplied with upgraded electronic equipment, identical to that used by the U.S. Air Force, in planes that would be manned by mixed Saudi and American crews, with compliance guaranteed under a secret protocol that would be kept in the President's safe. Baker suggested that we might have to accept the Glenn formula.

We were preserved from what seemed to me to be a mischievous solution by suggestions from both the Israelis and the Saudis that they were willing to be more flexible. Talk of providing a squadron of F-15's to Israel revived. To this was added the offer of $200 million in military assistance funds to be applied largely to purchases from their own defense industry. These were items that had earlier been agreed on, but for which the funds had not been available. There was little doubt now that Congress would appropriate the funds and eventually it did so. During this period, the first discussions of a form of strategic partnership with the Israelis took place. At least since the Ford Administration, the two governments had talked about a more formal understanding on questions of mutual defense. This would not be a full alliance in which either partner is obliged to go to war if the other is attacked, but rather, a cooperative arrangement to deal with external threats to the region. In short, it did not visualize coordination in Israel's regional disputes with the Arabs. This seemed a good moment to reassure them by taking the first steps. A memorandum of understanding that provided for limited peacetime military cooperation was drafted.

Soon afterward, following a visit by Weinberger to Riyadh, the Saudis at last agreed to conditions that would satisfy the Senate. In testimony before the Foreign Relations Committee, I described the agreements and understandings that had been concluded between the U.S. and Saudi governments. The U.S. would play a role in the development of Saudi air defenses; there would be complete and continuous sharing of information between the two countries but no data could be given to third countries without U.S. consent; Americans would be aboard the aircraft well into the 1990s; Saudi AWACS would not be operated outside Saudi air space; elaborate measures to protect the security of the secret equipment had been worked out.

On October 1, President Reagan sent the Saudi arms package to the Senate and expressed the widespread resentment that had been aroused by pro-Israeli lobbying by saying that "it is not the business of any other nation to make American foreign policy." In addition, he voiced American support of Saudi Arabia in unmistakable terms: "We will not permit [it] to become another Iran." The White House was engaged at last. A month of extraordinary effort followed. James Baker took over from Allen the prime responsibility for getting the arms package through the Senate. With great acumen and energy, he sought to persuade key senators to vote with the President. Reagan himself became fully engaged in the process, and in one of the most effective Presidential lobbying efforts of recent times, put the full weight of his office and the full persuasiveness of his personality into the fight. All three former Presidents gave their support; several recent Secretaries of State and all living ex-Secretaries of Defense came out in favor of the bill.

On September 14, according to the State Department's count, only fifteen senators had been in favor of AWACS, with eighteen leaning toward disapproval and the rest undecided. On October 15, the Foreign Relations Committee voted against the package, nine to eight. By the morning of October 27, the State Department counted forty-eight senators in favor. The President then revealed his final and decisive maneuver, worked out largely by Richard Fairbanks, the assistant secretary of state for congressional relations. Since early October, Fairbanks had been working behind the scenes with key senators of both parties and had perfected a letter promising Presidential certification of the safeguards on the AWACS before they could be delivered to Saudi Arabia. Delivered to Senator Baker on October 28, the letter provided the final margin. On the day of the vote, October 29, Senator Baker reported he had forty-nine firm votes in favor. Later in the day, the Senate approved the sale by voting against a resolution to disapprove, fifty-two to forty-eight.

This was a resounding victory for the President and a convincing demonstration of his political skills and his prestige and popularity. It was a victory, too, for a policy that was right for the United States, right for the Saudis, and, looking beyond the horizon, right for Israel. It enhanced the security of the Saudi oil fields, deterred external aggression against the nations of the Middle East, and benefited wider U.S. relations with the Arabs. The surveillance aircraft and the Sidewinder missiles and fuel tanks for the Saudi F-15's were not, in themselves, especially important. Saudi Arabia would not have perished without them, and unless the Israeli air force undergoes a precipitous loss of skill and nerve, Israel will not perish because the Saudis possess these systems. After many months of public debate and public diplomacy and private emotionalism, the following was accomplished: Saudi Arabia received nearly everything it had asked for in the way of defense systems and armaments, and so had Israel. The outcome was almost exactly the same as the proposals we had made, and the Saudis and the Israelis had implicitly accepted, in the first days of the Administration. No other outcome ever was possible. Nevertheless, the political fallout proved to be costly. At home, the President had to commit all of his prestige in behalf of a relatively minor issue because failure would have made it difficult for him to achieve anything else. Abroad, it irritated delicate relationships at the very time when we most wished to nurture them.

The entire AWACS experience contains several lessons. The first and most important of these is that when a thing starts out badly, it is likely to get worse. The second is that influence is a delicate plant whose early shoots must be tended carefully, and which can die before its season if it is subjected to too much rough handling. Here, organization and discipline are paramount. The third is that you must think long before moving in ways that disturb the natural balance of relationships between nations because it is never possible to foresee all the results. What happened, essentially, was that a simple issue got out of hand because of a combination of premature publicity, inadequate planning, the continuing organizational vacuum, and a superfluous test of political manhood.

The question of five airplanes is a tiny one when held up against the universe of American policy or even the solar system of American relations with Israel and the other nations of the Middle East. But every issue between two nations is a microcosm of their whole relationship, containing within itself, in a kind of genetic code, all the energy, all the goodwill and trust, all the resentment and suspicion and jealousy of the parent body. If it is not handled with care, it can break and release all these forces. This is seldom a good thing. In the case of AWACS, the Administration was too inexperienced fully to understand this, and the Israelis were too preoccupied with their history and its explosive new chapters to remember it. Many of the consequences await us both in a future in which, I fear, our old friendship and our shared values and mingled history will be more severely tested than ever they were on Capitol Hill.

BACKGROUND

The AWACS controversy, besides showing again what an important role the press plays in the making of policy, demonstrated what a powerful instrument of diplomacy it is. When the Israelis wished to make a point to the U.S. government in even plainer language than they used to talk to us in private, they would consult a friendly columnist on the *Washington Post*. When the Saudis wished to go on record as reserving the right to warn other Arab countries of an impending Israeli attack if such were detected on their radars, they spoke to the *New York Times*. When at last the President decided to vent his annoyance over Israeli meddling in the American policy-making process, he did so at a televised news conference.

Unless, like the President, you stand up before a news conference and speak your mind, this technique permits you to tell the unvarnished truth without being responsible for it. If some of the things that nations say about one another in the newspapers were delivered in a demarche, a break in diplomatic relations might follow. By using the press as a sort of code room to which everyone has the key, true feelings can be released and the risk of misunderstanding is reduced. It is, however, sometimes difficult to tell what is said for local consumption and what for the purposes of communication with partners in diplomacy. This is especially true in the Middle East, a region where the proximity of war can sometimes be scientifically judged by applying a mathematical formula to the emotive value of the words and phrases used in propaganda broadcasts. It is not uncommon for American ambassadors to note that the Arabs believe things that they read in the Israeli press that the Israelis themselves dismiss as rhetoric directed at the masses, and vice versa. This problem was especially acute during the AWACS controversy when Israel was in the midst of an election campaign.

On the whole, the press did itself proud in its coverage of this issue. It obtained the facts early, reported them accurately, and updated its information with remarkable efficiency. It presented both sides of the controversy fairly, and although the strategic reasons for the Administration's policy tended to get lost as the debate heated up, this, too, was reported and examined. The controversy was a good show, just the sort of thing the press loves and the public devours. The camera loved Reagan as it always had; it approached Menachem Begin more diffidently. The assonance between the two leaders' names, Reagan and Begin, was made poignant by the contrast in their television images. Perhaps there was a subliminal element of the story of David and Goliath in this. But the dramatic values never overwhelmed the facts. This was a serious issue, and to a remarkable degree, it was the press that kept it serious.

There was a dangerous potential for anti-Semitism, or accusations of anti-Semitism, in this situation. The American press never let this fire be kindled. This constituted a signal service to decency. The tribalistic suggestion that Arabs are somehow inherently untrustworthy was closer to the surface, as in the insistent demands that extraordinary oaths of secrecy be required of the Saudis. Here again, the press generally resisted those who may have been tempted to resort to the inflammation of bad impulses in order to make a point.

It was my impression, though I have no statistics or scientifically gathered data to support it, that the Israelis emerged from the controversy with their base of public support in Washington, in the United States at large, and in the media more or less intact. Paradoxically, this may be *because* they lost. Those who had opposed the sale did not cease to believe that they had been right, nor did they afterward fail to support other Israeli causes. Those who changed over to support the President did exactly that—supported the President. They saw that his defeat on a public issue as resonant as this one would be a far more serious matter for the United States, and therefore the world, than the stationing of radar surveillance planes in Saudi Arabia would be for Israel.

China:
"Why Are There Always Such Surprises?"

IN TERMS OF the strategic interests of the United States and the West in the last quarter of the twentieth century, China may be the most important country in the world. If the main threat to human progress and world peace is Soviet expansionism, as the Chinese along with many others believe, then it follows that this threat must be contained and drained of its energy. The Chinese contend that this can be accomplished through a strategic consensus among a sufficiently large and determined group of nations, the small as well as the large, the developed as well as those in the Third World, to resist what the Chinese call hegemonism—the Soviet determination to extinguish the history of other states and replace it with models of their own society. The Chinese do not believe that the United States and its allies can bring about the neutralization of Soviet adventurism without the participation of China, or that China can do so without the participation of the United States and the West, otherwise called the First World.

The Chinese do believe, and so do I, that American and Western wealth and technology, in combination with the irresistible force for economic change and social justice that drives the struggle for development in the Third World, can create a future in which the insistence on national survival is so great, because the future of each nation promises so much, that no force can overcome it. This requires not mere coexistence but active collaboration between nations with very different economic and political systems. The system in China is evolving from the impasse of Maoism toward a model that is designed to set free the enormous practical energy of the Chinese people. In other words, it is ceasing to be classically Communist. If the experiment works, and works to some degree because China and the United States are friends, then the rest of the developing world will face compelling evidence that nations may overcome their problems without surrendering their nationhood.

Our relationship with China is, therefore, a great opportunity for human progress. China is the bridge on which the First World and the Third World may meet. Her present leaders, practical men weary of impractical theory and revolutionary religiosity, are trying within the limits of prudence to bring about that meeting. And within the limits of prudence, the United States must join them. That is my conviction, and as Secretary of State I urged that it should be America's policy. In this I was stubbornly opposed by other men in the Administration who could not bring themselves to believe that not all Communists are the same, that national interests are at least as reliable a guide to national behavior as ideology, and that American interests can sometimes be served by arrangements with such people as the leaders of China.

The President himself was slow if not unable to see merit in my views. At first, I thought this was because he did not fully understand my arguments, but in the end I came to believe that, like his most trusted advisers, he simply did not agree with me. More than any other thing that happened in the eighteen months that I was Secretary of State, the China question convinced me that Reagan's world view was indeed different from my own, and that I could not serve him and my convictions at the same time.

At the time of Reagan's election, Sino-American relations, like so many others, were in a fragile state. This was the result of what a Chinese might call the Three Disappointments. First, China was disappointed by American passivity in the post-Vietnam period. More keenly than most capitals, Beijing was sensitive to the effects of the shrinkage of American power and influence. Fifty divisions of the

Red Army are stationed on China's northern frontier; battle-hardened forces of Vietnam, the Soviet client, are grouped to the south. After Korea and Vietnam, after Iran, after detente, the Chinese in their realistic way found ample grounds for questioning the fiber and the reliability of the United States. The depth of these feelings was revealed when one of my predecessors remarked to Deng Xiaoping, the Chinese leader, that the Soviet Union wanted only peace. Reportedly, Deng walked out of the room in disgust.

Second, China was disappointed in the fruits of her relationship with the United States. When normalization began, with President Nixon's visit to China in 1972, the Chinese hoped for substantial benefits. They remembered the cases of Japan and West Germany, in which the United States had literally built new countries for former enemies and, combined with their own hard work, propelled them into prosperity. If they did not envisage or desire anything quite so comprehensive as that, they nevertheless expected to receive large American loans and credits at reasonable rates of interest. Above all, they expected to benefit from a flow of American technology that would transform their backward and unproductive economy into a modernized, if not fully modern, enterprise capable of capturing the enormous creative energy of China's one billion people. "If I were born again," Deng Xiaoping is reported to have said privately to another Asian leader after visiting the United States, "China might have a market economy today." In line with her early expectations, China altered her five-year plan to emphasize heavy industry. But the United States of the 1970s was not the United States of the 1950s; even if America had possessed the resources to lift up China by massive aid, she hadn't the political will to do so. Instead of credits and technical assistance, China received an influx of American businessmen seeking profits. By 1980, having received nothing that she had expected to receive, China found herself with a $2.8 billion trade deficit with the United States. By then, she had been forced to modify her five-year plan to place primary emphasis on the development of light industry and agriculture—policies that could be pursued without significant outside help.

Third, China was disappointed that her relationship with the United States had not produced a solution to the question of Taiwan. Ever since Chiang Kai-shek fled from the mainland in 1949 with the remnants of his armies, the United States had recognized his regime at Taipei, which governed 17 million people on an island lying 100 miles off the Chinese coast, as the true government of all China. The "other" China, whose Communist government at Beijing controlled a population that approached one billion, did not exist, in diplomatic terms, for the United States and many of its allies. For nearly twenty years, America's Two Chinas policy kept China out of the United Nations and isolated her from all but a handful of countries. From the first moment of the negotiations that began under Nixon, even before his visit to Beijing (and, in effect, as a condition of his visit), the Chinese had insisted on discussing this "crucial and fundamental issue."

At the end of Nixon's visit, the United States had joined China in the Shanghai Communiqué, a summary of the differences and similarities in the foreign policies of the two countries. In this communiqué, the United States "acknowledge[d] that all Chinese on both sides of the Taiwan Strait maintain that there is but one China and that Taiwan is a part of China." On January 1, 1979, the United States and China reestablished diplomatic relations after a lapse of twenty-nine years. As part of the agreement that led to normalization, the United States ended diplomatic relations with Taiwan, withdrew from its mutual defense treaty with Taiwan, and agreed that "in the future, the American people and the people of Taiwan will maintain commercial, cultural, and other relations without official government representation and without diplomatic relations." In legal, if not emotional terms, that massive concession by the United States ended the Two Chinas policy.

However, the United States reserved the right to sell arms and other military equipment to Taiwan. China objected strenuously to this policy on grounds that Taiwan was a province of China and such sales constituted interference in her internal affairs and a challenge to her sovereignty. Many in the United States believed that the Carter Administration had gone too far in its concessions to China on the status of Taiwan and argued that Taiwan must have the means to defend herself until such time as the people of China had peaceably settled the question of reunification of island and mainland. This belief was enshrined in law when, on April 10, 1979, President Carter signed the Taiwan Relations Act, in which Congress defined the conditions of relations between the United States and Taiwan. The Act mandated continued sales of armaments to Taiwan, and within the year, the United States transferred more than $1 billion in military equipment to the Taiwanese. The government also granted permission to the manufacturers of the so-called FX fighter-bomber to make sales representations to prospective overseas customers, including Taiwan. China vigorously protested these transactions—and the Taiwan Relations Act itself—as intolerable interferences in the internal affairs of China.

It was this third disappointment—Taiwan, with all its complicated emotional and political baggage—that would bedevil the effort to create a China policy for the Reagan Administration that would eliminate Chinese doubts about our strength and steadiness of purpose, help the Chinese in the solution of their internal economic problems, and create the conditions for a strategic consensus that would have the power to frustrate Soviet ambitions in East Asia and the Pacific and thereby advance the stability and security of that region and the world.

Taiwan was a very difficult question for Ronald Reagan. He is an anti-Communist. For thirty years, Taiwan had symbolized the hope (it was not always regarded as an illusion) that the most populous and ancient civilization on earth would free itself of communism. The recognition of China shattered the illusion but left the hope intact. Reagan, like many others, had difficulty in grasping this truth—and, above all, in believing that a policy of American support for Taiwan's old adversaries on the mainland might accomplish, in less than thirty years, what thirty years of intransigence had not done. Reagan's emotions were deeply engaged in this question, and so was his sense of honor. Any suggestion of abandoning the Taiwanese, or of subjecting them to insult, deeply offended his sense of the loyalty that old friends and longtime allies owed to one another. He repeatedly said as much, in public and in private meetings with the Chinese, and he was absolutely right to feel as he did. I do not know that he ever understood that the abandonment of the Taiwanese was probably the last thing that Deng Xiaoping and his followers in Beijing wanted or expected from him. If one American President abandons the Shah, and the next betrays the Taiwanese, what then can be the expectations of the Chinese themselves?

During his campaign for the Presidency, Reagan left little doubt that he was one of those who believed that Carter had gone too far in his concessions on Taiwan. On August 25, 1980, in welcoming his running mate, George Bush, back from a visit to China, Reagan said, in a formal statement:

I felt that a condition of normalization, by itself a sound policy choice, should have been the retention of a liaison office on Taiwan *of equivalent status to the one we had earlier established at Beijing* [emphasis added]. . . . I would not pretend that the relationship we now have with Taiwan . . . is not official. . . . It is absurd and not required by the [Taiwan Relations] Act that our representatives are not permitted to meet with Taiwanese officials with fairness and dignity.

To Beijing, the words uttered by the Republican candidate, whom they perceived as a man of the right, suggested that Reagan harbored affection for the Two Chinas policy. His election, which the Chinese may not have foreseen—they treated Bush, during his campaign visit to Beijing, with a reserve bordering on coldness—was disquieting to them. Also, the Chinese had already had some experience with the confusion that can accompany changes in American Administrations. In its early negotiations on normalization, the Carter Administration—apparently unaware that the Nixon Administration had already agreed that the United States would have "unofficial" relations with Taiwan—had sought to keep "official" relations. In a stormy encounter, the Americans were advised to go back to Washington and do their homework.

This question of officiality is deeply important to Beijing because any official action toward a foreign state implies recognition and recognition implies sovereignty. Our affairs in Taipei are handled not by an embassy but by the American Institute in Taiwan, while the Taiwanese maintain the Coordinating Council for North American Affairs in the United States. Foreign Service officers who serve in Taiwan resign before taking up their posts and are reinstated without loss of seniority or pension rights when they complete their tours of duty. In Washington, the Taiwanese are not received in government offices and U.S. officials do not call on them in their offices. This diplomatic apparatus is designed scrupulously to preserve the unofficial nature of our relations with Taiwan.

Therefore, Beijing's anxieties were not eased when the Reagan staff, in its first handling of this question, included representatives of Taiwan among those who were provided with tickets to the inauguration as "invited guests." The Taiwanese press spoke of these people as "official representatives" of Taiwan. Beijing objected, and the Taiwanese were disinvited. This episode accomplished the feat of exciting both Beijing and Taipei, and of exposing American clumsiness and insensitivity, at the very outset of the Administration. After attempting to reassure the Chinese, I reminded Richard Allen and other White House aides that the Administration must be punctilious in its observation of the rules of contact with the Taiwanese. It was a question that could destroy our relationship with China.

Soon afterward, however, the Chinese embassy complained that representatives of Taipei had been received in official U.S. government offices, even in the White House itself. Discussing this episode with the President, in the presence of Allen, Deaver, and others, I once again emphasized the importance of conducting our affairs with the Chinese with propriety. It was understandable, I told him, that the Taiwanese, sensing a friendlier atmosphere after the freezing Carter years, were seeking symbolic gain from increased access to Administration figures. But this could not be permitted. Removing the fig leaf of unofficiality could provoke serious and possibly irremediable deterioration in our relations with the Chinese. Deng Xiaoping himself was concerned and had referred to the possibility of a breach in Sino-American relations. The Chinese were serious people who talked straight and did not bluff. Every improper gesture weakened a reformist government in Beijing that wished to have good relations with the United States and at the same time liberalize the economic and social conditions of life in China. The Taiwan question could threaten Deng's government. Deng would renounce the United States before he would accept such a threat to his own effectiveness. It simply did not make sense to lose the People's Republic of China in exchange for the personal or ideological pleasure of having a Taiwanese in for a nonsubstantive chat. This was especially true because Taiwan had applied for the purchase of F-16 fighter-bombers, aircraft that were overwhelmingly superior to any plane in the possession of the Chinese air force. Taiwan also wanted to buy $96 million worth of spare parts for military aircraft supplied in previous years by the United States. Neither request had yet been approved by the new Administration—or rebuffed by it, either. These were explosive issues.

Characteristically, the President listened, thanked me for my advice, and deferred his own comment and action. I knew that there were substantial differences of opinion on this question among his other advisers. But it seemed imperative to me that the Administration recognize that American relations with China was among the most important strategic questions of our times. If that principle could be established early, then the question of Taiwan and our relations with this island could be settled without doing violence to American honor, Chinese sensibilities, or Taiwanese dignity and security. Otherwise, it would become a sump that swallowed even more vital issues.

Before coming to office under President Reagan, I had had some experience with the Chinese—and not only as a soldier facing them across the frozen terrain of Korea. In January 1972, I arrived in Beijing—or Peking, as it was then called in the West—to assist the government of the People's Republic of China in its preparations for the forthcoming visit of the President of the United States. For many months before, I had coordinated the staff work in the White House that supported the hidden negotiations that led to Henry Kissinger's secret mission to Beijing in July 1971 and culminated in the invitation to Nixon to come to China. In their respective memoirs, both Nixon and Kissinger have described how a series of harmonized American signals to the Chinese produced the answering note that ultimately made the President's trip possible and ended more than two decades of bitter and sometimes lethal estrangement between two peoples who had a long history of mutual sympathy and every reason to be friends. The opening to China had been conceived by Nixon even before he became President and was personally managed by him, after he came to office, in such deep secrecy that even Secretary of State Rogers did not know about this historic initiative until, after the successful completion of Kissinger's mission, the President instructed me to inform Rogers of the facts.

The Chinese seemed to regard my visit in January 1972 as a dress rehearsal for Nixon's; everything that he would do when he came to China, I did first as his stand-in. On my first evening in Beijing, I was guest of honor at a huge banquet in the Great Hall of the People, just as Nixon would be on *his* first night in the Chinese capital. This affair ended, after innumerable toasts of mao-tai, a Chinese liqueur that produces (in me, at least) an instantaneous hangover but not intoxication, at about eleven o'clock. At midnight, in a most Mandarin gesture, Zhou Enlai summoned me back to the Great Hall of the People. He was surrounded by what appeared to be the entire Chinese cabinet and press corps in a room bright with klieg lights, and he immediately launched into a vitriolic denunciation of the United States. The television cameras were turning. I interrupted Zhou, saying that I had not come to Beijing to hear my country insulted, and if this were to be the character of my visit, I would take my party to the airport and depart at once. Zhou heard me out, then clapped his hands. Cabinet and journalists disappeared. For a moment, I thought that I had derailed the entire operation. But after the others had gone, Zhou remained. Until three in the morning, he and I were locked in discussion.

Zhou touched on every subject that was of interest to our two countries, but he dwelled on one in particular—Vietnam. Though he never stated the case in so many words, I reported to President Nixon that the import of what Zhou said to me was: don't lose in Vietnam; don't withdraw from Southeast Asia.

It may be thought remarkable that Zhou, as the head of a Communist government, would subtly reflect such sympathies to the representative of a capitalist state that was at war with a neighboring Communist nation. But Vietnam by this time had become a Soviet client, and then, as now, the leaders of China regarded an American presence in the Far East as a necessary counterweight to Soviet ambitions. At the same time, the Chinese were aware of the tendencies of American policy. Tapping his shoulders, Mao Zedong had said to Kissinger: "We see you are leaping to Moscow by way of these shoulders." Even after the death of Mao, his suspicion that the United States was attempting to use China as a pawn on the chessboard of Soviet-American relations continued to haunt our relations with Beijing. After his trip to Beijing, Nixon engaged in summitry with the leaders of the Soviet Union. Kissinger and his successors pursued an active policy of rapprochement with Moscow. New Soviet-American agreements on arms control in the Nixon years were followed by the era of detente. Three successive American Administrations entered into a whole series of agreements and understandings—and, finally, concessions—to Moscow.

During my time as NATO commander, the Chinese kept in touch with me. Their ambassadors in Brussels and Paris constantly sought explanations for American timidity. When, in 1979, Chinese troops carried out their punitive expedition against Vietnamese forces, the United States condemned China. A Chinese general asked me how this was possible, when the Chinese operation had probably prevented the final proof of the domino theory. In light of American behavior and its consequences, it appeared possible, if not likely, to the Chinese that they had been used—that the United States had held up the specter of a Sino-American rapprochement as a means of impelling Moscow toward a Soviet-American condominium. Further, the Chinese leaders may have read other auguries in the robust position the new Administration took with regard to the Soviets and made subtle adjustments in their own policies as a result. Because China's relations with the United States are so bound up with her anxieties about the Soviet Union, an American policy that has already approached the outer limits of rhetoric and resistance to Moscow tends to diminish the incentive in Beijing for good relations with the United States. It follows that those relations might be risked with greater confidence.

The sum of these considerations was certainly a factor in the atmosphere of my first meeting with the Chinese ambassador to Washington, Chai Zemin. Our talk had been scheduled for thirty minutes. It lasted for an hour and ten minutes. Chai told me flatly that China could not accept the Taiwan Relations Act. In China's view, the act violated the Shanghai Communiqué and the Communiqué on Normalization, infringed Chinese sovereignty, and affronted the nationalistic spirit of the Chinese people. I pointed out that this Act of Congress was the law of the land, which Reagan, as President, was sworn to uphold. "You must meet President Reagan within the next two weeks," I said. "This will dispel any doubts about the Administration's desire to develop positive relations with China." I hoped that a relaxed discussion between Reagan and Chai, creating a strong first impression of friendship, would reveal the similarity in world outlook that existed between the new President and the Chinese on many issues and lay the basis for a policy of mutual understanding on the Taiwan question. Unfortunately, my hopes for a meeting of the minds between Reagan and Chai were disappointed. Chai is no polished diplomat. He is an old revolutionary and party workhorse, rough-mannered and given to glowering at capitalists. Central casting could not have provided a more stereotypical Communist. Reagan was a little taken aback. Besides, the meeting in the Oval Office was attended by Vice President Bush, Meese, Baker, Deaver, and Allen in addition to Reagan and myself, and, as usual, lacked the requisite intimacy. In essence, the President told Ambassador Chai that he wanted good relations with China, but that Beijing must not expect us to throw our old friends overboard. Reagan's manner was attentive, his sincerity was evident, but it was in the nature of things that he could not tell the Chinese ambassador precisely what Chai wanted to hear.

The Chinese clearly were unsettled by this first contact with the President. It was obvious that the Administration must, by some concrete act, reassure the Chinese of its friendship and its steadfast intention to live by the understandings in the communiqués. At the same time, it must honor its friendship with Taiwan. There had never been the slightest doubt that the spare parts would be sold to Taiwan. The sale of an additional $100 million worth of search-and-rescue helicopters and other items was also approved, and the Pentagon was instructed to examine Taiwan's need for FX aircraft. It was thought that her defense needs could be met by an interceptor with limited avionics that would present no threat to China. At the President's personal direction, guidelines were adopted for Taiwanese contacts with the Administration that observed the understandings with China but eliminated the hints of ostracization that had obtained under Carter. Very strong assurances of American friendship and support, including personal assurances from the President, were conveyed to the Taiwanese. All these matters quickly, if not instantaneously, became known to the Chinese, who appeared to have enviable sources of information.

In the early months, a policy for China was hammered out on the Cabinet table. I proposed that the United States change China's trading status to that of a friendly but nonallied country. This would take her out of the same suspect category as the U.S.S.R. and its satellites, who are regarded for purposes of the Munitions Act (and some 200 other pieces of active legislation, mostly surviving from the 1950s) as potential enemies of the United States, and place her in a class with Yugoslavia. This modification would make possible the transfer of somewhat more advanced technology, including so-called dual-use technology, which had both civilian and military applications, and permit China to make requests to purchase from U.S. commercial sources any items on the U.S. munitions list, including defensive weapons. Chinese applications to purchase weapons would be examined by the government, in coordination with Congress, on a case-by-case basis, as with any other friendly country.

In making this overture to the Chinese, we could expect to encounter a certain skepticism. In 1979, Carter's very able Secretary of Defense, Harold Brown, had gone to Beijing and held out the possibility of increased technology transfer, as well as the sale of armaments. Geng Biao, the Chinese minister of defense, had subsequently traveled to Washington and presented a list of items desired by the Chinese. "Secretary Brown listened to me," Geng would tell me afterward, "but I could see that he was thinking about the election." The Chinese received none of the things they had requested. For example, the shipment of computers—which were no longer state-of-the-art equipment in American terms, but which could be useful to the Chinese in completing their census, among other functions—had been delayed in the bureaucracy through rigid interpretation of regulations governing the sale of electronic devices that have defense or intelligence applications. The failure of the Carter Administration to deliver a computer for use in the census had developed into a particular sore point with the Chinese, who were then engaged in counting their one billion people, and who are, for understandable reasons, preoccupied with population policies.

The change in China's status was approved in early June, and almost immediately leaked to the *Washington Post* and the *New York Times*. No one imagined that the news would please the U.S.S.R. That evening, I encountered Ambassador Dobyrnin at a social event. Notwithstanding the rules of affability that apply on such occasions, he did not fail to tell me that he was upset, and that he was sure his government would be upset, by these reports of a change. There was no practical change, I told him; American policy toward the U.S.S.R. was the same as it had been before. But I reminded him that the Soviet Union had recently given a full battalion of tanks to Nicaragua and assured him that he need not fear that the United States would apply the same arms-to-population ratio in its dealings with China.

In early June, Deng Xiaoping sent me a message expressing the hope that I would visit China soon. Such a visit had been under discussion for months. In some respects, the trip was an opportunity to drive the bureaucracy and the Administration toward the policy I had been struggling to establish. The change in status for China was the first gain in ground in this struggle. The time seemed right to go. It would be fine, Deng said, to talk in a general manner; all issues need not be settled in advance; China had some problems, but they need not embarrass me. The President instructed me to tell the Chinese leaders that the United States was following a comprehensive policy to counter expansionism by the U.S.S.R. and its proxies, and to emphasize the permanent nature of the American presence in Asia. Second, the decision to consider China a friendly nonallied country underscored the new conceptual basis of Sino-American relations, based on strategic association and a commonality of aims in Asia and other parts of the world. Finally, I was charged with exploring the question of finding a modus vivendi on Taiwan, including the parameters of unofficial relations and arms sales.

Deng Xiaoping, though he is the de facto leader of China, limits himself to the modest title of vice chairman of the Chinese Communist Party Central Committee. In speech and manner, Deng is plain and modest. In physical stature he is small, but he has a spacious intellect and an impressive grasp of detail. He is said to have a caustic tongue and a contempt for incompetence. It was Deng whose bold and heretical policies provoked the Great Proletarian Cultural Revolution. As general secretary of the Chinese Communist Party in the 1960s, Deng instituted pragmatic economic policies. Mao Zedong, believing that these measures betrayed the revolution and pushed China back toward capitalism, unleashed the Red Guards. In the decade of turmoil that followed, Deng was submerged. In 1975, he was reinstated to his party posts only to lose them again after the death of his protector, Zhou Enlai, in 1976. After the death of Mao, nine months after Zhou, Deng reemerged and was reinstated for a second time to all his party posts.

"I won't use diplomatic jargon, just straight talk," Deng told me when we met on my final day in Beijing. The site was the Fujian Room of the Great Hall of the People. Whether the choice of this room was happenstance or a subtle reminder that Taiwan lies opposite Fujian Province in the East China Sea, I do not know. Deng and I spent an hour and a half together. Premier Zhao Ziyang had already accepted an invitation to visit the United States and extended an invitation to President Reagan to visit China. Deng expressed pleasure over this arrangement and warmly repeated the invitation to President Reagan. For a passing moment, Deng did lapse into diplomatic subtlety, saying that he had heard about my "very good talks" with Foreign Minister Huang Hua and Geng Biao, the defense minister. He hoped that we now understood each other better. I was glad to have this authoritative evidence that the Chinese were pleased at the beginning we had made.

But Deng complained openly about the failure of the United States to deliver on the promises made during the Carter Administration. In 1979, Vice President Walter H. Mondale had come to China and offered $2 billion in Export-Import Bank credits and a more accommodating policy on technology transfer. But the Chinese never received the loans and now they could not even get the simplest items of technological or military equipment. It would have been much more convenient to conduct a census of China's vast population with the help of proper computers. Deeds were more important than words. I told Deng he would have the full support of the Reagan Administration with respect to old promises, including the $2 billion in loans, and that the new status of China was designed to ease its problems in connection with technology transfer and military purchases, but reminded him of the necessity for congressional approval and action when laws were changed or funds appropriated. At the time, publicity surrounded a visit to Taiwan by Maureen Reagan, the President's daughter. At the end of our official talks, a Chinese official drew me aside and asked a question or two about this situation. "Perhaps there should be a law about traveling daughters," he said with a touch of sarcasm. "You Americans are so good at passing laws, I'm sure it would be no trouble for you to arrange this with Congress."

At last Deng came to Taiwan. Earlier, Huang Hua, with a Chinese flair for analogy, had compared U.S. arms sales to Taiwan to the British policy, during the American Civil War, of shipping munitions to the Confederacy. Huang had spoken openly of the possibility of a rupture in Sino-American relations over this issue. Deng was less threatening, but still somber. No Chinese government, especially one confronted with controversy within the leadership over this issue, could mishandle the Taiwan question and hope to keep the confidence of its supporters. Arms, especially, were a sensitive question. China had been tolerant, said Deng, but there was a limit. If the United States went too far, relations might mark time or even backtrack.

Despite the emphasis placed on Taiwan, the talks in China had been cordial and had accomplished what we set out to accomplish: a reasoned advance in the cooperation between the two countries, and a reasoned explanation on both sides of the views of each about the future of our relationship. However, on my final day in Beijing, President Reagan remarked at a news conference that the Taiwan Relations Act would be carried out as the law of the land. This statement puzzled me. The timing suggested that the President felt that, in carrying out his instructions, I had somehow got out in front of him on our China policy. His ill-timed words were an increasing irritant and dispelled a good deal of the cordiality that the dialogue in Beijing had generated. Protocol indicated that the foreign minister himself should see me off at the airport. Instead, the Chinese sent a vice foreign minister. At the airport, this official drew me aside and, as we stood together on the tarmac, asked me earnestly: "Who makes American foreign policy? Why are there always such surprises?" This was a question I could not diplomatically answer.

As summer came on, Chinese pressure on the Taiwan question increased. In early July, the Chinese delivered a demarche to our ambassador in Beijing, Arthur W. Hummel, Jr.: if the United States continued to sell arms to Taiwan, this would force China into a very strong reaction with grave consequences for the strategic situation. Meanwhile, a press campaign began in China, denouncing the sales. There were other signs that the antireformists in China, who continued to doubt the practical and ideological soundness of the opening to the United States, had seized upon Taiwan as an issue with which to confront Deng and his followers. In the circumstances, it seemed wise to delay any decision on further arms shipments to Taiwan until after the Twelfth Communist Party Congress, scheduled early in 1982. I so counseled the President.

The Chinese ministry of defense had designated General Liu Huaqing, deputy chief of staff of the People's Liberation Army, as the person who would come to Washington to discuss arms purchases with Caspar Weinberger. He was expected to arrive in the latter part of September. By August 25, we were able to inform Beijing that we were prepared to discuss a considerable list of arms with General Liu. About a week later, in Beijing, an official of the Chinese foreign ministry informed our embassy that his countrymen in the military establishment needed more time to study the American list, so it would not be possible for General Liu to visit Washington as planned. This news was delivered with bland courtesy, but as it involved a decision by the Chinese military to ignore an opportunity to buy badly needed modern equipment, it was a significant development.

Soon after this incident, I encountered Zhang Wenju, a vice foreign minister, at the United Nations. Zhang was in possession of facts relating to the (supposedly secret) Taiwanese request to purchase FX aircraft. Solemnly, he told me that "a shadow hangs over Sino-

In January 1972, Haig with then Chinese leader Zhou Enlai in Beijing: "What Zhou said to me was: Don't lose in Vietnam; don't withdraw from Southeast Asia."

In October 1981, with former Chinese Foreign Minister Huang Hua. Asked one Chinese official: "Who makes American foreign policy? Why are there always such surprises?"

Greeting Britain's Prime Minister Margaret Thatcher.

Debating Soviet Foreign Minister Andrei Gromyko.

With West German Foreign Minister Hans-Dietrich Genscher *(center)* and
National Security Adviser Allen . . . and with former West German Chancellor
Helmut Schmidt.

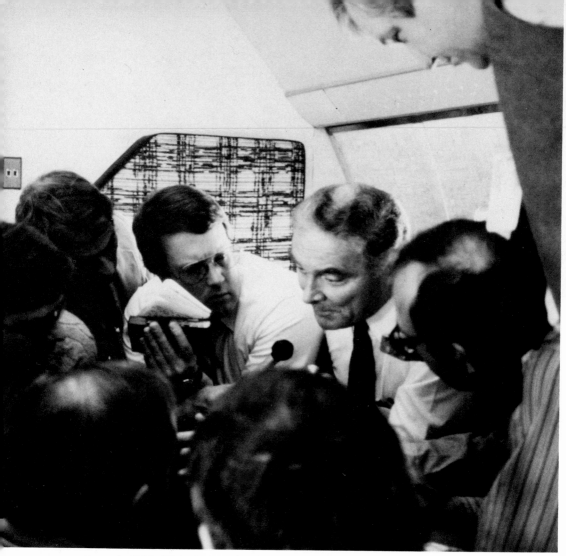

In early 1982, Haig *(center)* briefing the press while airborne on a hectic European trip.

Above: With the Saudi Crown Prince (now King) Fahd; *right*: Egyptian President Anwar Sadat; and Israeli Prime Minister Menachem Begin.

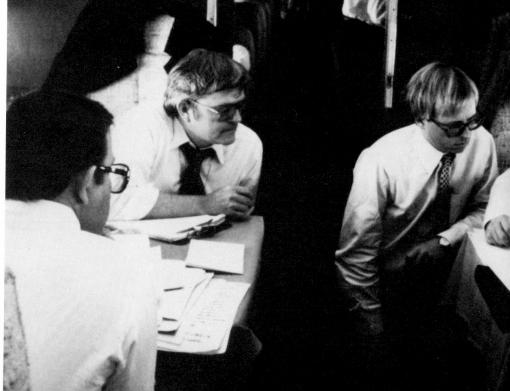

Haig *(far left)* as head of the American delegation attending the funeral of Anwar Sadat in Cairo. With Presidents Carter, Ford, and Nixon, and Mrs. Jihan Sadat.

In April 1982, shuttle-plane diplomacy between London and Buenos Aires. Haig and staffers fight a shrinking timetable while trying to avert war in the Falklands. "My efforts in the Falklands ultimately cost me my job as Secretary of State."

Secretary Haig announces his resignation.

American relations." The truth of this statement was confirmed in late October when President Reagan traveled to the Mexican island of Cancun for a summit meeting of North-South leaders. The Chinese premier, Zhao Ziyang, was present at the summit also. A private meeting between the two leaders was arranged. With the requirements of an international conference added to the normal burdens of his schedule, the President was even more pressed for time than usual; Zhao was invited to a luncheon in Reagan's hotel suite that was scheduled to last for precisely one hour. Once the pleasantries were over—Zhao made a joke about "the polar bear" that brought a smile to Reagan's lips—the Chinese made his country's insistent point: China wanted a long-term strategic relationship with the United States, but Taiwan was a problem. Reagan once again made the only possible reply: we wanted good relations with China, too, but the United States had been closely associated for a long time with the people of Taiwan and could not abandon old friends, just as we would not abandon China. Relations between China and Taiwan should be settled by the Chinese themselves without American or other outside interference.

Zhao then revealed that China was offering Taiwan a nine-point plan for reunification of the island province with the metropole (later rejected by Taipei and afterward broadened and reiterated). Under terms of Beijing's offer, Taiwan would be a special administrative region with complete autonomy. Beijing would not interfere in local Taiwanese affairs. The social system need not change; the Taiwanese could keep their life-style and their economic and cultural relations with other peoples; they could retain inheritance and property rights. They could have their own troops and national political bodies. This was an extraordinary offer. As Zhao recited it, pausing every few sentences while the interpreter put his words into English, he watched the President's face closely for a reaction. But the meeting was running overtime. Baker and Deaver reminded him that it was time to go. Zhao went on to the end despite the many interjections by the President's assistants.

Zhao slipped in a word about the danger of Soviet influence in Taiwan, should a power vacuum develop as a result of a delay in reunification. Reagan seemed startled. There was no danger of that, he said; the Taiwanese were not afraid of their countrymen across the Taiwan Straits. What they were afraid of was communism. Baker and Deaver were now fidgeting openly and looking at their watches.

With great self-possession, Zhao said that there had been one or two other things he wanted to discuss with Reagan, but as there was no time, Foreign Minister Huang Hua would tell me instead. The President said good-bye and turned his attention to his assistants and their schedule.

Perhaps it was just as well that Zhao's "one or two points" had not been raised in the impatient atmosphere of his last few minutes with the President. Even in much quieter circumstances, I was surprised by what Huang Hua had to tell me. In order to lay to rest the issue of American arms sales to Taiwan, he said, the United States must specify the period of time over which it intended to sell arms to Taiwan, undertake that sales in any given year would not exceed the level of the Carter years, and indicate that sales would decline year by year and then cease. I did not see how any American President could agree to such conditions and suggested that we discuss the matter when Huang came to Washington a few days later.

On October 29, in Washington, Huang repeated these demands and added the requirement that the United States give China assurances that sales would cease by a specified date in the future. This was an ultimatum. I could scarcely believe my ears. If ever there was an occasion for an unequivocal response, this was it. To make it, I raised my voice, and perhaps even thudded a fist on the table. "We have never insisted on an indefinite right to sell arms to Taiwan, but we have an obligation, and an imperative, to do so as long as reunification remains in the future," I said. "But to ask for a date-certain cutoff when the ultimate outcome of reunification, which we favor, is neither realized nor accomplished by your side, seems to be a profound departure. To have placed this new burden on this sensitive relationship will cause great problems. We, too, have our own imperatives! We, too, have a limit beyond which we won't be pushed! We have been shocked that you accepted the misconception that we were working toward two Chinas. That is absolutely untrue."

Huang seemed startled that he had provoked such a strong reaction. No American President—and especially not Ronald Reagan—could specify a day in the future on which the United States would stop helping a friend and former ally, not knowing what danger the friend might be in on that day. Leaving aside the moral question, the domestic political consequences—and the effect on Sino-American relations—would be devastating.

At this point both sides sensed that it was time to step back.

Huang had suggested high-level talks on the subject of arms sales to Taiwan. In our ambassador to China, Arthur Hummel, we had an extremely able and knowledgeable diplomat and negotiator. It was arranged that he and Vice Foreign Minister Zhang Wenju would talk in Beijing. It seemed to me that progress, even a solution, was possible; both sides wanted to avoid a breach. We must stand firm and not bend in the face of ultimatums. On the other hand, we could also give the appearance, at least, of making a concession: because more than a billion dollars in arms and military equipment had been transferred or allocated to Taiwan in the relatively brief period between the resumption of diplomatic relations with China and the end of the Carter Administration, it was unlikely that the Reagan Administration would wish to exceed these levels. Therefore, we could accept the Chinese position on this point even if rejecting all the others. That was a starting point. On December 4, talks began in Beijing between Ambassador Hummel and Vice Foreign Minister Zhang.

A week later, the Administration gave Congress informal notification that it intended to sell the spare parts to Taiwan. This leaked to the press, and the Chinese delivered strong protests in Beijing and Washington asking how the United States could take such action while talks were in progress. We told them that Huang's statement on October 29 had been a unilateral ultimatum that the United States did not accept. The talks continued.

The tenth anniversary of the signing of the Shanghai Communiqué would take place on February 27. In a letter to Zhao Ziyang, the United States suggested that the two signatories observe this anniversary with a visit by Zhao to the United States. No reply to this letter was ever received in Washington. In Beijing, Ambassador Hummel reminded the Chinese of the significance of this date and told them that the United States was not prepared to let such a historic decade end with a retrogression in Sino-American relations. As evidence of American good faith, he pointed to the fact that important decisions had been made to provide China with much of the military equipment and arms she had requested, and that measures to liberalize economic assistance, agricultural commodity assistance, import restrictions on furs and skins, and Export-Import Bank procedures would be submitted to Congress. A backlog of nearly 1,200 export licenses had been processed since July, with fewer than 50 denials. We also planned to ask Congress to repeal at least some of the legislation that restricted trade and other relations with China. On technology transfer, we made less progress as veto after veto was exercised by the Department of Defense. In communicating a decision to deny export of computers to China, the Defense Department explained that it did not accept the view that the sale of such technology to China involved no substantial possibility that it would not be diverted to the U.S.S.R. or otherwise used to America's risk. The fact that we knew that the Soviets possessed far more advanced computer technology than that which we wanted to sell to China did not seem to enter the equation.

Meanwhile, the Pentagon, after lengthy expert study of the matter, decided in mid-November that Taiwan did not need the FX aircraft in order to meet its defense needs, which could be met through continued coproduction of F-5E aircraft on a factory line that had existed in Taiwan for some time and by the provision of used F-104G's now in the possession of a NATO ally. Both these aircraft are interceptors that have little or no offensive capability. Holdridge went to Beijing to inform the Chinese of this development. He reminded them again of the proximity of the tenth anniversary of the Shanghai Communiqué and handed them a list of principles that the United States believed could form the basis of a joint communiqué settling the Taiwan question once and for all. During the early months of 1982, the United States and China exchanged many new drafts of the proposed joint communiqué. Small progress was made, and it was evident that agreement could not be reached before the communiqué's tenth anniversary.

The President had always believed that a frank statement of our good intentions toward Beijing, coupled to a manly explanation of our unshakable friendship for Taiwan, would produce results if only the right words could be addressed with sufficient authority to the Chinese leaders. With this in mind, he wrote to Premier Zhao, suggesting that Vice President Bush visit Beijing in May to discuss the matter of arms sales to Taiwan. The Chinese expressed pleasure and agreed. The prospect of receiving such a high-level emissary naturally raised hopes in Beijing that the American side had something new to offer. This, in turn, created the expectation that Bush would be armed with proposals and authority to settle the matter during his visit to China. But the President was not going to give. The staff at the State Department drafted new American proposals. Reagan worked over the draft and in his own hand—but with Bill Clark's assistance—toughened the American terms.

Bush went to Beijing, but he took nothing new with him. Nevertheless, Deng Xiaoping accepted the Vice President warmly. In speaking of the United States, he used the word *friend*, a significant choice of terms that had been avoided by other Chinese leaders. Deng's son was a university student in the United States; that, said Deng, showed the confidence he had in the nature of Sino-American relations. Now was the time to resolve the issue, said Deng; there should be no more delay. If the United States could not commit itself, he asked, then what was the way out? Bush said that the Taiwan Relations Act could and would be administered in a way consistent with the normalization communiqué. There was nothing new in this, and perhaps that was what was important about it. Deng may have seen that the United States could move no further. In any case, the Chinese foreign ministry presented new proposals to Ambassador Hummel within two hours of the interview with Deng. Obviously, Deng had decided to seize the issue if we could not. It seemed possible that the conditions for a breakthrough had been established.

There followed six weeks of silence and inaction on the American side. If Deng had his internal opposition, so did Reagan. Conservatives in Congress and elsewhere resisted any compromise with the Chinese that would further reduce the status of Taiwan. It was suggested in the press that Reagan had been "captured" by the liberals and the bureaucrats on this issue and was retreating from his campaign promises. Senator Strom Thurmond, Republican of North Carolina, and twenty-five other senators were said to be prepared to sign a letter asking the President to supply upgraded fighter planes to Taiwan. Senator Barry Goldwater wrote that he was "profoundly disturbed by the mounting evidence that we do not intend to honor our commitments to [Taiwan]," and stated his intention of going to the public on the issue.

Others felt as Goldwater did. In the emotional sense, at least, this company included President Reagan. The thought of abandoning Taiwan, or of giving the impression of doing so, was repugnant to him. In his inner councils as in the press, he was often reminded of the political cost of affronting his bedrock constituency. As late as March 1982, the President took the stance that we were going to sell spare parts to Taiwan whether the Chinese liked it or not; if they wanted to talk, then we would accommodate them, and if they did not, then there was nothing to talk about. While I agreed with the truth, if not the tact, of the first part of this statement, I was appalled by the second. I told the President and Bill Clark that if the President faltered in his relations with China, the Democratic opposition would leap on this question and turn it into a major issue in the 1984 elections. The refusal to search for a compromise on the issue of Taiwan could result in the most significant diplomatic disaster since the "loss of China" in 1949, and the party judged responsible for this failure would, and should, pay heavy political consequences.

This line of argument seemed to have some effect. Still, the negotiations had stalled, and I feared that if they did not begin to move again soon, the momentum generated by Deng Xiaoping's overture to Vice President Bush would be lost. In the months since these negotiations began, there had been an inevitable decline in my relations with the President. I realized that I had little capital left, and that I could not remain in the Administration much longer. But Deng was waiting for a response, and the future of Sino-American relations depended upon the answer he received. I sent President Reagan a memorandum recommending that he make a new proposal to the Chinese—and tell them that it was his final proposal.

The President's objectives all along, I reminded him, had been to preserve the strategic relationship with China, to preserve American honor, and to assure the continuing well-being of the people of Taiwan through a settlement that permitted arms sales to Taiwan with future reductions tied to China's peaceful approach to reunion with Taiwan. He must stake everything on these principles and make the Chinese understand that he could not move beyond them. The United States could not yield on the question of naming a date on which arms sales would cease. Any understanding with the Chinese on this issue had to be public; secret agreements cannot be defended before the public and the Congress. On the other hand, the Chinese had little room to maneuver. They must have an American statement that envisioned the goal of an eventual end to arms sales to Taiwan. But no such statement could firmly commit the United States to end such sales within a specific period of time.

The draft communiqué prepared for the President in the State Department affirmed, first of all, that the United States had no Two Chinas or One China, One Taiwan policy. Second, it reaffirmed Beijing's commitment to a peaceful resolution of the Taiwan question. Third, it offered the following language on the subject of arms sales: "The United States does not seek to carry out a long-term policy of arms sales to Taiwan and affirms the ultimate objective of ending arms sales to Taiwan. In the meantime, it expects a gradual reduction of its arms sales, leading to a final resolution of this difficult issue."

President Reagan approved the policy—after some subtle editing in his own hand—and, following the announcement of my resignation, this new and final offer by the United States was transmitted to Beijing. It was less than the Chinese had wanted, but with minor changes they accepted it. On August 17, 1982, the joint communiqué settling the question of arms sales to Taiwan was signed and issued. On reflection, it seems to me that my precipitous, albeit inevitable, departure from the Reagan Administration was the single act that made possible the solution of this critical question.

"Taiwan is important to us," a representative of the Chinese foreign ministry had told us months before, "but strategic cooperation is important to us, too." Those words also stated the American case with perfect accuracy. A compromise had been reached. A vital relationship had been preserved. The future with all its opportunities for the two principals and for many other nations had not been foreclosed. Emotions had been put aside and reason had prevailed. That is the purpose of diplomacy.

BACKGROUND

In Beijing, my executive assistant, Woody Goldberg, surprised by the forthright atmosphere of my talks with Geng Biao, the Chinese minister of defense, jotted down a remark to himself on the margins of his briefing book: "Haig is really being open with the Chinese." A page or two later, he recalls scribbling another thought: "I know why—the Chinese don't leak, therefore he can afford to be frank!" It was not until two years afterward, when Woody's doodles were resurrected in the preparation of this book, that either of us saw anything funny in the idea that the Chinese minister of defense was likely to be more discreet than some of our colleagues in Washington.

On the trip to the Far East in June 1981, we traveled 27,000 miles in sixteen days, visiting Hong Kong, the Philippines, and New Zealand in addition to China. We carried thirteen journalists with us on our aircraft and encountered many more when we were on the ground. At each stage, the press made it possible for us to footnote our diplomacy. It is not for nothing that every successful diplomatic encounter results in a communiqué. Diplomacy, as I have perhaps said often enough, cannot be carried out before the press. But it is also true that diplomacy, like justice, must not only be done, but be seen to be done.

A trip abroad provides a Secretary of State with splendid opportunities to explain his country's policies not only to the leaders and peoples of the countries he visits, but also to his own people back home. Sometimes, as in the announcement in Beijing that the United States would change its trade and arms relationship with China, the place where a decision is announced can add a certain dramatic weight. By separating the spokesman from the incessant background noise of a media center such as Washington, his statements sometimes become more audible. The traveling press knows this. My remarks in Manila, condemning the Vietnamese for their aggression in Cambodia, possessed a clarity that might have been lacking in a similar statement made in a routine news conference at the State Department, without suggesting, as Americans are wont to do, that the security of these states is more important to Washington than to their own governments.

Before I left Washington and after I left Beijing, I was able to reassure the Chinese on Taiwan arms sales by stating that the Administration felt no sense of urgency in supplying aircraft to Taiwan. Parallel assurances were telegraphed to Taipei through references to our commitment to its security. The President, of course, underlined this message in heavy black ink in his Washington news conference. The press also served as a medium for explaining, in detail, the difference China's new status would make to its ability to buy technology and such arms as we deemed it prudent to sell them.

Thanks to advances in electronics, the Secretary of State now takes the State Department with him when he travels. Cables, "scrambled" telephone calls, even photographic copies of documents, can be flashed at the speed of radio waves from any point in the world to the Secretary's aircraft. He is always in touch with everything, if he chooses to be. During my trip to the Far East, a debate took place in the United Nations Security Council on a resolution to condemn Israel for its raid on the Osirak nuclear reactor. The

United States understood that some sort of condemnation was inevitable. We did not wish to exercise our veto, but on the other hand, I saw no virtue in a resolution that might, through excess, further isolate Israel. The U.S. representative on the Security Council, Mrs. Kirkpatrick, and I had some differences of opinion on this question. As a result of a late-night conversation in a Wellington, New Zealand, bar between two members of my staff and reporters for the *New York Times* and the *Wall Street Journal*, self-serving details of the events connected to the resolution appeared, in dramatized form, in the newspapers.

In Hawaii, I tried to moderate the controversy, but as always, this was a hopeless task. The Kirkpatrick story, with its overtone of unchivalrous gossip, generated a controversy that obscured the results and the meaning of my mission to the Far East and spawned a whole new school of "think pieces" on strained relations between White House aides and me. Many ingenious analyses were offered. My favorite appeared in the *Washington Post*, in which "White House officials" were quoted as saying that the Kirkpatrick incident *"has damaged the Administration's ability to speak with a single foreign policy voice*[!]" [Emphasis added.]

" 'Tut, tut, child,' said the Duchess [in *Alice in Wonderland*]. 'Everything's got a moral if only you can find it.' "

ELEVEN

Nuclear Arms: "A Credible Western Deterrent"

IT HAS BEEN SAID of the Russians that they have suffered so many humiliating defeats at the hands of less numerous but qualitatively superior enemies, from the Asiatic Huns in the fourth century to the Germans in the twentieth, that they never feel reassured unless they have a five-to-one advantage in men and materiel, and never feel really comfortable until the advantage is ten to one. This is somewhat hyperbolic, but as a matter of fact, the West is aware of this Russian quirk and takes it into account—sometimes to its great cost—in calculating the balance of power with the U.S.S.R. There is, however, a point beyond which Russian paranoia—and the weapons that Russia requires as treatment for this malady—produces rational fear in others, especially when the shadow of Russian weaponry falls upon the backdrop of Soviet international behavior.

These are the motivations for the Western policy of deterrence. The subject of nuclear armaments is discussed by experts in terms that mostly do not occur in standard dictionaries. But *Webster's* has a plain definition for the verb *deter*: "to turn aside, discourage, or prevent from acting by fear or consideration of dangerous, difficult, or unpleasant attendant circumstances or consequences." The Western nuclear deterrent is designed to convince the Soviet leaders that any attack on the United States or its allies would result in a Western response that would cost the U.S.S.R. more than it could hope to gain by its aggression.

It is obvious that this essential element in the overall Western deterrent (which includes conventional as well as nuclear components) will only work if each side is convinced that the other has the means to survive a surprise nuclear attack and retaliate in an effective way. For thirty years and more, the United States maintained this certainty in the minds of the Soviet leaders through a combination of highly accurate land-based intercontinental ballistic missiles, B-52 bombers, and, later, a nuclear submarine fleet capable of launching somewhat less accurate ballistic missiles. Our superiority in these strategic nuclear forces was such that it had the added effect, over a period of more than three decades, of deterring Soviet use of conventional forces against us, our allies, and our friends.

So long as no doubt exists in the mind of an adversary, or in the minds of other nations, as to the adequacy of American strategic weapons to survive an attack and strike back, the overall deterrent is a force for peace. It is when doubt begins to appear on this score that the danger of war increases, because it is then that an enemy may calculate that he can limit damage to himself or even escape it altogether—or use what he sees as his own superior force as a means of blackmailing other nations into yielding to more conventional forms of aggression. By the beginning of the 1980s, the American deterrent had been placed in doubt. Over the previous decade, the Soviet Union had dramatically built up its own nuclear forces in terms of destructive power and technological improvement, while the United States had neglected to do so. It appeared to many—and, most dangerously, to the Soviet Union itself—that the U.S.S.R. might have achieved its long-standing goal of becoming at least the equal of the United States in the power and sophistication of its nuclear arms. If this was so, and if the United States failed to modernize its own arms, then logic dictated that superiority, if not already achieved, might soon lie within Moscow's grasp.

This question affected every aspect of American foreign policy and was reflected in all facets of Soviet international behavior. Military power remains the basis of foreign policy for all the nations of earth, whether they are benevolent or malevolent, as has been true throughout history. Nations accumulate military power in order to give themselves freedom of action and deny it to their rivals. In seeking the protection of stronger nations, weaker ones tend to choose (or at least not offend) what they believe will be the winning side. Strategic nuclear arms do not exist in a world of their own. They are much more powerful and terrifying than any of the weapons of the past, but fundamentally, they remain an expression of the strength of the nation that possesses them. A similar logic governs the relationship between arms control negotiation and other international policies. One may argue that nuclear arms control (and reduction) are such imperatives that linkage of negotiations in this field to Soviet behavior in other spheres ought to be irrelevant. But any such argument is likely to be dashed against the hard rock of reality; men, not weapons, make wars and conflicts arise from the pursuit of different interests, not the mere accumulation of weapons. No responsible American leader can assume that Soviet desire for reaching agreement on nuclear weapons means that Moscow will give up its habits of intimidation. Any such argument leads us back to the original premise: Moscow's international behavior is such that linkage cannot be dismissed, whether or not a given Administration declares a policy on the subject.

How can responsible American leaders assume, when the survival of the human species is at stake, that the Soviets have one type of behavior (benevolent and peaceable) when dealing with nuclear weapons and another (brutal and warlike) when invading Afghanistan or intimidating Poland or encouraging terrorism? It is Hobson's choice. Soviet expansionism and the almost heedless Soviet support for reckless proxies such as Qaddafi and Castro are, in turn, an expression of Moscow's sense of confidence in its strategic military power. Uncertainty about the future, which at the end of the 1970s was endemic even among nations that had been America's traditional friends, reflected a widespread perception that the United States was weaker than it used to be and the Soviet Union was stronger. Since there was nothing inevitable about this critical change in relationships, how did this happen?

In the 1960s, when the Soviets were building and testing huge rockets and very large, very "dirty" (i.e., characterized by large amounts of radioactive fallout) nuclear warheads, the leaders of the Defense Department convinced themselves, while overruling more experienced men, that the Russians were developing these clumsy systems because of technological backwardness. That was a mistake. These same leaders insisted also that the Soviets were building these systems simply to achieve a "more stable equality" with the United States, rather than superiority. Further, they insisted that we could keep ahead of them by means of our better technology (which we assumed would *always* be more advanced than the Soviets'), and especially through the development of miniaturization and what has come to be called MIRVing (for "multiple independently targeted reentry vehicles"), a technique that permitted us to attach several smaller warheads to each of our smaller rockets and guide them with greater accuracy to several different targets. This, too, was a mistake.

By the 1970s, the Soviets had mastered the technique of miniaturization, vastly improved accuracy, and MIRVed their own far larger systems, and were increasingly in a position to direct highly accurate and very powerful warheads onto our missile silos and destroy an ever larger proportion of them in a first strike. This produced a profound change in the balance of strategic power in the world and, I continue to believe, was the fundamental reason (the invasion of Afghanistan was merely the occasion) why the SALT II arms control treaty collapsed. SALT II risked giving the Soviets freeways for possible additional MIRVing of their nuclear weapons systems, employing their vastly heavier and more powerful warheads. This meant affording them the potential for dramatic improvement of their already superior capability of "killing" American ground-based missiles in a first strike. This multiplied an already worrisome Soviet ballistic missile advantage.

In the 1970s, the Soviets deployed an entirely new generation of land-based strategic missiles, three new submarine systems, and a new intercontinental bomber. In the same period, the megatonnage of American weapons was cut in half. America deployed no new ICBM's, no new ballistic missile submarines, no new bombers. Real U.S. defense spending shrank by 22 percent. The Army was reduced by three divisions and the number of Navy ships declined by half. During the Vietnam War, substantial proportions of U.S. defense expenditures were diverted to pay the operating expenses of the conflict, rather than being budgeted for overall force improvement. Today, according to the Secretary of Defense, three-fourths of U.S. nuclear warheads are carried on launchers fifteen years old or older, while three-fourths of Soviet warheads are carried on launchers that are no more than five years old.

Dealing with the reality of Soviet advances in the quality and destructive power of its warheads while negotiating a mutual reduction in nuclear arms presented great difficulties for the new Administration. The weakened position of the American deterrent and dissatisfaction with the results of the earlier SALT negotiations had convinced some that the negotiations were too dangerous to be undertaken at all. Conversely, I believed that we could not pursue policies that raised tensions with the U.S.S.R. and at the same time claim we were too weak to negotiate with them. Moreover, the American people would never agree to a posture that supported only a major arms building but ruled out negotiations that might produce greater security at less risk. What was required instead was a more realistic appreciation of what was to achieve arms control.

In 1979, testifying on SALT II, I had put forward three preconditions for a successful agreement with the Soviets:

(1) A modernization program for American strategic nuclear forces, (2) the improvement of what I described as the flawed elements of the SALT II Draft Treaty, and (3) the implementation of the NATO decision on the modernization of NATO's intermediate-range nuclear forces in Europe. By 1981, the building blocks were in place to resume the arms control process. President Reagan was, and is, committed as a matter of principle to reductions in strategic arms, and any perception to the contrary is mistaken. It was he who changed the name of the arms control negotiations from Strategic Arms Limitation Talks (SALT) to Strategic Arms *Reduction* Talks (START). In symbolic as well as real terms, this was an important departure from the past because it implied that the numbers of weapons would be systematically reduced, rather than *limited*, or reduced in selected categories. Early on, the President accepted the argument that the most stable deterrent should employ fewer weapons that are relatively invulnerable.

In the interdepartmental meetings to establish administration policy on START, the Department of Defense was understandably preoccupied with the disparity in destructive power ("throw weight," in the jargon) between Soviet and American weapons and argued for a decision that would have required an abrupt and fundamental change in the structure of the Soviet land-based missile force. The State Department advocated an approach that would require gradual reductions, with indirect restraints on the "throw weight" problem, on the grounds that this was negotiable while Defense's position probably was not. At the same time, we tried to adhere as closely as possible to SALT II, while identifying and correcting its flaws. In the end, the President decided, as Presidents are wont to do, to give each supplicant half the baby. On the basis of State's recommendations, he called for a reduction by one-third in the number of warheads (the previous measure of quantity) and conceded a basic point to Defense by stating that, during a second phase at a later time, the United States would seek a more direct reduction in the destructive power down to a level below current U.S. levels. More significantly, the President approved a limit of 2,500 ICBM's—a position that would require such drastic reductions in the Soviet inventory as to suggest that they were unnegotiable.

Unfortunately, the arms control process, like so many of the Administration's security-related and domestic initiatives in the early stages, suffered from the lack of a disciplined interdepartmental policy-making structure. The failure to delineate responsibilities clearly, or to establish bureaucratic authority at the outset, generated confusion and liberated a cacophony of vested interests that ultimately affected the quality of policy recommendations to the President. In arms control, the result was a flawed START position. Conceptual clarity was only achieved two years afterward with the formation of the bipartisan Scowcroft Commission. Because the commission operated outside the framework of the executive branch, it was able to cut across the interrelated disciplines and the competing priorities of foreign, defense, domestic, and arms control policy and achieve a coherent approach. But the device of the Presidential commission, successful in the cases of social security and the MX missile and arms control (the jury is still out, at this writing, on the Kissinger Commission on Central America), has a subtle but debilitating effect on the effectiveness of the Cabinet members who must ensure successful implementation at home and abroad of the policies that emerge from the commissions.

When, owing to its flaws, the initial U.S. position on START failed to elicit a Soviet response, the President, guided by the findings of the Scowcroft Commission, gave his negotiating team instructions to make our proposals more negotiable. In the fall of 1983, Reagan again modified the U.S. negotiating position through the introduction of the so-called build-down proposals that had been promoted by Senators Sam Nunn, Democrat of Georgia, and William S. Cohen, Republican of Maine. The difficulty with following a policy in which negotiating positions are publicly altered after negotiations fail to produce results is that the other side has little incentive to negotiate—it can achieve a retreat by its opponent without making concessions of its own. Ironically, many in Western Europe, who had initially believed President Reagan to be too inflexible on arms control, now suddenly began to fear that he might lack the determination to hold firm to a solid position.

By 1981, the danger to peace represented by the Soviet military buildup was obvious—indeed, was visible in Afghanistan and Central America and even in the streets of European cities, where every terrorist attack was a calculated insult to Western weakness and a contemptuous assault on Western ideas of the rights of the individual and the sanctity of life. In the late 1970s, the weight of a new arm of Soviet nuclear power was brought to bear on Europe itself, creating a situation in which Moscow might advance in a dramatic way toward its greatest foreign policy goal—splitting Western Europe away from the United States became more than an academic possibility.

It is common knowledge that the U.S.S.R. and the Warsaw Pact have always enjoyed a very large numerical superiority over NATO in conventional military forces. In the 1970s, the Warsaw Pact increased the strength of its conventional forces by one-third. These huge Eastern armies (in 1981: 60,000 tanks and more than 244 divisions for the Warsaw Pact, compared to 22,600 tanks and some 76 divisions [4.4 million men] for NATO) have been deterred, among other factors, by U.S. strategic nuclear forces, coupled to the declared American policy that any attack on any of its NATO allies is an attack upon itself. Yet from the beginning of the alliance, our European partners have been haunted by the perception that, in case of a Soviet nuclear showdown with the West, the United States would not actually be willing to risk the destruction of Washington or New York in order to save Berlin, Paris, or London. For three decades, this nagging European suspicion that the United States holds Europe's life cheaper than its own was kept under control by the reality of American nuclear superiority. When that superiority vanished, European anxiety grew stronger. Anxiety was redoubled when the Soviets introduced an entirely new element into the situation.

At the same time that Moscow was building up its strategic nuclear force, which is aimed essentially at the United States, it was constructing a second force of intermediate-range missiles, targeted on Western Europe. Beginning in the 1960s and early 1970s, the

Soviet Union deployed 350 SS-4 and SS-5 single-warhead, intermediate-range ballistic missiles. Earlier (and in my view, clearly related to the settlement of the Cuban missile crisis in 1962), the United States had removed its own considerable force of Jupiter intermediate-range ballistic missiles from Italy and Turkey and had never replaced them. Again in the 1960s, the West failed to provide an adequate response to the developing Soviet missile threat to Western Europe, a response that would necessarily have included the deployment of comparable new missile systems on European soil. Instead, Washington conceived the so-called NATO Nuclear Force, which envisaged a submarine-based nuclear force manned by multinational crews. This idea fell of its own illogic. In the end, the only U.S. response involved a certain number of F-111 fighter-bombers that were capable of delivering medium-range nuclear payloads. This failure in the 1960s, by the same leadership that misread the strategic nuclear equation, set the stage for one of the most serious threats to the core of the NATO deterrent since the founding of the alliance.

In the late 1970s, Moscow began to put a new and far more powerful and sophisticated missile system into the field. This was the SS-20, carrying three MIRVed nuclear warheads. The SS-20 had a range of some 5,000 kilometers (3,000 miles) and was capable of striking any city in Western Europe, the Middle East, or North Africa from bases on either side of the Ural Mountains. Moreover, the SS-20 is mobile and can be moved on short notice from one place to another. Militarily, this is an obvious advantage. From the point of view of verifying compliance with any possible agreement on reducing the number of SS-20's, it has equally obvious disadvantages.

By early 1981, the Soviets were installing SS-20's at a rate of two a week, and a total of 250 of these new missile systems (in addition to the 315 SS-4's and 35 SS-5's) had been deployed against Western Europe.* In addition to its missile force, the Soviet Union in the 1970s had modernized and dramatically increased the number of its warplanes, transforming its military aviation in Europe into an essen-

---

*The Soviets have continued to deploy SS-20's at the rate of approximately two a week while the European arms reduction talks have been going on in Geneva—and despite the fact that Brezhnev, in March 1982, had stated that Moscow would observe a moratorium on the placement of new SS-20's while the talks were in progress. By late September 1983, the number of SS-20's targeted on Western Europe had risen to 351, or 1,053 warheads. This meant that 1,100 Soviet medium-range nuclear warheads were aimed at Western Europe, which is, from the European point of view, a grave new strategic danger.

tially offensive force capable of delivering many hundreds of nuclear warheads to European targets. The Soviets had also developed a new shorter-range group of nuclear missiles designated as SS-21, SS-22, and SS-23, which the West anticipated would also be deployed. All this was accompanied by a major buildup of Soviet conventional forces and the deployment of an additional 100 SS-20's (300 warheads) against Asian targets, notably China.

This creation of a Soviet medium-range nuclear force, designed solely to threaten Western Europe and capable of utterly destroying all of her cities and infrastructure, turned European anxieties into a blazing fire. The debate broke into public view in 1977 when Chancellor Helmut Schmidt of the Federal Republic of Germany gave a speech in London in which he described the danger and called for an allied response to it. Schmidt's speech came as a surprise in Washington. In December 1979, with Schmidt's speech providing the initiative, NATO adopted its now famous "two-track" policy with respect to the Soviet missiles. On "track one," it invited the United States to install 464 new ground-launched cruise missiles and to replace the 108 obsolete shorter-range Pershing single-warhead ballistic missiles in Western Europe with the improved Pershing II type, which was then still in development. At the same time, on "track two," NATO committed itself to negotiations with the Soviet Union with the object of agreeing on a reduction in the number of nuclear weapons in Europe.

Out of this allied decision to counter a massive Soviet buildup of nuclear weapons that threatened the safety of the West, there emerged yet another European anxiety. Now many Europeans feared that the United States would, after all, be willing to fight a nuclear war with the Soviet Union, but would structure U.S. theater nuclear forces so as to confine hostilities to Europe. This new paranoia, which proved to have contagious appeal, brought tens of thousands of demonstrators into the streets in the cities of Europe. The Soviets were quick to see in this situation an opportunity for disturbing the internal political stability of the countries of Western Europe, and especially West Germany, thereby weakening the Western alliance. In a massive propaganda campaign, the Soviet Union played skillfully upon popular fears. Soviet leaders, including Brezhnev and high-ranking military figures, unanimously stated that in case of war the U.S.S.R. would regretfully have to eradicate the population of Europe, owing to the fact that the United States was threatening the

Soviet Union with the new missiles it planned to deploy in West Germany and elsewhere. Some of the rhetoric issuing from Washington on questions nuclear unfortunately helped to energize the frenzy.

The rhetoric was especially disturbing to me because it aggravated the European situation at its most delicate moment. Since the Second World War, the alliance had drawn on the strong roots of a popular transatlantic unity—the conviction that the destinies of the United States and its European partners were inextricably linked and that we could always do better by working together than by going separate ways. The European geopolitical spectrum, except at the fringes, had embraced the alliance as a fundamental fact of life. The disapearance of American nuclear superiority and the accumulation of economic troubles in the seventies had put great strains on this consensus. I have referred already to the new European "paranoia." But in the case of the great European Social Democratic parties, a new political dilemma developed. Earlier, these parties had been able to reconcile the rhetoric of socialism with a strong defense so long as the European economies prospered. Suddenly, the growing competition for resources aggravated by the economic turndown and the Soviet challenge drove the European Social Democrats toward unwelcome choices.

Unwise rhetoric from Washington facilitated the descent of these parties, especially Labor in Britain and the SPD in Germany toward anti-American rhetoric and outdated ideology. The consensus behind NATO on the part of the center left in Europe was and remains, today, in danger of disintegration. U.S. pronouncements on arms-control policy must take this factor into account.

The fact that new American Pershing II missiles based in Western Europe would be able to hit targets in Russia while Soviet SS-20's would "only" be able to strike European cities became the focus of the public discourse on the issue. It was the old argument that America cared more for Washington than for Paris turned inside out. Those 1,100 Soviet warheads, which were the real and present threat to Paris and every other European capital, apparently vanished from the collective memory. NATO's decision to temporize the issue by linking deployment to arms control, instead of merely proceeding with a long-overdue modernization, set a four-year propaganda clock running for the Soviet Union, distorted public debate, and turned the issue of the deployment of the Pershings from an unquestionable right of self-defense to a theological examination of the morality of weapons of mass destruction. In the latter case, the terms of the argument were so arranged that the moral question could be put freely to the West, which had deployed no missiles, and only gingerly to the East, which was putting missiles into position at the rate of one every 3½ days.

As I told Gromyko when we discussed these questions in New York in the fall of 1981, "The United States didn't force the Pershings on NATO—you did." The Russians did this because, in reality, the United States *does* regard any attack on its NATO allies as an attack on itself—and always has. But there was a bizarre side effect to this latest expression of a traditional bedrock policy. The fundamental issue—the threat of Soviet nuclear weapons—was overtaken by what may be called fear of Soviet fear.

The Soviets were eager to enter into arms control talks with the United States. Dobrynin raised the subject in his first talk with me and never failed to mention it in subsequent encounters. The Soviets were willing to talk on almost any basis. They naturally wished to consolidate the gains they had made in the SALT II negotiations, and so they spoke of reviving these talks. The Reagan Administration was not prepared to go ahead with this process, especially in light of credible information suggesting that the Soviets might already be in violation of some aspects of SALT II. Instead, the President decided to fall in behind the decisions of earlier Administrations to build and deploy the MX missile, develop the more powerful and accurate Trident II submarine, and, reversing the Carter Administration, build the B-1B bomber and further expand the U.S. cruise missile capability. With this reinforcement of the deterrent, Reagan would feel able, eventually, to propose a new round of Strategic Arms Reduction Talks that would seek more substantial reductions in nuclear arms levels and—most importantly—address in a more effective way the question of the Soviet advantage in first-strike capability against hardened U.S. targets.

Negotiation of the European nuclear question also presented difficulties. Inasmuch as the Russians had overwhelming modernized forces in place and we had no equivalent nuclear capability in Europe, our bargaining position was not ideal. It was made even more complex by the European political situation—the fracture of the Social Democrats over the alliance itself. Nevertheless, we decided to proceed. The West Germans thought they had a way out. The Schmidt government huckstered an ingenious basis for negotiations:

the United States would not deploy new missiles in Europe if the Soviets would dismantle the SS-20's and perhaps the SS-4's and SS-5's they already had in place. This came to be known as the Zero Option. It was enthusiastically championed by the Department of Defense. I opposed it, telling the President that it was a mistake that he would have to modify within the year.

The fatal flaw in the Zero Option as a basis for negotiations was that it was not negotiable. It was absurd to expect the Soviets to dismantle an existing force of 1,100 warheads, which they had already put into the field at the cost of billions of rubles, in exchange for a promise from the United States not to deploy a missile force that we had not yet begun to build and that had aroused such violent controversy in Western Europe. Caspar Weinberger, in his enthusiasm for the Zero Option, could not concede this point. In his hardheaded, repetitive way, he argued for adoption of the Zero Option on the basis of its potential for attracting public support [and like benefits]. I replied that we wouldn't want a Zero Option even if we could have it—it would risk uncoupling the U.S. strategic force from the defense of Europe and intensify the very doubts among our allies and miscalculations on the part of the Russians that we had wished to abolish or avoid in the first place. Furthermore, proposal of the Zero Option would, as it has, generate the suspicion that the United States was only interested in a frivolous propaganda exercise or, worse, that it was disingenuously engaging in arms negotiations simply as a cover for a desire to build up its nuclear arsenal. These were false suppositions that would needlessly weaken the President's credibility. In the end, however, Weinberger's arguments carried the day, and on November 18, President Reagan announced the Zero Option as the American negotiating position. It was ironic, if not predictable, that many of the European advocates of the Zero Option quickly became its most vociferous critics.

Dobrynin called the first meetings between Andrei Gromyko and me in New York in the autumn of 1981 "the most important Soviet-American talks in twenty-five years." That was a gratifyingly expansive opinion, but I did not think there was any prospect of agreement on any important issue in this first encounter, apart from setting the date and place of the Geneva talks. It had been arranged that there would be two meetings, the first on September 23 at the United States mission to the United Nations, the second five days later at the Soviet mission. There would be no dinner, no cocktail hour, no hint that a

glass of vodka or champagne could brighten the atmosphere of Soviet-American relations. As a symbol of hospitality, both sides laid
out tea and coffee, cookies and cigarettes, but these were left untouched.

Of Gromyko, the inimitable Nikita Khrushchev said, "He will sit
on a block of ice with his pants down until he's told to get up—or
lose his job." Gromyko has been foreign minister of the U.S.S.R.
since 1957, a longer tenure than any other foreign minister in the
world. Lord Home of the Hirsel, the former prime minister of Great
Britain, tells of a conversation about sporting guns with Mrs. Gromyko. She said, "If you buy a gun for my son, buy a better one than
you buy for my husband, because my son lets the ducks rise off the
water." Gromyko was ambassador to Washington during World War
II and was his country's first ambassador to the United Nations. He
joined the Soviet Communist party in 1931 and ever since has served
it doggedly and sometimes brilliantly, but he is no ideologue. When,
in the course of negotiations, he makes an ideological statement or
engages in a fit of temper, it is safe to assume that he does so on
instructions from Moscow or for tactical reasons. The Germans say
that Gromyko has "an Anglo-Saxon sense of melancholy," and if this
is so, it may be explained by the fact that he knows that he works for
men who will blame him if he permits himself to be tricked by the
Americans. In fact, Gromyko has a lively if utilitarian sense of
humor, marked by the weary sarcasm of a man who, in half a century
of diplomatic life, has dealt with every human folly—and expects to
go on doing so until the shrimp whistles.

"If we talk more about Afghanistan," Gromyko told me as we
discussed the agenda for our first talks, "nothing will be left but the
bottoms of our shoes." With an allegorical wink that reminded me of
the Soviet preoccupation with American strength, he spoke of his
first meeting, some forty years before, with W. Averell Harriman, the
wartime American ambassador to Moscow, and the impression this
tall capitalist had made on the young Gromyko: "*Very* big and
powerful . . . strong." Our delegation included Arthur Hartman, the
American ambassador to Moscow, who stands well over 6 feet. Gromyko gazed upward at Hartman and said jovially, in English, "He is
even bigger at home than in Moscow; Hartman is growing, always
growing." I pointed out that Dobrynin, who stood next to Gromyko,
was large also, so that there was no ambassador gap.

A good deal of edgy banter had already passed between us on the subject of a proposed joint press statement announcing the beginning of Soviet-American talks on the missiles in Europe. Because nuance is the language of diplomacy, agreement on the simplest statement of this kind always involves tortuous discussion. My aim was to keep the text short, factual, and neutral. Gromyko would have liked to introduce some history and a Soviet principle or two in order to play to the growing disarmament audience in Western Europe and the United States. Finally, he threw up his hands in mock despair: "This is unclarity on top of unclarity. One cannot go farther into the twilight without being in the black night!" There followed a steady murmur of "nyets" as I proposed modifications. At last I said, "Very well, Mr. Foreign Minister, we simply won't have a statement." After that, agreement came quickly.

On that same morning, before driving to the United Nations from my hotel, I telephoned Paul H. Nitze, inventor of the vicar principle in the conduct of foreign affairs and one of the most experienced and expert negotiators on strategic arms in the United States, and asked him to head the U.S. negotiating team with the rank of ambassador. Nitze, Reagan's choice for the job, accepted. The details of negotiations were now his province, but I wanted to tell Gromyko, in the unvarnished language that must be used in situations in which misunderstanding can be fatal, what the American position was.

I said nothing to Gromyko in private that President Reagan and I had not said to the Russians in public. "For a number of years," I told him, "there has been a lack of reciprocity on strategic arms control. While we were negotiating SALT II with you, and showing restraint on theater nuclear forces in Europe, you upgraded your European nuclear missile force. Now it is time to walk the cat back." Although Gromyko speaks and understands English, he prefers to listen in English and respond through an interpreter. The slower pace this introduces has its advantages: it gives time for thought and reduces the probability of emotional reactions. On this day, Gromyko appeared to want to establish an atmosphere of sweetness and reason. Without rancor, he made the expected point that the SS-20's and other Soviet nuclear systems targeted on Europe did not threaten U.S. territory, but the Pershing II would be within range of major Soviet cities. I told him that a threat to our allies was a threat to ourselves: that was the foundation of our policy. Taking existing British and French missile systems (162 warheads) into account, Gromyko added mildly, an effective balance existed.

It would not do, I suggested, for the Soviets to assert that a balance existed, then build up their forces while the United States stayed as it was, and then insist that a balance still existed. In fact, the Soviets at this point enjoyed an advantage of at least three to one in all types of nuclear delivery systems in Europe. Gromyko countered that Soviet calculations showed a 50 percent NATO advantage. If the United States intended to abandon the principle of equality and equal security, then the prospects were grim indeed, said Gromyko. I replied that the principle of equality was the very basis of negotiations, but "equality" could not be, as it had seemed to be to many in the United States in recent years, a formula for Soviet advantage. After this single exchange, we left the subject.

In the two years and more that have passed since these first conversations with Gromyko, the issues and the language have not changed, and the negotiators at Geneva have not yet found a formula to reconcile the fundamental differences that were exposed in that first talk. Subsequently, the President modified his Zero Option proposal to provide for the deployment of fewer Pershing II's, but that did not meet the objective of the Russians—which is to prevent the deployment of any modernized ballistic missile system in Western Europe—and it caused thoughtful European leaders to worry that the flexibility Europe had urged on the United States had been carried too far. A second proposal, which emerged after Paul Nitze and his Soviet counterpart went for a well-publicized "walk in the woods," involved abandoning the deployment of the Pershing II's altogether in return for a reduction in the numbers of SS-20's. If the objective of the talks is a balanced reduction in missiles, if the aim of Western policy is deterrence, if the American goal in Western Europe is to allay the anxieties of our allies and restore their confidence in our leadership, then the "walk in the woods" proposal works against our purposes on all three counts.

It cannot be the purpose of the United States and the West to accept the status quo: a situation in which the Soviet Union has more than five times as many warheads in Europe as all other nations combined is by definition a dangerous and unstable state of affairs. The same conclusion applies to strategic nuclear forces; there, Soviet advantages in destructive power and, possibly soon, numbers of warheads produce doubts about American capabilities and Soviet intentions that have already deeply disturbed the political and psychological equilibrium of the world and have the potential of doing far greater damage to the peace. Nothing in the history of our negotiations with the Soviets suggests that they are likely to surrender an advantage in the service of an abstract principle. The suggestion that nuclear weapons on both sides should be frozen at present levels is emotionally and politically seductive, but a freeze would not relieve danger. It would exacerbate the peril by freezing instability and uncertainty and making the anxieties it is designed to correct a permanent feature of international life. Any renunciation of the right to first use of nuclear weapons would have a more serious effect: deterrence is based on the threat that you will use your weapons and the belief on the part of your adversary that you will do so; if you abandon the threat, you relinquish the power to deter, and you also give the other side the option of waging a large-scale conventional war, or even launching a first strike of its own. Of all solutions, this is the most likely to produce the fatal miscalculation that has haunted the sleep of mankind since the invention of nuclear weapons. The Russians, who demand both these concessions by the United States, want to keep their missiles and be regarded as a peace-loving nation at the same time.

To a remarkable degree, they are succeeding in this paradoxical desire. Not everyone in the West is convinced that deterrence has, in fact, kept the peace. Some doubt the reality of Western fears about Soviet aggressive intentions. It is possible to theorize about the Soviet mind, but it is not possible to read it, or even to read Soviet archives. We lack reliable information on which to make a judgment. As a general rule, the trustworthy have little to hide; the Soviet Union is obsessed by secrecy; that is, at least, a reason to be cautious. Many critics, who include eminent thinkers and religious leaders as well as a large number of intelligent and sensitive citizens, question the morality, if not the effectiveness, of deterrence. They argue that we cannot defend human values by threatening to destroy them, and say that it is folly to build additional nuclear weapons when the two superpowers already possess enough missiles and warheads to kill everyone on earth several times over.

It is good to raise these questions. In answer, one must concede that deterrence must be morally acceptable to a free people or it cannot work. Self-defense has always presented man with a moral conundrum. To preserve our own lives, we must threaten to take the lives of others, and this threat puts our own lives at risk. The pacifist is prepared to lose his own life rather than take another. The current debate raises these alternatives to the level of civilization. When the values and peoples and institutions of the West were threatened by conventional weapons in the hands of an expansionist, ideologically extreme power in the 1930s, many believed that a policy of appeasement—giving Adolf Hitler the territory he wanted and the superiority in arms he required to allay his paranoia—would prevent war. The result was the greatest war in history, with some 45 million dead and the creation of conditions, which included the rise of an implacable tyranny at the center of the Eurasian land mass and the invention of nuclear weapons, that threatened the continuation of the civilization that the war was fought to save. In pondering the morality of defending ourselves against nuclear weapons, we must consider the consequences to earlier generations of questioning the morality of self-defense and basing policies on the unanswered question. To our own generation, the possible consequences include the epidemic spread of nuclear weapons. Suppose the nations of the world conclude that the United States cannot deter the Soviet Union and, instead of meekly bowing to the inevitable, decide to build minideterrents of their own? What would the prospects for civilization be on a planet with seventy nuclear powers?

The definitive answer to the moral question is: the only moral policy for the United States and the other free nations is a policy that prevents war. For nearly forty years, deterrence and peace between the superpowers have existed at the same time. This suggests that there is a connection between the policy of making war unthinkable through deterrence and the absence of war. Before breaking the connection, we should think long and deep.

BACKGROUND

In this chapter about nuclear arms, I have attempted to discuss the issues in standard English, and I expect that in so doing I have laid myself open to the charge of oversimplification. It is true that the artificial vocabulary that specialists in nuclear arms and nuclear arms reduction and control have developed has a certain precision that is useful within the priesthood, but the basic facts are easily understandable.

Public misunderstanding of these basic facts can only lead to suspicion and opposition, and contribute to a tendency to believe the deliberately flawed version of reality offered by the other side. A failure of communication on the part of the United States and the Western alliance is the only reasonable explanation for a state of affairs in which the Soviets, who enjoy a substantial advantage in missiles in Europe and unquestionable advantages in the destructive power of their ICBM's, are regarded as underdogs and the victims of Western threats by a great many sincere and intelligent people who live in the West.

The Soviets are simplistic in their propaganda. They describe their own fears and say how reasonable they are. This sets up a sympathetic response in frightened people in the free world and establishes an emotional bond. They say that the United States invented nuclear weapons and thereby started the arms race; the U.S.S.R., therefore, is a victim of circumstances. In the minds of free persons who believe in the value of self-criticism, this sets up a perverse equation of self-accusation and reassurance: if the West is worse than the Soviets, then it is not necessary to fear the Soviets because we know that we ourselves are not very frightening. The West, with its philosophical attachment to objective truth and its tendency to explain that things are more complicated than they seem, has been unable to develop a primer of its own that would serve the facts as well as the politics of the situation. It is not too late to do so.

Even between Republicans and peace marchers there are natural bonds of sympathy, though neither may easily realize it. In the Reagan Administration, I resisted the view, which was sometimes expressed by the President's more dogmatic advisers, that people who opposed American nuclear policies were wrong-headed or soft or unpatriotic. The peace movement and the Administration have precisely the same objectives: the reduction of nuclear arms. Members of the NSC and citizens who attend rallies against nuclear weapons may differ on methods, but they push on toward the goal of disarmament because all perceive that these weapons threaten the continuation if not the survival of civilization and the human species as we have known them. The most basic of all human instincts, survival, is engaged in the peace movement and in the President's councils—no matter who runs the peace movement and no matter who happens to be the President.

It is the duty of any Administration to listen to the messages contained in great popular movements and to try to understand their deeper meanings. But if the demands of a popular movement are likely, if adopted, to bring about results opposite to the ones desired by the movement itself, then leaders must not yield to popular pressure. Early in the Administration, when the nuclear freeze movement was at its apogee, some of the President's advisers urged him to consider calling for a freeze after the level of weapons had been reduced and equalized. This I opposed, and would oppose again, because only the word *freeze*, not the qualifier "after reduction and equalization," would have registered on the superheated surface of the disarmament issue. The United States cannot freeze if its deterrent is in question; the U.S.S.R. would never negotiate the conditions that would permit a freeze if it knew in advance that an American President was committed to a freeze. It would merely wait for him to institutionalize the Soviet advantage. Any commitment to a freeze, at present unstable levels of force, would be a cynical exploitation of a vulnerable popular mood and a signal to the Soviets of precisely the weakness and erosion of integrity that can lead to miscalculation and its unthinkable consequences.

In regard to the peace movement, the leaders of the United States must be understanding, sensitive, patient. The rank and file of the movement are sincere people. But a belief in the unthinkableness of nuclear war, no matter how passionate, cannot change the statistics or the reality of the balance of weapons or the meaning of historical experience. The American President must use Theodore Roosevelt's "bully pulpit" to explain, to reason, to repeat the truth. Political leaders must be realistic about the movement, understanding that, though at times it may seem to adopt the arguments and the vocabulary and the objectives of the other side and vilify them and their governments, it represents something deeper than an exercise in agitation and propaganda. The fact that its pressure has been directed almost entirely against the West, and almost never against the East, expresses the movement's underlying judgment as to where reason and the possibility of progress lies. Only the democracies can eliminate the possibility of nuclear war because only the democracies read messages from the people. Nobody seriously believes that the Soviet Union, if it came into political control of the whole planet, would eliminate nuclear weapons. They would simply convert them from a military to a police weapon and use them to control the populations of China and the United States and Western Europe.

If democratic governments have an obligation to listen, they have no mandate to yield, and must remember that even if there are a million demonstrators in the streets, they remain demonstrators. The leaders of democracies are the trustees of their governments from election to election; they are not vested by the voters with a quit-claim deed that entitles them to deliver the nation into the hands of any minority that has a sufficiently forceful argument with the decisions of the majority.

In the 1950s, an American journalist suggested that newspapers, when they quoted demagogues, should insert the words "this is not true" after every mendacity. Most saw the utility of this suggestion, but nobody has discovered a way of putting it into effect in a democracy. Nevertheless, there are ways to oppose falsehood with the truth, distortion with correction, and hysteria with reason. Once that happens, the peace movement will have the effect it wants in the place that counts: the Soviet Union. The fact is, a credible Western deterrent is the only thing that will make the demands of the movement as credible to the Russians as they are now audible to the West, because it is the only thing that will let democracy live long enough to deal with this fearful issue. The bomb will be banned only if democracy survives.

TWELVE

Poland: "What Now Exists Cannot Endure"

FOR the Soviet Union, Poland is a *casus belli*, a question on which she would go to war with the Western alliance. The Polish plain, that vast maneuver ground lying between the Oder and the Vistula, is the highway over which the armies of Gustavus Adolphus, Napoleon, and Hitler approached the Russian heartland, and it is the way west for the Red Army. Though many would disagree, it has always been my belief that the United States can influence Soviet behavior toward Poland, but it cannot break the political and strategic connection between these two unequal neighbors without taking up arms. The Poles themselves, though they have preserved a vibrant sense of nationhood by some miracle of ethnic will while enjoying only twenty years of independent existence and seven years of democracy since 1795, cannot be the masters of their own fate so long as the U.S.S.R. disposes overwhelming power and wills otherwise.

For the moment, those are the melancholy realities. Almost surely, they will not obtain over the long course. Where the indomitable spirit of a nation is involved, there is always the potential for evolution and for explosive change. As President Reagan came to office, nobody knew whether evolution or explosion would be the result, but it was clear that the Poles had decided to make history. A dynamic popular movement had arisen under the banners of the trade union Solidarity and, by means of a series of strikes and other actions that ignited the political imagination of the Polish people, had shattered the orthodoxy of the Marxist-Leninist regime. Solidarity was officially recognized as the representative of the workers, separate from the apparatus of the workers' state and the United Workers' party of Poland. The party itself elected a new chairman of the central committee, Stanislaw Kania, by secret ballot, with more than one candidate being nominated. These were truly Lutherian challenges to the dogma and the authority of the Kremlin and showed that the Polish situation was something entirely new and altogether more powerful than previous instances of restiveness in the satellites. The uprising in Hungary in 1956 and the Prague spring of 1967 were appeals for a better and freer life within the established system; Solidarity was a schismatic movement and changed the system, possibly forever.

Theoreticians of the reform movement in Poland spoke of establishing a second house of parliament to insure that Solidarity's reforms would be institutionalized, and discussed reducing the role of the Communist party to something resembling that of a constitutional monarch. The reformers had the open sympathy of the church in the most profoundly Catholic country in Europe. "For Moscow and the Soviet bloc, this is the most dramatic situation ever facing them—more than Yugoslavia, more even than the Sino-Soviet split," said Hans-Dietrich Genscher, the West German foreign minister, during a talk with me and the foreign ministers of Britain and France. Moscow knew that if the reforms in Poland survived, a contagion of democracy could sweep through the satellites and finally threaten the Soviet Union itself. The Soviet leaders could not permit this to happen. Therefore, there was never any question that the popular movement in Poland would be crushed by the U.S.S.R. The only questions were: when will this happen, and with what degree of brutality?

In the councils of the Administration, I spoke of postponing the day and of minimizing the brutality by discouraging direct intervention by Soviet troops. To some of the President's other advisers, these policies were not sufficiently red-blooded, despite the fact that the United States alone hadn't the military power or the interrelated diplomatic influence to go farther. It was clear, in the very first discussions of the Polish situation, that some of my colleagues in the NSC were prepared to look beyond Poland, as if it were not in itself an issue of war and peace, and regard it as an opportunity to inflict mortal political, economic, and propaganda damage on the U.S.S.R. These same men seemed to imagine that the United States could control Soviet behavior toward Poland, or even defeat her purposes, through the application of economic and trade sanctions that would "bring her to her knees."

This was a questionable proposition. Total American trade with the U.S.S.R. amounts to less than 1 percent of the Soviet gross national product. The extent to which the Russians are dependent, or willing to reveal their dependence, on imports from the United States was illustrated by the results of lifting the grain embargo. Although, as we have seen, the U.S. Secretary of Agriculture and others looked on the termination of the embargo as a way of rescuing the financial position of the American farm industry, the Soviets in fact bought no grain from the United States in the two years following the lifting of the embargo—and then only after the United States gave Moscow the astonishing guarantee that there would be no future interruptions, motivated by foreign policy considerations, of contracted shipments from U.S. suppliers.

This did not mean that the United States could have no influence on the outcome in Poland. But the Polish situation was heavy with the possibility of death and repression on a horrifying scale. Ever since the hand of Russia fell on Eastern Europe at the end of World War II, many have predicted that the people of the satellites would one day rise up and, in the resonant phrase that expresses this state of mind, "roll back communism." In 1956, the freedom fighters of Hungary (for whom the term was invented) had battled Soviet tanks in the streets, but the United States had not rescued them. This memory was a stark warning to us. If the Poles were to rise in response to what they took to be a signal of encouragement from Washington and fight their own government or the Red Army or both, the outcome could be no different than it had been in Budapest. I detected no willingness on the part of the hardliners around the Cabinet table or in the NSC to risk international conflict or shed American blood over Poland, nor would any rational official have advocated such a policy.

What, then, could we do? American aims were simple: to keep Soviet troops out of Poland, and to preserve the reforms achieved by

Solidarity. First, we could avoid any statement or action that might encourage a hopeless armed resistance on the part of the Polish people. Second, we could tell the Soviets, in plain words and on every possible occasion, that intervention in Poland would severely damage Soviet-American relations and imperil the prospects of agreements on questions vital to Moscow. Third, in full consultation with our European allies, and in concert with them, we could alleviate Poland's desperate economic situation through financial measures and the shipment of food to the Polish people. Fourth, should the Polish people be suppressed, we could—again in concert with our allies—apply sanctions to the U.S.S.R. and those in Poland responsible for the outrage.

In the end, Reagan accepted the broad outlines of this policy, and thereby largely avoided making the dangerous mistake that many urged upon him. But to appease them, and also because his sympathies were often with their arguments even if his good sense was not, his Administration took other steps that started the most serious squabble within NATO in recent memory and placed self-generated strains on the alliance at the very time when Western unity was essential in order to deal with a whole range of politically explosive issues. Each of these issues—the introduction of a new generation of nuclear missiles into Europe, arms control and reduction, East-West trade, the interrelationship between the American economy and those of its European allies—was to some extent hostage to events in Poland.

It was, therefore, supremely ironic that when the hammer of American economic power finally smashed down, it did not strike the Russians or the military government of Poland, as the hardliners had wanted, but instead battered our friends and allies. In its anxiety to conduct an exemplary public punishment of the Soviet Union, Washington first demanded that its European allies stop supplying American technology for the building of the trans-Siberian pipeline that was designed to carry natural gas to Western Europe, and when the allies demurred on grounds of legality, economics, and sovereignty, applied sanctions to *them*.

Until Western unity collapsed in the early months of 1982 over the pipeline issue, however, the official American approach to the Polish situation was consistent and firm and coordinated with the allies. This process began in the last year of the Carter Administration when, alerted at last by Afghanistan, it joined the Europeans to put in place excellent NATO contingency plans in case of a Soviet invasion of Poland. Plans for dealing with an *internal* suppression were, however, very much less satisfactory, an omission that was not repaired, to our cost and Poland's and Europe's, during my period as Secretary of State. We were, however, worried from the start. The very first communication addressed to the Soviets by the Reagan Administration, a letter from me to Andrei Gromyko on the day after the inauguration, expressed American concern over the possibility of Soviet intervention in Poland. In every meeting with Gromyko and Anatoliy Dobrynin, from beginning to end, I said emphatically that all hope of progress on every question involving the United States and the Soviet Union depended on Soviet behavior toward Poland. "We will stay out," I told Dobrynin in the early spring of 1981, "and we want you to do the same." Always, in reply, I heard from the somber Russians some version of the earliest words Dobrynin spoke to me on this subject: in Poland, the Soviet Union would do what it had to do. But often, too, I heard suggestions that the Soviets had taken our concern into account.

When Andrei Gromyko and I met in New York on September 23, 1981, in my first encounter with him as Secretary of State, I seized the occasion to tell Gromyko that the Polish situation was a matter of great concern to the United States: "Any external involvement in the internal affairs of the Polish people will lead to grave consequences in connection with everything we have spoken of, in connection with everything we hope to achieve." Gromyko made no reply. The talks went on to the end of a gray and overcast afternoon. At that time, Gromyko was seventy-two years old. At the beginning of the meeting he had seemed fit and younger than his years, but at the end he looked aged and tired, and wiped his brow with his bare hand in apparent fatigue and relief. Perhaps he was glad that nothing worse had been said about Poland, and realized that when he and I met again, the subject in all its danger for the world and shame for the Soviet Union would not be so easy to avoid.

In the meantime, Moscow was following a policy designed to squeeze Poland economically and politically in the expectation that the resultant collapse would open the way to replacing the present leadership in Warsaw with a new regime that would reverse the reform process and, by following instructions from the Kremlin, put a Polish face on a Russian solution. Poland was close to bankruptcy. The interest and principal due in 1981 on its foreign debt amounted to nearly $12 billion. The Polish treasury was unable to pay any meaningful part of this sum. The country's reserves of food were 44 percent lower than in the previous year, and it suffered from serious food shortages. Owing to strikes and work stoppages, among other factors, some sectors of Polish industry were operating at a rate 30 percent below capacity. An unprecedented decline of 15 percent in gross national product was forecast for 1981. Imports had fallen by 20 percent in a year because Poland had no hard currency with which to pay for foreign goods. Without the West, Poland could not finance imports, and the lack of food and goods would heighten unrest.

The possibility that Poland might default on her foreign debt was extremely disturbing to the West Europeans, especially the Germans, whose banks had risked very large sums throughout Eastern Europe. If default by Poland led to default by other countries in the bloc, the consequences to the German financial community, and to the wider European and American banking systems, would be severe. Attractive as default may have seemed to some as a demonstration of the utter failure of Poland's Marxist economy, it was not an option the West could exercise. Quite apart from the huge financial loss it represented for Western lenders and the shadow it would cast upon East-West trade, default was in Moscow's interest because it weakened the Polish government and thereby brought Soviet intervention so much closer.

The Soviets withheld credit, lined up a new military government for Poland, and maneuvered troops near the Polish frontier. Within Poland, the mood remained bleak. All across the country, women organized hunger marches to protest the shortages of food. Agitation by the workers continued in a spirit of reckless defiance. A leader of Solidarity told an American diplomat that the reform movement acknowledged that there was no more slack in the economy, "but, as the horse has run away, the rider has no choice but to hang on." The potential for violent unrest, and for the almost certain intervention of Soviet tanks that popular disturbances would provoke, was very great.

For a few hours, early in this tumultuous Polish year, it seemed possible that intervention had come. In late March, the Warsaw Pact staged large-scale military exercises, called Soyuz 81. These were described as routine springtime maneuvers, and routine monitoring by our intelligence system suggested nothing to the contrary. Then on April 3, as President Reagan lay in the hospital recovering from his wounds, the intelligence community reported unusual Soviet troop movements toward the Polish frontiers from East Germany, Czecho- slovakia, and the U.S.S.R. itself. These included infantry and ar- mored columns and airborne formations. The twelve Soviet divisions normally stationed in and around Poland appeared to be in a high state of readiness. Soviet aircraft evaded Polish radar by flying be- neath it and entered Polish airspace. Soviet troops had been moved into Warsaw to protect the compounds in which Soviet personnel were housed. In a number of West European capitals, Soviet embas- sies that were, at the moment, untroubled by demonstrators, had asked for extra police protection from "Trotskyites." Leonid Brezh- nev was en route to Prague for a summit meeting of the Warsaw Pact. Czech airspace had been closed.

These were ominous signs, but did they constitute a pattern? In the State Department operations center, we asked ourselves the ob- vious questions: were the Russians moving in? were they raising the level of intimidation? was this a prelude to a declaration of martial law by the Polish government? I considered postponing my trip to the Middle East, scheduled to begin that evening. At the end of a long day, however, it appeared that Soviet troop movements had abated. Whatever Moscow's purpose had been, it did not on this particular Friday include an invasion of Poland. We stood down the watch and I boarded my plane for Cairo. But the Soviet actions of the day had reminded us, if any reminder was needed, of the power realities in Eastern Europe and of the sword that hung over Poland's head.

The Europeans were keenly aware of power realities, and the alliance was profoundly disturbed by them. More than anything else, the Soviet leaders want to split the United States away from Western Europe. American vacillation in the 1970s gave them their best op- portunity since World War II. The Soviets knew that the kind of action they took in Poland could have a good or bad effect on their goal. They had also witnessed the belated awakening of the Carter Administration and were now faced with a new American leadership that was even more dedicated to challenging Soviet behavior. If they proceeded in ways that did not unduly alarm the West, then possibly they could preserve some of the gains they had made in winning the esteem of important elements in West European society.

If these considerations had the good effect of moderating Soviet behavior toward Poland, they also revealed disquieting evidence that detente had opened a gap between America and its allies. Where the strategic vision of the United States detected wars of liberation and Soviet adventuring at the margins of the Free World as the result of a policy of accommodation with the U.S.S.R., the Europeans looked eastward and saw increased trade, renewed contact with their ancient neighbors in what used to be called Central Europe, and the possibility of relief from the remorseless psychological pressure that Soviet military power and hostile Soviet diplomacy have exerted on the European mind since 1945. It is well to remember what war has meant to Europeans in this century: over 50 million dead in two "conventional" world wars, the wanton destruction of cities that were the very symbols of Western culture, more civilians dead in Berlin between 1942 and 1945 than the total of American battle deaths in all theaters of operation for the entire war.

If Poland had become the freest country in Eastern Europe as a result of the reforms achieved by Solidarity, it was also the most economically troubled. It was clear that Poland could not pay higher wages to the workers and also pay her debts. As the months passed, the West struggled to find a way for the reforms in Poland to survive the terrible problems of debt and shortage that beset the country. On every possible occasion—as at NATO ministerial meetings in Rome and Brussels—I met with the foreign ministers of Britain, France, and Germany to discuss the problem. The U.S. Treasury Department and the finance ministries of our European allies were continually engaged in examining complex details of the Polish debt. In August, Poland reported a $1.5 billion deficit in hard currency. The Europeans estimated that she would need as much as $700 million worth of food before the end of the year. The West Germans had lowered the down payment on food exports from 15 percent to 5 percent, but the Poles could not even pay that. France reduced its own down payment to zero and sent meat, grain, sugar, and oil to Poland. I recommended to the President that the United States provide immediate food aid to the Polish people as a means of buying time for their experiment in liberalization. Eventually, an additional $50 million was allocated to this purpose.

Finally, a way was found to postpone the crisis of Poland's debt. By late August, $9 billion of Poland's foreign financing needs for 1981 had been met, with the United States providing $1.1 billion in credits and our allies furnishing the rest. Warsaw still needed an additional $1.6 billion, which had been expected from Moscow but did not materialize. We estimated that similar or greater sums would be required from Western treasuries for the next several years to sustain Poland's economy. In the end, the Polish debt for 1981 was rescheduled with a four-year grace period; repayment would now take place over an eight-year period beginning in 1986. We and our allies urged membership for Poland in the International Monetary Fund (IMF), which could promote and monitor economic reforms, but the Poles needed to apply for membership on their own behalf. Understandably, they did not choose to do so without Soviet approval. This was not immediately forthcoming.

In September, the Soviet Communist party warned Poland that anti-Soviet activities by its citizens must be curbed. The Polish prime minister, General Wojciech Jaruzelski, told Solidarity that its actions were jeopardizing the "independent existence" of the country, and instructed the army and police to take steps to end anarchy and anti-Sovietism. In October, Jaruzelski, who had generally followed a policy of accommodating Solidarity, became head of the Polish Communist party while keeping his post as premier. The central committee of the party, on October 18, authorized the government to use military force against striking workers. This gave the Warsaw government the power to impose martial law. These were clear danger signals. On November 13, I wrote to the President saying that the progress made by the Polish people was still fragile, but the importance of Poland's peaceful revolution as a demonstration that Moscow's power could be challenged and confounded could not be overestimated. If what had happened in Poland could be consolidated, this would be a historic event for the people of Eastern Europe and for Western values. Once again, I reminded the President that our ability to influence events was limited.

As the year approached its end and the worst still did not happen, a deceptive calm settled over the Polish question. On the evening of Saturday, December 12, 1981, I dined in Brussels—where I had stopped for a meeting of the North Atlantic Council en route to the Middle East—with a Belgian friend, Baron Leon Lambert, who asked me with the skepticism of old acquaintance what had ever happened to my predictions of a wave of repression in Poland. "It will still come," I replied, "and when it does, it will come on a weekend, when the factories are closed." Though I did not know it, and had no foreknowledge of events, suppression would come that very night as General Jaruzelski declared a "military government of national salvation," suspended the operations of Solidarity, closed the borders, broke communications with the outside world, and rounded up and arrested a large number of citizens. We recognized at once that, for the time being at least, martial law, rather than something worse, had been imposed upon Poland.

The news was flashed to me at three o'clock Sunday morning in Brussels. The timing of this action, which obviously had been meticulously prepared—and which we knew had been planned in minute detail in the U.S.S.R.—came without forewarning to the United States. For a period of many days, Poland had been covered by thick cloud, so the movement of troops and militia and the other signs that might have been observed by space satellites were undetected. We had expected that the suppression would come at the hands of internal Polish forces, but discussions with allied governments failed to develop a consensus on the actions that might be taken by the West in this contingency. We had known for many months what we would do in case of direct Soviet intervention; but there was no certain plan of action in the more ambiguous case of internal crackdown.

A secure telephone had been placed in my room at the Hyatt Regency Hotel, and I used this instrument to reach the American embassy in Warsaw. Over a crackling connection, the chargé d'affaires told me that he had been called into the Polish Foreign Ministry a short time before and told that "the reforms will continue." However, the government had rounded up some leaders of the dissident movement in Warsaw and perhaps elsewhere, and there were indications that the People's Militia, an organization of toughs whose mission was control of the population, had been activated. There was an unconfirmed rumor that a Solidarity meeting in Gdansk had been surrounded by troops. But Lech Walesa, the leader of Solidarity, had not yet been arrested, and this suggested a policy of caution and a fear of popular resistance on the part of Jaruzelski. On the surface, it appeared that the action was being taken by the Polish government without the overt participation of the Soviets. So long as that state of affairs continued, the events in Poland were an internal matter. But, though they were almost ostentatiously not in a state of alert, massive Soviet forces were in position in case of violent resistance within Poland. The question was, could the Polish government control the violence if it occurred? The next twenty-four hours were a period of great danger for the Polish people.

President Reagan was spending the weekend at Camp David. Bill Clark, who would soon replace Richard Allen as National Security

Adviser, told me on the telephone that the President's staff was weighing the possibility of calling Reagan back to the White House for a special NSC meeting on Poland. I advised against this. A hurried return by helicopter, followed by a crisis-style meeting, might prematurely raise international temperatures. Our objective was to remain calm and steady. I phoned Vice President Bush and repeated this opinion. It was just after two in the morning. "Nothing will happen in Washington for now, Al," Bush replied, presumably over his bedside phone. "No one is up yet." Caspar Weinberger was somewhere above the Atlantic, returning to Washington from one of his many missions abroad. I took the opportunity of calling him aboard his aircraft and mentioning that it behooved us all to speak cautiously in public, and especially to the press, on this issue.

Lord Carrington, the British foreign secretary, was already in Brussels, while Claude Cheysson, the French foreign minister, and Genscher of West Germany were expected shortly. At first light, I phoned all three to ask their opinions of the situation and suggest a meeting. Fortunately, Genscher had not accompanied Helmut Schmidt to East Germany, where the chancellor was visiting over the weekend—a circumstance that produced signs of concern in Genscher. Poland was a crisis that took priority, while it lasted, over almost any other issue. It was essential to preserve allied unity and produce action on the part of the unified West that would send a signal of warning to the Polish government and the Soviets without, at the same time, further inflaming passions within Poland. The fact that the foreign ministers of our principal allies were present in Brussels, or soon would be, persuaded me that I must postpone my trip to the Middle East and remain in Brussels, close to the situation, and close to our allies, for the next twenty-four hours, and then return to Washington.

In these early hours we were handicapped by the absence of information. Our allies seemed to have no better data than we, and the press had so far been effectively muffled by the cutoff in telephone and telegraph traffic to and from Poland. Though we made many attempts to establish contact with our embassy in Warsaw over a secure satellite link, we were unsuccessful. Communication with the Vatican revealed that the Holy See had been as surprised as everyone else in the West by the combination of stealth and clockwork action that had overtaken the reformists in Poland. In Washington, Poland had not been a topic of urgent discussion for several days. For many months, in the State Department, we had discussed contingency plans, mulled over checklists, speculated on the form the action against liberalization would take. Now that the inevitable had happened, we were, in our surprised state, far from the operations center in a hotel suite in Belgium, with no files of memoranda, no indexes of plans, no checklists. We had to rely instead on memory, experience, and the broadest policy considerations. I was very glad to have Larry Eagleburger, who had a steady hand and experience in abundance, at my side, along with the other seasoned members of the traveling staff.

After five hours of activity, it was still quite early in the morning in Brussels. The hotel suite had filled up with aides and the coffee cups and tobacco smoke that are the signs of busy people attempting to remain alert at unnatural hours of the night. I put on my coat and went for a walk in a nearby park. The morning was sunny, cold, and crisp. On the icy surface of a pond, a flock of ducks waited patiently for whoever usually fed them. The exercise and the cold air cleared my head but did not alleviate my anxiety for the people of Poland. I knew how little the West could do to help them. Until some agreed approach emerged, we could do little but maintain our unity and cool our rhetoric.

In the early afternoon, I attempted to reach President Reagan, but it was still barely eight o'clock on a Sunday morning at Camp David, and he hadn't yet gotten up. The French had already issued a statement warning against outside interference in what they regarded as an internal affair of the Poles and postponing a visit to Warsaw by the French premier. The foreign ministers of the European Community would meet in London the next day. Dr. Joseph Luns, secretary general of NATO, had called a meeting of the foreign ministers of NATO and had formally called the foreign ministers of "the Quad"—Britain, France, West Germany, and the United States—together for consultation that afternoon. These events would also make a public impression. It was true that the Polish government, by acting on a Sunday, had taken advantage of the normal weekend news brown-out in the West, but nevertheless, I felt that the United States, partly because of the time difference, was somewhat behind the action. It was important that Washington take such initiatives as it could as early as possible, and it was important that it lead the alliance in these important hours.

On my next attempt, I reached the President. He agreed that he had awakened to an atmosphere of excitement and agreed, too, on the importance of a calm, reasoned public posture on the part of the United States government. I gave him such information as I had. We could not be sure where this situation would lead. We must avoid committing ourselves to any line of action, avoid excessive provocations to the Soviets, while not abandoning our sympathy for Solidarity and our hopes for the survival of the reforms in Poland. Bloodshed was a clear possibility. Above all, we must do nothing that might lay us open to a charge of triggering it. We must offer humanitarian aid to the Polish people, but not even hint that the United States would under any circumstance go beyond that. Those were the broad outlines of the policy we discussed. The President authorized me to meet the press in Brussels that day and state the American position.

"The political experiment in Poland should be allowed to proceed unimpeded," I said at a news conference. "The United States reiterates that the people of Poland should be allowed to find a solution to their current difficulties through a process of negotiation and compromise among the parties involved." But if Budapest and Prague and the whole clouded history of the Soviet bloc had taught us anything, it was that political experiment and negotiation and compromise are not the language of totalitarianism.

If there had been any question about Soviet responsibility for events in Poland, it was dispelled by reports that Moscow had informed the governments of every country in the Soviet bloc that martial law would be imposed in Poland *before the Russians told the Warsaw government*. This contemptuous exercise illustrated the first reality of the situation. In the Polish crisis, we were not seeing the collapse of the Soviet empire. Moscow's difficulties with the Poles were a sign of trouble and decay, but the situation was not irreversible. Solidarity could be snuffed out. Solidarity had declared a general strike. Walesa and most of the leadership of Solidarity had now been imprisoned. Refugees streamed into Austria and Western Europe. The Polish ambassadors to Washington and Tokyo were soon to defect. Though there was no fighting in the streets against the overwhelming show of force mounted by the Jaruzelski government, the potential for violence and for Soviet intervention was high.

In Brussels, I had urged a policy of systematic unity on our allies. It can be argued that this policy had until then served us well in Moscow. When the Soviet Union at last "did what it had to do"—

cauterize this outbreak of nationalism and liberalization—it acted in a fashion that was risky to its own interests and designed to be as unalarming to the West as possible. For its own reasons, Moscow feared the consequences of a bloody uprising in Poland, but it also believed what the Carter and Reagan administrations had repeatedly told it—that any more violent action would jeopardize arms control, eliminate the possibility of American cooperation on a Soviet escape from Afghanistan, and prejudice every other question that depended on American cooperation for its solution. Of all the actions that might have been taken against the Polish people, a state of martial law engineered by the Soviets, instead of an invasion by the Red Army, was familiar confirmation of the limits of Soviet toleration of threats to what it regards as its essential sphere of influence. On this occasion, it was also confirmation of the Soviets' essential weakness. The heavy apparatus of the totalitarian state, after forty years of grim success, had failed to frighten a people who had no defense against it except their convictions.

In Washington, the mood of the President's advisers was, as usual, a reaction to the press. At meetings in the White House, the hardliners spoke of draconian measures. I kept on telling the President to remember Hungary. Bush and Weinberger and their supporters urged tough talk to the Russians in private and to the world in public. It was suggested that the President publicly demand the release of Lech Walesa and insist on internal reforms in Poland. What happens, I asked, if he does so and Walesa remains in prison and the reforms do not occur? The President had already sent a strongly worded letter to Brezhnev over the hotline. Mrs. Kirkpatrick, not unnaturally, wished to take the Polish question into the United Nations. I urged the President not to render Western action subject to a Soviet veto in the Security Council, and he accepted my advice.

Sanctions against the Soviet Union and the Jaruzelski government, even a total embargo by the West, were discussed. But reimposition of the American grain embargo would cost the treasury at least $3 billion in payments to farmers in compensation for taking 30 million tons of wheat off the market. Canceling the export licenses for International Harvester equipment that had already been sold to the Soviet Union could push a troubled company toward bankruptcy. "If Defense has its way," I told my staff, "we'll have the United States in a war scare and the Europeans off the bridge by Christmas." Christmas, at this point, was three days in the future.

The question before the President was not: what is the most we can realistically do? It was: shall we be like Carter and waffle or shall we lead the world? I doubted greatly that the world would follow any President in some of the actions that were being proposed—and yet only through unified action could we achieve results within the range of reactions rationally available to us. Although some of Reagan's advisers clearly did not think he was being tough enough, he took a balanced line, even speaking at one point about offering the East a Marshall Plan for the eighties and suggesting to the Soviets a new era of world cooperation.

Meanwhile, I suggested that the President articulate first principles: nothing for the Polish government, a cutoff of Polish imports into the United States, a policy of providing food for the Polish people if we were guaranteed that the food would reach them. Defense and most of the President's staff, out of genuine outrage but also because of a reflexive belief in the power of the public relations gesture, urged the President toward sanctions. I was not opposed in any way to sanctions; indeed, I thought they were indispensable. We simply could not punish the victims of aggression while leaving the aggressors untouched. But sanctions had also to be measured and practicable, and they had to hurt the Soviets and the Polish government more than they hurt the West, while hurting the Polish people as little as possible. Some spoke of calling the Polish debt into default. This course of action, with all its potential for calamity, was put forward on one level as an effective measure in its own right, and on another level as a means of pressuring our European allies to suspend construction of the trans-Siberian pipeline.

To the advocates of this policy, the pipeline was just the sort of highly visible issue that would focus and dramatize Western reaction. Furthermore, the Polish crisis provided a convenient pretext for dealing with the pipeline issue, which had long nettled their strategic sensitivities. From the beginning of the Administration, Weinberger had been alarmed by the pipeline, arguing that it would make Western Europe dependent on a potential adversary for a significant part of its energy supplies and also provide the Soviet Union with a bonanza in hard currency with which to finance a continued arms buildup. In this judgment he was correct, and as NATO commander I had urged the Administration of the day to oppose construction of the pipeline. But President Carter had chosen not to oppose it and the

Europeans had made massive financial and political investments in it. It was, quite simply, too late to say no.

As had happened before, the confusion over this issue within the Administration owed something to a lack of historical understanding. The pipeline had its genesis in the oil shortage of 1973 and the second explosive increase in energy costs imposed by OPEC in 1979. The countries of Western Europe, and especially France and Germany, were almost entirely dependent on the Persian Gulf for their petroleum. They regarded this as a dangerous situation. An alternative source existed in the North Sea, but the undeveloped offshore fields there were largely controlled by Norway, and the Norwegian people, concerned about the impact that large-scale development might have upon the environment and their traditional national life, had made it impossible for their government to proceed with further exploitation of the oil beneath the seabed. Large fields of natural gas also existed in Siberia, and the Russians were willing to sell the Europeans 1.37 trillion cubic feet of gas a year for twenty-five years—under conditions favorable to Moscow. The Europeans met the entire cost of construction, estimated at $15 billion. The pipeline, running 3,300 miles from the Arctic Circle to the western frontier of Czechoslovakia, would supply about 5 percent of Western Europe's total energy needs and between 20 and 30 percent of its natural gas, at current rates of consumption.

In the NSC and the Cabinet, alternative energy sources for Western Europe were discussed. The United States possesses an 800-year supply of coal, but in order to make its export to Europe economically feasible, an extensive and costly program of port modernization was necessary. There was little chance of approving such a project in an Administration so devoted to cutting federal budgets that the White House, at one point, decided to remove $30 billion from the defense budget without telling an apoplectic Secretary of Defense about it in advance. During the Carter years, the United States had largely got out of the business of exporting technology and expertise for nuclear power plants. In the final analysis, Washington had no alternatives to offer.

Had it been otherwise, the West Europeans might have been interested in a quiet discussion of substitute sources of energy. They had signed contracts for the pipeline at a time when energy costs were at a historic high, only to find a couple of years later that prices had dropped and supplies had risen. In 1981, the pipeline was less of a necessity, and much less cost-effective, than it had been when it was conceived. The original plan, to build a two-strand pipeline, was modified to provide for a single strand. All of these considerations notwithstanding, the pipeline remained important to the economies, the national pride, and the security of Western Europe.

When, on December 29, the President announced a list of sanctions against the U.S.S.R., he stated that he was ending Aeroflot service to U.S. airports, closing the Soviet Purchasing Commission, suspending negotiations on the new long-term grain agreement and the maritime agreement, and refusing renewal of exchange agreements. He also announced the suspension of the issuance or renewal of export licenses for electronic equipment, computers, and other high technology items. Finally, Reagan suspended the issuance of licenses for "an expanded list of gas and oil equipment. . . . This includes pipelayers."

This was a direct challenge to the continued ability of the Europeans to build the pipeline. Pipelaying machines, essential for its construction, were being manufactured by Caterpillar, an American firm. Other essential components were being fabricated in Western Europe by the foreign subsidiaries of U.S. corporations or by European companies operating under license from American firms. Our allies in Europe were given five hours' advance notification of the President's action, a procedure that transformed the perfunctory to the curt. Though this was a decision that would deeply trouble the alliance, I had acquiesced in it, thinking that the Europeans had enough machinery and materiel in the process of manufacture to provide time to find some sort of solution. I never imagined that the President's decision would be retroactive, requiring manufacturers to renege on existing contracts. I doubt that this was the President's intent either; certainly the issue never won support in discussions around the NSC table.

However, when the decision was applied by the Department of Commerce, one of its officials, going beyond the letter and intent of the President's policy, interpreted it as being retroactive. Inexplicably, the Administration accepted this bureaucratic fiat. This meant that equipment already contracted for, even equipment already manufactured or in the process of being manufactured, would not be licensed for export to the U.S.S.R. This applied equally to items manufactured abroad by the subsidiaries of American companies or under American license. Leaving aside the legalities, the value of the contracts amounted to many hundreds of millions of dollars as well as hundreds of jobs in a time of general economic trouble in Western Europe. On my urging, with the support of the always sensible Regan, Baldridge, and Brock, the President decided to delay imposition of these measures and sent Under Secretary of State James L. Buckley to Europe to discuss the question with our allies. The Europeans reacted with all the bewilderment and vexation that such an invasion of their sovereignty might have been expected to produce.

Though I was unable to persuade the President and his staff that this was so, this policy had the potential of shaking the alliance. Just how high feelings ran I discovered on January 29, a month to the day after the President issued his statement on sanctions, when I stopped in London to discuss the pipeline, and the question of the Polish debt, with Prime Minister Margaret Thatcher. Mrs. Thatcher is a most intelligent and courageous and politically gifted leader, utterly devoted to the West and to her country's friendship with the United States. She is also among the Reagan Administration's best friends in the world. I was in Cairo, completing a round of talks with the leaders of Israel and Egypt, when Mrs. Thatcher's invitation came. I amended my flight plan so as to be able to lunch with her and members of the British cabinet at No. 10 Downing Street.

It was my practice, while Secretary of State, to be as frank with our friends and allies as with my own government; in diplomacy as in life, it is far easier to tell the whole truth than to try to remember inventions. This is also Mrs. Thatcher's practice, and she told me at once that she was uncertain of American intentions with regard to the sanctions and worried over rumors of even stronger action to come. The prime minister had heard alarming reports that some in the United States wanted to put Poland in default. She pointed out that any such action would likely put other Eastern European countries in default with consequences for the Germans and the rest of the Western banking system that could not be calculated. The cost of breaking the trust on which Western banking was based would be far greater to the West than to the Soviet Union.

The United States must understand that the continental Europeans profoundly believed that they needed the pipeline and would desert the United States on this issue rather than abandon it. Mrs. Thatcher did not believe that France and Germany could be persuaded to give it up. The pipeline would go through. It affronted the

Europeans to be asked to make enormous sacrifices while the United States made none. Suspending Aeroflot flights, for example, cost the United States nothing because no American airlines flew into the U.S.S.R. and the Russians could not retaliate by banning American landings at Soviet airports. It seemed to Europeans that, at worst, Americans had little to lose. The total annual value of American industrial exports to the U.S.S.R. was $300 million. The total value of contracts held in part by a British firm, John Brown, Ltd., alone, for the manufacture of pipeline components that depended on American technology affected by the President's ban, amounted to $400 million. It would be very damaging to Britain if John Brown, Ltd., failed to fulfill the contract. Similar situations applied in France and Germany and other allied countries. Yet the United States had not mentioned the possibility of suspending wheat shipments to the Soviet Union. There was a lack of symmetry in burden sharing. Were the President's actions sanctions or were they merely signals to the Russians?

I had to tell Mrs. Thatcher that, on the subject of sanctions, the President meant what he said. On the question of default, the rumors she heard were correct; some in Washington did contemplate such a course, but I didn't think they would prevail. The President was thinking of doing more. It was possible, I said, that he would impose a total embargo on the Soviet Union, even call the Polish debt into default. At these words, a silence fell over the luncheon table.

Mrs. Thatcher gasped: There would be nothing left to do were we to go the whole hog at once, suggesting that in such circumstances the Soviets might as well go into Poland.

I profoundly agreed. In the course of this luncheon, Mrs. Thatcher, with her usual perspicacity, had identified the fundamental issue that would trouble the alliance for the remainder of my time in office, and well beyond, and warned of the consequences of the United States expressing its policies by gestures instead of actions. Britain, and the other members of the alliance, wanted desperately to follow the American lead on Poland in a policy that would protect the Polish people and discomfit the Soviets and the regime in Warsaw. But it was too much to ask that they punish their own economies and their own interests in support of policies that would inflict no noticeable wound on Moscow's interests. After months of acrimony in which Poland, the object of the policy, was largely ignored, the entire episode came to its conclusion at the summit at Versailles, but I will deal with that in a later chapter.

In January 1982, however, no one could ignore Poland. Gromyko and I had agreed in New York to meet again in Geneva in mid-January for two more days of talks. Because of the Polish situation, the United States reduced the talks to a single day. There would be no business as usual with Poland as long as martial law lasted. In January, the NATO foreign ministers had called for the lifting of martial law in Poland, the release of political prisoners, and a dialogue among the Jaruzelski regime, Solidarity, and the Catholic church. These three principles formed the basis of allied and American policy on the crisis in Poland. At the Geneva talks, I told the press, "Poland is the only item on the U.S. agenda." Gromyko, arriving at the airport in Geneva, said, "I have no intention whatever of discussing questions relating to Poland or the domestic situation in Poland."

But, of course, the subject did arise. Gromyko's demeanor through the talks was apprehensive, apologetic. Finally, unbidden, he addressed the Polish question in the form of an apologia: allegations of Soviet troops massing, of Soviet interference, were false. Martial law was strictly constitutional. The United States only accused Moscow in order to cover up its own interference, as, for example, with its provocative radio stations that Gromyko, to his distress, sometimes had to listen to in the line of duty. Washington was not alone in this meddling, but it was playing first fiddle. The Soviet Union did not have to apologize because it was not interfering, not interfering, not interfering. . . . Gromyko repeated this phrase over and over. The Poles should be let alone. Of course, along with all decent people, the Soviet Union wanted to help.

This was not a subject for petty squabbling. I told Gromyko, who looked exceedingly uncomfortable, perched on a sofa in a sitting room of the mission in Geneva, that I would not debate with him. The situation in Poland had now become dangerous to the world and to our future relationship. No one could argue that Moscow had not acted with great restraint so far; the President knew this and so did I. But the three principles enunciated by the NATO foreign ministers remained the basis of United States policy. The outcome in Poland must be based on compromise. There was a paramount need for safety valves. It was in the interest of each of us to seek social and economic remedies. Credible, demonstrable moderation was in everyone's interest. I said this, I told Gromyko, by way of expressing America's goodwill. We did not seek to interfere in Poland.

Gromyko, though he had certainly understood every word I had said, waited for the interpreter. He told me that I was totally incorrect and that the situation in Poland was improving, and improving quite successfully. No one should hamper this, and this gloomy American information was quite inaccurate.

However, we both knew the facts, and so did everyone else in both Europes. A few days later, after watching the Polish chairman of the Madrid human rights conference attempt to stifle all debate on the circumstances in which the Poles were being ravished of their human rights, I visited the capital of Romania. The streets of Bucharest, darkened by the energy shortage, teemed with armed soldiers and police. My wife, visiting the local markets, saw few vegetables except for a couple of wan cabbages and onions, and virtually no meat and was cheered, after several hours in which no one she met would make eye contact, to have received a fleeting smile from a young couple in the street.

We had been invited to lunch in a hotel by the foreign minister, but evidently President Nicolae Ceausescu himself decided to act as host. Ceausescu remained for four hours, chatting, and though the Romanians had declined to translate my arrival statement, which contained strong language on Poland, this subject was not omitted from the conversation. Ceausescu was frank, but he hardly mentioned the Soviet Union. In his tone and his opinions, he sounded remarkably like the leader of a nonaligned Third World country. Ceausescu spoke of Romania's need for $1 billion in American aid. My reply, explaining the role of Congress in foreign aid appropriations and the budgetary policies of the Administration, must not have been wholly satisfactory to him because he said, in a gruff tone, wagging a finger, "We have other alternatives!"

"Be realistic, Mr. President," I replied. "Look out the window and you will see the alternative."

And that, of course, is the ultimate meaning of the Polish question to the East Europeans and the present leaders of the Soviet Union. Each has only to look out the window to see the reality of the present, and try to imagine it as the reality of the future, in order to understand that what now exists cannot endure.

BACKGROUND

The television camera is the siege machine of the twentieth century. Nobody understands that better than Lech Walesa, the leader of Solidarity, who possesses the great man's gift for the simple gesture. When Walesa signed the solemn agreement with the government of Poland that gave Solidarity legal status, he used a gaudy souvenir pen left over from the recent visit to Poland of Pope John Paul II. Scribbling his name with this implement, which was about the size of a carrot, a rumpled, good-natured Walesa managed to flash a wordless but powerful political message to the world: Solidarity was a very human organism connected to the Pope and therefore to the humanitarian European Christian tradition. Walesa's antic pen also punctured the pomposity of the party officials who were sitting at the table with him and, with a gentle humor that was far more convincing than bombast, demonstrated that the all-powerful state was vulnerable to the ordinary desire of ordinary people for an honest life.

It may well be said, when the history of the Polish crisis of the 1980s is finally written, that the most important thing about it was that it let the camera into the East. The men and women who supported Solidarity doubtless would have struggled in obscurity with equal courage. It is doubtful that they would have struggled with equal effect in the absence of the pictures that appeared on television screens and in newspapers and magazines in Poland and throughout the world. The global community of sympathy that the cameras created for Solidarity was the most powerful protection the movement had. The world was literally watching and, more than anything else, that made Moscow hesitate.

"Pictures don't lie." In a society ruled by lies that everyone must pretend to believe as a matter of survival, an outpouring of pictures that show things as they really are must be a great catharsis. It is taken for granted that there is a hunger for information in the Soviet bloc because information is embargoed. But there is a concomitant thirst for expression. Fundamentally, Solidarity was a device for forcing government and party and, ultimately, the Kremlin to listen to the truth about the Polish people. The camera made the message universal. The object of imposing martial law was the control of Solidarity, but it was also designed to shut off the cameras. History may also decide that Jaruzelski and the Kremlin acted too late in both cases.

The Falklands:
"Do Not Urge Britain to
Reward Aggression"

ON March 28, 1982, a Sunday, the British ambassador, Nicholas ("Nikko") Henderson, brought me a letter from Lord Carrington. A party of Argentinians, wrote the foreign secretary, had landed nine days earlier on the island of South Georgia, a British possession lying in the South Atlantic a few degrees above the Antarctic Circle and some 600 miles to the east of the Falkland Islands, a British crown colony. The Argentinian government had refused a British request to remove its citizens from South Georgia or regularize their presence by having them report to British authorities and had subsequently landed additional supplies and issued a statement that the landing party would be given all necessary protection. "I should be grateful if you would consider taking up the matter with the Argentines, stressing the need to defuse the situation," Lord Carrington wrote. "If we do not find a solution soon, I fear the gravest consequences."

This was the beginning of the Falklands crisis, a confrontation between the heirs to the British Empire and a Latin American military junta that was perceived by some, before the killing started, as an amusing anachronism, but in fact was a case study in miscalcula-

tion, national rivalry, war fever, and the way in which the leaders of
nations can be driven by the most basic human emotions toward
fateful decisions. On March 28, I hardly imagined that Peter Carrington's letter presaged events that would contain such trenchant
lessons, but I saw at once that it had the makings of a troublesome
problem. I asked our ambassador in Buenos Aires to express American concern to the Argentinian government, urging that it take no
further steps to aggravate the situation. In my reply to Carrington, I
expressed admiration for British patience. The Bureau of Inter-American Affairs, which had been maintaining a routine watch on the
Falklands situation, was instructed to remain alert and report any
unusual developments to me at once.

I was aware of a long-standing dispute between Britain and Argentina over ownership of the Falklands—or the Malvinas, as this
windswept archipelago of about 200 islands off the coast of Argentina is called in Spanish. The British based their claim on discovery of
the islands in 1592 by the English captain John Davis and on the
continuous presence of British settlers since 1832. Argentina maintained that the islands had been administered by Spain as part of the
Vice Royalty of the Riode la Plata, and sovereignty passed to Argentina when it attained independence in 1816. In 1965, after 133 years
of contention, Argentina brought the question to the United Nations.
The General Assembly found that sovereignty was in dispute and
created a negotiating framework. The resulting talks continued for
seventeen years, but did nothing to resolve the question of sovereignty. In 1978, an Argentinian destroyer fired warning shots at a
British research ship in Falklands territorial waters. A new round of
talks began in February 1982, a year that marked the 150th anniversary of British sovereignty (in British eyes) or trespass (in the Argentinian view) in the islands.

An earlier Labour government in Britain had suggested that the
British might eventually relinquish sovereignty. This created a political controversy in London. The Falklanders, about 1,200 ethnic Britons who had mostly been born in the islands and made their living as
sheepherders, were polled and chose to remain British. The Argentinians felt that they had been dealt with perfidiously and expressed
their frustrations at the February negotiating session at the United
Nations. President Leopoldo Galtieri, head of the ruling military
junta in Buenos Aires, demanded a permanent negotiating commission, and in mid-March Argentina issued a public ultimatum that

Britain accept this proposal or face the end of the talks—together with other, unspecified Argentinian action. London refused, the talks floundered, and on March 19 that landing party of Argentinians who so troubled Lord Carrington—and who Galtieri later told me were in fact Argentinian military personnel in civilian clothes—came ashore on South Georgia.

The United States had not paid a great deal of attention to the Falklands situation. During a visit to Buenos Aires in early March, Thomas O. Enders, the assistant secretary of state for inter-American affairs, had urged the Argentinians to continue negotiations; he reported that they were noncommittal on this point, but not negative. There was a widespread impression that the junta was creating a foreign distraction to give itself a respite from domestic economic problems, including severe inflation. The fact that 1982 marked the 150th anniversary of the British presence in the Falklands, and the patriotic significance of this sesquicentennial for Argentina, escaped my notice—and was perhaps not sufficiently appreciated by the British.

On March 30, two days after receiving Carrington's letter, the United States picked up signs of an unusual state of force readiness in Argentina. The following morning, a Wednesday, the brilliant and studiously rumpled Ambassador Henderson called on me at the State Department. "They are invading," he said in astonished tones, and placed before me an array of information that indeed suggested that an Argentinian military operation against the Falklands was imminent. I asked our own intelligence community to check the British information, and by late afternoon our analysts confirmed that it was probable that an Argentinian task force would strike the Falklands in a matter of days or hours.

Immediately, I ordered our ambassador in Buenos Aires, Harry W. Shlaudeman, to deliver a strong warning to the Argentinian government that any military action would heavily damage U.S.-Argentinian relations. In the meantime, I called in Estaban Takacs, the Argentinian ambassador, and gave him the same message. The chief of intelligence of the Argentinian army was visiting Washington, and he, too, was officially warned. In Buenos Aires, Shlaudeman experienced difficulty in arranging an appointment with the Argentinian foreign minister, Nicanor Costa Mendez, and when finally he saw him, Costa Mendez refused to make any direct response to the American request for assurances. I ordered Shlaudeman to see

Galtieri himself and tell him that should any Argentinian military action occur, for whatever reason, it was a simple fact that overwhelming internal and external pressure would be brought to bear on the Reagan Administration to abandon the new and promising relationship it had been building with Argentina. We waited anxiously for Galtieri's answer, but Shlaudeman reported that Costa Mendez appeared intent on delaying his interview with the president.

On hearing this, I urged President Reagan to phone Galtieri and issue a strong personal warning. That afternoon, March 31, Prime Minister Thatcher informed President Reagan that the British government believed that the Argentinian navy was preparing to invade the Falkland Islands within forty-eight hours. Britain could not, she said, acquiesce in any Argentinian occupation. Mrs. Thatcher asked Reagan to talk urgently to Galtieri and ask him not to authorize a landing, let alone hostilities. Meanwhile, the British would not escalate the dispute or start fighting. Britain called a meeting of the United Nations Security Council.

After a good deal of stonewalling on the part of the Argentinian foreign ministry, Shlaudeman was finally admitted to Galtieri's presence and delivered our demarche. Galtieri, who seemed to Shlaudeman to be in a state of high emotion, bluntly informed our ambassador that he was not going to tell the United States whether or not he intended to use force against the Falklands. He handed Shlaudeman a paper in which the situation in the islands was described as intolerable and impossible to maintain in terms of Argentinian national honor.

At about 6:30 on Thursday evening, President Reagan attempted to place a telephone call from the White House to Galtieri in Buenos Aires. Galtieri's aide stated that his chief was "unavailable" to speak to the President of the United States. After a two-hour delay, however, Galtieri consented to come on the line. During a conversation that lasted for no less than fifty minutes, Reagan reiterated our concern, offered the good offices of the United States, and volunteered to send Vice President Bush to Buenos Aires for discussions. Galtieri declined both the good offices and the Vice President; he appreciated Reagan's concern, he said, but the British had refused for 150 years to relinquish sovereignty and time had run out. "Do you intend to use force?" Reagan asked. Galtieri replied that Argentina felt free to use whatever resources it possessed unless Her Majesty's government, that very night, recognized Argentinian sovereignty over all the islands and turned over control within the next few months. Reagan warned that the British would certainly fight in case of an Argentine landing on the Falklands. "I must have your assurance that there will be no landing tomorrow," Reagan said. Galtieri responded with a portentous silence.

In other words, it was too late. Even as Galtieri spoke to Reagan, the invasion was being launched. During the night of April 1–2, an assault force of about 300 Argentinian marines went ashore near Port Stanley, the capital of the Falklands, and in a short time secured the airfield and the port and raised the Argentinian flag. The British garrison, which consisted of a small detachment of Royal Marines, fired on the invaders. Four Argentinians were killed and two wounded. There were no British casualties. The Argentinians, under orders not to harm the British defenders, did not fire back.

Britain broke diplomatic relations with Argentina, froze Argentinian assets in London, and asked its partners in the European Economic Community (EEC) and the United States to impose financial sanctions and a trade embargo—an action that would exhaust Argentina's economy in a matter of weeks. The very accomplished Lord Carrington, who was subjected to the charge that he had not read the signs of trouble aright or brought them soon enough to the notice of the prime minister (and who may have taken a slacker line after the invasion than Mrs. Thatcher), resigned as foreign secretary and was replaced by the former defense minister, Francis Pym. In Parliament, Mrs. Thatcher took a very strong position, giving the house assurances that her government would not yield on the question of British sovereignty over the Falklands and that the wishes of the British citizens resident in the Falklands would be paramount in deciding the future of the islands. It was clear that the survival of Mrs. Thatcher's government was at stake. As David Steel, leader of the British Liberal party, put it, "The facts speak for themselves. After unsuccessful foreign ventures, prime ministers have been replaced."

In a reawakening of the spirit of the Blitz that exhilarated Britain, warships were withdrawn from NATO, civilian ships, including the liner *Queen Elizabeth II*, were requisitioned and refitted, troops were embarked, and in an astonishingly short time a task force of over 100 ships and 28,000 men was steaming under the British ensign toward the Falklands. On April 3, the U.N. Security Council adopted Resolution 502, calling for cessation of hostilities, Argentinian withdrawal from the Falklands, and a negotiated settlement of the dispute. On April 4, Argentina invaded and took South Georgia; three Argentinians were killed, but once again there were no British casualties.

The British government immediately called on the United States for support, asking on the day following the invasion that Washington issue a strong statement condemning the Argentinian action, withdraw its ambassador to Buenos Aires, take the issue of Argentinian aggression to the Organization of American States (OAS), and embargo arms shipments to Argentina. While my sympathy was with the British, I believed that the most practical expression of that sympathy would be impartial United States mediation in the dispute. The honest broker must, above all, be neutral. We chose to preserve our useful neutrality by avoiding extremes of language, declined to withdraw our ambassador on grounds that such an action would eliminate our ability to communicate with Argentina as a friend of both belligerents, cautioned the British that Argentina would win any votes in the OAS as a matter of inter-American solidarity, and informed them that the sale of arms to Argentina was already forbidden by Congress under a policy linking such sales to progress by the recipient on human rights violations.

At the State Department, in the early hours of the crisis, most of the staff shared the amusement of the press and public over what was perceived as a Gilbert and Sullivan battle over a sheep pasture between a choleric old John Bull and a comic dictator in a gaudy uniform. Among the White House staff, there was little sense of urgency. Though I was virtually alone in this, I viewed the situation from the very beginning with the utmost seriousness and urged the bureaucrats of the department to do the same. The Falklands was not an isolated problem. Among other things, it involved the credibility of the already strained Western alliance, the survival or failure of a British government that was a staunch friend to the United States, the future of American policy and relations in the Western Hemisphere as well as in Europe, the possibility of yet another dangerous strategic incursion by the Soviet Union into South America, and most important of all, an unambiguous test of America's belief in the rule of law. Moreover, in Latin America, the rule of law as the basis for change is more than a theoretical imperative. The map of the continent displays many territorial disputes that, under the rule of might-makes-right, could inflame the region. Few in the U.S. government saw this in those early hours. None doubted it at the crisis's bloody conclusion.

Margaret Thatcher never saw the problem as a narrow issue exclusively between Britain and Argentina. Almost messianically, she viewed it as a test of Western fiber and determination. In this, she was correct. The Argentinian junta, in the first of many miscalculations, invaded the Falklands because it believed the European democracies were so decadent that Britain would never fight and the United States would decide that its vital interests and its political and economic future lay not in an exhausted Europe but in a nascent Latin America. In short, the junta, displaying a pattern of behavior typical of many militarized, authoritarian, xenophobic regimes, thought it could get away with it because Britain was weak and the United States was corrupt.

Adolf Hitler and the militarists of imperial Japan had made precisely the same miscalculation about the democracies in the 1930s. Forty years of Western deterrence and diplomacy had been designed to prevent the totalitarian U.S.S.R. from making the identical miscalculation. It was vital that the Argentinian miscalculation be exposed as a fundamental mistake lest it be made by a greater power over a greater issue, with far graver consequences. Had Britain collapsed in the face of this petty aggression, it would, in Mrs. Thatcher's words to me, have sent a signal round the world with devastating consequences. Had the United States, for reasons of selfish advantage, retreated from the principle that the status quo must not be changed by the use of force, and, however subtly, connived at rewarding aggression, it would have confirmed the corruption of the West.

The whole of the West, therefore, was engaged in the crisis on both moral and practical planes. All Western leaders understood this, though more than a few may have wished that the test had somehow come in another place over a very different issue. Great Britain's partners in the EEC and NATO supported her, but in some respects this was a fragile unity; Italy has special historic ties to Argentina based on consanguinity and important economic and cultural factors, while the Socialist governments of France and West Germany, sympathizing with Mrs. Thatcher on principle, had their own deep ideological reservations about entangling the alliance in what might be perceived as an anticolonialist war in the Third World.

Actually, the Falklands war had little to do with colonialism.

Britain was prepared to decolonize the islands; she was not prepared to hand them over to Argentina, population and all, for recolonization under another flag. The negotiations to prevent the war ultimately broke down because Argentina was not prepared to give the Falklanders independence if they wanted it, while Britain insisted that the islanders must have freedom of choice. Simply put, Argentina clearly violated international law by seizing the territory of another nation by force. Britain, in exercise of its right of self-defense under Article 51 of the U.N. Charter, was legally entitled to use reasonable force in preserving its rights by retaking the islands. Argentina was legally obligated under U.N. Resolution 502 to withdraw. If she refused to do so and hostilities resulted, then the United States would have no choice, as a matter of principle and unambiguous historical precedent, but to support Britain. Knowing the technological capabilities and the state of training of the two sides, there was never the slightest doubt in my mind that if it came to a fight—as I feared it must—Britain would win. This was not an opinion that was universally held among the White House staff, the American military, or our intelligence analysts—or even by every knowledgeable Briton.

Even in the National Security Council, there was confusion over the underlying causes of the conflict. Recent geological exploration had revealed that the Falklands were situated above a large pool of undersea oil. Some of the President's aides deduced from this that the dispute in the Falklands had to do with oil and could be resolved by reaching an agreement to split up the drilling rights. Nothing could dislodge this notion. The aides listened attentively to explanations about the real cause, but could not seem to grasp that such simple things as pride and patriotism could apply when billions in oil revenues were not involved. Finally, I told the President, "Oil is not the issue. The British say they don't give a damn about that, and it's the last thing on Galtieri's mind." The President thereupon closed the subject, at least when I was present.

In the NSC, I argued that the United States must do whatever it could to avoid further bloodshed and bring the crisis to a negotiated solution, but if this was not possible, it must support Britain and the rule of law. In this view I enjoyed the enthusiastic, if uncharacteristic, support of Caspar Weinberger. Mrs. Kirkpatrick, a specialist in Latin American questions, vehemently opposed an approach that condemned Argentina and supported Britain on the basis of international law. Such a policy, she told the President, would buy the United States a hundred years of animosity in Latin America. Even after the policy was approved, Mrs. Kirkpatrick, in the eyes of the British, at least, continued to attack and undermine it, notably through a series of misleading signals to the Argentinians, a course of action that risked influencing the Argentinians into thinking that American policy differed from the one I was describing to them, and thereby affecting the outcome of negotiations. Before the end of the first week of the crisis, the British were telling us they believed that Mrs. Kirkpatrick had told the Argentinian ambassador to the U.N. that if his country continued to support the United States on Nicaragua, there would be no American criticism in the U.N. on the landing in the Falklands. I assured an agitated Ambassador Henderson that, no matter what his evidence, this statement bore no resemblance to official U.S. policy. Mrs. Kirkpatrick continued to assure me that she was not engaged in such activity. Nevertheless, the British went on complaining till the end about Mrs. Kirkpatrick's public statements ("The Argentinians have been claiming for 200 years [sic] that they own those islands. If they own those islands, then moving troops into them is not armed aggression.") and her private conversations with the Argentinians.*

---

*Much was made during the Falklands crisis, and in other situations, about disagreements between Mrs. Kirkpatrick and me. It is true that we had a number of frank conversations, but, in general, I held the same views as Mrs. Kirkpatrick on broad issues and most specific ones. I admired her intelligence, respected her scholarship, and was impressed by her debating skills. In the Falklands crisis, however, our positions were unreconcilable—not because of any personal issue or special taste in allies, but because each of us believed that the other's position was contrary to the interests of the United States. Ordinarily, when a President, after hearing the arguments on both sides in a contested issue, adopts a policy, an adviser who disagrees has the choice of closing ranks and supporting the President's decision even though he does not like it, or resigning. That Mrs. Kirkpatrick chose to keep on pushing her own view should not be taken to suggest that she had departed from honorable practice, because the concept of closing ranks had no meaning to the President's aides. The necessity of speaking with one voice on foreign policy, discussed so exhaustively in the earlier pages of this book, simply never took hold among Reagan's advisers. In the Falklands crisis, while I was shuttling back and forth from Washington to London to Buenos Aires carrying the details of the negotiations in my own mind while reporting the broad outlines to the President for his eyes only, Mrs. Kirkpatrick was describing the progress and the meaning of the talks, about which she knew little, in a variety of public forums—and, if the British are to be believed, in a very active pattern of private contacts. Because she held Cabinet rank and was known to have access to the White House through channels that excluded the Secretary of State, her words were given considerable weight. How were the Argentinians to know that hers was not the authentic text on Presidential policy? Mrs. Kirkpatrick was in no way to be blamed for this unfortunate state of affairs. She was merely acting according to the rules of the system which had at its heart an evidently irresistible desire

It remained essential, in the early stages of the crisis, for American neutrality to be preserved. If the prospects for a peaceful solution were not great, they still must be seized. With the British fleet steaming down the South Atlantic at a steady 18 knots and the Argentinians daily reinforcing their garrison in the Falklands, the opportunity for negotiations would last only a few days. We had to assume that both sides wanted to find a way out and a mechanism to make the escape possible. We knew that American mediation was a mechanism acceptable to both. It was my opinion, tested in a series of freewheeling staff discussions, that the United States alone had enough influence with both sides to provide an outside chance of success. The United Nations, with its vociferous anticolonialist coalition of Third World and Marxist members, would probably not be able to act quickly enough to be effective, and the debate was certain to digress into issues that would exacerbate a situation that could only be resolved by quiet diplomacy. The OAS was unsatisfactory for similar reasons. There was no time to form a consortium of European and American states, and besides, this was not a problem ideally suited to the methods of a committee. The President had offered the good offices of the United States in finding a basis to negotiate a resolution of the dispute. It was important that Reagan himself not be involved in the mediating process. The chances of failure were too high, and I argued strongly against suggestions that Reagan should go on the radio to appeal for a settlement or involve himself publicly in other ways. We examined the possibility of assigning Admiral Thomas C. Hayward, the chief of naval operations, who happened to be in Argentina on Navy business, to the role of mediator, but decided that this might not be a job for a military man. Henry Kissinger and Ellsworth Bunker were mentioned. So was Mrs. Kirkpatrick, who was much admired in Argentina, but she had persevered in her intention to attend a dinner in her honor at the Argentinian embassy on April 2, the day of the invasion. This raised, at the outset, a doubt in the minds of the British as to her impartiality, and no doubt underlay their subsequent consternation about her activities.

In a series of conversations with the British and the Argentinians,

---

to save the President's popularity even if this meant undermining the President's policies. Mrs. Kirkpatrick herself acted out of a deep loyalty to her own principles and very intelligent opinions. The populist instincts of the White House staff, quick to adjust appearances to shifts in public mood and opinion, were the real cause of the problem.

it became clear that both sides hoped that I would serve as intermediary. Once again, I was under no illusion as to my chances of success. Both sides had gotten themselves into positions from which it would be very difficult to retreat. But each development in the crisis strengthened the conviction that the most vital interests of the United States and the West were at stake. It also seemed to me that a sincere, high-level effort by the United States could do much to strip away the confusing ambiguities of the situation and help to establish who was right and who was wrong.

It was clear to me also that if I undertook this mission and did not find a way to stop the hostilities, I might have to resign. By now it was clear enough that there were men and women around the President who would urge my departure. "If the situation cannot be saved, and this is very possible," I told my wife, "then whatever I do will be seen as a failure, even if it is a success in larger terms than the conflict itself. I'm going to take this on because I have to, but it may turn out to be my Waterloo."

As evening fell on April 6, I called the President and suggested that I go to Buenos Aires and London in an attempt to find a solution. The alternative was a war that would drive Galtieri from office and perhaps inflict something far worse on the Argentinian people and the Americas. "If you order me to try, and if we prevent more bloodshed, it will be worthwhile," I said. "It involves a high risk for you, but I don't think we can sidestep the issue. If we fail, all we have worked for in Latin America will be up in the air." Reagan, who was on the point of leaving for summit meetings in Jamaica and Barbados (and for a brief vacation at the home of the Reagans' old friend Claudette Colbert on Barbados), agreed that I should try. It was decided that I would go first to London, in order to know what was possible, before traveling to Argentina and talking to its unpredictable leaders.

By now, after a series of intensive staff meetings, the State Department had produced the bones of a solution. This involved diverting the British fleet, withdrawing Argentine military forces from the Falklands, and interposing on the islands a peacekeeping force consisting of personnel from Canada and the United States and two Latin American countries. Negotiations would follow. The Argentinian ambassador, when I shared this paper with him, told me that he thought it was at the extreme of what the junta might be able to accept. Ambassador Henderson was unequivocal: Argentina must withdraw; anything less would mean the fall of the Thatcher government. Britain would prefer to see the United States alone, rather than a consortium of nations, as the guarantor of the security of the Falklands.

On Thursday April 8, the day of my arrival in London, Britain imposed a blockade of the Falklands, announcing that any Argentinian ship within 200 miles of the islands after dawn on the following Monday, April 12, risked being sunk. There were no unseemly celebrations in the streets of London, but there was a certain suppressed patriotic effervescence, a sense of emancipation from the years of postimperial frustrations. Our excellent deputy chief of mission, E. J. Streator, told me that his conversations with figures in the British government portrayed Mrs. Thatcher as being set on the principle of "unconditional withdrawal" and as seeing the situation as a simple matter of right and wrong. In Streator's opinion, Britain was in a bellicose mood, more high-strung and unpredictable than we had ever known it. I could believe this. In Washington, Nikko Henderson, ordinarily the most insouciant of British ambassadors, had assured me that the support for Mrs. Thatcher was the greatest for any British leader since 1939, that the government and the country were determined not to back down, and, what's more, "we wouldn't mind sinking the Argentine fleet—something that can be done relatively easily."

In the drawing room at No. 10 Downing Street, after I had explained the American proposals to Mrs. Thatcher, she rapped sharply on the tabletop and recalled that this was the table at which Neville Chamberlain sat in 1938 and spoke of the Czechs as a faraway people about whom we know so little and with whom we have so little in common. A world war and the death of over 45 million people followed. She begged us to remember this: Do not urge Britain to reward aggression, to give Argentina something taken by force that it could not attain by peaceful means and that would send a signal round the world with devastating consequences. Britain should not be considered on the same level as Argentina, the aggressor.

Before dinner, Mrs. Thatcher had shown me and the other Americans portraits of Wellington and Nelson. She was in a forceful mood, embattled, incisive, and with the right indisputably on her side. It was evident from the beginning of the five hours of talks with Mrs. Thatcher and members of her government that the prime minister, as I afterward reported to the President, "had the bit in her teeth." The working dinner at No. 10, which followed an earlier private talk with Mrs. Thatcher, included the new foreign secretary, Francis Pym; the minister of defense, John Nott; my old colleague Admiral of the Fleet Sir Terence Lewin, chief of the British Defence Staff; and other officials. At one point, during a discussion about the capabilities of the British task force, Pym murmured, "Maybe we should ask the Falklanders how they feel about a war." Mrs. Thatcher heatedly challenged him: Aggressors classically try to intimidate those against whom they aggress, saying that things far worse than the aggression itself could happen. Had I been Francis Pym, I would not have counted my chances of remaining in the cabinet as being very great if I persisted in suggesting to this prime minister that a retreat from her principles might be desirable.

I had not come to London with the idea of urging a compromise of principle on Mrs. Thatcher. My purposes were the opposite. I wished to assure her that she had the support of the United States in a right course of action. It was supremely important that the democracies demonstrate their strength, their uprightness, and their statecraft in resolving this crisis, and I was quite certain that Mrs. Thatcher would do this. Immediately on arrival, I assured the prime minister, in so many words, that there would be no repetition of Suez, in which the United States had coerced Britain and France into retreating from a military expedition in 1956. "I am in London to help the British," I told Mrs. Thatcher. "We are fully sensitive to the depth of British feeling on the Falklands issue. But we must, if possible, avoid armed conflict." In these early hours of the crisis, it was evident that while Mrs. Thatcher, though she was strongly backed by Nott and also by Admiral Lewin, did not enjoy the full support of the other members of her government. In the days that followed, other doubts surfaced. In hindsight, the American mediation effort clearly contributed to Mrs. Thatcher's ability to maintain a spirit of national unity on the Falklands question during the critical mobilization period.

I pressed on the question of interposing an international force on the islands and setting up some sort of interim administration and providing for self-determination. The notion was too wooly, Mrs. Thatcher said. The House of Commons would never accept it because she was pledged to restoration of British administration, which meant the courts, public services, and all the normal apparatus of government. No vague international presence could substitute for this essential authority. She feared that we were talking about negotiations under conditions of duress, which would be a terrible insult to Britain. In any case, she felt that Argentina would never accept self-determination because all the islanders wanted to remain British. As for sovereignty: British sovereignty was a fact. It continued no matter what the Argentines had done or may do.

Mrs. Thatcher and I had met when she visited NATO headquarters in 1979, just before she became prime minister; if I had been impressed then by her muscular intelligence, I had been aware ever since of her ability to absorb facts and see the lessons in them. My experience with her suggested to me that though compromise came hard for her, it did come. She had given me her message: self-determination for the islanders was her irreducible requirement for settlement. She would not impose on British citizens a solution that deprived them of their freedom of choice, and she would go to war, if need be, to defend the rights of a thousand shepherds because their liberties could not be divided from the freedom of all Britons. As the evening ended at No. 10, Mrs. Thatcher gave me her hand. "Only true friends could discuss such an issue as this with the candor of feeling that has characterized this dinner," she said. Then she laughed and said, "We are nice to other people."

In reporting to the President, I emphasized that unless some way could be found to alter British authority and provide for an Argentinian role in the government of the Falklands, Mrs. Thatcher's terms ruled out Argentinian acceptance. If Galtieri accepted her terms, it would be the end of him. Just as Mrs. Thatcher must show that the junta got nothing for its use of force, Galtieri must be able to show that he got something. Here I will say again, because it was constantly in my thoughts at the time, that many young lives hung in the balance. The question was, could I bring enough back from Buenos Aires to satisfy Mrs. Thatcher?

In April, it is spring in England but autumn in Argentina. Here there was no British understatement. Buenos Aires throbbed with excitation. After a flight of eighteen hours, with stops to refuel in Dakar, Senegal, and Recife, Brazil, we arrived at night. The foreign minister, Nicanor Costa Mendez, met me at the airport as protocol demanded. In the distance could be heard an indistinct roar of voices and what sounded like many automobile horns being honked in unison. I asked what the noise was. "Argentina is welcoming you," Costa Mendez said. He rode with me, formal and somewhat withdrawn, into the city. Every street was lined with people, and every person seemed to be holding a flag. The flag of Argentina, blue and white, hung also from every window, transforming the colorful city into an even brighter aspect. While hundreds of automobile horns blasted the rhythm, the crowd uttered a deep-throated, repetitive cry: "*Ar-gen-tina! Ar-gen-tina!*" Costa Mendez smiled with pleasure at this demonstration of patriotic emotion. Yet as the car moved slowly through the crowd and faces looked in at the windows, I thought that I saw in the eyes of the people, for all their frenzied display of belligerent spirit, the haunting fear that Argentina was facing unknown dangers. This country had not known a foreign war since 1870.

In the late 1970s, after the junta overthrew the government of President Isabella Perón, the Argentinians had fought a bitter civil war in which radical terrorism was rampant and thousands of leftists died or disappeared. It is possible to view this conflict, as many do, as a brutal suppression of a legitimate political opposition. On the other hand, it may be seen as a victory by defenders of Western civilization over Marxist guerrillas in a putative war of liberation—and that is the way the rulers of Argentina saw it and saw themselves. The Carter Administration took the position that human rights violations by the Argentinian government were so extreme as to exclude her, as a practical matter, from normal relations with the United States. The Reagan Administration believed that a policy of friendship and persuasion was more likely to encourage the restoration of full human rights in Argentina than one of hostility and public condemnation. If results rather than self-congratulation are the aim of policy, this proved to be the correct judgment. "Disappearances," a hateful process under which the politically suspect are arrested and never seen again, with their fate never being disclosed to their families, declined dramatically. Political arrests dwindled, the death rate from political conflict approached zero. There were other signs of liberalization and evidence also of a will on the part of the junta to be a responsible partner in hemisphere affairs. To Ambassador Shlaudeman, in fact, Galtieri had suggested that Washington should acquiesce in the invasion as a quid pro quo for Argentinian support for the United States in the Southern Hemisphere. Galtieri never really understood that the

United States, as a nation of laws, could not have one rule with regard to the use of force for its friends and another for the Soviet Union and its proxies.

On the first morning in Buenos Aires, as I drove with Costa Mendez to the Casa Rosada, the presidential palace, I learned a new meaning for the word *crowd*. The media had urged the population to gather in the Plaza de Mayo to "show Haig the spirit of Argentina." Overnight, the government had transported thousands of demonstrators, many of them militant Peronists, from the provinces. The streets were jammed with surging masses of shouting men and women who appeared and disappeared into a sea of flags in a kind of tribal dance. Again, the rhythmic cry of "*Ar-gen-tina!*" and the counterpoint of car horns reverberated from the stones of the buildings. Men and women shouted at Costa Mendez, calling him "the Iron Chancellor." He slowed the car "so that we will have longer to talk before we reach the Casa Rosada," but really, I suspect, to let the hired crowd produce in me an impression of its frenzy. In fact, it reminded me of newsreels taken in Rome and Berlin in the 1930s. By now, people had begun to drum on the top of the automobile with their fists. There was nothing threatening in this; the crowd was merely exuberant. Costa Mendez and I continued gamely with our conversation, as if we were having a relaxed chat in a quiet salon.

Inside the Casa Rosada, with its presidential guards wearing shakoes and carrying drawn swords and its grim female security agents in gray shirts, Galtieri, a tall handsome man with a strong nose and a hearty drill-ground voice, greeted me with a bear hug and a cry of "*General!*" We had never met before, but I had brought an old friend of Galtieri's with me, Ambassador-at-large Dick Walters. Walters, a linguist of amazing fluency, is on good terms with many of the important men and women in the world and speaks to most of them in their own languages. Galtieri, who speaks halting English, talked at first in this language, then lapsed into Spanish. "I will call you 'general,' " he said in English, gripping my shoulders, "because there is a brotherhood among military men and a commonality of values that makes blunt talk easier among us."

He ushered me into the cabinet room. Already standing around the burnished table were uniformed representatives of the army and air force (but not Admiral Jorge Anaya and Lieutenant General Basilio Lami Dozo of the air force, the other members of the junta) and a sprinkling of foreign ministry people—including one symbolic, graying functionary who had spent his entire career negotiating with the British over the Malvinas to the exclusion of all other assignments. Galtieri opened the discussions with an exhaustive review of the history of the dispute. What he said next, while the British fleet moved down the South Atlantic like the weight on a clock, made me realize that the mixture of bravado and apprehension I believed I had seen the night before in the eyes of the crowd also existed inside the Casa Rosada. "The Argentinian government is willing to find an honorable solution that will save Mrs. Thatcher's government," Galtieri said with grandiose diction. "But we cannot sacrifice our honor." Then he lowered his voice, looked around the table at his colleagues, and added, "You will understand that the Argentinian government has to look good, too."

Because direct quotation of Galtieri's sentences, translated from a more plangent language than English, may leave an impression of theatricality, I should like to say that Galtieri was a man of considerable presence and bluff goodwill who was caught in the difficult position of trying to save a situation he did not create. The Falklands adventure was a navy operation, conceived and urged upon the junta by that service. The air force, realizing it must bear the brunt of any battle with the British navy and air force, was unenthusiastic. So, to a lesser degree, was the army. On at least three occasions, Galtieri prevented offensive operations from taking place, and there is reason to speculate that when the invasion finally was put in train, in deepest secrecy and employing only naval forces, the air force, and perhaps the army, may not have known exactly what was happening until it was too late to stop it. The extraordinary security measures surrounding the preparations for the landings kept both Britain and the United States in the dark, but the blackout may well have been equally designed to surprise the Argentinian army and air force. We were informed that four out of the five army commanders were not informed of the pending invasion.

The reasons why this should have been so go deep into the Argentinian political past. Rivalry between the army and navy has been simmering nearly as long as the Falklands question. Historically, the army has been the preeminent service in Argentina and the maker of presidents. The navy, proud of an aristocratic Spanish tradition, has always chafed at being in second place and, in the Falklands, found an opportunity to do something about it. Faced with a fait accompli and an impossible situation, Galtieri loyally attempted to preserve his country's safety and honor—meanwhile fighting hard to save himself from removal from power and disgrace. Had he been vested with the power to act alone, I think he might well have succeeded. But, as we shall see, he lacked that authority. In view of some of the alternatives to Galtieri, the world ought to have been happy enough to see him survive and guide Argentina back to democratic civilian rule.

Galtieri made it plain that similar considerations were on his own mind. As the crowd chanted under the windows of the palace, he said, "We have an internal situation that you will already have felt. Our crisis today can easily result in the destabilization of South America and thereby weaken the defense of the West. The consequences can go far beyond the local problem between Argentina and the United Kingdom. The result is uncertain."

Galtieri evidently had some political need to interlace sensible talk with bombast when in the presence of men who represented the other armed services. Hard on the heels of this clear-eyed estimate of the possible consequences of the situation, he recalled the capture of Lord Beresford, the leader of a British expedition against Argentina in 1806–1807, and his imprisonment in the religious shrine at Lujan. "If the British wish to send another army," he said with a flourish, "we will receive this anachronistic colonialist expedition with the appropriate honors."

Galtieri, with heavy meaning, then told me, "I cannot fail to express to you that I have received offers of aircraft, pilots, and armaments from countries not of the West." While flying from London to Buenos Aires, I had been informed that an aircraft carrying a high Cuban official had been forced to land in Brazil for repairs, and then had continued on to Argentina. This was interesting, if unsurprising, news because the Cuban ambassador had been absent from Buenos Aires for a year as a result of Argentinian charges that Havana had given aid and comfort to Marxist guerrillas in Argentina. "Last night at midnight," Galtieri continued, "a Cuban plane arrived in Buenos Aires carrying [Emilio] Aragones, the Cuban ambassador to Argentina, who brought an urgent letter to me from Fidel Castro. I have not yet received this letter." That the Soviets, despite their preoccupations in Poland and Afghanistan, should have sent the Cubans to scout a target of opportunity as tempting as Argentina was hardly astonishing.

Now that all the scenery was in place, the dialogue began. I told

Galtieri what the American proposals were and assured him that it was the purpose of the United States to work out an interim solution that would provide two important and friendly leaders with a success. Galtieri listened, nodding as I made my points. "In this pleasant conversation," he said, "I will say something once and then I will not repeat it again. As far as Argentina is concerned, there is no question of Argentinian sovereignty. Everything else, Argentina is disposed to negotiate."

I told him that if he insisted on having an Argentinian governor on the island, there would be war. For the first time of many, I expressed my judgment that the British were the superior force and would prevail in case of hostilities. "I must be frank," I added. "In the United States, the support for Britain is widespread. In the liberal world the sentiment is overwhelmingly in favor of Great Britain and would remain so if it comes to a confrontation." Galtieri replied, "I am truly regretful, but the government [of the islands] must be Argentinian. Argentina will not step back from what it considers to be its rights."

However, as the conversation continued, the Argentinians spoke of withdrawing from the island as if this were a possibility they were willing to consider, and there were other signs that progress might be possible. The two sides agreed to work out a draft agreement modifying the American proposal to reflect the needs of Argentina and meet again at six o'clock in the evening.

Galtieri then drew me toward an open French window leading onto a balcony. The crowd, later estimated at 300,000, seethed below. Galtieri obviously loved the sight of so much aroused humanity. He invited me to step onto the balcony with him while he addressed the Argentinian nation. Naturally, I declined, but I discovered on emerging from his office that he had arranged a bit of theater anyway—a helicopter to fly me back to the American embassy. As this craft, bearing the American negotiator, lifted off the roof of the Casa Rosada and circled over the crowd, Galtieri stepped out onto the balcony and gave his speech. According to the press, he referred to "peace with nobility and honor," but warned that "at the same time, anyone who dares touch one square meter of our sacred soil will regret it." There were cries from the crowd of "Peru, Peru," for a possible ally, and also shouts of "War! War!" and "Perón!" The United States was booed, and Mrs. Thatcher was called a rude name.

After the meeting, I played a couple of sets of tennis on courts at the American ambassador's residence and, after a restless night on the plane, attempted to take a half-hour nap. But even if I had not been disturbed by the rumble of tank treads in the street outside, I doubt that I would have been able to sleep with the situation as it was. Already I felt a glimmering of understanding that Galtieri, for all his imperious manner, was not a free man politically and diplomatically. Admiral Moya, chief of the president's military household, and other senior military officers had seemed to have some sort of watchdog role. Beyond that, the grandiloquent language, the posturing, the pretense of dealing from strength when disastrous weakness was the truth of the matter, filled me with dismay. Machismo appeared to be the style of the Argentinian leadership. This would mix dangerously with the icy scorn and iron will of Mrs. Thatcher. Even after all that I had said to the contrary, I feared that Galtieri and his colleagues were unable to believe that the British would fight. In one final attempt to convince them, I sent Dick Walters to see Galtieri alone and to tell him in crystal-clear terms, in the Spanish language, that if there was no negotiated settlement, the British would fight and win—and that the United States would support Britain. Gualtieri listened and replied: "Why are you telling me this? The British won't fight." In this judgment, I believe, he had the agreement if not the tutelage of Costa Mendez, who was reportedly the main opponent of my advice.

That afternoon, after hours of intensive drafting and redrafting by a brilliant young Foreign Service officer named David Gompert and other staffers, we presented a proposed agreement to the Argentinians. This draft suggested, on the basis of U.N. Resolution 502, that all military and security forces of both sides be withdrawn from the islands and an agreed surrounding area no later than two weeks from signature, and that no new forces be introduced. A consortium composed of the United States, Canada, and two Latin American countries would send observers to monitor compliance. Communications and movement of people between the island and the mainland would be maintained. The British and the Argentinians would undertake to negotiate a final settlement of the dispute, taking into account the rights and interests of the inhabitants, no later than December 31, 1982. The final paragraph read, in part, "The traditional local administration shall continue, including the executive and legislative councils. Argentina shall name a senior official as its coordinator on the islands to act as liaison with the consortium and to assist it in its tasks."

Officials of the Argentinian foreign ministry, in a working session with Assistant Secretary Enders, bitterly resisted this approach. They demanded that the Argentinian presence and authority on the island be preserved. If they insisted on that, Enders repeated, there would be no agreement and there would be war. Costa Mendez himself took the draft and asked for a short time in which to work on it. At 8:30 on Saturday evening, after an absence of more than two hours, Costa Mendez reappeared, apologizing for having kept us waiting. He had been with his president. Argentina was now proposing changes that had the effect of establishing its sovereignty and authority over the islands regardless of the outcome of negotiations. To Costa Mendez I said, "I'm afraid we'll have to go home. Your proposals will be utterly unacceptable to the British."

I asked for a meeting with Galtieri and this was arranged. There ensued eleven hours of intensive and often tumultuous negotiation. That day, the ten nations of the European Economic Community had imposed an embargo on trade with Argentina, and this had had a staggering effect. Argentina's annual exports to the EEC were valued at $2.3 billion, a large percentage of her total foreign sales. Without these revenues, it would be difficult for Argentina, which had reserves of about $5 billion, to pay the nearly $10 billion in annual interest and other charges on its foreign debt. If bankers refused to refinance short-term debt as a result of the crisis and export earnings were further limited by British pressure, Argentina could be bankrupt in a matter of a few weeks—unless, of course, the Soviets stepped in with, say, massive purchases of Argentinian wheat and came to dominate the economy through a system of long-term agreements.

Galtieri, though he never once conceded the slightest Argentinian military disadvantage, seemed keenly aware that the movement of the British fleet was also the movement of a historical clock that was striking the hours of these negotiations. Argentina had reinforced its landings with thousands of fresh troops. Any man who had passed through a military academy understood that every soldier the Argentinians put ashore in the Falklands was another potential hostage to the Royal Navy. At one point, Galtieri confided that the Russians had insinuated that they might be prepared to have one of their submarines sink the British carrier *Invincible* with Prince Andrew aboard and let Argentina take credit for the action. I was incredulous, but when imaginations begin to skid out of control, so do events.

In one of the most grueling sessions I have ever experienced, we worked hour after hour in the Casa Rosada with Galtieri and Costa Mendez and other officials. Small progress was made. Finally, between midnight and one in the morning, the impasse broke. Galtieri, face to face with the prospect of war and economic ruin, took me aside and, all bravado abandoned, said that only soldiers could understand how critically important it was to avoid conflict. Then, with moving candor, he told me that he could not withdraw both his military and his administrative presence from the Malvinas and last a week. If the British attacked, he would have to accept help from whomever it might be obtained.

Now that we knew Galtieri's requirements, the work went quickly. In less than an hour, we produced a new draft that was essentially the same as the one I had brought from London, except for two important modifications. Argentinian troops would leave the islands and the British administration would be restored. But economic and financial measures against Argentina would be terminated within two weeks, the flags of the six nations would be flown at the headquarters of the consortium, and, finally, national flags could be displayed at the residences and on the official automobiles of all countries represented on the islands. Galtieri attached great importance to the flags.

Early in the morning, I drove several blocks through the quiet streets to the nearest church. Other early risers, mostly women, had come to pray. I was recognized, and when I rose from my place, several woman approached me. These were quieter and more kindly faces than the ones I had seen in the crowd, and truer, I imagine, to the real face of Argentina. One by one they took my hand. Several murmured the same phrase: "Bring us peace." A young mother with a child in her arms pressed a religious medal into my palm. This would have been a moving experience at any time; on Easter morning, knowing better than anybody what obstacles lay in the path of peace, it was poignant indeed.

At the airport, Costa Mendez, showing the fatigue of our long session of the night before, awaited me. We had parted at one o'clock, and it was only a little after eight. Costa Mendez handed me a paper. It contained some personal thoughts of his own, he said. He hoped that I would read them on the plane. Aloft, I scanned the paper Costa Mendez had given me. It constituted a retreat from everything we had accomplished at the Casa Rosada the night before. The Argentinians were demanding either de facto authority over the islands through administrative arrangements that would give them immediate control of its government, or a British promise that sovereignty would be transferred to Argentina no later than December 31, 1982, regardless of the outcome of negotiations. This was a formula for war.

As I arrived in London, it was my hope that Mrs. Thatcher would see that while her strategy of pressure and threat was having the right effect in rattling the Argentinian leaders, it could not produce an Argentinian withdrawal from the islands. Only diplomacy could do that, short of military action. We were two minutes early at No. 10. Mrs. Thatcher convened the meeting at once. Though it was abundantly clear that her determination was as strong as ever, she and her ministers negotiated fully and responsibly every point of the draft we had produced with Galtieri and the junta. It was even clearer than before that self-determination for the islanders was the paramount consideration. Then, in the midst of the talks, we were informed that the New York Times, in its editions of that day, had carried an article describing the "personal thoughts" that Costa Mendez had handed to me at the airport in Buenos Aires as the official policy of the Argentinian government. This threw everything into doubt. At about 2:30 in the afternoon, I placed a telephone call from No. 10 Downing Street to the Argentinian foreign minister in Buenos Aires and asked for an explanation. Costa Mendez suggested that we talk later, after he had had time to discuss the matter with the Casa Rosada.

At nineteen minutes after midnight, April 13, Costa Mendez phoned me at my hotel. He told me that Argentinian islands must be governed under the Argentinian flag by an Argentinian governor. The junta could not tell the Argentinian people that it would discuss self-determination after all the risks they had taken. "These two points are essential, either one or the other," Costa Mendez continued. "That is what my president said." This finally confirmed the blatant double-cross. I clung to my temper and replied, "I didn't understand that from your president. All I got from him was the importance of flying the flag. This is a tragedy for everyone."

Perhaps, said Costa Mendez, it was just a matter of how the proposal was worded and presented; perhaps it was just a matter of "cosmetics." Costa Mendez, an able diplomat of long experience, surely knew how disingenuous this statement was. "There is a very, very serious prospect of war," I said. "The results will be felt within hours if I do not continue with this process." I asked again if I should come to Buenos Aires on the following day. Costa Mendez offered to send a man to Washington or come himself. I told him that would be a mistake. "Think it over tonight," I said. Costa Mendez said he would think it over with Galtieri. "Talk to your president," I urged. "Tell him we are close to a workable solution if we are not faced with these kinds of alternatives. I'll call you in the morning." Costa Mendez, in an abrupt change of mood and tone, suddenly began speaking of resuming negotiations early. "I will do my homework now," he said, and hung up.

When I called Mrs. Thatcher at 1:20 A.M., immediately after completing my talk with Costa Mendez, she listened sympathetically to my account of his words and said, "What a sad thing!" That day, a British paper published the results of a public opinion poll: 83 percent of the British people approved of the dispatch of the battle fleet, 67 percent were in favor of landing troops, 51 percent thought that the loss of military life was justified, and 60 percent were satisfied with the government's handling of the crisis thus far. As noted earlier, support for the prime minister was not universal. Questions were being raised about the wisdom of a fight, about the readiness of the British military, about the possibilities of failure.

Just before noon, Costa Mendez called back from Buenos Aires. His government was now willing to modify its demands. It would not insist on an Argentinian governor if the agreement contained a British acknowledgment that it intended to "decolonize" the Falklands in compliance with the 1964 United Nations Declaration on Decolonization. However, Buenos Aires was not prepared to submit this proposal formally without some advance indication of flexibility from London. Argentina also required a guarantee that the British fleet would limit its movements and, from the United States, a firm statement that the U.S. was not assisting Britain militarily in any way. I replied that it was unrealistic to expect the British to limit the fleet's freedom of action before an agreement had been reached. On military cooperation with the British, I could give firm assurances at once. Since the outset of the crisis, the United States had not granted British requests that would go beyond the scope of our customary patterns of cooperation. This would continue to be our practice while the diplomatic effort continued.

Francis Pym was cautious when I spoke to him a few minutes afterward about the new Argentinian offer. Neither of us was immediately familiar with the U.N. Declaration mentioned by Costa Mendez, and while our respective staffs tried to find a copy of it, we could only agree that there was a basis for hope that we might keep the dialogue going. I interpreted the Argentinian proposal to mean that Buenos Aires accepted autonomy and self-determination for the Falklanders. Pym, emphasizing once again that self-determination was crucial, did not reject the matter out of hand. Later, I spoke to Mrs. Thatcher, whose wariness and reservations were as great as Pym's; but she, too, believed that there was a basis for continuing the process. When Costa Mendez called back at two in the afternoon, I was able to tell him that I had spoken to the highest figures in the British government, and that I saw grounds for a breakthrough. Costa Mendez agreed that I should return to Buenos Aires. He sounded deeply tired. The British, too, were showing signs of fatigue. My staff and I had had very little sleep over a four-day period. I reflected that instantaneous modern communications and swift modern transport have drawbacks as well as advantages and decided to stop over in Washington for a night, in part so that I might arrive in Buenos Aires at an hour when our hosts would normally be awake.

The leaks and indiscipline that had vexed other diplomatic efforts were intensified in the Falklands crisis. Secret negotiations, which depended for their success on remaining secret, were repeatedly leaked from the White House and elsewhere and were seldom accurate. One report, on ABC's "Nightline," alleging that the United States was offering extraordinary intelligence support to Britain, very nearly wrecked the talks. This report was false. I informed ABC that it was false before it was broadcast. My day in Washington, which I had hoped to devote to a fresh examination of the Falklands crisis and other acute problems, was spent instead in trying to convince an outraged and deeply nervous Argentina that the U.S. government was telling the truth and that my return to Buenos Aires should not be canceled as the result of a mischievous press report based on a mendacious leak. Finally, I succeeded, but it was an arduous process. In addition to being the enemy of results, leaking is the thief of time.

On Thursday, April 15, we were airborne again. In Buenos Aires, the atmosphere was distinctly more ominous. The press had taken on an even darker and more bellicose tone, and the signs of self-hypno- tizing war hysteria had intensified. The prospect of military defeat, political isolation, and economic ruin—which was understood if not admitted at the heart of the Argentinian government—continued to be obscured by patriotic fervor. The day before, Galtieri had phoned President Reagan again and asked him to intervene with the British to stop the fleet; his rising anxiety was obvious.

I carried with me a proposal, approved by Mrs. Thatcher, that called for Argentinian withdrawal from the islands, a halt by the British fleet at a distance of 1,000 miles from the Falklands, an in- terim administration by Britain and Argentina with the United States also present in the islands, an immediate end to economic and finan- cial sanctions, and guaranteed completion of negotiations on the question of sovereignty by the last day of 1982. It seemed inconceiv- able to me that any rational government could reject these terms. I handed them over to the Argentinians as soon as I arrived and awaited their reaction.

The hours before midnight seem to be the late afternoon of the Argentinian official day. Costa Mendez called on me near 11 P.M. on April 15 in my rooms in the Sheraton Hotel. He had just come from a meeting with the junta. Argentina had rejected the British terms. Costa Mendez handed me new proposals. Once again, the Argentin- ians had reversed themselves and abandoned the compromise Costa Mendez had offered during our telephone conversation. Now the junta wanted shared administrative control of the islands during a transition period, with provisions for saturating the Falklands with Argentinians and for pushing out the existing population, plus condi- tions for a final settlement that would automatically result in a decla- ration of Argentinian sovereignty.

"I am sure the British will shoot when they receive this message," I told Costa Mendez. Visibly shaken, the foreign minister asked if I wanted to see Galtieri or the junta; I replied that I believed that I had earned the opportunity of seeing them and telling them the con- sequences of their decision. By now I was beyond surprise, but hardly able to bear the weight of my pessimism. It was clear that I was not dealing with people who were in a position to bargain in good faith. Time after time, Galtieri and Costa Mendez had agreed to condi- tions, only to have the ground cut from under them. Apparently, some invisible force held the power of veto over the duly constituted authorities of the government. "My advice is to wait until you see the junta before you send the British any messages," Costa Mendez said. Then, with a quick shake of his head, he uttered a phrase that demonstrates how large was the gulf that separated the two sides. "I am truly surprised," he said, "that the British will go to war for such a small problem as these few rocky islands."

As soon as Costa Mendez left, I reported to President Reagan, telling him what had occurred and saying that if, as I anticipated, I made no headway with Galtieri in the morning, I would depart immediately for Washington. It would be fruitless to carry these latest proposals to London. To do so, moreover, would be unfair to the British government because it would shift the onus for ending the negotiations onto it, when in truth the fault lay in Buenos Aires. "I can understand your personal frustration and disappointment," Reagan replied. "You undertook an extremely difficult task and have carried the burden to its fullest potential at great personal sacrifice. For that you have my deep personal thanks, Al." The President instructed me to return to Washington the following day unless overnight enlightenment occurred.

In the Casa Rosada the next morning, April 16, Galtieri listened magisterially while I explained the advantages to Argentina of the proposals worked out before Argentina's new demands shattered the matrix. Galtieri made no response. I asked him if I should present the American estimate of the situation and explain the proposal to the full junta. Again Galtieri was silent. Instead, he complained, "with the frankness that is possible between members of the family," that a number of people in the American embassy were asking for visas to go to Uruguay; this made Argentina look like Iran instead of a civilized Christian nation. Suddenly, Galtieri abandoned pretense and for a moment the underlying panic showed. "You must seek a peaceful solution," he said, in a tone of urgent appeal. Then, without further discussion, he suggested that I meet with the full junta on the following morning.

But when the meeting convened at 10:00 A.M. on April 17 in the Casa Rosada, I found that thorny intransigence and the lush foliage of heroic speech had grown up again during the night. I had not previously met Admiral Anaya and Lieutenant General Lami Dozo. For the record, Galtieri said that Argentinian sovereignty over the islands had never been up for discussion. Visualizing the end of negotiations, he said, rather mistily, "I can visualize a ceremony with the raising and lowering of flags by an honor guard of Royal Marines and San Martín Grenadiers while the British band plays the Argentinian national anthem and the Argentinian band plays 'God Save the Queen.' " Unfortunately, Galtieri added, he had not seen a draft expressing British concessions that would lead to this happy result. Admiral Anaya, an unsmiling man with a hard voice and harder opinions, spoke of his son, an army helicopter pilot who was serving in the islands. "My son is ready to die for the Malvinas," he told me, "and it is my family's point of view that we would be proud to know his blood had mingled with this sacred soil." By then I was very tired and I could not smother my feelings. "Let me assure you, Admiral," I replied, "that you don't know the meaning of war until you see the corpses of young men being put into body bags."

Lami Dozo, third in influence on the junta but also clearly its most realistic member, said that it was vital that both British and Argentinian forces be withdrawn, so long as the situation was resolved by December 31. I seized on this. "There is nothing in the agreement that precludes Argentina from saying that it received satisfaction," I said. "We must put this thread of history through the eye of a needle. I believe that withdrawal is achievable." Galtieri paused, threw back his head, and gave each of his colleagues a look of Caesarian authority. "I agree," he said. After a weighty pause, Anaya joined in. "Our concept is not far from yours," he said. "We must find an acceptable solution." We adjourned to draft yet another new set of proposals.

Again the result was an impasse. When, late at night, it seemed that progress had become impossible, I played a wild card. Although the British in fact told us nothing of their military plans, the Argentinians plainly believed that we knew everything they did. Possibly this misconception could be useful. I called Bill Clark at the White House on an open line, knowing that the Argentinians would monitor the call, and told him in a tone of confidentiality that British military action was imminent. At 2:00 A.M. on April 18, new proposals were delivered to me at the hotel together with an invitation to resume the negotiations at the Casa Rosada at two o'clock in the afternoon.

We met in a frigid, air-conditioned conference room, hung with maps and furnished with gleaming modern tables and chairs, on the second floor of the Casa Rosada. Frigidity extended beyond the room: members of my staff, waiting outside, were left for nearly twelve hours without food and were escorted to the lavatory by armed guards. Gradually, it became apparent what the difficulty had been. If Galtieri did not hold the power of decision, neither did the junta. On every decision, the government apparently had to secure the unanimous consent of every corps commander in the army and of their equivalents in the navy and air force. Progress was made by syllables and centimeters and then vetoed by men who had never been part of the negotiations. Ten hours of haggling failed to produce a workable text. The Argentinians could not agree on the very point the junta had granted the day before: withdrawal of forces. The staffs on both sides were half asleep.

At ten in the evening, Galtieri again drew me aside. "If I lay it all on the line," he said, "I won't be here." I asked him how long he thought he would survive if he lost a war to the British. Just before midnight, Galtieri reconvened the junta, and by 2:40 A.M. on April 19, we had produced a draft, acceptable to the Argentinians, providing for an immediate cessation of hostilities and the withdrawal of forces, an Argentinian presence on the island under a U.S. guarantee, and negotiations leading to a resolution of the question by December 31, 1982. I believed that Mrs. Thatcher would have great difficulty in accepting this text. Later in the morning, I met again with the Argentinians to clear up a number of unresolved points. This, too, was a strenuous session, but by 1:00 P.M., we had in hand a modified text that anticipated some of the British objections.

Leaving the Casa Rosada, I ordered that our airplane be ready for takeoff at 4:00 P.M. Our destination was undecided. If Mrs. Thatcher, after seeing the Argentinian proposals, wanted me to come to London for further talks, I was prepared to do that. Otherwise, I would return to Washington. Costa Mendez remained with Galtieri, but assured me that he would meet me at my hotel at two o'clock. He did not keep that appointment and, after a number of telephone calls, arranged to meet me at the airport. Recalling our last airport meeting, I was deeply apprehensive as my car passed, in a pouring rain, through the streets of Buenos Aires.

The engines of the jet were already turning when Costa Mendez arrived. As in our earlier airport encounter, he drew an envelope from his pocket, advising me to open it and read the message inside after I was airborne. As the wheels lifted off the runway, I read Costa Mendez's message. "It is absolutely essential and *conditio sine qua non* that negotiations will have to conclude with a result on December 31, 1982," it said. "This result must include a recognition of

Argentinian sovereignty over the islands." Once again, in an exercise of bad faith that is unique in my experience as a negotiator, the Argentinians had gone back on their word and returned to their original, impossible terms: the British must either give Argentina sovereignty over the Falklands, or approve an arrangement for governing the island that amounted to de facto Argentinian sovereignty. This Mrs. Thatcher would never give them because it rewarded aggression and betrayed the islanders. The British fleet would be within gunnery distance of South Georgia within forty-eight hours.

In the face of the latest Argentinian refusal, the United States could either abandon the negotiations or make one final attempt to resolve the situation. President Reagan approved my suggestion that we abandon good offices, discard the earlier draft agreements, and present an American proposal to Argentina and Britain. On April 23, Francis Pym arrived in Washington for two days of talks and told me that Mrs. Thatcher was willing to try again. At the State Department we had produced a proposal that called for an eventual negotiated transfer of sovereignty, but preserved the basic British position by providing for free choice by the islanders as to whether they would be associated with one or the other of the parties, opt for independence, or even accept compensation for leaving the Falklands.

It was my plan to present this draft to Pym, negotiate down to the British bottom line, and then pass the proposal on to the Argentinians. However, before I had an opportunity to discuss the substance of the paper with the British foreign secretary, Bill Clark confided its details to him at a breakfast meeting. Pym told me that Mrs. Thatcher would not be able to accept the American draft; even her most ardent supporters in the Conservative party would not support it. Nevertheless, Mrs. Thatcher, after considering our draft, very reluctantly agreed that the United States might put it forward to Argentina. Her action did not imply acceptance of all of its provisions, but it showed again that Britain was prepared, as she had been from the start, to negotiate a settlement as long as the islanders were given the opportunity of deciding their own future. Once again, we had a reasonable alternative to useless bloodshed—and once again, its fate was in the hands of the Argentinians.

Costa Mendez, who was now in Washington himself, had told me that the Argentinians would withdraw from negotiations should the British attack South Georgia. Again, I told him that while British military action appeared to be imminent, there was nothing the

United States could do to stop it: the British did not tell us their plans. On April 25, the day Costa Mendez had planned a meeting to discuss the American proposal, British forces invaded South Georgia. Costa Mendez phoned me to cancel the meeting. Argentina, he said, was in a state of shock. "You warned of British action," he said. "But we didn't believe it." Argentina, Costa Mendez added, was considering taking the conflict to the U.N. He said he would call me again at nine the following morning.

The next day, April 26, while awaiting Costa Mendez's call, I heard from Francis Pym. New ideas were coming from Britain, he told me. Washington lay under gray skies, and I drove through a soaking rain to the headquarters of the Organization of American States, which had convened a meeting of foreign ministers to consider the Falklands question. My speech, a reiteration of the position I had stated on so many occasions in Buenos Aires and elsewhere—that the rule of law, not the rule of force, must govern international conduct—was greeted by stony silence.

Afterward, I met with Costa Mendez, telling him that within forty-eight hours, the British would almost certainly strike again, bombarding airfields, launching commando raids. "We have no more time," I said. "The American proposal is fair and reasonable. If necessary, we will go public with it and let the world judge why these negotiations have produced no result." In Costa Mendez, I sensed a reluctance to forward the U.S. proposal. He told me that there was a virulent anti-American and anti-Haig atmosphere building in the country and in the junta. I offered to return to Buenos Aires and deliver the text to Galtieri and the junta myself. Although I did not disclose the thought to Costa Mendez, I believed that the British would not carry out further attacks if the American Secretary of State was in Argentina or en route.

I asked that the junta inform me within twenty-four hours whether they could receive me. Costa Mendez promised to pass on the message, but as the hours passed, no reply came. On the telephone, Costa Mendez said that he was awaiting Galtieri's decision. As the deadline approached, we phoned the Argentinian embassy and were told that Costa Mendez was dining with the ambassador and could not be disturbed. Finally, Costa Mendez informed me that his government could not receive me in Buenos Aires at this time.

We were not certain that Costa Mendez had transmitted the American proposal to Galtieri. I instructed Ambassador Shlaudeman to deliver the draft to the Argentinians. We asked that the Argentinian government inform the United States government by midnight April 27, Buenos Aires time, whether it could accept the agreement. Galtieri, receiving this message, seemed to Shlaudeman to be tired but composed. He remarked that no one wanted war, but if Britain attacked, Argentina would resist with all her means. "I do not understand," he said wearily, "why the United States government, with all its resources, cannot stop Mrs. Thatcher from launching this attack."

Meanwhile, Francis Pym informed me that he had (without prior consultation with the U.S. government) conceived a plan to convene an international conference on the Falklands crisis, possibly in Mexico City, under the sponsorship of the Mexicans and perhaps some other Latin American states. This seemed to be the "new idea" from London that Pym had promised earlier. I was surprised by it because, during an earlier discussion with Pym, he had assured me that he had had no contact with the Mexicans. Now Pym told me that President Lopez Portillo had expressed an interest in being helpful. The British were prepared to offer to stop their task force and turn it back if the Argentinians first withdrew from the Falklands, and to forego sending back their governor while accepting an Argentinian resident at Port Stanley to look after the interests of Argentinians living on the islands, as well as other provisions, including a U.S. guarantee of the security of the islands. The Argentinians regarded this offer as surrender terms dictated by the British, other Latin American states looked upon it as an effort to manipulate opinion in the hemisphere, and Pym's plan came to naught.

Meanwhile, the deadline approached for the junta's answer to the final draft that had been delivered by Shlaudeman on April 25. Britain declared a total air and sea blockade for 200 miles around the Falklands, effective at 7:00 A.M. on Friday, April 30. A steady flow of messages came from Buenos Aires, suggesting that the junta was "favorably disposed" to the newest draft. It was impossible to know if this meant that the junta was serious or if it was buying time. We pressed for an answer. At fifteen minutes to midnight, the Argentinian minister of the interior telephoned from the Casa Rosada to say that his government had not forgotten the time, but there was no answer yet; the junta was still meeting. In Washington, Costa Mendez had stopped returning my telephone calls. As the deadline approached, I waited in vain with my staff in the office for word from Costa Mendez. Finally, a telephone call to the Argentinian embassy produced the information that Costa Mendez, once again, was point-edly dining with the ambassador while we awaited his reply. I left the office and went home.

Then, on Thursday, long after the deadline and only hours before the blockade went into effect, Costa Mendez brought the junta's reply to the Department of State: "Argentina's objective is the recog-nition of its sovereignty over the Malvinas . . . for us, [this] is an unrenounceable goal. . . . The document that you sent falls short of Argentinian demands and does not satisfy its minimum aspirations." Argentina could not accept a binding referendum among the inhabi-tants of the island on its future status.

War was now inevitable. The Argentinian government had simply been incapable of responding; now it would fall like a house of cards, with unforeseeable consequences. On April 30, I announced the breakdown of negotiations to the press and stated that the United States would support Britain. We suspended military exports to Ar-gentina and withheld certification of Argentinian eligibility for mili-tary sales, suspended Export-Import Bank credits and guarantees and Commodity Credit Corporation loans, and adopted a policy of responding favorably to British requests for military materiel.

The next day, May 1, the British bombed the airfield at Port Stanley. The following day, with hostilities raging, President Fer-nando Belaunde Terry of Peru telephoned me from Lima with the proposal that one final attempt be made to stop the fighting and find a peaceful solution. It was a Sunday, and he found me at home. Speaking over an open line, we worked all day on a new draft. Belaunde believed that the proposals had become too complicated. "Simplify," he said, "and we can still do it." Finally, largely due to Belaunde's gift for clarification, we reduced the proposal to five sim-ple points. He presented these to both sides and encountered, as he said "a certain obstinance" in the Argentinians. Nevertheless, he gained acceptance in principle from both parties, and on May 4, sent an official of the Peruvian foreign ministry to Buenos Aires with the new paper. But while the junta was in the act of considering it, the submarine HMS *Conqueror* sank the Argentinian cruiser *General Belgrano* outside the blockade zone. The submarine captain, acting on rules of engagement issued long before, deemed that the *Belgrano*, which was equipped with Exocet missiles and other armaments highly dangerous to British ships, was steaming in a threatening manner toward the British fleet. Out of a crew of 1,042, 308 died.

The early reports of casualties reaching the junta were even more serious than this, and the Argentinians, reacting angrily to the bad news, rejected the new peace proposal. Three days later, the British destroyer *Sheffield* was set afire by a radar-seeking Exocet missile fired from an Argentinian aircraft and abandoned with the loss of twenty lives.

One final attempt was made to resume negotiations. Javier Pérez de Cuéllar, secretary general of the United Nations, responding, as he told Mrs. Kirkpatrick, to appeals from the king of Spain, the president of Colombia, and other dignitaries, attempted to bring the parties together. It did not seem to me that there was much prospect for success in this initiative, and I informed the secretary general that the United States would oppose any settlement that appeared to reward aggression or derogate from the rule of law, but encouraged him to try. After a valiant effort, Perez de Cuellar also failed to reconcile the parties to a peaceful outcome.

During the negotiations, Galtieri had told me repeatedly that, in case of hostilities, he would be forced to accept the assistance, including munitions, that had been offered by the Cubans and the Soviets. It was important to turn him away from this action, if in fact he was seriously contemplating it. It was important, too, to see if the tragic events of the first days of fighting had created an opportunity to return to the peace process. In the second week of May, Dick Walters flew secretly to Buenos Aires for a final talk with the junta.

Galtieri, in an elegiac mood, spoke of the loss of the *Belgrano*. After that, he said, Argentina had needed a success very badly. The *Sheffield* had been a considerable success, Walters responded; was it not possible to abandon fighting and break through, now, with honor intact? Galtieri spoke again of sovereignty. "Hundreds have been killed," he said. "What can I tell my people they have gained by their sacrifices?" Walters said that he did not know who would be the winner of the battle for the Malvinas, but the U.S.S.R. would be the only winner in this war. After a pause, Galtieri said, "I agree." He would seek help, he said, but not at the price of letting the Soviets have any say in Argentina. The Soviets, said Lami Dozo, were "offering military equipment and assistance at low prices—but money is only part of the price, and Argentina will never pay that price." "No matter what happens," Admiral Anaya said, "I will never, repeat never, turn to the Soviet Union. It would betray everything for which I stand." Anaya spoke of his dead sailors and of his long friendship with Galtieri; they had been comrades since the age of twelve. But there was no hope of saving the situation. It was already irretrievably lost, and so were the men who had created it. Nevertheless, Walters, as always, had performed brilliantly and bravely: his mission eliminated any possibility that the desperate leaders of Argentina would collaborate in their last moments with the Soviet Union.

Three and a half weeks after British troops went ashore in the Falklands, the Argentinian defenders, cut off from supplies and faced with a better-trained and better-led force, surrendered. The fighting men on both sides showed great bravery and humanitarian feeling for wounded enemies and prisoners. Altogether, about 1,000 died and over 1,700 were wounded. The loss in ships and aircraft and other materiel was enormous, and the destructive power of modern conventional weapons shocked and sobered the whole world. Galtieri resigned on June 17, and after the war was over, he was arrested and placed in custody. The currency of Argentina was debauched, and political consequences that no one can predict began to unfold.

Many believe, and all hope, that the return to civilian rule in Argentina will produce a more stable atmosphere within the country and that the bellicosity that characterized the episode over the Falklands will permanently subside. It would be wise to temper these hopes with the knowledge that the junta, in its most mulish moments, was in touch with civilian politicians as well as military officers. All three members of the junta complained, throughout their conversations with me, that it was unjust that military men should have to deal in this way with a political question. The harshness, the unyielding position on the question of sovereignty, I was told, came not from the military but from some of the civilian political parties and most especially from the Peronists. There is another cautionary factor. In the midst of a moment of heated advocacy by Mrs. Kirkpatrick early in the crisis, it was pointed out that many experts believed that Argentina would soon develop a nuclear weapon. This possibility is now public knowledge. To place such devices in the hands of a country that was willing to resort to aggression, and suffer a crushing humiliation as a result, is to change strategic perceptions in Latin America in a serious way.

Why did it all happen? There are obvious answers: the Argentinian leaders did not read British reaction, British military capabilities, and especially the character of the British prime minister aright. The British did not appreciate the depth of Argentinian feeling about "a few rocky islands" in the South Atlantic. The United States, preoccupied with great events elsewhere in the world and with its own economic troubles, failed to see that conditions were right for a war between two of its friends in its own hemisphere. It has been suggested that the Argentinians believed that the United States would tolerate their aggression. There is absolutely no basis for this misconception since no sane U.S. official could have contributed to such a cataclysmic misunderstanding. In fact, the Argentinians were specifically warned against military action against the islands by officials of the United States. Almost certainly, the Argentinians also believed that the United States could control the military and diplomatic actions of the British and that the British depended on us for intelligence and logistic support. Admiral Anaya seemed convinced that we were telling the Royal Navy the locations of Argentinian ships. In fact, we could not influence British operations, we provided no intelligence support before the collapse of negotiations, and, as Dick Walters told Anaya, British success in locating Argentinian ships might have been due to Argentinian bad luck or British technology, but it had nothing to do with American technology.

The real causes of the war lie deep within the collective minds of Britain and Argentina. It may be that the explanation for the war, like the emotions that fanned its flames, is exceedingly simple: the time was right. Argentina faced overwhelming economic problems and had passed through a period of terrorism and counterterrorism that had deeply frightened and divided the nation. The Falklands diverted the attention of Argentinians from the worrying problem of inflation and provided a longed-for opportunity for unity and national reconciliation; the legends and facts of Argentinian history made it possible for left and right to unite in hatred of a "colonialist" foreign power.

Britain, too, had its economic problems and social rivalries and its legends and traditions. It is not easy, in the psychological sense, for a people living in the afterglow of great empire and unquestioned power and authority, to exist without these things. Mrs. Thatcher's objective, after all, was to demonstrate that Britain was still Britain. It is a noble thing to defend principle at the cost of great sacrifice, and a willingness to do so and pay the price is thread and dye in the tapestry of British history. Cynics in Argentina and America might make jokes about 1,000 sheepherders on an antipodal island, but the shepherds were Englishmen and, therefore, by the long tradition and fearless practice of the British crown, safe from the threats of foreigners.

Last and first, the war was caused by the original miscalculation on the part of the Argentinian military junta that a Western democracy was too soft, too decadent, to defend itself. This delusion on the part of undemocratic governments has been, and remains, the greatest danger to peace in this century. The cacophonous self-criticism of the democracies and their standard of living, added to the unwavering insistence of their people that peace must be the paramount goal of their elected governments, are signs of great strength. Autocrats persist in mistaking them for signs of weakness. The British demonstrated that a free people have not only kept a sinewy grip on the values they seem to take for granted, but are willing to fight for them, and to fight supremely well against considerable odds. The cost was great, but not as great as the cost of a miscalculation by Moscow should it forget these truths. The Falklands crisis was the most useful and timely reminder of the true character of the West in many years. Indeed, Britain's action in the Falklands may have marked a historic turning point in what has been a long and dangerous night of Western passivity.

The reader will not have failed to see the lesson. The mixture of history, passion, miscalculation, national pride, and personal egotism that produced a "little" war that everyone knew was senseless and avoidable also contains the ingredients for a much larger conflict. It was by no means impossible that the fighting in the Falklands could have escalated into a general war. Wars are not made on the basis of abstract principle but as a result of anger and the failures of judgment that rise out of human nature. The tendency to be carried away by the emotions of the moment is not peculiar to Argentina and the tendency to underestimate the uncontrollable power of the emotions of a faraway people and the folly of their leaders is not confined to Britain.

If the Falklands war put us on our guard against these things, then we should be grateful. But we should remember, too, that despite the fact that peace was possible, and the basis for peace was evident to everyone involved, war was the conscious choice of the Argentinian leaders and, therefore, the only resort of the British. In my last communication to the Argentinian government before the shooting started, I wrote, "There can be no greater tribute to leadership than the will to make a reasonable but hard decision." I was asking the junta to abandon pride and embrace reason. That is the request that diplomacy has always made to rulers, and I was not the first diplomat to be answered by an unyielding silence.

In the Falklands, the West was given a great victory by Great Britain. I do not mean the defeat of Argentinian soldiers by British soldiers. Every man who fell on either side represented a loss to the free world. British arms prevailed, but principle triumphed. The will of the West was tested and found to be equal to the task. The rule of law was upheld. The freedom of a faraway people was preserved. For this, the free world may thank the men of the British task force and Mrs. Thatcher, who was by far the strongest, the shrewdest, and the most clear-sighted player in the game. In times of acute national crisis, a leader will always hear advice that clashes with his inner convictions. Easier courses than the right course will be thrust upon him. It is the leader who, knowing where the true interest of the nation lies, resists such counsel and perseveres in his principles, who deserves the name of statesman. Margaret Thatcher belongs in that company.

The United States, by involving itself in the negotiating process at a high level, had helped to make it possible for Mrs. Thatcher to do what she did. In the beginning, she did not command, even in her own cabinet and party, the widespread support for her vision that she later enjoyed. The opportunity to seek a negotiated solution through the good offices of Britain's best friend, and for a systematic ordering of the facts by a third party, gave Mrs. Thatcher the time she needed for opinion to anneal around her policy. Although the Reagan Administration attached great importance to the survival of the Thatcher government, the United States doubtless would have behaved as it did, placing its prestige on the line, no matter who was prime minister of Britain or which party was in power. The course we took was right for our mutual interests and for the collective interest of the West.

As for me, my efforts in the Falklands ultimately cost me my job as Secretary of State. As I had forewarned my wife, the work I had done was perceived to be a failure, and those in the Administration who had been looking for an issue on which to bring me down recognized that I had given them one. Knowing that this would be so, I accepted the consequences when they came, very soon afterward. In my own mind, I regarded American diplomacy in the Falklands crisis as a success. It is a matter of personal sorrow that we were not in the end able to prevent the shedding of blood, but on every other count we succeeded in acting with honor and in upholding the principles that we set out to defend. Withdrawal from public life was, for me, an acceptable price to pay for this result, which I had hoped, above all others except peace, that the United States and the West could achieve.

BACKGROUND

After a short dry period following the resignation, in January, of Richard Allen as National Security Adviser, the Falklands crisis let loose the leakers once again. Until the Argentinians made their landing, I had been scheduled to accompany the President on his trip to the Caribbean for a summit meeting of regional heads of state and government. Summits always generate a lot of press coverage, and for those members of the White House staff who think in such terms, media exposure for the President was the primary objective of the trip.

I would agree that it was a very important objective. Those who work for Presidents understand that their chiefs are entitled to a clear field when they decide to go before the public. No sensible member of the Cabinet would schedule a news conference on the same day as the President or testify in an open hearing on Capitol Hill on a day when the chief executive had scheduled an important public statement. Even after all my months in the trenches with the President's aides, therefore, I was startled to hear reports from the White House that I had undertaken the Falklands mission as a means of upstaging Ronald Reagan in his visits to Jamaica and Barbados. The White House term for my peace mission, I was told, was "grandstanding." This was a charge that might better have been leveled at Leopoldo Galtieri and his comrades in Argentina, but I saw no point in bringing this to the attention of the President's ruffled aides.

On April 10, the New York Times reported that I had refused to accept an airplane from the White House fleet because it had no windows and had demanded a more luxurious aircraft. It is true that a KC-135, a cargo transport refitted for passenger use and one of several military versions of the Boeing 707, had been allocated for my use and that this aircraft has no windows. It is also true that I had asked that it be replaced, if possible, with a VC-137, another variation on the Boeing 707 that does have windows.

Windows, however, were not the issue. The issue was working space and communications. The VC-137, an aircraft traditionally used by the Secretary of State, is equipped with desks, typewriters, copying machines, and the most advanced communications gear. As my staff and I would be engaged in drafting and redrafting innumerable versions of a Falklands agreement and would require fast, secure communications in order to report to the President (who was staying in a private house on Barbados) and communicate with the parties to the dispute, this gear was indispensable. The KC-135 is much less well designed and equipped to be used as a flying command post during a spell of shuttle diplomacy.

I asked Bill Clark to make a change, thinking that this would be a routine matter. It did not seem likely that any American official apart from the President, who was using Air Force One, would have greater need of airborne office facilities or advanced communications; so far as I knew, nobody else in the Administration was flying back and forth across the ocean trying to prevent a war. Clark told me that James Baker was in charge of assigning aircraft and that he guarded the prerogative jealously. It was he who had chosen my plane, and only he could change the order. "Well, then," I said, "ask him to change it."

Evidently Baker hesitated to do so. It turned out that the only available VC-137 was being used by a congressional delegation headed by Representative Jim Wright of Texas. If I wanted the plane, Clark said, I'd have to call Wright and ask him for it. I did so; Wright graciously swapped aircraft with me, and after adjusting to a consequent schedule change that required a 3:00 A.M. takeoff, I flew to London to talk to Mrs. Thatcher.

That ought to have been an end to the matter, but one of my aides, offended by the newspaper item, made the fundamental mistake of complaining to the *Times*. "This is typical of the sort of sniping Secretary Haig has had to endure from the beginning of this Administration," he was quoted as saying, with a beguiling truthfulness that makes it easy for me to forgive him everything. He went on to say, with admirable loyalty but shaky judgment, that he believed the story had been "planted" by James Baker. This (like earlier suggestions that there was a "guerrilla" in the White House who was out to get me), implied that there was some sort of plot against me.

"Ludicrous," said an unnamed White House aide. Untrue, said the *Times* reporter who had written the original item, thus bending if not violating the code of anonymity that governs the relationship between leaker and leakee; if the reporter did not actually identify his source, he narrowed the circle of suspects by one, an incremental sacrifice of confidentiality that may simply have indicated how highly he thought of Baker and how little he was able to control this admiration.

This is the sort of story democracy loves. Ridicule, when it is earned, sticks a needle into the pompous, gives everyone a chuckle, does nobody any harm—and frequently does the fellow getting the needle a world of good. The press took it up and had a good time with it, as was right and proper. The fact that this particular story wasn't accurate made no difference to the entertainment value.

Because I took no reporters with me on the VC-137—there was simply no room for them, and besides, a mission that depended on secret diplomacy, with bloodshed as the alternative, could not be served by public relations—very little news about the negotiations emanated from me or my staff. This created a vacuum that was quickly filled by leakers and spokesmen and even an enterprising reporter or two. Jack Anderson printed the transcript of an aircraft-to-ground conversation between President Reagan and me that had been intercepted by one of Anderson's myriad sources. CBS News reported (inaccurately) that the United States was giving satellite intelligence to Argentina on the movements of the British fleet, one of many intelligence-related stories that had no basis in fact but an aggravating impact on negotiations. (The only satellite pictures we gave either side, so far as I am aware, were Landsat pictures of the Argentinian coast and the Falklands, which are unclassified and available for sale to any government or person; both the British and the Argentinians received these.) Much information in the press was based on leaks, but not all. Galtieri complained throughout the crisis about quotations of Caspar Weinberger, whose anglophilia led him, *inter alia*, into statements that did not have the effect, as Galtieri put it, of "tranquilizing the press."

Possibly the most gorgeous leak of the month of May was authored by Dr. Norman Bailey of the NSC staff who, at breakfast in

Washington with a group of newsmen, including the correspondent
of the British *Guardian*, described the details of a draft agreement,
some of which were correct, some of which were not, and some of
which, accurate or inaccurate, were so sensitive as to jeopardize not
merely the negotiations but the future of Anglo-American dinner-
table conversation. As Dr. Bailey was speaking for quotation, it may
be that he can be credited with the invention of the on-the-record
leak.

On April 15, while I was en route to Buenos Aires with a British
proposal that many believed might bring peace and, incidentally,
success to my efforts, the term "grandstanding" found its way into
print. Hedrick Smith reported in the *Times* that:

Once again, White House aides are grumbling privately about Mr. Haig's
"grandstanding." Some say he has not only taken center stage but "even
stolen the limelight" from President Reagan by making an extended public
statement this afternoon on the Falklands crisis after the President was
cautioned by Mr. Haig . . . to say almost nothing during a quick morning
session with reporters. . . . "You can say Haig needs a win," a White House
official agreed, asking not be quoted [*sic*]. ". . . He seems to be reveling in it.
But if this one doesn't work out, I think it would be going too far to say he
loses everything. . . ." "It's really [Haig's] baby," commented one Administration foreign policy specialist. "He didn't even have to share the responsibility with the crisis management committee under Vice President
Bush. . . ." "He only hurts himself with his grandstanding."

The tone and methodology reflected in this item were familiar
enough, and the message was quite clear: when I came back to Washington, with or without peace in the Falklands, I could expect to read
a lot about myself. In the end, as the world knows, I did not come
home with peace. Nor was there peace for me at home. The intensity
of the anonymous gossip reported in the press increased steadily.
Shortly after my return, a lifelong friend who has never failed to tell
me the truth, and who is in a position to know the truth, called to say
that there had been a meeting in the White House at which my future
had been discussed. "Haig is going to go, and go quickly," James
Baker was quoted by my friend as saying, "and we are going to make
it happen."

"Mr. President, I Want You to Understand What's Going On around You"

ABOARD Air Force One en route to Paris, the first stop on a ten-day diplomatic visit to Europe, President Reagan broke his reading glasses. I loaned him an extra pair of my own, and he discovered that he could see perfectly well with them. "That proves it, Mr. President—we have the same vision," I said. We laughed together over this mild joke, but by the time the trip was completed, I saw with final clarity that however similar our views might be on certain issues, we were hopelessly divided on other, vital questions, and the confident personal relationship that might have bridged this difference would always be denied to Reagan and me.

The President's trip to Europe was overdue. The Ottawa economic summit, a year before, had not allayed the anxiety of our allies over the effect of high American interest rates and an abnormally strong dollar on European recovery from economic recession. In the five months and more since martial law was imposed in Poland, the questions surrounding the trans-Siberian pipeline had remained unresolved. The threat of retroactive sanctions, linked to "extraterritoriality" (i.e., U.S. action to prevent the export of American technology to the U.S.S.R. even if it was fabricated abroad by foreign firms), with the loss of jobs and revenue that such policies implied for U.S. subsidiaries in Europe or European manufacturers of U.S.-licensed pipeline components, remained an acute concern to the Europeans. They seemed as determined as ever to build the pipeline with Western credits and technology, and the Reagan Administration was equally fixed on the principle that the West should not spend billions to defend itself against the Soviet military threat while at the same time subsidizing the Soviet economy. The time had come to resolve this question, which had so sorely tried the unity of the alliance, by sitting at the conference table with our allies and friends and finding a formula that preserved both the logic of the American position and the political and economic requirements of the Europeans.

We expected, with some confidence, to be able to do this at the seven-nation economic summit at Versailles June 4–6. It was difficult to persuade the President and his staff or the Defense Department of the serious effect that unilateral American actions on the pipeline, trade, economic and monetary policies, and nuclear policies were producing among our allies. Nevertheless, I had tried to insure that the ground was well prepared. While the uproar over the American plan to impose retroactive sanctions was still at its height, the President had agreed to send Under Secretary of State James L. Buckley on a mission to discuss the issue with European governments. After exhaustive—and sometimes overly frank—talks, Buckley had made some progress, but the principal questions remained unresolved. It could hardly have been otherwise because the pipeline sanctions, as our friends bluntly told us, had the effect of punishing our allies, at least in the near term, more than the Soviets. It was clear to all on the American side that if the Europeans remained intransigent on the question of credits, it would be difficult for the United States not to be equally intransigent on the pipeline question.

I advised President Reagan to study the mood of the alliance very carefully before making his final decision, and as early as February, after the first NSC meeting on the pipeline, urged him to send George Shultz, who was well regarded among European financial experts, ahead of him to talk to allied leaders. The hope here was that an atmosphere of calm and reason could be restored to the dialogue. In May, Reagan finally moved and sent Shultz on a round-robin mission to the heads of state of the other participating nations—Canada, France, Italy, Japan, the United Kingdom, and West Germany.

Shultz's mission, carried out with the skill and intelligence that is characteristic of him, in some ways confirmed my own reporting to Reagan over a long period of time. Shultz had found sympathy for American principles and puzzlement over American methods. He had also found a desire on the part of our friends and allies for American leadership. "They want a leader," he told Reagan succinctly. "You're elected." Europe could not, however, accept crudely publicized American decisions that had the effect of overruling the policies of sovereign European governments.

Yet sentiment within the Administration for taking just such measures continued to run high. Around the NSC table some of the President's advisers insisted that Europe was not doing enough on the question of sanctions against the Soviet Union, especially on the question of limiting future official or officially backed credits to Moscow. The belief, always strong, that the United States must somehow shock its European allies into an acceptance of the Soviet threat had grown stronger as a result of differences over the pipeline. As I have said, I believed that sanctions were essential in response to the brutalization of Poland, that the pipeline prefigured an unwise dependence on energy from Western Europe's primary enemy, and that the West (and Europe in particular) was overextended in its lending to the Soviet bloc. These considerations were important. But in the fundamental order of Western goals, allied unity remains supremely important.

We needed a policy to preserve that unity and restore the equilibrium and the spirit of the alliance. In Ottawa, President Reagan had made the entirely reasonable point, accepted by the other heads of government, that the West should not make financial transactions with the U.S.S.R. on more favorable terms than Western countries gave one another. Nevertheless, some European governments had continued to do just that. As Versailles approached, I made it plain to the European foreign ministers that if we did not at least have progress on a cooperative policy to limit future government-backed credits to the Soviet Union, the United States would find it difficult not to apply retroactive sanctions that would prevent the manufacture of American technology for the pipeline.

Out of these consultations, an initiative developed. The weakness of the French franc threatened not only the domestic programs of the Mitterrand government but also the efforts of other European governments to control inflation and unemployment. The French asked that the United States commit itself publicly to bolster the franc by intervening in the foreign exchange market as a clearly stated matter of policy. Not unexpectedly, this proposal excited opposition among Reagan's advisers. Secretary of the Treasury Donald Regan and other monetary conservatives argued, correctly, that intervention of this kind, though it costs the United States a great deal of money, does not solve the basic problem. The real solution lies in the development of a concert of economic policies among and within the industrialized nations that will control imbalances in currency values. However cogent, this was a moot argument, as no mechanism existed for making such cooperation possible and differing economic philosophies made it unlikely that one would soon be created. If we did not help the French with the distressed franc, we were unlikely to get help from them or the other Europeans on the limitation of financial credits to the U.S.S.R. Our first priority at Versailles was to link these two questions and, by doing so, to apply sanctions that would hurt the Soviet Union without fracturing the sense of equality and unchallengeable nationhood on which the Western alliance rested.

If agreement at Versailles was the goal of the President's trip to Europe, which also included a speech in London, a visit to Rome and Vatican City, a NATO summit in Bonn, and a visit to Berlin, it was not the most urgent issue before us. The Falklands war was entering its final stages as British troops prepared for full-scale landings in the islands. And, as the Presidential plane crossed the Atlantic on June 1, it appeared certain that Israel would invade Lebanon in a matter of hours, days, or weeks, touching off a dangerous and destructive war that had the potential of becoming a much wider conflict.*

The handling of these problems during the trip was complicated by the fact that William Clark, in his capacity as National Security Adviser to the President, seemed to be conducting a second foreign policy, using separate channels of communication. In Washington, George Bush's crisis management group went into session over the Lebanon situation and established communications with Clark, bypassing the State Department altogether. Such a system was bound to produce confusion, and it soon did. There were conflicts over votes in

---

*I will not pause here to describe the situation in Lebanon, which dominated my thoughts and energies for the remaining days of June, and my final days as Secretary of State, but will deal with it at length in the next chapter.

the United Nations, differences over communications to heads of state, mixed signals to the combatants in Lebanon. Some of these, in my judgment, represented a danger to the nation and put the President into the position of reversing decisions already made. After several such rattling incidents, I asked Clark, who had been such an agreeable deputy to me in my early days at the State Department, what was going on. Clark, drained of his old good fellowship, gave me a cryptic answer. "You've won a lot of battles in this Administration, Al," he said, "but you'd better understand that from now on it's going to be the *President's* foreign policy."

I understood. In the few days since my last trip to Buenos Aires, my prediction to my wife that the Falklands might be my Waterloo had taken on the character of prophecy. With the collapse of the Falklands peace effort, my "image" had suffered. Detractors in the White House evidently sensed a new vulnerability and were mounting their final onslaught on my authority in foreign affairs and on the President's confidence in my advice. During the President's progress through Europe, it became plain that the effort to "write my character out of the script" was underway with a vengeance. As always, all roads led through the press. In an early, and telling, sign of quarantine, photographs were banned at my meeting with Prime Minister Zenko Suzuki of Japan. At official events in Europe, last-minute changes in seating and other curious breaches of protocol engineered by Baker, Deaver, and their apparat thoroughly baffled our European hosts, many of whom had not previously had the experience of a guest, as it were, shuffling the place cards of the other guests.

Nevertheless, I continued to attempt to give the President counsel. The necessity to do so arose almost immediately after our arrival in Paris. In an assay into diplomacy-by-photo-opportunity, the President's assistants decided to ban cameras from his meeting with Mrs. Thatcher. Evidently the White House feared the impact in Latin America if the press carried pictures of Reagan and Thatcher meeting together. But the press was bound to make much of a refusal by the President of the United States to be photographed with the British prime minister. In recent days, such a large number of unofficial feelers had been sent out to the Argentinians by officials of the government that I had warned the President of the danger that the junta, grasping at straws, might believe that the United States was so sympathetic to Argentina that it might prolong the war. To Clark, who listened with some impatience, I made this point anew, repeatedly, and with emphasis, adding that it was unheard of for heads of government to meet together without being photographed. The cameras were admitted. As to the meeting itself, the advice that I wished to give the President—to seize the moment when British forces were close to victory and urge a policy of magnanimity upon Mrs. Thatcher—had to be passed through Clark, who told me that Reagan "was not going to be assertive with Mrs. Thatcher or ask her any unpresidential questions."

The issue of Presidential assertiveness on the question of the Falklands arose again at a working luncheon given at the Élysée Palace by President Mitterrand. The French leader was visibly disappointed when Reagan would respond only with generalities to his questions about U.S. support for the British in the Falklands. Reagan avoided specific answers to other French probings as well. Rising from the table, Mitterrand invited Reagan to accompany him upstairs for a private chat. The luncheon, which had taken place around a huge circular table, had been crowded with Presidential aides from both countries, producing a babble of conversation that made confidential exchanges between the principals unlikely. Like others before him, Mitterrand failed in his bid for a high-level tête-à-tête. Reagan's aides reminded the American President, with no less insistence than on similar occasions in the past, that his schedule would not permit even a short diversion with the head of an allied government and hustled him outside for a meeting with reporters. Swallowing this affront to French hospitality and sense of place with difficulty, the French foreign minister, Claude Cheysson, complained to me with Gallic acidity that the conversation had been "shallow."

Entering the summit, troubling questions about American intentions on pipeline sanctions remained in the minds of our allies. I had urged the President to clarify his position before the summit and to make explicit the linkage between intervention to help the franc and allied cooperation on the credit question. But Clark—who, with Weinberger, vigorously opposed any compromise on this issue—told me, on the eve of Versailles, that the President had decided to put off his decision until the NSC meeting scheduled for mid-June, after our return to Washington. I received this news with some dismay. If this action—or, rather, lack of action—did not preclude a settlement of the issue at Versailles, it narrowed the ground for negotiations in a significant way.

The preparatory meetings preceding the summit had failed to

produce clear-cut agreement on the question of credits, technology transfer, and intervention in currency markets. On the day before the plenary summit meeting, the finance ministers of.the seven countries involved had failed to find a basis for an agreement by the heads of state. In a final effort to achieve agreement and preserve unity, I insisted that the foreign ministers join the finance ministers that night. Very late, we reached an understanding: the United States would bolster the franc on a case-by-case basis in return for restraint by the other governments on future credits to the Soviet Union. This ministerial agreement, if sustained by the heads of state and government at the plenary, would by implication trigger a decision favorable to the Europeans on the pipeline issue.

Next day, June 6, when the heads of government met with their foreign ministers and a recorder for each side in the Salle du Sacre in the Palace of Versailles, President Mitterrand, in a very long and detailed presentation, seemed to ignore completely what the ministers had tortuously achieved the evening before. Prime Minister Pierre Elliott Trudeau of Canada mischievously joined Mitterrand. This behavior was mystifying, but it is possible if not likely that, owing to the late hour at which the ministerial meeting concluded, some heads of state had not been informed of the result. However, with the doughty support of Mrs. Thatcher and Prime Minister Giovanni Spadolini of Italy, the agreement was confirmed—but only after a long and far too testy exchange in which the President left me to play the role of American arch-villain.

Though the pipeline question was not covered in the exchange, it was implicitly understood that the United States would not apply retroactive, extraterritorial pipeline sanctions. A solution was now in sight.

Then everything collapsed. Secretary Regan, who had not been present for the full plenary meeting (it is quite possible that he was not aware of the agreement), was asked by reporters whether the United States had agreed to "intervening against the long-term thrust of the [foreign exchange] market." Regan replied, "We have not agreed to any such thing." This statement, which ran directly counter to the understanding of the other participants at the summit, would have serious, if unsurprising, consequences a few days later when an angered President Mitterrand called a news conference in order to state that the European participants at the summit had made no agreement on credits, either. In diplomatic terms, we were back where we started, not only on the questions of intervention and credit, but on the pipeline sanction question as well. As the U.S. delegation went on to the other cities on the President's itinerary, and finally headed back to Washington, I hoped that the result would be no worse than that.

The party arrived home on Friday afternoon, June 11. After the long, eventful trip through Europe and the plane ride home into another time zone, we were all tired. The President went to Camp David for the weekend. The Lebanon war was raging, but it appeared possible, if we acted quickly, to achieve a cease-fire, to prevent a further widening of the conflict, and to begin the political process that was necessary if Lebanon was to emerge from this shambles as a sovereign state once again. Philip Habib, shuttling between Damascus, Tel Aviv, and Beirut, urgently needed new instructions. On arrival at the State Department, I called Clark and told him that I would draft Habib's instructions and send them over for the President's approval. Because of the vital importance of these instructions, which would enunciate basic U.S. policy for the crisis, I meant to give them careful thought; even working with the staff at full speed, the task could not be completed before the following afternoon. Neither Clark nor I liked to disturb the President on a weekend after his exhausting trip, but Habib's need was so urgent and the instructions were so significant that the President had to see them before they were sent. On this much, Clark and I agreed.

The instructions were ready by early evening of the following day, Saturday, June 12, and listed what subsequently became U.S. policy: withdrawal of all foreign forces; a strengthened central government for Lebanon; arrangements to preclude further attacks on Israel's northern border. As soon as it was complete, I sent the one-page draft over to Clark at the White House. Over the phone, Clark told me that he would immediately "Datafax" the paper to Camp David—meaning that it would be sent to the President through an electronic device that instantaneously transmits facsimiles of entire documents. At about 7:30 P.M., Clark phoned me and reported that the President had seen the draft instructions but had not approved them, judging that the issues were of such import that Reagan wanted to clear them at a formal NSC meeting the following Monday. Because Habib was to leave for Damascus and Beirut in a few hours and would need the instructions to carry out his mission, I told Clark that we must have a decision immediately.

It hardly seemed possible to me that the President really meant to delay for two days, inasmuch as the point at issue involved a war that was daily claiming hundreds of lives. Clark assured me that this was, in fact, the President's decision. Astonished, I phoned Reagan at Camp David and explained that Habib was already en route to Damascus to keep an appointment with Syrian President Hafez al Assad, and was committed to return to Beirut with the results of his conversations there and in Jerusalem; he simply could not wait until Monday. Reagan heard me out, but when he responded I detected a note of puzzlement in his relaxed and amiable voice. He knew nothing about the instructions to Habib, and I gained the impression that he had not even received them.

Tired, and more than a little disillusioned, I explained once more the urgency and danger of the situation. There was nothing in the instructions, I reiterated, that departed substantively from the positions prepared for him during the several meetings of the crisis management team while we were in Europe. Reagan remained detached, friendly, and still clearly a bit puzzled by my call. "That's all right, Al, don't worry," Reagan said at last. I hung up the telephone and sent Habib his instructions without the President's formal approval.

I immediately tried to call Clark to inform him that I had sent Habib's instructions on my own authority, but was informed that he had retired for the night. The next morning, Clark, with vexation in his voice, told me that he would have to report my actions to the President. I invited him to do so and asked for an appointment with the President on Monday morning. I felt that the end had come.

When we met on Monday, June 14, in the Oval Office, Reagan was in a troubled mood, his usually sunny countenance drawn into a worried frown. This time no aides crowded into the Oval Office with us; we were alone. Even before we sat down, he brought up the matter of Habib's instructions. Clearly he was disturbed by my action. "Al, what would you do if you were a general and one of your lower commanders went around you and acted on his own?" he asked.

"I'd fire him, Mr. President," I replied.

"No, no, I didn't mean that," Reagan said. "But this mustn't happen again. We just can't have a situation where you send messages on your own that are a matter for my decision."

The President gave no indication that he disagreed with the policy embodied in Habib's instructions or understood their urgency.

I related the details of my encounter with Clark and recalled the conversation Reagan and I had had over the telephone the previous Saturday. I recounted the episodes of the trip to Europe and told Reagan that I believed that the cease-fire he had proposed in Lebanon had been delayed, and loss of life had needlessly continued, as a result of the petty maneuvering by his staff. As he listened to the details, the President's frown deepened.

"Mr. President, I want you to understand what's going on around you," I said. "I simply can no longer operate in this atmosphere. It's too dangerous. It doesn't serve your purposes; it doesn't serve the American people."

Then I told the President that while I could not desert him and the country in the middle of a crisis, under the present arrangements I could not continue as his Secretary of State nor could his policies survive for four years. If the President could not make the necessary changes to restore unity and coherence to his foreign policy, then it would be in the country's interest to have another secretary. I suggested that the best time for my departure would be after the midterm elections in November, so as to minimize the political impact of a Cabinet resignation.

Reagan listened intently to my words, but did not react. His aides were waiting outside his door. His expression was set; he said nothing. I took my leave in silence.

Days passed; I awaited the President's reply. Weeks earlier it had been arranged that Andrei Gromyko and I would meet in New York on June 18 and 19. Knowing that I would not be able to attend, Clark then scheduled a meeting of the NSC to consider the question of pipeline sanctions. As my deputy, Walt Stoessel, was also unavailable, Larry Eagleburger represented the State Department in our place. By now fearful of the worst, but determined that the historical record would show that the State Department had fought for a rational course of policy, I instructed Eagleburger to oppose the extension of sanctions to overseas manufacturers. Eagleburger did so with his usual capability, but when the moment for decision came, Clark placed only the strongest option paper before Reagan, who uncharacteristically approved it on the spot. There had been little discussion of the issue, and virtually no participation by the President himself, before this decision was formalized. It had been made before the meeting convened: Mitterrand's repudiation of the summit agreement on credits to the Soviets, following Donald Regan's unaccountable retreat from support of the franc, had made the outcome inevitable.

I had told Eagleburger to insist that announcement of the decision to the press be delayed until we had had time to notify our allies that it had been taken. There was no way, after all the misunderstandings that had attended this issue, to minimize the damage, but we owed this minimum courtesy. Inasmuch as sanctions were directed primarily against the Soviet Union—a point that tended to be lost as analysis concentrated on the damage to the British, German, and Italian economies—the President's decision was a matter of no small interest to Gromyko. At our Friday session, I did not raise the pipeline with Gromyko; though I foresaw the outcome of the NSC meeting, it would have been wrong to tell the Soviets of such an action before telling our allies and before the decision had been formalized.

All my experience with the White House public relations machinery notwithstanding, I trusted that the decision would not be announced before the flash cables Eagleburger would send to our allies had been delivered. I planned to inform Dobrynin in the normal way on Saturday, but when I returned to the hotel, Eagleburger informed me that despite his cautions, Clark had already informed the press.

Next day, Gromyko confronted me angrily, suggesting that I had either withheld the truth from him or did not speak for the United States government.

"Mr. Foreign Minister," I replied in my weariness, "I'm afraid it is the latter."

The President had not yet responded to the points I had raised in our last meeting. I discussed this with Clark on Sunday. Toward the middle of the week, after a meeting in the situation room, I raised it again with Clark and asked for an answer. On Thursday, June 24, Clark told me that the President wanted to see me.

The lack of warmth that had characterized Reagan's behavior during our last meeting had vanished. In its place, as we greeted each other in the Oval Office, was a mixture of apprehension and what seemed to me to be almost fatherly concern. I asked the President if he had thought over what I had said to him on June 14.

"Yes, I have," he said. "You know, Al, it's awfully hard for me to give you what you're asking for."

In preparation for this meeting, a member of my staff had drawn up a bill of particulars, listing the occasions over the past weeks on which the cacophony of voices from the Administration and the seeming incoherence of American foreign policy had created dangerous uncertainties. To this I had added a second memorandum, detailing a similar story of mixed signals during the Falklands crisis. These documents, though more forthright in tone than communications to Presidents usually are, had the virtue of being accurate reflections of the frustrations produced by these events. I handed the paper to Reagan. He glanced at them.

"I'm going to keep this, Al," he said. "This situation is very disturbing."

"It has been very disturbing from the first, Mr. President," I replied. "If it can't be straightened out, then surely you would be better served by another Secretary of State."

The President, sitting behind his desk, made no reply. It may have been that he was still struggling with his decision.

Next day, after a working NSC luncheon on arms control, I was asked to step into the Oval Office to see the President. He was standing at his desk as I entered.

"On that matter we discussed yesterday, Al," he said. "I have reached a conclusion."

He then handed me an unsealed envelope. I opened it and read the single typed page it contained. "*Dear Al,*" it began. "*It is with the most profound regret that I accept your letter of resignation.*"

The President was accepting a letter of resignation that I had not submitted.

I had not recovered from this surprise before Reagan asked if I would stay on as Secretary of State and manage the Lebanon crisis until my successor was confirmed by the Senate. Reagan sat down at his desk and motioned me to a chair.

"I'll talk shortly to George Shultz, who is in London," he said in warm conversational tones. "I'm confident he'll take the post."

"I think it would be a great mistake for me to stay on, Mr. President," I said. "You can't have a lame duck as Secretary of State in a crisis of this magnitude in the Middle East."

Reagan insisted, saying that the country needed me, and so did he. Against all instincts and judgment, I reluctantly agreed to do as he asked.

But there was yet another important question involved. As the President outlined the scenario, it appeared that I had suddenly quit at the height of the Middle East crisis.

"The precipitous way in which you're conducting this, Mr. President," I said, "means I can't just up and leave. I will have to make it clear publicly, in the least damaging way possible, that I simply no longer support your policies and that is the case."

The President appeared to be surprised and shocked by my testiness. Once again, his aides had briefed him badly, evidently leading him to believe that I would meekly accept the decision and meekly depart. As always in moments of emotion, the President's eyes shone with moisture; he was at once nonplussed and angered, but he made no effort to dissuade me, and when I asked him for two hours in which to draft an appropriate letter of resignation and deliver it to him before the matter became public, he agreed. He noted that he was leaving for Camp David at 3:00 P.M.

Returning promptly to the State Department, I began drafting my letter to the President. It passed through several versions, until finally it read as follows:

Dear Mr. President:

Your accession to office on January 20, 1981, brought an opportunity for a new and forward-looking foreign policy resting on the cornerstone of strength and compassion. I believe that we shared a view of America's role in the world as the leader of free men and an inspiration for all.

We agreed that consistency, clarity, and steadiness of purpose were essential to success. It was in this spirit that I undertook to serve you as Secretary of State.

In recent months, it has become clear to me that the foreign policy on which we embarked together was shifting from that careful course which we had laid out. Under these circumstances, I felt it necessary that you accept my resignation.

I shall always treasure the confidence which you reposed in me. It has been a great honor to serve in your Administration, and I wish you every success in the future.

While I was still at work on this letter, the President appeared in the White House briefing room and announced that I had resigned as Secretary of State. Then he boarded a helicopter and flew to Camp David.

A little later, saying good-bye to my staff, I made the necessary joke, remarking that I had called the meeting to discuss the question of excessive overtime at the department. Then, for the last time as fifty-ninth Secretary of State, I appeared before a news conference to read my letter of resignation. The reporters were in good form, their sympathy becomingly tinged with cynical wit. It was a pleasant, even an affectionate farewell. Because the President had gone on television before me, there were no surprises. The press already had the story and was eager to get on to tomorrow's news.

FIFTEEN

Lebanon:
"Mixed Signals Bedevil
Our Diplomacy"

MEANWHILE, Lebanon was in flames. During Reagan's trip to Europe, the war we had hoped to prevent, with all its incalculable peril to American and Western interests in the Middle East and its all too calculable consequences for the suffering people of Lebanon, had finally come. For more than a year, Israel, goaded by the bombardment of her northern settlements by Palestinian gunners from fortified sanctuaries in southern Lebanon and by terrorist attacks on her citizens at home and abroad, had wanted to send her ground forces into Lebanon and destroy the PLO. On June 6, 1982, despite the strongest possible warnings by the United States, Israel launched her offensive at last. In less than a week, her armies had shattered the PLO, destroyed Syrian air power while inflicting stinging local defeats on Syria's ground forces, and redrawn the map of Lebanon. Thousands had died. The remnants of the PLO, trapped in Beirut, could hope for nothing better than surrender on terms that would minimize their humiliation.

Dangerous and tragic though this turn of events was, it provided a historic opportunity to deal with the problem of Lebanon by re-

moving the causes of a national crisis that had long threatened to be
mortal. The primary obstacle to peace in Lebanon had been the
presence of two foreign armies—the Syrian "peacekeeping" force
and the military arm of the PLO—each in its own right stronger than
the Lebanese army. This de facto occupation had stripped the central
government of its authority and created the conditions for strife
among the religious and ethnic communities of Lebanon. The Israeli
invasion added a third foreign army and, in the worst case, threatened to create, in southern Lebanon, a new zone of occupation. But
Israel's military incursion also created circumstances in which it was
possible, during the fleeting moments in which the former equation
of power had been overturned, to remove all foreign troops from
Lebanon and restore the powers of government to the Lebanese.
Beyond that, a settlement in Lebanon would have significant consequences for Arab-Israeli peace: Syria and the PLO, the heart of the
Arab opposition to Camp David, had been defeated. With the PLO's
"military option" gone, Israel's arguments against granting a wider
measure of autonomy to the Arabs in the West Bank and Gaza would
be negated. There would be a fresh opportunity to complete the
Camp David peace process, including measures that would have
given the Palestinians in the West Bank and Gaza political control
over their daily lives. Indeed, in my last meeting with Menachem
Begin in Washington in June 1982, I told him that the United States
expected, after resolution of the Lebanon problem, that Israeli settlement activity in the West Bank would come to an end and rapid
progress toward an agreement on autonomy would be realized.

In the final hours of my incumbency as Secretary of State, even
after my resignation, this opportunity was seized. Through intensive
negotiations, the necessary agreements were reached. The Syrians,
the PLO, and the Israelis were prepared to leave Lebanon at the same
time. Lebanon's security would have been internationalized. The
Lebanese government was ready to function on behalf of all the
factions in Lebanon. Peace was within our grasp. Then, in a series of
miscalculations that divided American diplomacy and dissipated
American influence, peace was thrown away. The situation we now
face in Lebanon is the result.

How did this happen and why? The Lebanon crisis is a dramatic
illustration of the truism that, in the Middle East, all things are
related. It is impossible to deal with one question in this ancient

region, defined as imprecisely by its geography as by its myths, without affecting all the others. Americans are preoccupied with the Arab-Israeli conflict, but it is no isolated phenomenon. Animosities between Muslim and Muslim, or Muslim and Christian, are in some cases at least as heated as those between Arab and Israeli. No less than those of Judaism and Christianity, the schisms of Islam have produced great political disturbances, and continue to do so. The fundamentalism of the Iranian revolution is a Shiite Muslim phenomenon that has its roots in a seventh-century dispute over the descent of true authority in Islam after the death of Muhammad. More than 1,300 years later, it is a rampant political force that threatens the stability of every Arab state in the region having a substantial Shiite population, including Lebanon. In addition to being a theological phenomenon, fundamentalism is also a struggle between tradition and modernization, and it is that aspect of it that eliminated America's two greatest friends in the region, the Shah and Anwar Sadat. Enmities may be suppressed, dogmas may slumber, and suffering minorities may be quiescent for a time, but they are always just beneath the surface in the Middle East, and when they break forth, as in the war in Lebanon, they have the potential to wreak geopolitical changes that involve factors and peoples far from the point of eruption.

Overlaid on the region's own tumultuous history of conflict is the superpower competition. Quite simply, the Soviet Union wants to displace the United States as the most influential foreign power between the Caspian Sea and the Indian Ocean. From her point of view, the prizes are enormous—population, wealth, energy, the strategic position of the Middle East as a bridge linking three continents. But in the last decade, following its banishment from Sadat's Egypt, the Soviet Union has been on the periphery of events in the Middle East. Throughout that period, Moscow has been trying, with little success, to recapture the center. It was only natural that the Soviets would see Lebanon as an opportunity to advance their interests through her ally, Syria, and her ofttime agent, the PLO. The danger that the U.S.S.R. might become directly engaged was, and is, by no means negligible. Conflict in the Middle East had brought the Russians close to military intervention in the past. As noted earlier, the Yom Kippur War in 1973 involved a direct, if little-known, superpower confrontation when President Nixon, in response to a Soviet threat to land airborne troops in the Sinai, alerted U.S. nuclear forces and thereby persuaded Moscow to step back.

After that war, the United States had engaged in its most determined effort to reduce the threat to peace and stability from conflict in the Middle East. This effort yielded a treaty of peace between Egypt and Israel that provides a point of diplomatic contact between Arab and Israeli and is the only existing mechanism capable of advancing toward the solution of the wider Arab-Israeli conflict and the Palestinian question. All Arab states except Egypt have been, and remain, opposed to the Camp David Accords and to Egypt's treaty of peace with Israel. This animosity isolated Sadat's Egypt, representing roughly half the population of the Arab world, from the rest of the Arab nations, including America's friends, Saudi Arabia and Jordan. The Palestinian Arabs themselves refuse either to join in the peace process or to acknowledge Israel's right to live in peace.

Historic Middle Eastern conflicts, the superpower rivalry, and the fate of the peace process all came together in the Lebanon crisis. Although there has been no official census since 1932, it is believed that Lebanon's population of about 3 million is almost evenly divided between Muslims and Christians. The National Covenant of 1943, an unwritten agreement that established the political foundations of independent Lebanon, provides that the president, who appoints the cabinet and chooses the prime minister, shall be a Maronite Christian, the prime minister shall be a Sunni Muslim, and the president of the chamber of deputies shall be a Shiite Muslim. This system has produced periods of internal stability and economic progress, but the delicate balance of interests, which is by its nature susceptible to foreign meddling, has frequently broken down and plunged the country into turmoil. Sometimes the Lebanese have called for foreign help, as in 1958 when President Eisenhower sent U.S. Marines ashore to help the country safeguard its independence in the face of an insurrection.

In the 1970s, as internecine conflict escalated, new factors from outside Lebanon aggravated the situation. The PLO, expelled from Jordan in 1970, attached itself to the quarter of a million Palestinian refugees long resident in the country and the Palestinian "state within a state" took shape. Combat between PLO guerrillas and the forces of the Lebanese government metastasized into battles between Muslim and Christian militias and a general atmosphere of terror. Syria had been invited into the country, with U.S. encouragement, in 1976; the Israelis invaded the south briefly in 1978. The central government was unable to control these events. Thousands died as a patrimony of hatred and bloodshed accumulated.

Meanwhile, both Egypt and Israel were beset by profound fears and ambivalences regarding the peace process. Egypt had agreed to a separate peace with Israel even though the Palestinian issue remained unresolved. Sadat had put his trust in the benefits of political, military, and economic support from the United States, believing that this support would help overcome Egypt's subsequent isolation and restore what Egyptians had always regarded as their natural leadership of the Arab world. Israel believed that she had conceded much at Camp David—the return of the strategic Sinai, captured from Egypt in the 1967 war, and autonomy for the 1.3 million Palestinians living in the West Bank and Gaza—in return for recognition of her existence by Cairo and the removal of the most powerful of the Arab states from the ranks of her enemies.

This three-cornered peace process depended not only on the tentative and often fractious relations between Israel and Egypt, but also on their faith and confidence in the United States. For a variety of reasons, this confidence had been shaken. For Egypt, American economic and military support had been slow to come and even slower to make a difference. The AWACS controversy and the measures taken by the Administration in response to that series of sad events— the attack on the Iraqi nuclear reactor, the air strikes on PLO targets in Lebanon, the annexation of the Golan Heights—had exacerbated U.S.-Israeli relations in the first year and a half of Reagan's Presidency. To both countries, American response to the challenges of Soviet expansionism and the Ayatollah's fundamentalism had seemed weak and ineffectual.

A date, April 25, 1982, had been set for the return of the Sinai. As this day approached, fears mounted on both sides. When the Reagan Administration took office, it was by no means certain that the transfer would take place on time, if at all. At the best of times, the return of the Sinai would have been regarded as a tremendous risk by the Israelis. It meant the removal of Israeli settlers who had established farms and towns and families there, and it meant giving up a strategic buffer zone between Israel and the nation with which it had fought four major wars in the space of thirty years. Above all, Menachem

Begin, reflecting the misgivings of most Israelis, saw Palestinian shells
and Katyusha rockets falling into Galilee and chaos in Lebanon and
pondered the wisdom of shrinking his defensive perimeter.

Yet peace was advanced by a human intangible—the growing
trust between Menachem Begin and Anwar Sadat. As men, Sadat and
Begin appeared to have little in common. In many ways, their mutual
regard was a triumph over personal chemistry. Begin is a lawyer,
absorbed in legalism, detail, and nuance; Sadat gloried in the grand
conception and the silent understanding and had a mystic's contempt
for detail. Begin won respect, even if it was sometimes grudging,
because of the force of his character and the tenacity of his mind.
Sadat had the charismatic gift of winning the admiration and friendship of statesmen and former enemies; few left his presence without
believing that they had just parted from a great man. Yet Sadat and
Begin were similar spirits. If Sadat's Koranic vision gave him the
strength to break the mold of Arab thinking, there was something of
the Old Testament prophet in the single-minded eloquence of Begin
and in his testy righteousness. Both men had fought with ferocious
patriotism against the British in the underground, and this was a very
strong bond. Each believed in the unique historic destiny of his people and country, and each thought of himself, with perfect accuracy,
as a maker of history. In short, they understood each other, and I am
convinced that both men believed that, with the help of the other and
the support of the United States, they could complete the peace. The
fact is, these two exceptional men had personalized the peace process, and its success depended on their trust in one another.

Then, on October 6, 1981, Sadat was assassinated. He had been
reviewing a parade when he was attacked by Muslim extremists
dressed as soldiers. The first news from our embassy in Cairo repeated Egyptian government reports that Sadat had received two
gunshot wounds, and stated that these were not life-threatening. I
telephoned this information to President Reagan at 8:55 A.M. on
October 6. At 12:30 P.M., during a luncheon at the White House with
Reagan and General Prem Tinsulanonda, the prime minister of
Thailand, Woody Goldberg handed me a note containing the information that Sadat had, in fact, died instantaneously of wounds to the
head and body. I passed the note to Reagan. His eyes grew misty. I
myself was deeply affected. In the decade that I had known him,
Sadat had spoken often about his own death, as if he lived with a
recurring premonition. He had mentioned it again with his old fa-

talism in April, when I saw him in Cairo. "I know the risks I take among my Arab brothers who do not understand my purposes," he told me. "They may be fatal risks—but that is of no consequence. Remember what is at stake."

It was not simply the loss of an admired friend that moved me. I felt very strongly that the former leadership of my country had failed Sadat. I knew that he believed this, too. In Cairo, Sadat had spoken to me in his subtle way about the fall and subsequent death in exile of the Shah, as a means of suggesting a second American failure without actually leveling the charge that America had exposed another of its friends—himself—to an unhappy fate. He would have been justified in taking a sterner line with us.

President Reagan, though I had assumed that he would personally lead the Americans who would pay their respects at the grave of this great friend to our country, decided that I would head a delegation that included Caspar Weinberger, congressional leaders, Henry Kissinger, Mrs. Kirkpatrick, and others. All three living former Presidents had known Sadat, and I urged that they be included in the delegation. Aboard the Air Force VC-137 that carried the entire delegation on the eleven-hour flight to Cairo, the former Presidents segregated themselves according to party, with Nixon and Ford seated at one table in the lounge along with Kissinger, and the Carters with Jody Powell, the former White House press secretary, at the other. Nixon, wearing the comfortable cardigan of the seasoned traveler, was very much his old self, entertaining the Republicans with anecdotes. Kissinger had brought the manuscript of his memoirs with him and marked the pages, as if correcting the thesis of a promising graduate student. Sociable Gerald Ford conversed with everyone. After supper, the Carters slipped off their shoes and stretched out, head to foot, on a narrow bench that ran along the corridor outside the stateroom door. My aides, bringing cables and other business to me, tiptoed past their sleeping forms.

Jimmy Carter believed, in common with virtually everyone else who had fallen under the spell of Sadat's personality, that he had had a special relationship with him. This assumption complicated the knotty problems of protocol involved in introducing, seating, and deciding other matters of place for three ex-Presidents. Carter asked for a private meeting with Mrs. Jihan Sadat, and this was arranged. At the funeral, held some distance outside Cairo, the ladies were seated apart according to Muslim custom; they were positioned in the very row of seats occupied by Sadat during his last moments of life, and included Mrs. Sadat's close friend, the recently bereaved empress of Iran.

The male guests, including numerous heads of state and government, were collected in a tent in an open field about a mile from the crypt. Few Arab countries had sent delegations. No Soviets or Eastern Europeans or Cubans were present, though some of their African friends had come. Menachem Begin had chosen to attend despite many warnings that he was risking his life by doing so. The tent was, of course, a great temptation to terrorists. Security was so heavy as to introduce an element of chaos; in addition to the large detail provided by the Egyptians, every leader had brought his own bodyguards. The tent was crowded and hot. There were a great many flies. The wait before the ceremony lasted for nearly two hours. We had all been urged to wear bullet-proof vests, and in the stifling atmosphere beneath the sun-scorched canvas, I was glad that I had chosen not to do so. The many famous men present were obviously conscious of the uniqueness of the moment and the circumstances that had brought the leaders of the Western world and the Third World together in a tent in the desert. Everyone, it is fair to say, wanted to have a look at everyone else.

Yet decorum obtained until the cortege formed for the walk to the crypt. Outside the tent, television cameras and news photographers waited, and there was a scramble among some of the security men to get their presidents and prime ministers to the front of the crowd, where the lenses were. Some of the bodyguards hooked arms and moved in lockstep, roughly pushing aside eminent world figures as they strove for the limelight. Other security men tried to shield the more decorous leaders, but largely failed, and the jostling continued. It occurred to me, as I trudged along with Nixon and Ford and Begin (Carter, more nimble, had moved toward the front of the pack), that these people had not been jostled in years. I was concerned about Helmut Schmidt, who seemed to be suffering from shortness of breath, and lagged behind to be near him and Begin, who walked with the aid of a cane. Most went through the experience with affability—President Alessandro Pertini of Italy, eighty-five years old, seemed positively to enjoy it—and the ceremony of interment restored the simple dignity that Sadat himself had exemplified.

If there was sorrow among the great of the world at Sadat's graveside, there was little evidence of mourning in Cairo. Sadat, who had risen from a poor village, had always been more empathetic to the peasants than to the urban masses, but the indifference of the Cairenes was shocking to the outsider. In these streets there were none of the signs of national grief that had overwhelmed Americans after the assassination of President Kennedy or the South Vietnamese following the murder of President Ngo Dinh Diem. Sadat, who lived for peace and believed that only the greatness of the ancient Egyptian nation could achieve it in the Middle East, had lost the love of his people. Toward the end, even Sadat's supporters felt that he had gone too far and had been duped by a combination of Israeli guile and American impatience. The United States, which could have helped him achieve results that would have reassured his people, had instead let him face the consequences of his ambiguous situation alone. Sadat was a deeply religious, even a saintly man; when I remember him, I always visualize the *zabiba*, a callus formed in the center of the forehead by pressing the brow to the prayer rug five times daily.

Sadat's vice president and protégé, Mohamed Hosni Mubarak, told me that he had warned Sadat about the danger presented by Muslim fanatics who in the end murdered him, but Sadat, who had encouraged the growth of such groups in the early seventies to counteract the leftist and Nasserite tendencies of his opponents, believed that he could manage the religious extremists. Sadat's popularity was adversely affected also by rumors that some members of his family had exploited their kinship for profit. Mubarak, who had been sitting next to Sadat before the fatal shots were fired, told me that all during the parade, Sadat had been discussing his plans for the future, especially after the final Israeli withdrawal from the Sinai the following April. It was almost, said Mubarak, as if Sadat foresaw that something might happen to him and wanted his successor to know all his thoughts. Those who believed that Sadat's policies would change after the return of the Sinai, Mubarak said, were completely wrong.

These were loyal words, but they could not hide the reality: if Mubarak continued to follow Sadat's policies without modification, he was likely to share Sadat's fate. Nobody, probably including Mubarak, could know whether it would be possible for him, in light of the situation within Egypt, to go forward with the peace process. Any delay in returning the Sinai to Egypt, let alone a failure to do so, would have incalculable consequences. It was vital to demonstrate that it was not fatal to be a friend of the United States.

Menachem Begin seemed to understand at once that the best

moment to extend the peace process had probably passed. Nevertheless, he was anxious to save what could be saved. When I met him at the Hyatt Prince Hotel in Nasser City on the day after the funeral, I said at once that we needed to move quickly on the peace process. Begin replied that Israel was willing to proceed without delay. But when I told him that the Europeans were willing to join the Sinai MFO (Multinational Force and Observers) if Israel announced a policy of no new settlements in the West Bank, the old problem took hold. "No," he said. "I never promised Carter or anyone else that there would be no new settlements, only a ninety-day hiatus."* Begin then spoke of the difficulties involved in returning the Sinai. "It would be a disaster, alienating Israel from the United States and isolating her in the world, if she reneged on this agreement," I said. Begin held up a hand in reassurance. "I will meet my commitment or resign—and there may be such turmoil over the issue that I will have to resign," he said. I asked if he could not return the territory sooner. Begin shook his head—such a thing was impossible. In that gesture, one could read the reality: if the situation deteriorated in Egypt in a way that threatened Israeli interests, Begin's will to return the Sinai, or his freedom to do so in the face of domestic political realities, might disappear.

Begin then told me that Israel had begun planning a move into Lebanon that would not draw Syria into the conflict. This was the first time he or any other Israeli had been quite so specific. "If you move, you move alone," I said. "Unless there is a major, internationally recognized provocation, the United States will not support such an action." He was only talking about contingency planning, Begin said; the general idea was to push the PLO back from the border area and then go to the U.N. and ask for a guarantee that

---

*At Camp David, Begin agreed to halt settlements during the peace treaty/autonomy negotiations, which were originally expected to be completed within three months. Carter apparently concluded that Begin's pledge extended to the end of the negotiations—in other words, an indefinite freeze. During the first 3½ years under Begin, Israel established thirty-nine new settlements in the West Bank (or Judea and Samaria, as Begin insisted that this territory be called), four in Gaza, and seven in the Golan Heights; the number of Jewish settlers increased from 5,000 to 14,000. Although President Reagan, in an offhand remark to the press early in his term, had suggested that these settlements might be legal, the United States has never formally conceded their legality. Desettlement leading to PLO control of these territories occupied in the 1967 war, Begin maintained, would pose a mortal danger to Israel by bringing two-thirds of her population within range of the same sort of Soviet-supplied howitzers and rockets that were now bombarding her northern towns.

Israel's border would not be attacked. "Does that make sense to you, Al?" he asked. I repeated that while it might make sense from the Israeli point of view, "Israel will be alone if it carries out such a plan." We dropped the subject.

In the months ahead the subject would arise again and again. My response, and Reagan's response, was always the same: the United States would never tell Israel not to defend herself from attack, but any action she took must be in response to an internationally recognized provocation, and the response must be proportionate to that provocation.

In the wake of Sadat's murder, the opponents of the Camp David peace process made their most determined efforts to upset what had been achieved. Even before the assassination, I had found European governments reluctant to participate in the Sinai force—the French less so because President Mitterrand wanted to reestablish a relationship with Israel, the British more so because Lord Carrington appeared to be devoted to the idea of bringing the PLO into the peace process. Throughout the summer, the result had been a sort of hanging back from the dance floor: no European country would join the Sinai force unless another government went first. There was another diversion: Crown Prince (afterward King) Fahd of Saudi Arabia put forth a plan that enunciated the principle that "all states in the region should live in peace" and called for Israeli withdrawal to pre-1967 lines, a Palestinian homeland with Jerusalem as its capital, and other objectives that could only be achieved, if at all, by negotiation. As the plan had no concept of a direct Arab-Israeli negotiating process, it had little realistic prospect of achieving results. Yet President Reagan, who was interested in the possibility that Fahd's reference to "all states in the region" living in peace included Israel, was induced to praise the plan on the day after the AWACS vote in the Senate. Mubarak spoke well of the Fahd plan during visits to the gulf. Carrington praised the plan and, while in Riyadh, criticized Camp David.

Against these threats to the peace process, I moved rapidly to counteract any notion that the United States would move away from the peace for which Sadat had given his life. During King Hussein's visit to Washington on November 2, the President publicly reaffirmed Camp David. A vigorous protest was sent to London over Carrington's remarks. Prince Fahd was reminded again that we did not regard his plan as a practical peace proposal. Begin was reassured that we intended to go ahead on the Camp David peace path. The result was that the Saudi plan, the centerpiece of the Arab summit in Fez on November 26, so clearly lacked American support that the summit adjourned without a vote. The effort to repudiate Camp David had failed.

Meanwhile, the European participants in MFO, seemingly aware at last of the stakes in the aftermath of Sadat's murder, decided to join without preconditions. The Israelis and the Arabs understood, as we all did, that European participation in the force implied European support of Camp David. The commitment of troops and national honor meant more than any words.

Despite this achievement, the peace process was in serious trouble. In Egypt, Mubarak began the inevitable reorientation of Egyptian policy. By late November, Egypt's reluctance to go forward at the negotiating table with arrangements for autonomy was clear to both the Israeli and the American teams. Too late did Israel begin to offer practical arrangements that might have given autonomous Arab governing authorities in the West Bank and Gaza a veto over the allocation of public land and water.

As for U.S.-Israeli relations, the downward spiral that had begun with AWACS continued. Then, on December 14, 1981—the day after martial law was imposed in Poland—Begin decided, without warning, on the de facto annexation of the Golan Heights. This astonishing act inflamed Israel's critics within the Administration. "How long do we have to go on bribing Israel?" Caspar Weinberger demanded angrily. "If there is no real cost to the Israelis, we'll never be able to stop any of their actions."

In this instance, the President decided that the cost would be a suspension of the U.S.-Israeli agreement on a Memorandum of Understanding (MOU), establishing limited strategic cooperation between the two countries, which had been concluded only two weeks before. He also suspended some $300 million in potential benefits to Israel through arms sales. Begin had set great store in the MOU; coming soon after the AWACS vote, it was a timely reassurance to Israel of the American commitment to the future security of Israel against attacks from forces outside the region. Even so, Begin had been concerned that the MOU might be halfhearted. Noting that it contained no provision for joint military exercises of the kind that were conducted by Egyptian and U.S. troops in Operation Bright Star, he said that American behavior reminded him of "the old poignant story about the German aristocrat who has an affair with a poor Jewish girl and tells her: 'But don't greet me [on] Unter den Linden.' "

The suspension of MOU, culminating a series of penalties, provoked a memorable outburst from the Israeli leader. This he delivered on December 20, 1981, to our ambassador to Israel, Samuel W. Lewis. "What kind of talk is this— 'penalizing' Israel?" Begin asked, livid with anger. "Are we a state or [are we] vassals of yours? Are we a banana republic? . . . You have no right to penalize Israel." Lewis had told Begin that resumption of the MOU talks would depend on progress in the autonomy talks and the situation in Lebanon. "The people of Israel lived without the memorandum of understanding for 3,700 years, and will continue to live without it for another 3,700 years," Begin replied.

Disturbed by these events, I traveled again to Cairo and Jerusalem on January 12–15. In Egypt, Mubarak told me that any agreement on autonomy would have to be "reasonable and acceptable"—implying that the Palestinians would have to accept it before Egypt would sign it. In Israel, Shamir said, in the rising tone of emphasis that had begun to characterize these exchanges, it was felt that Israeli concessions at Camp David had been disproportionate; it was now time for Egypt to show some flexibility.

Defense Minister Sharon railed at me on the subject of the suspension of MOU. Sharon is a brawny man who uses his bulk, his extremely loud voice, and a flagrantly aggressive manner, which I suspect he has cultivated for effect, to overwhelm opposition. "We are your ally and friend and should be treated as such!" he shouted, pounding on the table so that the dishes jumped. "If you act like an ally, General," I replied, "you'll be treated like one."

Before I left, Begin himself, in obvious pain from a broken hip suffered only a short time before, gave me his final answer. Yes, the Sinai would be returned on time, but Egypt would be held strictly to account by Israel for subsequent events. And, once again, Begin delivered his warning about the PLO in Lebanon. I responded in the cautionary phrases with which the Israeli prime minister was by now very familiar.

After this visit and a subsequent trip in late January, it was obvious that the achievement of both the Sinai withdrawal and an autonomy agreement was impossible. Nevertheless, we could not allow the negotiations on autonomy to collapse and neither Egypt nor Israel wanted the process to end. Richard Fairbanks, my former assistant secretary of state for congressional relations, was therefore appointed a special representative to the talks, with a mandate to keep the discussions alive while seeking ways to bridge the differences between the parties on questions that might be pursued after the Sinai withdrawal.

True to its word, Israel returned the Sinai on April 25, 1982. This was, as I wrote to Begin, "an act of the utmost courage, statesmanship, and vision. . . . Above all, Israel's decision is an inspiring example of the commitment of you and your government to the future."

The Sinai issue settled, Israeli fixation on the threat from southern Lebanon intensified. On May 28, I wrote to Begin and told him, in so many words, that I hoped there was no ambiguity on the extent of our concern about possible future Israeli military actions in Lebanon. The President and I wanted to make it very clear that we sincerely hoped that Israel would continue to exercise complete restraint and refrain from any action which would further damage the understanding underlying the cessation of hostilities. Israeli military actions, regardless of size, could have consequences none of us could foresee.

In reply, Begin expressed himself in language that testified to the depth of his feelings: "You advise us to exercise complete restraint and refrain from any action . . . Mr. Secretary, my dear friend, the man has not been born who will ever obtain from me consent to let Jews be killed by a bloodthirsty enemy and allow those who are responsible for the shedding of this blood to enjoy immunity."

Reading these phrases, I understood that the United States would probably not be able to stop Israel from attacking. On May 7, while I was in London for the first contacts with the British in the Falklands crisis, Prime Minister Begin, stating that he did not wish to "surprise" the United States, had sent us an oral message warning that it might well become "imperative and inevitable" to remove the threat against Israel.

I never believed that mere words would restrain Israel, tormented as she was by fear of her enemies and by her enervating quarrel with America, her historic protector. Throughout the tense and eventful period that began with the death of Sadat and ended with Israeli withdrawal from the Sinai, we had taken a whole range of actions in our determination to keep Lebanon from exploding into an even more destructive war. The cessation of hostilities achieved by Phil Habib in the summer of 1981 had bought time. I tried to use it to change the conditions that made war likely. The crisis in Lebanon could only be brought under control by a Lebanese government strong enough to settle the country's internal quarrels and restore the rule of law.

Therefore, the Lebanese presidential election, scheduled for the fall of 1982, must take place in an atmosphere reasonably free from Syrian influence. By late August 1981, we had set up a three-part plan to achieve this, calling for the development of an Arab consensus leading to a withdrawal of Syrian forces (then face to face with Phalange militia), the solution of the problem of Syrian SAM-6 missiles in the Beka'a Valley, and a strengthening of the cease-fire in the south through a more effective U.N. presence and the simultaneous phased removal of PLO heavy weapons and the Israeli military presence from the enclave commanded by Israel's Christian friend, Major Saad Haddad.

The foreign ministers of Kuwait, Lebanon, Saudi Arabia, and Syria formed a quadripartite commission to deal with consultations among the Arabs, including the PLO, in what came to be called (after a town in Lebanon where it began—in both Arabic and Hebrew, the words mean "house of judgment") the Bait a Din process. Immediate problems developed. The Syrian objective, as communicated to the other Arabs, was the "arabization" of Lebanon and its incorporation into the Syrian defense structure—in short, permanent occupation and the exclusion of the Christians from their share of political power. The Syrians did not want to leave Lebanon, and not even the Saudis had the means to persuade them to do so. The PLO meant to remain also and enjoyed the support of Syria and at least the acquiescence of the other Arabs in this intention.

Throughout the late summer and fall and into the winter of 1981–82, the Israelis continued to complain of a buildup of artillery, rockets, and other heavy arms by the PLO in southern Lebanon. In mid-August, Begin reported that "since the cessation of hostilities on July 24, the PLO has exploited the situation to place eighteen new 135mm guns with a range of 27 kilometers [among the best in the Soviet arsenal]. . . . How long can this horror continue while we hold our fire everywhere?" In early November, President Elias Sarkis of Lebanon was telling us about "the most intensive buildup ever of weapons in southern Lebanon, including more 135mm artillery." These weapons, of Soviet origin, were being passed by Syria to the PLO. In late November, Habib toured Arab capitals and reported that all Arabs, including the "mainstream PLO," wanted the cessation of hostilities to continue. However, the Bait a Din process, though it was brokered by the influential Saudis, could not produce a formula for changing conditions that most of the participants did not want to change.

Meanwhile, the bitter struggle between the Syrians and the Christian Phalange intensified; Israeli support for the Phalange continued. In January 1982, President Reagan wrote to Begin, urging restraint. In his lawyerly fashion, Begin sought to redefine the conditions under which the United States would consider an Israeli attack justified. Pointedly, I repeated my formula: only in strictly proportional response to "an internationally recognized provocation." Begin agreed, then changed his mind, and in one of his exercises in creative nuance, told Reagan that there would be no major Israeli action "unless [Israel was] attacked in clear provocation."

Begin interpreted the cessation of hostilities between the PLO and Israel as being universal and regarded any terrorist attack anywhere in the world, as well as the violation of any Israeli frontier, as a breach of the agreement meriting retaliation. The United States held that the agreement meant precisely what it said: "There will be no hostile activities from Lebanon directed at targets in Israel [and vice versa]." In late January, just as I was leaving the Middle East after the last round of autonomy talks, Israeli forces captured a team of six heavily armed terrorists who had infiltrated from Lebanon through Jordan. They were members of Fatah. Either Yasir Arafat did not know what risks he was running or his control of the PLO was being threatened by the cessation of hostilities. Word reached me that Sharon had recommended heavy attacks on PLO bases in retaliation, followed by an invasion if the PLO escalated in reaction.

On February 3, Begin sent General Yehoshua Saguy, the director of Israeli military intelligence, to call on me in Washington. Since the cessation of hostilities slightly more than six months before Israel had lost 17 dead and 288 wounded in ten PLO violations. Israel was prepared to attack the PLO in Lebanon if there were any further incidents. A large-scale force would advance from the Israeli border to the southern suburbs of Beirut. Its target was the PLO infrastructure; the Syrians would be avoided if possible.

We had already heard that Sharon had visited Israel's Phalangist allies in Beirut. War seemed very near. Our duty to attempt to pre-

vent it was obvious; our ability to do so, questionable. After informing the President of this latest development, I sent Ambassador Lewis
to Begin with instructions to tell him that an Israeli operation along
the lines described to us would have far-reaching consequences for
our relationship. The Israelis should not misjudge American public
opinion; it would not tolerate such an operation in current circumstances. Begin interrupted. "Don't use those words, Sam!" he
pleaded. But in his reply, sent after he had consulted the cabinet,
Begin said that he and his colleagues had decided to accept my request for restraint: "We agree that you will make, in the near future,
diplomatic and political efforts, provided that no attack whatsoever
on Israeli citizens or territory or any border or sector is carried out."
Though the United States carried on no direct communications with
the PLO, we had channels to its leadership through Saudi Arabia and
Jordan, and I asked Crown Prince Fahd and King Hussein to urge a
policy of restraint on Syria and the PLO. Habib pressed the same
message, and there were no more incidents for a time.

Soon afterward, the New York Times carried a remarkably detailed account of the Israeli plan. It was no longer much of a secret;
nor was it any secret that time was running out. At this delicate
juncture, Caspar Weinberger, while on a tour of Saudi Arabia and
Jordan, was reported to have stated that the United States needed
more than one friend in the Middle East and revealed to the press
that the Administration might provide F-16 fighter-bombers and
mobile I-Hawk antiaircraft missiles to Jordan. The Israelis were outraged. Begin wrote to the President: "I do not understand why it was
necessary for the Secretary of Defense to make his worrying statements . . . while he was visiting Arab countries that, but for one, are
in a state of war with us. . . ." Neither did I.

In March and April, as we worked through the final details of the
Sinai withdrawal, the storm continued to gather. We heard reports of
increased Soviet support for Syria and increased Syrian support for
the PLO. An Israeli diplomat was assassinated in Paris, and an Israeli
officer was killed in the Haddad enclave. Israeli planes attacked PLO
targets in Lebanon on April 21 and again on May 9; the PLO shelled
northern Israel but in such an obviously ineffective way as to give no
excuse for an Israeli escalation.

We were running out of time, and I tried to get the diplomacy
moving again, this time through an attempt to tie together the three

major issues confronting us: the Iran-Iraq war,* autonomy, and Lebanon itself. The best hope for preventing a new war in a Lebanon already being torn to shreds by war lay in internationalizing the crisis. I seized upon the idea of calling for a conference composed of the European countries participating in the U.N. peacekeeping force in Lebanon (France, Ireland, the Netherlands, and Norway); Saudi Arabia and Kuwait, as the gulf states represented in the Bait a Din group; and the United States. Syria would have been invited to attend, but not the U.S.S.R. This group, which had excellent communications with Israel, the PLO, and all factions in Lebanon, might have been able to move on the fundamental issues and perhaps arrest the tumbling current toward war.

While I had little hope that these theatrics would succeed, I believed that they would impose another inhibition on the Israelis in their military intentions and perhaps even help to bring the Syrians and the PLO to their senses. The fact that diplomatic alternatives to war existed weakened the will to war. But even this limited attempt to control the crisis before it burst into being was frustrated. The Administration was already divided over its policy toward Israel. Some of my colleagues were little inclined to sympathize with Israeli reminders that the bargain underlying the cessation of hostilities— that the United States would arrange for removal of the Syrian missiles from the Beka'a Valley in exchange for a guarantee that Israel would not attack the missiles—had not been fulfilled; twelve months later the missiles were still there. The foreign policy bureaucracy, overwhelmingly Arabist in its approach to the Middle East and in its sympathies, saw the crisis as an opportunity to open direct negotiations between the United States and the PLO.

Now the cessation of hostilities itself was threatened. As tensions mounted, I repeatedly warned the President that we must act or face the consequences of war in the Middle East. On May 21, I sent the President a detailed plan of action for my three-part initiative for the

---

*My proposal to internationalize the Iran-Iraq war (though this time with no U.S. participation in any peace conference) as a means of avoiding further destruction and bloodshed in the two countries and worse destabilization of the gulf region, failed to win the attention of the White House. The war was then at a critical stage, an Iranian offensive having recovered nearly all of Iran's lost territory, and it is possible that a properly designed initiative could have succeeded in ending the hostilities. At the very least, it would have reassured the gulf states that they would not be alone in confronting a revolutionary Iran bent on subversion of Shiite populations on one side and a resurgent, Soviet-backed, Baathist Syria on the other.

Middle East and asked him for an NSC meeting to discuss it before
we left for Europe eleven days later. But my efforts came to
nothing—memoranda, telephone calls, confrontations with Bill
Clark all failed to drive the message through the incoherent NSC
system. In the absence of approval, my speech before the Chicago
Foreign Policy Association, which I had regarded as an opportunity
to make a public policy statement on the Middle East, could only
hint at possible action to come.

As a result, we were reduced to "exploratory diplomacy." I asked
Philip Habib to raise the question of a Lebanon conference with the
President when he made his report on the progress of his negotiations
in the Middle East. Habib found the President amenable to his "exploration" of the conference idea and to that part of my proposal
that dealt with autonomy. On May 22, Reagan wrote to Begin invit-
ing him to Washington on June 21 for a general discussion of that
subject and U.S.-Israeli relations.

Late in May, while on an official visit to Washington, General
Sharon shocked a roomful of State Department bureaucrats by
sketching out two possible military campaigns: one that would
pacify southern Lebanon, and a second that would rewrite the political map of Beirut in favor of the Christian Phalange. It was clear that
Sharon was putting the United States on notice: one more provocation by the Palestinians and Israel would deliver a knockout blow to
the PLO.

In a strenuous argument with Sharon in the presence of my staff, I
challenged these plans, and after the meeting, so that there could be
no question that I was playing to an audience, I invited Sharon into
my office and told him privately, in the plainest possible language,
what I had repeated to him and Begin and their colleagues many
times before: unless there was an internationally recognized provocation, and unless Israeli retaliation was proportionate to any such
provocation, an attack by Israel into Lebanon would have a devastating effect in the United States. "No one," Sharon replied, in his
truculent way, "has the right to tell Israel what decision it should
take in defense of its people."

On June 3, the *casus belli* the Israelis had been waiting for mate-
rialized. In London, Arab terrorists shot and grievously wounded
Sholom Argov, the Israeli ambassador to Great Britain, in the Dor-

chester Hotel. Argov's assailants were armed with a mint-new Polish machine-pistol and fragmentation grenades, among other weapons, and were found to be carrying a list of targets that included diplomats from moderate Arab nations as well as a plan for an attack on the London Jewish School for the Blind. The next day, Israel bombed the empty sports stadium in Beirut, exploding the ammunition dump the PLO had established beneath the grandstand. Israel also carried out air attacks (which Begin described as "surgical") against other PLO targets inside Lebanon.

The PLO reacted promptly. On June 5, the Israelis reported that twenty of their towns in the Galilee had been bombarded by PLO artillery, and three civilians had been wounded.

The President, in a message from Versailles, urged Begin not to widen the attack after the stadium bombing. The Saudis told us that Arafat was willing to suspend cross-border shelling. It was too late. Begin's deepest emotions had been engaged. "Military targets . . . are completely immune," Begin wrote. "The purpose of the enemy is to kill—kill Jews, men, women, and children."

Facile analysts of Begin's character and motives have written that he is afflicted with a Masada complex, implying a romantic psychological attachment to the Jewish zealots who, when they were overcome by a Roman siege of the fortress of Masada in A.D. 73, committed suicide en masse rather than surrender to their enemies. In my opinion, this is nonsense. Begin certainly believes that Israel is besieged, but his entire motive is to preserve the lives of Jews. He has no "complex"—only the inescapable memory of the Holocaust. "[In my generation], millions of Jews perished for two reasons," Begin wrote to me, "(a) because they did not have the instruments with which to defend themselves, and (b) because nobody came to their rescue." His letters, his conversation, his speeches—and, unquestionably, his thoughts—were dominated, when he was prime minister, by the sense that the lives of his people and the survival of Israel had been personally entrusted to him. He once said, when asked what he wanted to be remembered for, that he wished to be known to history as the man who established the borders of the state of Israel for all time. To Begin, and to most other Jews, Israeli sovereignty is no abstract idea; the state of Israel is where Jews need not depend on rescue that never comes, but are defended, in Begin's phrase, "by a valiant Jewish army." As to how that army should operate, once it engaged the PLO, Begin had no doubts. "In this connection," he said,

"I will always remember the masterful saying: 'Hot pursuit? Right up to their hangars!' "

On June 5, in Jerusalem, the Israeli cabinet approved a large-scale invasion of Lebanon. The Israelis named their operation Peace for Galilee, and Begin informed us that the objective was to drive the PLO back 40 kilometers (24 miles) from the Israeli border, "so that all our civilians in the region of Galilee will be set free of the permanent threat to their lives." It was expected that the operation would last no more than three or four days. Israel asked us to tell Syria that its forces would not attack Syrian military units unless they attacked the Israelis.

Comparing Israeli action against the PLO to the British operation in the Falklands, which was then in progress, he asked, "Do we not have an inherent right of self-defense? Does not Article 51 of the U.N. Charter apply to us?" By the end of the first day of operations, the Israeli defense forces had advanced northward 32 miles into Lebanon along a 35-mile front extending from the foot of Mount Hermon to the coast. They had lost 8 killed and 17 wounded; the Lebanese government estimated that 300 Arabs had died in the first day of fighting. So far, the Syrians had not moved to oppose the Israeli advance.

Philip Habib, who had been in London en route to the Middle East, was summoned to Paris on June 6 by Bill Clark, who immediately ushered him into the presence of the President. I was not present at this meeting and do not know what instructions, if any, the President may have given Habib. Later, in Clark's presence, I asked Habib to go immediately to Begin and urge an immediate end of hostilities before the conflict widened, which was what the President himself had urged on Begin in his message the day before, June 5. The United States had voted that day for U.N. Resolution 508, which called for Israeli withdrawal and a cross-border cease-fire. While we were talking, the President entered, accompanied by Deaver and Darman, collected Habib, and went outside for a "photo opportunity."

Meanwhile, the Israelis, though they encountered stiff resistance around Tyre and elsewhere, continued to drive northward. Syria moved an additional 16,000 troops into Lebanon, bringing her total forces to nearly 40,000. The Israelis continued to send messages that they did not wish to engage the Syrians, but at the same time their columns continued to advance up the coast toward Beirut in a way that might well develop into a link-up with the Phalange that would cut the main body of Syrians off from their contingent in the capital.

On June 8, Habib, then in Jerusalem, was asked by Begin to carry an unwritten personal message to President Hafez al Assad of Syria: if PLO artillery in the Syrian lines was pulled back to the 40-kilometer mark, there would be no need for Syria and Israel to fight. The next day, while Habib was in Damascus waiting to deliver this message, a second message arrived from Begin to Assad, warning Syria that the Syrians should withdraw the additional SAM batteries that the Israelis claimed were being brought in to reinforce Syrian positions. Habib delivered both messages to the Syrian government, but while he was still in Damascus waiting to see Assad, the Israeli air force attacked the SAM-6 sites on both sides of the border in the Beka'a Valley, destroying them all; Israeli pilots also shot down twenty-three Syrian MIG's while losing no Israeli aircraft. It is still not clear what prompted this sudden Israeli attack, which changed the whole character of the conflict. Later, in Washington, Begin told Reagan and me that the Syrians had moved some of their missiles as Israeli forces advanced, posing a threat that the Israeli military chiefs deemed it essential to remove. However that may be, this dramatic widening of the war demonstrated once again the truism that political leaders tend to be carried away by the greatness of their responsibilities and the urgent nature of military advice once a conflict begins.

During a dinner given by the queen in Windsor Castle on June 8, the Presidential party having flown to England, Bill Clark passed me a note informing me that a resolution had been introduced in the U.N. condemning Israel for its invasion and threatening sanctions. Clark's note suggested that the United States might vote in favor of the resolution. This would have been an unprecedented step for the United States. It was also entirely out of character for the President. The resolution would come to a vote in New York in a matter of minutes.

Upstairs, in the quarters that had been allocated to the Presidential party, I asked Clark who had made the decision to support the resolution. "The President of the United States, Al; we've got the decision and there is no more discussion," Clark replied. But I doubted that the President fully understood the implications of the vote and asked for a meeting with him. As we went into the President's rooms, Clark told me that Reagan had acted on the basis of a recommendation from Vice President Bush's crisis management team in Washington. In my conversation with the President it seemed clear that he had been under the impression that this recommendation reflected the unanimous judgment of his advisers. After telling President Reagan that his Secretary of State had not been consulted, I advised him that the United States must veto the resolution not only because it placed the entire blame for hostilities on Israel but also because sanctions were implied. If the United States took this step against Israel, then it must be prepared to take the next, much more serious steps. Reagan, listening intently, agreed that we must veto.

Eagleburger informed us that only fifteen minutes remained before the vote. By now Clark understood that a vote for the resolution would bring about a major break with Israel and explained to me that he had supported a U.S. vote in favor of the resolution only if Israel was not named as the object of condemnation and sanctions. As no other country except Israel could possibly be the object of condemnation and sanctions, the value of this nuance eluded me. Therefore I instructed Eagleburger to tell Mrs. Kirkpatrick to veto the resolution whether or not Israel was mentioned by name in the text. That, said Eagleburger, was not what Clark's deputy, Bud McFarlane, was telling him to do. This new confusion required another meeting with Clark, this time in Deaver's bedroom, where acquiescence if not agreement was reached after a stormy exchange of words. With only minutes to spare, I telephoned Mrs. Kirkpatrick and instructed her to veto the resolution, regardless of any other instructions she may have received, whether or not Israel was named in the resolution.

Clark had advised me, in the course of our first confrontation that evening, that it would be "best to go to bed, and maybe it will all blow over in the morning." When I did go to bed, a long time afterward, my thoughts were deeply disturbed by the dangerous implications of a situation in which a Presidential assistant, especially one of limited experience and limited understanding of the volatile nature of an international conflict, should assume the powers of the Presidency.

Whatever the confusions among his staff, the President himself now understood the dangers of a widening war. On June 9, he turned aside a hotline message from Brezhnev with a succinctly worded indictment of Soviet policy, especially its failure to support the Camp David accords and its readiness to arm the PLO, and urged him to use Moscow's strong influence on Syria to bring about a cease-fire.

On the same day he wrote, in his own hand, a strong appeal to Begin, asking Israel to accept a cease-fire at 6:00 A.M. the following day. Habib delivered a similar message to Assad.

Understandably, Assad was interested in a cease-fire, but insisted that it could take place only in connection with unconditional Israeli withdrawal, something that was beyond Assad's power to command or Habib's to promise. As for Begin, he was not inclined toward a cease-fire until Israeli objectives had been achieved. But what were these objectives? Were they the ones we had heard earlier in the war or were they now the more ambitious goals of the Sharon plan?

When Begin called me at 5:30 on the morning of June 10, the Presidential party had moved on to Germany. Begin was in voluble form, providing detailed information on the Israeli-Syrian air battle over the Beka'a. Saying that Israel would stop her forces only after they had cleared a safe 40-kilometer zone and withdraw them only when an agreement had been reached to safeguard her northern border, he asked me to come to Israel immediately. In his view, only a high-level U.S. involvement could produce results in a new situation. Obviously, Begin was playing for time. Certainly we were at a critical juncture. If I went, the war might be halted. Balanced against that was the impression of collusion that might result from the appearance of the American Secretary of State in Jerusalem at the height of the Israeli attack. We were already being accused of that. I therefore instructed Larry Eagleburger to send Sam Lewis to Begin with a precondition: before I could consider coming to Jerusalem, there must be an immediate cease-fire and withdrawal to the 40-kilometer line. It would also be necessary for Syria to understand and accept my role.

Lewis's report on Begin's reaction came back while I was meeting again with the President, and Clark brought the paper in to us. Lewis, who is one of the most brilliant men in the Foreign Service, had quite properly appended a sort of postscript to Eagleburger expressing the opinion that Habib might feel that his role had been usurped if I came to Israel, and he might resign as a result. Certainly it was possible to read Begin's invitation to me as suggesting that he was not entirely comfortable with Habib, and in view of recent events, that feeling might be reciprocated. Lewis's comment appeared to trouble the President when he read it. I had already sensed a reluctance to accept Begin's suggestion. In the end, he chose to instruct Habib anew to press for a cease-fire in both Syria and Israel.

I told a news conference that I was not going to fly to Israel (Meese had already told the press, without mentioning this to me, that I would not be going to the Middle East) because the Israelis had not shown sufficient flexibility.

Later in the day, having been called to meet with the President, I found that he had already signed a letter to Begin calling in harsh terms for an unconditional Israeli withdrawal from Lebanon. Once again, Clark had delivered this draft to Reagan without showing it to me beforehand. I reminded the President that this letter, expressing demands that the Israelis could not possibly meet, gave them justification for inflexibility. The President agreed and did not send it. I then phoned Habib, who was still in Damascus, and instructed him to determine the Syrians' bottom line and then go to Jerusalem to press the Israelis hard for a cease-fire.

Later that day, Begin told us that he planned a unilateral cease-fire on all fronts at noon on Friday, June 11. Like many a cease-fire in Lebanon, it did not last long. First against the Syrians, later against the PLO, the Israeli advance settled into a holding position, but there were recurrent exchanges of fire. On June 13, Israel closed the ring around Beirut. Sharon's objectives had now been achieved: the PLO was trapped in Beirut, Israeli forces had linked up with the Phalange, cutting off the Syrian forces in the capital, the Syrians themselves had been badly defeated in the air and in the lower Beka'a Valley. To all appearances, the Israelis had cast off restraint entirely. Operation Peace for Galilee had become an Israeli-Syrian war and, now, the siege of an Arab capital.

"We do not worry about victory," Menachem Begin had told us before the operation began. "We worry about casualties." The Israelis had lost 170 killed and 700 wounded thus far (by Israeli estimates, Syria had lost approximately 1,000 killed, the PLO 2,000). On the basis of comparative populations, Israel's battle losses were the equivalent of the United States losing 10,000 dead and 40,000 wounded in a week. To capture Beirut in street-to-street fighting would have cost many more lives. Ambassador Moshe Arens had told me that Israel did not want to go into Beirut and pay this price. For obvious reasons, he did not want the PLO to know that. Israel's objective was to create an atmosphere of pressure and threat that would persuade the PLO that it must either come to terms or be annihilated. By air attack and artillery barrage, by loudspeaker and leaflet, Israel carried out a powerful exercise in psychological warfare to convince her adversaries that she meant to attack West Beirut and smash the PLO if there were no other alternative.

In this tragic situation lay the great opportunity to make peace. Syria and the PLO, the two forces that had destroyed the authority of the Lebanese government and brought on the fighting, had been defeated. The Syrians and the Soviets were at each other's throats in the aftermath of Syria's humiliating defeats at the hands of the Israelis. The Syrians blamed the destruction of their air force (the Israelis claimed a total of eighty-seven Syrian planes downed, against no Israeli losses) on the inferiority of Soviet aircraft; the Soviets, whose MIG's had once again been swept from the skies by American-Israeli technology and Israeli manpower while the whole world (and especially the Arab world) watched, charged the Syrian pilots with incompetence.

The moment had come to move all foreign forces—Syrian, Palestinian, and Israeli—out of Lebanon and return the country to the Lebanese under suitable international protection and guarantees. I was convinced that such a moment might never come again if it was not seized. That was the reason for my sense of urgency in sending Habib his instructions after the contretemps with Clark on June 12. Phil's work was vital, but he needed the support of a strategic plan. The elements of this plan were clearly defined: withdrawal of all foreign troops, reestablishment of effective government in Lebanon, a safe northern border for Israel. The strategy was to use the shock of the Israeli attack to force the PLO out of Beirut, to make the feuding Lebanese understand at last that their collective peace and security could be achieved only through unity, and finally, to reinforce the incentives for both Syria and Israel not to prolong their adventures in Lebanon.

I believed that if we acted quickly and with a sure hand, the United States could achieve all this. We had the right channels. Already, encouraged by Habib, a Lebanese Council of National Salvation had been formed and had a good chance of including all elements in Lebanon. The Saudis could talk to, and influence, Syria and the PLO. We could weigh in with the Israelis. And among our European allies, the French, keenly sensitive to their historic role in Lebanon, were anxious to play a leading part.

In Washington, though he was displeased with me for the unauthorized dispatch of Habib's instructions, the President never disagreed with the instructions themselves. But the constant bugaboo of the Administration's foreign policy—divided councils, different voices—rose up again. On June 13, King Khalid of Saudi Arabia died and was succeeded by Crown Prince Fahd. Without consultation with me or the State Department, the White House delegated Vice President Bush, Caspar Weinberger, Senator Percy, and Bud McFarlane, who had become Clark's deputy on the NSC staff, to offer the official condolences of the United States. The three men traveled to Riyadh in order to carry out this mission. Early on the morning of Wednesday, June 16, they were received by King Fahd, and later they breakfasted with the Saudi foreign minister, Prince Saud. When I read the cable reports of these meetings, I feared that words Bush and Weinberger had uttered to the Saudi leaders would have the effect of undercutting the pressure we were bringing to bear on the PLO. On June 19, at a news conference in New York, I reiterated our policy in plain terms:

The United States view is that we would like to see ultimately all foreign forces out of Lebanon so that the central government can conduct the sovereign affairs of a sovereign government within its internationally recognized borders. . . . This recent crisis was a culmination of a long period of unacceptable instability in southern Lebanon and perhaps throughout Lebanon. There will have to be very careful analysis of events associated with this recent crisis before any value judgment would be appropriate.

Yet on the very next day, Cap Weinberger, appearing on national television, drew an analogy between Israel's actions in Lebanon and Argentina's in the Falklands, adding that "it is very premature and probably totally wrong to say what is our policy right now." His words were not contradicted by the White House.

The effects were immediate. On the same day that Bush and Weinberger met with King Fahd and Prince Saud, the Lebanese had informed Phil Habib that Arafat and other leaders of the PLO were ready to begin negotiations leading to the disarmament of the PLO and its submission to Lebanese government authority. They asked for a forty-eight-hour cease-fire to work out the details. I told Habib that the United States supported such negotiations, and the Israelis, after I spoke to Arens and urged acceptance, agreed to the cease-fire.

The next morning, it seemed that American diplomacy had achieved the breakthrough that was the key to ending the war and creating a stable peace for Lebanon. The PLO was going to be disarmed and would probably leave the country. The siege of Beirut would be over. I received an unverified report that Yasir Arafat was already aboard a ship that would carry him to Cyprus. But by late afternoon, we heard that the PLO was hardening its position; the Lebanese attributed this change to Saudi advice, which was in turn based on what the Saudis had heard from the Vice President's party. Then came the Weinberger remarks. As talks continued, drained of their urgency, it was possible that the Saudis, after interpreting these "signals" from the United States, had advised the PLO to play for a better outcome. The opportunity for a quick, clean withdrawal of the PLO and an end to bloodshed in Beirut had been destroyed.

Mixed signals continued to bedevil our diplomacy. When Begin met President Reagan in the Oval Office on the afternoon of Monday, June 21, the President was, as Bush and Weinberger had predicted in Riyadh, "firm and stern." As the talks took place, Israeli artillery and naval guns pounded West Beirut. An expressionless Reagan read off the American position from typed file cards; Begin responded with equal coldness. There was no exchange of pleasantries, no dialogue, no hint of the warm sympathy that had up to now characterized their relationship. At a later, larger meeting in the Cabinet room, Begin attempted to discuss the reasons for the Israeli actions, but by now, nothing he could say could change the mood of the Administration. In a heated outburst, Weinberger attempted to scold Begin and received a tongue-lashing in return. "Be quiet!" Begin said. "You're wrong again!" A majority of the President's advisers, exasperated by Begin's unpredictability and outraged by the attack on Lebanon, were determined to punish Israel. Yet the communiqué issued by the President and the Israeli prime minister reaffirmed the policy outlined in the instructions I had sent to Habib on June 12.

The negotiations for the withdrawal of the PLO continued in Beirut. Arafat, in his meetings with the Lebanese, had demanded with near-hysterical insistence that the Israelis withdraw to a distance of 5 kilometers as a precondition in any deal. On June 22, thinking that the effort to get the PLO out of Lebanon might be revived by an Israeli gesture, I asked Begin to consider a fallback as part of a package. Begin replied that he would take the matter up with his cabinet. In a matter of hours, the PLO in Beirut was under the impression that Israel had *agreed* to the disengagement unilaterally. Israel had done nothing of the kind. Arafat's information came from the Saudis, whose ambassador in Washington evidently had gone away from a meeting with Judge Clark that afternoon under a misapprehension. (The meeting had been called by Clark to discourage a plan by Ambassador Alhegelan's wife to picket the White House over the Lebanese crisis.) The PLO withdrawal was derailed again. I called in Alhegelan, told him the facts, and repeated that only a PLO withdrawal could create the conditions for peace.

The President's anger with Begin, fed by the greater anger of Weinberger (who was reportedly exploring ways to cut off military deliveries to Israel) and others, seemed to grow by the day. Senator Percy introduced another reason for dismay in the White House when he told the Administration that the Senate Foreign Relations Committee would recommend cutting off arms to Israel if it went into West Beirut, and he asked the President to telephone this warning to Begin. Advising the President against any such call, I tried to reassure Percy, as I continually attempted to reassure the President and Clark, by explaining that Israeli pressure, and it alone, could produce a solution that would end the fighting. There was little chance that Begin would squander lives in the rubble of Beirut unless he had no other choice. Israeli casualties, as Sharon would soon report, had by now risen to 270 dead and 1,470 wounded. Nevertheless, the PLO and its friends must not be allowed to believe that they could escape an eventual Israeli attack.

This strategy of keeping up the psychological pressure depended on good communications with Israel and strong nerves in Washington. Despite the obstructions put up by Weinberger and others, there was every reason to fight through the difficulties of the situation. I was convinced that the logic of our strategy must overcome the opposition to it. We fended off attempts to relieve the PLO's dilemma, such as a French initiative in the U.N. Security Council that would have interposed a U.N. observer presence between the PLO and the Israeli forces. The French, who were anxious to appear as friends of the PLO, were offering valuable support for our position on PLO withdrawal. Realizing that the alternative to withdrawal was annihilation, sooner or later, the Saudis, too, were drawing closer to our position.

By the evening of June 24, after a day of intensive discussions with Bandar, Cheysson, and Arens, among others, I was able to telephone the President and tell him that King Fahd supported our position on West Beirut: the PLO must lay down its arms in Beirut and depart. The French also agreed that the PLO must disarm. Both the Saudis and the French would convey this view to the PLO.

The pressure on the PLO was dissipated further on June 24 when Larry Speakes, the official White House spokesman, told the press that Begin had promised President Reagan on June 21 that Israel would not go farther into Beirut. No such promise had been made. Begin had merely said that Israel "had no intention" of attacking. I spoke forthrightly to the President, urging him to discipline his Administration. "Above all, Mr. President," I said, "we must not clarify our position publicly. We can tell the Israelis privately how upset we are with them, but we don't need a public break with Israel. What we do need is a PLO withdrawal. By tomorrow, we'll know what the PLO decision is."

Reagan received my remarks without comment, and with what seemed to be embarrassment and unease. Only that morning, we had had our last tense confrontation in the Oval Office and I had handed him my list of particulars on the ineptitudes of the past weeks. By now, no doubt, he had decided to "accept my resignation" on the following day, June 25.

At four o'clock in the morning of Friday, June 25, Habib phoned Larry Eagleburger at home to report West Beirut was under heavy Israeli bombardment. The Israelis, perhaps believing that the cumulative impact of the Bush, Weinberger, Clark, and Speakes incidents had convinced the PLO that the danger was receding, had decided to increase the military pressure. It was a heavy-handed act that nearly shattered the fragile political consensus in Lebanon. Saying that they would not be part of the massacre of Lebanese civilians, Muslim leaders were resigning from the National Salvation Council and the cabinet, and there was a danger that the Lebanese government would collapse altogether. We immediately contacted Arens and asked for a cease-fire. After contacting Jerusalem, Arens reported that Israel was ready to accept the cease-fire. At 8:00 A.M., I spoke to Habib on the radio-telephone. Phil, understandably agitated, told me that while the bombardment of West Beirut had stopped for the moment, a battle was raging a mile and a half from the presidential palace. Israeli military pressure, he said, was destroying the hope for an agreement: if there was no Lebanese government, there would be no one to negotiate with the PLO. We agreed that he must encourage the Lebanese to put together a new government that represented all Lebanese factions while we worked for a general cease-fire and a settlement of the PLO question with the Saudis and the French.

Soon after I finished speaking to Habib, Ambassador Arens arrived with an assurance from the Israeli government that its forces would not enter West Beirut for at least forty-eight hours and would notify the United States before they decided to go. I knew my President and his White House. I sent a message back to Begin: if Israel went into Beirut, the United States would abandon her. Begin already knew this; he had understood what had happened in Washington. The Administration, however, did not seem able to realize that Begin would not throw away the sacrifices of his troops and abandon his irreducible objective—the removal of the PLO from Israel's northern frontiers—merely because of pressure from Washington. If he could not get the PLO out in any other way, he would do it at the point of a bayonet.

That afternoon the President announced my resignation. Nevertheless, at the President's insistence, I continued to deal with the crisis. On the morning of June 26, Arens reported a conversation with Sharon, who said that if Israel could "do more" in West Beirut, it could bring the PLO to its knees in twenty-four to forty-eight hours. I expressed my disapproval; it was not our idea to bring the PLO to its knees under the guns of Israeli soldiers, but to rid Lebanon of the PLO under circumstances that would enhance the prestige and influence of the Lebanese government.

The present cease-fire would run out at noon the following day, before a scheduled meeting of the Israeli cabinet. Fearing that Sharon would recommend an escalation of military pressure, and possibly carry the day, I told Arens that we needed another twenty-four hours of general cease-fire. I believed that we were within hours of settling the crisis on preferable terms.

By June 28, however, Arafat's actions amply suggested that as he played for time, he was also playing for advantage. Habib reported that the PLO was demanding a "symbolic" military presence in Lebanon and a political presence in Beirut. It was time to clear the air and get both the PLO and Lebanon to understand our bottom line. On June 28, we sent Habib new instructions: there must be a cease-fire in place; all PLO leaders must leave Lebanon; all PLO rank-and-file must quit Beirut, leaving all but personal weapons behind; Israeli lines will be readjusted after an agreement is reached and its implementation is in progress; the Lebanese armed forces will take control of all Beirut and other armed elements in West Beirut will hand over their arms to the Lebanese military; as a matter of policy, all foreign military personnel—Syrian, Israeli, or PLO—must leave Lebanon in the final arrangements.

These details were leaked by the Israelis, further complicating negotiations. Habib had reacted with considerable emotion to the Israeli bombardments of West Beirut, and this, combined with other incidents on both sides, magnified Israeli suspicions that Habib's sympathies were with the Arabs. While I did what I could to allay Israeli doubts, it was necessary to deal with repeated shifts and turnings in the Arab position. Pressure developed in Riyadh and Cairo to keep the disarmed PLO rank-and-file in Beirut while sending the leadership away. The entire process would have collapsed if this happened, and we managed to turn the idea aside.

Pressure mounted again on the PLO. On June 30, the President reiterated U.S. goals in a news conference and conceded that Israel had given no promises about entering Beirut. The President added that, once Lebanon was settled, the United States expected to resume its efforts to resolve the Palestinian problem in the context of Camp David. Again the Israelis squeezed the PLO, cutting off water and electricity to West Beirut. This brought a fresh storm of protest but also a new sense of immediacy to the flagging negotiations.

On Friday, July 2, the breakthrough came. I had gone to the Greenbrier, an isolated resort in West Virginia, to escape the post-resignation curiosity of Washington, but continued, minute by minute, to manage the Middle East crisis. As Reagan prepared to leave for California, he had reaffirmed his wish that I continue to act for him in this until George Shultz had been confirmed by the Senate. Under this unusual if not unprecedented arrangement, my resignation would be held in abeyance and I would still be the legal Secretary of State until Shultz's confirmation. As was normal when the Secretary of State was out of Washington, Deputy Secretary Stoessel technically became acting Secretary of State, in charge of the day-to-day administration of the department, but in accordance with the President's wishes, I continued to exercise the powers of my office. At 8:24 A.M., Walt Stoessel and Larry Eagleburger phoned to pass on Habib's information on a new meeting with the Lebanese government. After talks with the PLO and the Saudis, the Lebanese were united on a plan based on the U.S. nine points: as soon as a country could be found to accept them, the PLO would withdraw, leaving a small political office and a token residual force of about 600 men in the northern city of Tripoli; phased withdrawal of all foreign forces would begin with the adjustment of the Israeli lines following the departure of the PLO. The government of Lebanon demanded an international peacekeeping force, but not a U.N. force, in Beirut, and requested that the United States contribute troops to this force.

The linchpin of these arrangements was the international peace-keeping force in Beirut. Lebanese confidence had been battered. Neutral military forces would be needed to give confidence and time to rebuild. In the greatest secrecy, I began to discuss with the French the possibility of inserting an international force, in which France and the United States might participate. Two weeks before, Reagan had agreed in principle to the inclusion of American troops in such a force.

At 9:45 A.M., I phoned Cheysson, the French foreign minister, and he agreed in principle to the inclusion of French troops in the international force. It seemed possible to both of us that Italy and Morocco would be willing to follow our lead. That evening, in a telephone conversation with me, President Reagan again accepted the principle of American participation.

It was essential to maintain the momentum. Above all, the PLO must be moved out quickly. It was important that the PLO leave in a single group, rather than piecemeal, so that the Lebanese and the Israelis could have confidence that the problem had been solved before the eyes of their peoples and the world. On July 4, the PLO, eager once again to the point of panic to escape the certain destruction that awaited them, entered into a signed agreement with the government of Lebanon to leave Lebanon. All during Friday, I had worked to achieve this, asking the Saudi government through Prince Bandar to deal with the Arabs on the question of finding a country or group of countries to accept the PLO and to explore the question of Syrian withdrawal. But whatever the fears and wishes of its leaders, the PLO in fact had no place to go. One after the other, Jordan, Egypt, Syria, and even Libya refused to accept Arafat or his followers.

Fortuitously, the Arab League was meeting at Taif, in Saudi Arabia. Once again, I spoke to Prince Bandar and at 8:30 P.M. received word that President Assad of Syria, after talks with King Fahd, had agreed to receive the PLO, leaders and rank-and-file, in Syria. Moreover, assurances were received that once the government of Lebanon restated its request to Syria to leave, Syria would withdraw its own military forces from Lebanon. Though this action would be carried out in phases, the withdrawal would be total. After making arrangements with the government of Lebanon for the future of their ally, Major Haddad, the Israelis agreed to withdraw to the 40-kilometer line as a preliminary step to a phased total withdrawal from Lebanon.

At last, all of the pieces were falling into place. Now it was vital to act on the agreement while the will and the sense of urgency to do so were at their height. To all parties I spoke of a total withdrawal of the PLO, either by ship from Beirut or Tripoli or overland to Damascus, four days hence, on Friday, July 9. The Syrian battalions in Beirut would also leave. There was no demur. After the PLO withdrawal, but not before, the international peacekeeping force, including an American contingent, would enter Beirut. Israeli forces would fall back. The government of Lebanon would once again control its own capital, and as the Syrians and the Israelis withdrew, the Lebanese would take responsibility for their own future. By the end of the day on Monday, I believed that by that Friday, the conditions for peace in Lebanon would have been established.

The President had, of course, been kept informed of these developments as they occurred. George Shultz was with Reagan in California, and in the early evening Shultz called me to discuss what he described as "future arrangements." Shultz said that he saw an arrangement in which Walt Stoessel would continue to be acting Secretary of State while I became a "consultant," providing guidance and counsel. I told Shultz that I was prepared to step aside whenever the President wanted, but I could not accept the role he was describing. As a result of the President's decision, I was still Secretary of State, responsible to Congress and the American people. I would continue to make decisions as Secretary of State until my successor was sworn in, as the President had ordered me to do, until the President wanted me to do otherwise. Shultz replied that he, or perhaps the President, would call me back shortly. He said that he, Shultz, took his hat off to me—a great deal had been accomplished in the past week.

About an hour later, Shultz phoned again. The President had decided that I should leave. My resignation was accepted, effective immediately. Shultz had been given an uncomfortable duty, one that I had performed myself for other Presidents, and I sympathized. But in the circumstances, with this message coming at the hour in which we were on the verge of achieving peace in Lebanon, I felt that I must hear the words from the President himself. I could not abandon the negotiations on lesser authority.

Pat and I went to dinner in the hotel dining room. At 9:45, a messenger summoned me to the telephone. The President was calling. I took the call in an empty room off the lobby; the strains of orchestra music floated in from the dining room. Reagan's voice was warm, his manner affable. "Al, George Shultz tells me he's had a discussion with you," Reagan said. "I just wanted to tell you that what he told you had my approval."

Very little more was said. The entire conversation lasted for less than one minute. Reagan thanked me for what I had done for the country and for his Presidency, saying that he hoped that he could call on me from time to time for advice. I replied that I had served the United States all my life and would always be ready to do so again. Then the two of us said good-bye and I went in and finished my dinner.

The next day, on July 6, in response to press reports from Jerusalem, Reagan announced that he had agreed to commit U.S. troops to a peacekeeping force in Lebanon. With this ill-conceived announcement, attention was diverted for several vital days from the peace effort and focused instead on the meaning of committing American troops to a peacekeeping force. Superpower rivalry was reawakened. Brezhnev, protesting the introduction of U.S. troops, said that the U.S.S.R. would "build its policy with due consideration of this fact." Soviet policy, as it emerged, was to regard the situation as a confrontation between the superpowers; the breach between Syria and the Soviet Union was mended by huge new shipments of arms, including improved SAM missiles for the Beka'a Valley—some of them manned by Soviet crews. Syria announced that under present circumstances, it could not accept the PLO; the PLO reneged on its agreement to withdraw from Lebanon and spoke of redeploying to its camps under the protection of the international peacekeeping force. The Israelis announced that they were making logistical preparations to spend the winter in Lebanon, if necessary. On July 13, George Shultz, during his confirmation hearings before the Senate, put special emphasis on "legitimate needs and problems of the Palestinian people." American policy seemed to be changing again. And again the PLO decided to play for time.

Vision without discipline is a daydream. All that we had labored so hard to grasp, and had come so close to grasping, slipped away, with consequences not yet wholly revealed.

Conclusion

Nations, like individual human beings, should live by a system of affirmations, not by a code of taboos. In 1980, Ronald Reagan was given a historic opportunity to lead America back to a life of national affirmation after a long period of doubt and timidity on the part of its political leaders. As the end of his first term approaches, it is possible to say that he has contributed greatly to the revival of America's confidence and pride in itself, and in the restoration of the economy and in beginning the process of rebuilding the nation's military strength. Thanks to the President's fundamental good judgment and his many acts of political courage, the United States is stronger now than it was in 1980, its voice is more clearly heard and on the whole better understood, and if our friends have suffered shocks and surprises, they have also been reassured that America will no longer choose the sensibilities of its adversaries over the interests of its allies and itself. These accomplishments abundantly justify the second term which, as now seems almost certain, the American people will bestow on their fortieth President.

In other respects, and especially in the conduct of foreign policy,

President Reagan has accepted flawed results. This did not have to be. It need not continue. Indeed, it must not continue, because the opportunity to rebuild our foreign policy on the basis of realism will not survive much longer in the absence of a policy that recognizes the prime reality of our time: nations cannot live at the expense of other nations and will no longer live on the sufferance of greater powers. The world, as I have said, is not as it was; the United States alone cannot control history by overwhelming international problems with its wealth, its military power, and its diplomatic influence. But in concert with its friends, and in realistic understanding of its own interests as these are inextricably bound in the aspirations of mankind, it can act in the world according to the rule it has always applied at home: that the present is the means of creating a better future.

That is the message of this book. It was the reason for writing it. In an earlier passage, I remarked that above everything else, a servant of the President owes his chief the truth. This obligation, even more than the confidential relationship between President and subordinate, is permanently binding. The atmosphere of truth—of realism, if you will—in which a President must operate had been clouded. To a significant degree, this had deprived President Reagan of the opportunity to lead the nation in foreign policy. That opportunity still exists. The President, and he alone, can teach us to have patience as we seek to understand the world in its profound changes; he alone can inspire us to have faith in the power of freedom and political honesty to overcome the problems of hunger and ignorance and spiritual deprivation that tyranny only exacerbates.

All Presidents learn as they serve; the office itself, unique and mysterious, is the only possible teacher. President Reagan came to office, like most Presidents, relatively unschooled in foreign affairs. Like all good Presidents, he has learned much, and he has learned it before it is too late to apply the lessons. If his policies have contributed to the restoration of the economic and military strength of the United States after a long period of decline, it is even more important to remember that his confident example has revived the moral strength of the nation. These are great assets in the conduct of American foreign policy. Our principal adversary, the Soviet Union, disposes military power to a dangerous degree, but otherwise it is adrift in a sea of troubles. Its economy is questionable, its moral capital is a fiction, and its capacity to kill dissent is in decline: who would have imagined, on the day that martial law was imposed in Poland, that Lech Walesa, two years later, would have survived to become the recipient of the Nobel Peace Prize and the living symbol of the unbreakable strength of the idea of freedom?

President Reagan understands this symbolism. There is nothing lacking in his vision. Where his instincts have been thwarted, where his policies have not succeeded, the problem has lain elsewhere. The problem, almost unspeakably complicated in its consequences, is very simple in its essential nature. It lies in an absence of discipline on the part of some of his advisers; there is no adequate structure to enforce discipline upon the system.

"The flesh is not weak," the priest tells Lara in *Doctor Zhivago*, "it is very strong, and only the sacrament of marriage can contain it." So also the drives of human beings who find themselves in the exhilarating service of presidents and princes: only the most specific description of duty, only the most rigid rules will overcome the temptation to mistake the President's power for one's own. Only a disciplined structure makes it possible to channel the ambition, rivalry, and competitiveness which are natural in men toward constructive ends. In the absence of such a structure, the chief executive must exercise a lonely and nearly superhuman monitorship of the whole system—an undertaking that is beyond the limits of individual knowledge and energy.

For Reagan, the problem started on Inauguration Day, when in that famous encounter in Ed Meese's office, the President's aides decided that he must not be given the opportunity to sign NSDD1, the draft document that established the structure of the foreign policy establishment. The document in its original form was never signed. As a result there was no description of duty, no rules, no expression of the essential authority of the President to guide his subordinates in their task. This failure arose from ignorance: Reagan's assistants saw a routine act of government as a novel attempt to preempt power. In fact, it was a plan to share and coordinate those duties in the field of foreign policy that express the President's powers under the Constitution.

In the absence of such a charter, there can be no other result than confusion. The grand purposes of the nation to keep the peace, to hold up the standard of loyalty to our friends and allies, to defend social justice and the rule of law, and to admonish our enemies, fall victim to schoolboy scuffles for personal advantage in the corridors of the White House. What begins in uncertainty nearly always ends in chaos.

The three pillars of the foreign policy that I advanced to President Reagan were balance, consistency, and credibility. These cannot stand when shaken by the Samsons of populism and petty ambition. Where the policy failed to achieve desired results in the first years of the Administration, these two factors were almost always present. The impulse to view the Presidency as a public relations opportunity and to regard government as a campaign for reelection (which, of course, it is, but within limits) distorts balance, frustrates consistency, and destroys credibility. This very mischievous force need never have been let loose. In his second Administration, President Reagan will, I hope, give his Cabinet and his staff their instructions in no uncertain terms, no later than Inauguration Day.

Above all, the President must decide (though I doubt that he will wish to revive this term) who will be his "vicar." My friends at the State Department will perhaps be shocked to have me say so, but it does not really matter whether the Secretary of State or the National Security Adviser, or some other official carries out the President's foreign policy and speaks for the Administration on these questions. What does matter is that the person chosen by the President must be seen to have his total confidence and that he be his sole spokesman, once policy has been decided through the free but unbreakably confidential discussion of advice within the National Security Council.

It matters greatly also, as Dean Acheson (and probably every other Secretary of State) perceived, that the President and his vicar for foreign policy must see each other regularly and frequently. They need not be old friends, they need not even be friends in the personal sense, but they must understand each other and speak frankly to each other. As Secretary of State, I was mortally handicapped by lack of access to President Reagan. Not knowing his methods, not understanding his system of thought, not having had the opportunity of discussing policy in detail with him, I had to proceed on the assumption that our principles and our instincts were roughly the same, and that the integrated framework of policy that I advocated would therefore be acceptable to him. It was not, as we have seen, fully acceptable. Yet he is now largely pursuing it, and where prior to my departure he abandoned or modified critical portions of it, he has tended as time went by to return to the original concepts.

Experience has begun to demonstrate the fundamental rule that a policy must be coherent: every part of it is related to every other part, and the way in which our nation behaves and speaks must be everywhere the same and in pursuit of the same clearly understood goals. The President's aides, in the first days of the Administration, appeared to believe that foreign policy did not matter much: the problems of the nation were essentially domestic and if the economy was made healthy and the government trimmed down, all else would follow naturally. But the United States is not an island, entire to itself; it is dependent in some way on every other nation on earth. The very purpose of a foreign policy is to express and defend the domestic interests of the nation and to accommodate these to the domestic interests of other countries without resorting to war or destructive rivalry.

Our foreign policy must reflect the values of the nation. Military power and economic strength are important, but they are not everything. Americans will support a policy that demands a world of peaceful change, the defense of human values, the liberation of human genius, the advancement of social justice. The world will believe in an American that defends these values and asks other nations to share the burden and the promise of defending them. This is no idle dream. At a dark hour in the history of Western civilization, Winston Churchill reminded us that facts are better than dreams. The fact is that the human race, though the toil is sometimes bitter, chooses the upward path when it is given the choice. Together with the rest of mankind, we have everything that we need to make the future, as we have made the American past, a celebration of the possible.

If Ronald Reagan wishes to be among the makers of the future, he will grasp this truth. In December 1980, when he asked me to become his Secretary of State, I saw in him a figure who possessed great gifts of leadership—an honest mind, a good heart, a sound conception of America, and the common touch. I repeat, nobody needs more to be a great man except the vision and the courage to seize the opportunities God gives him. America and the free world will welcome Ronald Reagan's leadership if he will seize his opportunity—and if they are convinced that he is a servant of the truth. At the end as at the beginning, it remains my hope as an American that history will have reason to call Reagan great.

John Greenleaf Whittier wrote: "Of all sad words of tongue or pen, The saddest are these: 'It might have been!' " It is wise to live in the present and look to the future. In this book I have looked back into my experiences in an attempt to illustrate the lessons they contained while those lessons are still relevant to the current situation. My frankness may startle, and, at moments, it has been painful to write the truth as I saw it during the eighteen months that I served President Reagan. But in my regard for him and in my duty to my country I could not do otherwise, and those who read what I have written will make their own judgments according to their own lights.

INDEX

(Continued from front flap)

the substance of American policy—region by region—around the world and then provides his own reasoned views of where America has gone wrong.

The problems that General Haig confronted during his tenure at the State Department remain—and, as we look to the future, we see that his proposals for solving them are even more valid today than when he felt compelled to submit his resignation.

Alexander M. Haig, Jr., a graduate of the U.S. Military Academy, holds a master's degree in international relations from Georgetown University. He has served as vice chief of staff of the Army, White House chief of staff in the Nixon Administration, and the supreme allied commander of the NATO forces in Europe, as well as Secretary of State in the Reagan Administration. He is currently a lecturer, and a consultant and board member of several domestic and international corporations. He and his wife, the former Patricia Fox, reside in the Washington, D.C., area.